Your

Soul's

GIFT

The Healing Power
of the Life You Planned
Before You Were Born

ROBERT SCHWARTZ

*Whispering
Winds
Press*

This book contains an excerpt adapted from *Your Soul's Plan: Discovering the
Real Meaning of the Life You Planned Before You Were Born*
by Robert Schwartz, published by Frog Books/North Atlantic Books,
copyright © 2009 by Robert Schwartz. Used with permission of publisher.

ISBN: 978-0-977-67946-1
Library of Congress Control Number: 2011963331

Printed and bound in the U. S. A.

10 9 8 7 6 5 4 3 2 1

QUANTITY DISCOUNTS are available on bulk purchases of this book.
Please contact the publisher at:
Whispering Winds Press
www.yoursoulsplan.com
e-mail: rob.schwartz@yoursoulsplan.com
Your Soul's Gift by Robert Schwartz

Cover Design by Jan Camp
Cover Illustration by Bruce Rolff
Interior Book Design by Jill Ronsley, suneditwrite.com

~

Publisher's Cataloging-in-Publication data
Schwartz, Robert M., 1962-
    Your soul's gift : the healing power of the life you planned before you were
born / by Robert Schwartz.
    p. cm.
    Includes bibliographical references.
    ISBN 9780977679461
1. Spiritual healing. 2. Reincarnation therapy. 3. Pre-existence --Case studies. 4.
Mind and body. 5. Spiritual life. 6. Life change events. 7. Soul. I. Title.

RC489.R43 .S375 2012
616.89/14 --dc23   2011963331

A Note to Readers

THERE ARE MANY PEOPLE WHO truly cannot afford to buy books. My mission is to make the healing information in this book available to as many people as possible, including those who cannot afford to purchase it. Please ask your local library to carry this book, or after you finish reading it, please consider donating your copy to your library. This simple act of kindness will touch many lives.

Thank you for helping me to bring a healing awareness of pre-birth planning to the world.

With gratitude,
Robert Schwartz
rob.schwartz@yoursoulsplan.com

Would You Like to Know Your Life Plan?

ROBERT SCHWARTZ IS A TRAINED hypnotherapist who offers both past life and between-lives regressions. In a past life regression, you can experience the previous life or lives that best help you to understand your current lifetime. In a between-lives regression, you may experience your pre-birth planning session, thus discovering specifically what you planned before you were born and why. These sessions are invaluable in assisting you to know the deeper purpose of your life: what your experiences mean; why certain patterns reoccur; why certain people are in your life and what you sought prior to birth to learn from those relationships. Physical and emotional healing, forgiveness, greater peace and happiness, and a profound knowing of who you are and why you are here can come from these sessions.

If you prefer not to experience hypnosis, Robert also offers general spiritual guidance sessions in which he draws upon his knowledge of pre-birth planning to help you understand the deeper meaning of your life. Often, these sessions make use of the Divine Virtues Exercise, a powerful tool developed by Robert to help you understand the qualities or Divine Virtues you sought to cultivate and express in this lifetime. Prior to birth, most people plan to develop several specific qualities, and life challenges play an important role in this process. Through the Divine Virtues Exercise, you gain an understanding of what those qualities are; that is, you acquire an expanded awareness of your life purpose and plan.

For more information please visit Robert's website at www.yoursoulsplan.com or write to him directly at rob.schwartz@yoursoulsplan.com.

Soul-inspired Jewelry

TO VIEW A LINE OF soul-inspired jewelry that will help you and those you love to focus on and express the Divine Virtues you are cultivating in this lifetime, please visit the Online Store at www.yoursoulsplan.com. These beautiful gifts serve as heartfelt reminders of what your life is truly about.

Dedicated to

Dad and Mom
I love you

and

Rebecca & Calvin
Bob & Kathryn
Marcia & her pets
Kathryn
Jim
Debbie
Carole
Rolando
Carolyn & Cameron
Beverly
Mikæla

and
Their loved ones

We never know how high we are
'Till we are asked to rise
And then if we are true to plan
Our statures touch the skies.

—Emily Dickinson

Contents

Acknowledgments

I AM FOREVER GRATEFUL TO the individuals whose stories are in this book. Bravely, you opened yourselves to me and to the world. You spoke freely, honestly, and poignantly of the most difficult challenges you have faced. You inspired me. You touched me. You were teachers to me. For that I thank you.

To Barbara Brodsky and Aaron, Pamela Kribbe and Jeshua, Corbie Mitleid, and Staci Wells and her spirit guide: Thank you for being my teachers as well. Your wisdom and love flow throughout these pages. You have given so much of yourselves in service to the world. It is my great honor to collaborate with you.

To Liesel, the love of my life: Thank you for your love, encouragement, and insights. Thank you for believing in me and my work. I chose well in my pre-birth planning when I chose you. Though I'm a writer, I will never be able to express in words how much I love you.

To my sister, Deborah; my brother-in-law, Jerry; and my adorable nieces, Sydney and Riley: Thank you for all your love and support throughout the writing process and, indeed, throughout my life. Thank you for always being there.

To Debbi Mayo and Dr. Greg Karch: Thank you for reading and commenting on some of the chapters. Your insights were invaluable, and your healing touch will be felt by all who come to these pages. Thank you for caring.

To Deborah Bookin: Thank you for allowing me to write much of this book in The Crystal Bee (www.crystalbee.com), a place of sweetness, warmth, and inspiration. Thank you for the walks, the lunches, and the wonderful conversation.

To my cousin Emily Fleisher: Thank you for your eagle-eyed proofreading and extraordinary kindness and generosity. To Debbi

Mayo and Kathleen Webb: Thank you for your invaluable proof-reading as well.

Thank you to Sue Mann for yet another brilliant editing, to Jan Camp for yet another exquisitely beautiful cover, and to Jill Ronsley for yet another gorgeous interior design. Working with all of you once more was like reassembling an all-star team. Thank you to Jaine Howard, the newest member of the team, and to Edna Van Baulen for your wonderful transcriptions.

Thank you to Rita Curtis and Sylvia Hayse for helping me to bring my books and an awareness of pre-birth planning to the world. Rita, I wish you much joy in your retirement. I will miss you.

This book would not have been possible without the contributions of many others who shared their wisdom and offered their support. In particular I thank John Friedlander, Bob and Cynthia Dukes, Jill Caro, Serenity Meese, Omiri, Kathy Long, Joyce Fricke, and Josh Mendel.

I often say that I am not the sole author of the books I write, but simply the member of the writing team who happens to be in body. Thank you to the many nonphysical beings who work with and through me. This book is as much from you as it is from me.

Prologue

"I WAS FOUR OR FIVE years old when the nightmares started. On some nights a huge, black spider dropped from above, its underbelly opening to devour me as its talons curled around my face. On other nights a massive shark rushed up from somewhere below, with rows of glittering, razor-sharp teeth around a mouth that became an immense dark abyss about to engulf me. Another time, a primeval bird of prey, with a beak like a knife, swooped down from the ceiling to plunge into my heart. Sometimes my nightmares didn't coalesce into creatures, though. Instead, the walls of my bedroom crawled, or foggy clutches emerged from the night air. But always I felt the certainty of death.

"Terror surged through me as I awoke in the middle of those nights. Then I knew I was in my bedroom, but the creatures were still there—I saw them, heard them—clearly impossible, but just as clearly still about to kill me! Screaming, I clawed the sheets as I scrambled across the bed, until finally I found myself on the floor: heart pounding, gasping for air, in a dark, empty room.

"In Harry Potter's world, a creature called a Boggart erupts from its hiding place to take the form of your deepest fears. To conquer it, you have to imagine the object of your terror in a way that you will find silly or laughable. My decades of nightmares (accompanied by crushing depressions and inescapable obsessions) seem that way to me now: a bad horror movie, ridiculous. I wish Harry Potter's techniques had been around when I was that terrified little girl.

"Many people imagine that the goal and reward of true healing are to be found in peak moments of divine ecstasy—an opening onto eternity as the Universe lifts us into its galactic swirl ... or as a profound stillness breathes with us—and we know God. But

1

no, that isn't it. Those moments come out of nowhere and usually disappear as mysteriously as they arrived. Awakening is inspired by such moments, and we all seek to prolong them. But in my experience no therapy, meditation, knowledge or practice will invariably take us to the mountaintop, much less keep us there.

"Evolving to reach a place where we are serene, joyful and enthusiastic about daily life, every day (or almost): that's the real goal and the real reward. The day I knew I had 'made it' was the day I realized that I had not had any nightmares in ages. Even more important, I also realized that I had not felt depressed, obsessed, invaded or out of control for years. It dawned on me that I was no longer a seeker. I had found what I was looking for, and it had become a way of life where I am happy nearly all the time, and often for no particular reason.

"Life requires much less effort now. I appreciate the people, places and things that give color and richness to my world, as I see that all of them do. I often feel joyous and free. This is the kind of healing that happens when we follow our soul's plan. This is the kind of healing that is possible, not just for me, but for everyone.

"It is the kind of healing that, for me, has created a Heaven on Earth."

—Mikæla Christi
(Chapter 13: Mental Illness)

Preface

AS A CHILD I WAS severely emotionally abused by my mother. I planned this abuse before I was born.

When I say that *I* planned the experience, what I really mean is that my soul planned it. I am not separate from my soul; my soul contains my body, energy—indeed, the entirety of my consciousness. Yet, my soul is also more than me, just as the sun is more than any one ray of light it emits. My soul, like yours, is vast, expansive, limitless, and ever aware of its oneness with all beings. As I learn and grow, I bring my frequency closer to that of my soul and thus allow my soul to express more of its wisdom, love, and joy through me. My soul, your soul—in fact, all souls—are literally made from the energy of unconditional love. I *know* this to be true, because as you will read in Chapter 1, I have experienced it myself.

My greatest challenges, including the abuse I suffered as a child, were planned at the soul level before my birth to foster my evolution. If my soul is love, why would it plan for me to be abused? A fair question, one I have asked repeatedly throughout my life. In many ways the search for an answer is the driving force behind this book.

The abuse was intense and extreme, and though not literally unremitting, it was enough a part of daily life to feel so. The details are not important here. What is important is to understand how and why such things happen. For millennia humanity has learned through suffering. If we want to move beyond the learning-through-suffering paradigm, then such an understanding is essential.

Much of the planning between my mother's and my souls was based upon a past life in which I was a woman and my current mother was my son. In that life I was in a very difficult marriage. I eventually managed to extricate myself and take my son with me, but my decision to leave my husband resulted in our impoverishment. My son blamed and deeply resented me for our poverty. I died at a relatively young age, and my son, though an adult at the time of my death, was then left both poor and alone. He felt abandoned by me.

Before he died, my son (my current mother) was unable to resolve the rage he felt toward me for the poverty and perceived abandonment. His anger, therefore, became part of his soul, an energy his soul wished very much to heal. Out of love my soul chose to give his soul the opportunity to heal that anger in a relationship in which our roles as mother and son would be reversed. Symbolically, this reversal represents the soul-level intent to "reverse" (heal) the rage. Such healing could perhaps best be accomplished, and is perhaps most meaningful, in circumstances in which my former son would have the power to act on his anger. Why? Because profound healing occurs *in the moment* in which negative emotion is felt but not acted upon. (Suppression is the choice to push "negative" emotion out of conscious awareness. Here, I refer instead to feeling the emotion but not acting upon it.) Had my former son not been in a position of power over me, he might not have had the opportunity truly to choose whether or not to express his anger. Such was our souls' plan—a plan to which I agreed before I was born.

My soul had other motivations for creating this plan. In at least some of my other past lives, I was unable to love myself. Because we as souls learn through opposites, my soul chose for me to cultivate self-love by having an abusive mother. (Both our souls felt that at least some abuse was highly likely but hoped that healing would eventually occur.) From the level of the personality this decision may appear to be contradictory, even nonsensical, but it is not. Often, our souls forge life plans that are intended to get our attention, to put our "issues" front and center where we simply cannot ignore them. My mother's *apparent* lack of love—she did and does, in fact, love me deeply, just as I love her deeply—mirrored to and for me my own lack of self-love. My soul intended to motivate and even force me to learn to love myself through the seeming lack of love from my mother. In choosing my former son to be my mother, it was as though my soul had placed an enormous billboard in front of me that read: "Self-love is what you are here to work on."

My father, who died during the writing of this book, was a key part of my soul's plan. Though he utterly loved (and loves) me, and though he was not abusive, he was unable during my childhood to tell me that he loved me or to show affection in a way I could recognize as love. In addition, at my soul's request he agreed to judge me repeatedly over the course of my life, and many of his judgments felt quite harsh to me. His judgments and early lack of affection were intended by my soul to have the same effect as my mother's abuse: to drive me inward, where I would discover, and then spend a lifetime fanning, the flame of self-love. That flame, once but a small, barely perceptible spark, has grown considerably. As I continue to learn more about my life plan, I see ever more clearly both the courage it took for me to agree to it and the courage it takes for me to live it. And so, self-respect blossoms, and self-love grows stronger still.

Significantly, and also I believe by mutual pre-birth agreement, my father was unable to fathom the idea of pre-birth planning. Nevertheless, during his last years, as he sensed death approaching, he became increasingly supportive of my life path and writing. (He also told me often that he loved me, and I told him that I loved him, too.) In the weeks before he returned to Spirit, I read passages from this book to him. Each time he listened attentively, then looked at me and said, "I don't understand a single word you're saying, but your writing is brilliant!" He genuinely meant both parts of that statement. I couldn't help but laugh, and I was deeply touched by his support. After his death, in a gesture that is both wonderfully loving and delightfully ironic, he joined the team of nonphysical beings who helped me write this book. Indeed, these words may very well be his.

In other incarnations I have been unable to achieve emotional independence, and these lives, too, played a role in my soul's decision to choose my mother. What is "emotional independence"? When I put that question to Spirit, I was told that it means looking to oneself as the primary source of one's well-being. By designing my life as it had, my soul had created circumstances that would powerfully motivate me to become, and know myself as, the primary source of my own well-being. Like self-love, emotional independence is a life lesson I am still in the process of mastering.

In yet other past lives I believed myself to be powerless. Our souls seek to heal false beliefs, including, most certainly, beliefs that contradict what the soul knows about itself to be true— and the soul knows itself to be tremendously powerful. My soul designed for me, and I agreed to incarnate into, a family that would reflect to me the belief in powerlessness. Again, my soul had placed squarely before me an issue in need of healing.

There were also lives in which I felt and believed myself to be unworthy. Our souls are sparks of the Divine, and because we are sparks of our souls, we, too, are Divine. As you will read, feelings or beliefs of powerlessness or unworthiness are primary motivators of a soul's decision to plan experiences that will mirror these aspects of self to us. Such feelings and beliefs are often largely or entirely subconscious, but as life reflects them to us, they trickle into the light of conscious awareness, where they may then be healed. Life blueprints that are intended to shine light on issues of powerlessness or unworthiness are often some of the most difficult learning-through-opposites plans, and experiences such as child abuse, incest, and rape are among them.

This book is the second I have written about why before we are born our souls plan to have specific experiences during our lifetime. It differs from my first book, *Your Soul's Plan,* in three ways. First, although in *Your Soul's Plan* I explored only the planning of life challenges, this book looks at two topics, pets and spiritual awakening, that do not necessarily fall into the category of challenges. The pre-birth planning we do with our beloved animal companions is the topic most often requested by readers. Because we live in a time of widespread spiritual awakening, that subject, too, is worthy of inclusion.

Second, this book focuses to an even greater extent on healing. Our souls do not wish us to become permanently enmeshed in trauma. If a traumatic experience does occur, however, regardless of whether or not it was planned before birth, our souls will seek to guide us to and through healing. Healing actually taking place depends upon many factors, not the least being our tenacity and resourcefulness, but our souls are always there, nudging us, leading the way. The fact that you found this book indicates you are open to the promptings of your soul.

Third, this book explores the pre-birth planning of several particularly difficult subjects, among them incest and rape. You may be repulsed or horrified that a soul would plan to participate in such experiences as either perpetrator or victim. But know that my intent is not to repulse or horrify, but rather to bring an awareness of this aspect of soul planning into the collective consciousness so we can heal the wounded parts of ourselves—the underlying issues of unworthiness, powerlessness, and rage—and in so doing bring an end to incest, rape, and other forms of violation. Whether to include these chapters was a decision I agonized over for a very long time. In the end I felt a responsibility to share what I had found. We can, if we like, deny that the Earth is round, but that will not make it flat. It will still be round. Similarly, we can deny that these traumatic experiences are often (though certainly not always) planned before birth, but that will not mean such planning doesn't occur. It does. If we wish to create a world that is free of such trauma, then we must look bravely and honestly at what motivates the pre-birth planning of those experiences. And then heal.

I have not experienced either incest or rape in my current lifetime and so cannot possibly know the suffering that results. Yet, as someone who was abused as a child, I do know what it's like to feel oneself to be a powerless victim, and I am intensely motivated to learn and heal. My childhood experiences have focused me on what I need to do, and what my soul wishes me to do, during my time on Earth. But, in addition to motivation and focus, my awareness of pre-birth planning has given deep *purpose and meaning* to what I experienced as a child. I know to the very core of my being that none of it was random or arbitrary. I know that I was not being punished by a wrathful God or a cruel Universe. I know that what happened is ultimately for my highest good.

In the Prologue you read about Mikæla. Her suffering was beyond anything I can imagine, yet it led her to a profound realization of herself as soul. When I asked Mikæla how she felt about everything she had gone through, she replied, "To get here, it was worth it."

That is how I view my childhood experiences: may they be a path to healing and awakening for me as Mikaela's experiences with mental illness were for her. May we also take all other challenges, and rather than misperceive them as empty, meaningless suffering, see them instead from the perspective of our souls and heal the wounds that underlie them. May all the experiences discussed on these pages and offered by life serve as tools of healing, awakening, and enlightenment for each and every one of us.

Introduction

IN THIS BOOK I OFFER to you a perspective that has been immeasurably helpful and healing for me. My hope is the same for you. You will know if this perspective is part of your spiritual path if the words on the pages ahead resonate with you. *Resonance* may be thought of as a feeling of intuitive rightness. But, what is it and where does it come from?

It comes from your soul. Your soul is aware of every thought you think, every word you speak, every action you take. Certain thoughts, words, and actions feel good; others do not. These feelings, these intuitive promptings, are communications direct from your soul. It is right there, peering over your shoulder, saying "Yes, this is the way" or "No, this path is not for you." Trust these feelings. Notice when a feeling of resonance is present and when it is not. If it is not present as you read this book, then gently lay the book aside. But if it is present, I ask you to consider the possibility that your soul has guided you to this book. And I ask you to keep reading, even if your logical mind has difficulty with the notion that certain experiences, or perhaps any experiences, are planned before birth.

A Course in Miracles teaches that "perception requires the right instrument." To read—that is, to perceive—this book with your mind is like trying to perceive weight with a thermometer or temperature with a bathroom scale: it's the *wrong instrument*. What is the right instrument? Quite simply, the heart. The heart has a higher form of knowing than the mind. It may not make logical sense, but it will feel right. Trust that feeling.

You will read stories of people who—like you—planned their lives before they were born. I talked with these individuals at length about a particular life experience, then researched their pre-birth plans with the assistance of four exceptionally gifted mediums and channels. In most instances I provided them with the person's full name and birthdate, the names of the family members and relevant others whom we wished to discuss, and a brief description of the life experience on which I wanted to focus. This information was necessary so the medium or channel (and the channeled consciousness) could access the relevant portion of the Akashic Record, a complete nonphysical record of everything that transpires on or is related to the Earth plane, including our pre-birth planning.

The Akashic Record is not static like a physical library on Earth; it is a living, dynamic tapestry that, when queried, responds to the specific needs and intentions of the questioner as well as the specific circumstances under which the questions are posed. Too, mediums and channels are unique in their gifts and in the ways in which they access information from Spirit; consequently, different mediums and channels will access different elements of the same person's pre-birth planning. It is for this reason that most interviewees had sessions with more than one medium or channel. In this way we were able to bring forth a fuller, richer picture of why a particular experience was planned before birth.

In the sessions with the mediums and channels, I typically began by asking Spirit this central question: "Was this experience planned before birth, and if so, why?" Further discussion and inquiry evolved organically from the response. Often during these sessions, the interviewees permitted me to ask most or all the questions. Both the individual interviews and the sessions with the mediums and channels are presented in dialogue format. I begin a new paragraph each time the interviewee or channeled consciousness starts to speak about a new subject. In keeping with convention, the preceding paragraph does *not* end with quotation marks, thus indicating that we are still listening to the same speaker.

Both in the discussions with Spirit and in other sections of the book, I use terms such as *higher* and *lower, good* and *bad,* and *positive* and *negative*. These terms are used to reflect and discuss our human perspective, but they are not intended to indicate judgment on the part of our souls. Our souls do not judge, rank, or view the Universe in hierarchical terms; rather, they are acutely aware that all is One.

From the moment we are born, we have free will and are therefore able to deviate from our pre-birth plan whenever we like and as much as we like. All of us do so, and in doing so we create— we vibrationally attract—experiences that were seen as unlikely before we were born. As you read the stories, you will be tempted to ask if you planned a particular experience in your own life. A more helpful question to ask is, "If I planned this experience before I was born, why would I have done that?" Asking this question empowers you to extract from the experience all the learning and expansion of consciousness you sought if you did, in fact, plan the experience. This growth is more important than knowing whether the experience was indeed planned.

To understand the stories in the pages ahead—and, indeed, to understand life—it is helpful to know that everything in the Universe is energy vibrating at a certain frequency. Every person, animal, plant, object, word, thought, feeling, belief (whether conscious or subconscious), and action has its own unique vibration. The food you eat and the clothing you wear vibrate at specific frequencies. The car you drive has its particular vibration. If you were to paint your car a different color, it would then have a different vibration. In a Universe based on vibration, like attracts like; that is, the vibration of your words, thoughts, feelings, beliefs, and actions magnetically draws to you experiences that are the same vibration. Colloquialisms like "Everything's coming up roses" and "When it rains, it pours" reflect an intuitive understanding of this principle. When you are happy or unhappy, you draw to yourself experiences of equal vibration that perpetuate your happiness or unhappiness. Vibration plays an important role in both pre-birth planning and healing, and we will explore its role in the pages ahead.

You may be inclined to proceed immediately to the chapters that appear to be directly relevant to your life. Yet, because the stories build on each other, you will gain the fullest, richest understanding if you read them in order. Moreover, very different sorts of life experiences are often planned for the same or similar underlying reasons; therefore, you may gain greater insight into the deeper meaning of your experiences by reading the story of someone whose life is—on the surface—completely different from yours.

Some experiences in this book are highly traumatic. If you have had any of these experiences, please have social support around you when you read about them. The stories are offered to you in loving support of your soul's journey, but there is no substitute for the loving, in-person support of one who cares for you. Before we are born we choose with great wisdom and care those we will love and who will love us. We intend for our lives to be a shared voyage. I encourage you to extend your hand to a loved one and ask to walk this path hand-in-hand with you.

That, too, may be part of your pre-birth plan.

Your Guides

In deciding to read this book, you have embarked on a journey that will shine light on, and therefore bring deeper meaning to, your life. As you begin this journey, you may naturally wonder who your guides are. The following are the wise and loving mediums, channels, and spirit beings with whom I was honored to collaborate and from whom I have learned so very much. It was through them that I discovered what the people in this book planned before they were born—and why. Because this book focuses primarily on the pre-birth planning of life challenges, I asked the mediums and the beings they channel to speak openly and honestly of their own challenges.

Barbara Brodsky and Aaron

"I lost my hearing suddenly in 1972, when the first of my three children was born. Losing the ability to hear was a traumatic experience for me—imagine not being able to hear the laugh or cry of your newborn baby!—and also for my husband, who could no longer speak to me easily. I had the love of my husband and some good friends, and I continued to teach sculpture at my local university, so my life was full and joyful in many ways. Still, I felt cut off from the world. I was living a nightmare of isolation. 'Why me?' I asked. 'Am I being punished? Has God abandoned me?' Finally, in a place of great anguish and anger, I prayed for help.

"Sitting in meditation in my living room the next morning, as had been my daily practice for over two decades, I was aware of a strong energy presence. I could actually see his face. I thought, 'Either I'm hallucinating or this is real, and I don't know which possibility is more frightening.' He radiated a white light so brilliant that at first I had to look away. It was hard to tell if he shined out of that light or if it radiated from him. His features were clearly visible: piercing blue eyes, high cheekbones and forehead, and white hair and a flowing beard that came to his chest. I trembled in his presence, yet I felt a deep love pouring from him, a love so familiar but unlike any I have known in this life. There was a comfort and joy in his presence that washed away all fear.

"I'm not going to suggest that I took this casually. I went into the kitchen to get a cup of tea. When I returned, he was still there. I wondered if I was hallucinating. But every time I looked, I saw him patiently waiting for me to be ready to move ahead. There was both power and ease in his presence. I wasn't frightened because I felt so much love from him, as well as a gentleness and a connection dimly remembered from some unknown past. The white light was also comforting, like a brilliant torch in the darkness.

"I sat in meditation with him for two days before I ventured to talk again. Then I asked him who he was. Very simply he told me he was my teacher.

Barbara:	Why are you here now?
Aaron:	You are ready. You are learning to see the responses that build more karma. You can hear these words without ego adding karma. Listen for ego. Don't let it block your openness.
Barbara:	Where do we start?
Aaron:	You are suffering. Let us start there to investigate together the causes of this suffering and find the end to it.
Barbara:	Does it ever end?
Aaron:	It does. Yes, it certainly does.
Barbara:	With death?
Aaron:	Do you imagine that walking through a doorway will change your experience? No, suffering ends when you know who you are, when you realize the totality of being. Not of "your" being, but of being. Then you will cease to believe in this limited identity, this self, as the whole. I do not deny the existence of this self we call Barbara, but she is not what you think she is. Humans know the self as a collection of form, feelings, thoughts, perceptions, and consciousness. All of these are only the surface. When you take them as your whole identity, then there is a grasping for things to be different in this body, with these thoughts, this consciousness. Then there is suffering. [But] let us not get ahead of ourselves. We have as long as is needed to do this work together. Let us better prepare the foundation before building on the upper floors.

"Aaron gave me more information on what I need to work on. Then he stepped back, and I again experienced that brilliant, all-encompassing light. I was crying.

Aaron:　　　　　Don't be so solemn. Be joyful.

"Following this initial meeting, every time I sat to meditate Aaron was there, patiently waiting for me to deal with my fears. Each time I could see him sitting before me. I could also feel the energy vibration of his presence. It was clear to me that to accept and learn from him meant a deeper level of commitment. I would have to be increasingly honest with myself and more responsible.

"I wanted to learn, and especially to move past my suffering, but I was afraid. I wasn't afraid of Aaron, but [rather] of the changes that accepting his reality and his teaching could bring to my life. I didn't know if I was ready to give up all those old props of blame, anger, and fear to which I had clung. I was like a timid and scared little child, yet wanting to pat the big dog.

"There was never any pressure to accept Aaron. He gave me all the time and space I needed. Slowly, I trusted, as I understood that I would never be coerced. Each step was always my choice, to be taken only when I was ready.

"He also reassured me, although I did not understand it then, that there was nothing to give up. 'Just open,' he told me, 'to the truth of your innate kindness, goodness, and compassion, and these old forms [emotions] will drop away. There will be nothing remaining to support them.' There was such a strong feeling of loving acceptance from him. Everything he said seemed very wise and led me to new insights. I had nothing to lose by trusting and seeing where the experience would take me.

"With this simple beginning, I met Aaron and began a journey of life-changing discovery and healing. It was equally vital for my husband and our relationship. Now, after forty-four years of marriage, we can look back and laugh at the difficulties and hold

that time with tenderness, but in those early years both the deafness and our anger and bewilderment about it were very painful.

"Soon, friends began to ask if they could speak with Aaron.
I said yes, but had no idea how. Aaron asked me just to repeat
aloud what I heard him saying. Then someone pointed out to
me, 'You're channeling.' 'What is channeling?' I replied. The
channeling was difficult at first, because I had to be sure my own
ego and preferences didn't interfere with Aaron's messages. With
time I gained confidence, and increasing numbers of people
sought his guidance. It felt like what I needed to do.

"People also asked me to teach them the meditation practices
Aaron was teaching me. I had been practicing vipassana meditation (a type of meditation in which one observes thoughts,
feelings, bodily sensations) for twenty years. Now, Aaron was
giving me a way to deepen the practice and to articulate it. This
form of meditation is central to his teaching; it allows us to
deepen presence and thus witness life, rather than be buffeted
about by it. After many years of work as a sculptor, I felt moved
to let it go and devote myself fully to this new direction.

"Shortly thereafter, with so many people coming to my door
for meditation classes and work with Aaron, some of them suggested creating a nonprofit organization to support the work.
Thus, Deep Spring Center for Meditation and Spiritual Inquiry
was born. We continue now, more than twenty years later, with
classes, retreats, and community outreach in hospices and prisons.

"It's been a great joy to watch my three sons grow up with
Aaron as a member of our family, to watch their growing comfort
with the realities of the spirit plane. It has also given me enormous joy to share Aaron's teachings and see people benefit from
them. Everywhere people ask the same questions: Who am I?
Why am I here? How do I do the work I came to do? Why is
there been so much pain? I finally understand that this work was
my soul's plan."

An Introduction from Aaron[1]

"Greetings and love to you all. I am Aaron. What and who am I? What and who are you? What is the difference between us? Or is there none?

"We are all beings of light. What does that mean? Some of you may be familiar with the meditative experience of the dissolution of ego and body. Those who have experienced that have ascertained that what remains is light. That's all; just light, energy, and awareness. There is no ego. There is no sense of self or other. There is no permanence of form, no individual thought, no selfish will, no personal consciousness. Beyond all the attributes of separate self, there is pure awareness, pure heart-mind. Essence expresses as radiant light, pure sound, awareness, intelligence, and energy. This is what you are. This is what I am.

"As we evolve, we materialize in whatever form is best suited to our growth and present learning needs, as directed by karma. This Earth is a schoolroom. You are here in material form because it is here you will find the next lessons you need. I have evolved beyond the need for material form, and so I have none. Nevertheless, I am still learning and am in the form best suited to those lessons I now seek to learn.

"I do have a different perspective than the human one. I can call on the knowledge and wisdom of all my past lives, as well as the wisdom I've gained in these five hundred of your Earth years since I passed from your plane. On my plane we have passed beyond any illusion of the separate, small ego self. We communicate telepathically, one spirit with another or with many others. As there is no ego, there is no need to protect from embarrassment

---

1 Derived from Barbara and Aaron's book *Presence, Kindness and Freedom*. Although Aaron's tone is serious in this introduction, he has a delightful sense of humor, which he uses to convey his great wisdom. Once, for example, I asked him how many minutes per day I should spend meditating. "Rob," he replied, "how many minutes per day should you spend eating?"

or to cover up unskillful choices. Thus, our sharing is complete and honest. Each spirit shares its own understandings and experiences completely, and I can learn from another's experiences just as well as from my own. I also learn deeper compassion, and it is partially for this learning that I choose to teach. You remind me of the pains of being human; remind me not to judge another, but to keep my heart open in love.

"I have the advantage of the perspective of many lifetimes. My final lifetime on your human plane was as a Theravadin Buddhist monk in Thailand, a meditation master. The wisdom and understandings of many lifetimes came together then, enabling me to find freedom [liberation from reincarnation] for myself and also to help many beings to discover that path. Yet, I do not teach you only as that Thai master. I have been a monk in many lifetimes. Through many lives I've practiced most forms of Buddhism, but that is only a small part of it. I have been a Christian monk in just as many lifetimes, a priest, and in positions that are higher in the hierarchy of that church. I have been Muslim, Jew, Sufi, Taoist, and so many more. I have lived in all colors of skin, in male and female form, in many and diverse cultures. I have wandered forests, dwelled in caves, and lived in magnificent temples. I have prayed in hovels and palaces. I have starved, and I have lived in luxury while those around me starved. I have been a nobleman and a murderer. I have loved and hated, killed and cherished. In short, I have done just about everything in the realm of human experience. So have all of you.

"What does it mean to have compassion for another? Can you see that the potential for negativity exists in you also? Can you move from judgment of the tyrant to compassion for his pain and situation? This does not mean condoning his acts. It means having compassion, acceptance, and unconditional love.

"Remember that this learning is a process. If you had already arrived at that space of unconditional love and perfect compassion and acceptance, you would not need to be here learning in a human body.

"Let me return to my present perspective. I teach you as all of those beings that I was, the murderer and his learning so painfully gained as well as the beloved meditation master and his learning. Beyond that, I teach from my present perspective that knows the illusion of all form, that sees clearly that all any of us are is light and energy, slowly evolving to a brilliance and clarity as all self and ego are dissolved.

"As such I do not teach Buddhism or any 'ism' separate from the Truth. I know of only two Truths with a capital T: God and Love. All formal religions are merely paths to the understanding of these two truths, which are in fact one.

"We begin as sparks of that perfect light [God] and experience material form as a way of evolution. As we evolve, we grow in brilliance and clarity, losing all shadow until we shine as a small sun. If you were to take my essence at this phase of my evolution and place it in front of that perfect light, you would see the barest edges of form and a gray shadow cast against that brilliance. If you were to take the essence of a perfectly evolved being and put it in front of that perfect light, it would be invisible. That is what each of you is evolving to: perfect invisibility, immaculate emptiness.

"What I teach you must be filtered through your own processes. I can only guide you. The real learning must come from your own experiences. If what I say is of help and provides guidance, use it. If it doesn't help, put it aside and follow your own inner wisdom.

"I thank you for this opportunity to speak with you. I hope I have left you with more questions than answers. Perhaps one day we will meet and I can speak to some of those questions, but please remember that the answers are all already there, within your own hearts. Practice well and find them for yourselves.

"Go with my love."

Corbie Mitleid

"Hello, friends. I'm Corbie Mitleid, and I'm honored to be part of Rob's second volume of discovery, as I was part of the first. Rob has asked me to share a bit about who I am and how I got here with you. It's a two-part story: the first deals with how I developed the metaphysical abilities that enable me to work with clients. The second part deals with decades of self-challenge, self-examination, and shadow work. Different they may be, but they have become inextricably intertwined.

"I've investigated different ways of teaching, counseling, and healing since 1973. In 1994, working on some past-life investigations proved to be a catalyst for my abilities. Without formal instruction of any kind, I found myself able to do hands-on healing and long-distance energy work. I found, too, that I was able to act as a liaison between discarnate entities and those of us currently in body. I proved to be a doorway Home for souls caught in the Gray Space—those who have died but, for one reason or another, cannot get to the Light on their own. And I discovered that I could channel souls (Higher Selves) for those who would like to know the hows and whys of their life challenges.

"Today, my intent is not only to continue to learn more technique but also to go within myself to eradicate fears, bias, judgment, ego—anything that can get in the way of unconditional love and compassion.

"And that second part? Many of you already know it, for if you read Rob's first book, I shared it there. My story and challenges were explored as the person we called Doris. I have lived the Examined Life to the hilt.

"I started with a dysfunctional birth family, centering around an alcoholic mother who agreed in our pre-birth planning session to be the trigger for my major life decision: Would I cherish myself, honor my sexuality (and therefore that of all women), and love my body as I created it—or not?

"If I had chosen to love myself from the beginning, life would have been quieter and calmer. But, I took the harsher road, familiar from many other lives, and therefore generated decades of challenge: two bad marriages, three dances with breast cancer (including a double mastectomy), and a life filled with countless experiences around sexuality that reflected my feelings of deep unworthiness. Still, I was not willing to give up on myself. Through it all I kept asking: *If God is a loving God, and if I am completely certain of our connection, then how does all this serve me? Because it must!*

"I used many tools to discern the meaning behind that profound question. And on my journey, I discovered my 'sentence of passion,' which is how I now live my life and what I teach others in my work: *Cross the bridge from fear to fearlessness—and fly!* By embracing *all* of myself, flaws and magnificence alike, loving all of it and accepting that every experience came from a benevolent Universe intent on helping me to heal, I have lived my pre-birth plan in fullness, coming to a place where what I have accomplished helps others through their own challenges.

"My part in this book is that of 'priestess-storyteller'; my gift is being able to access past lives with detail and nuance. I see people's other incarnations like a movie: backdrop and costumes, plot and dialogue, arc and journey. And, I channel Higher Selves—souls—to offer fuller, deeper insight into why someone's life has unfolded along a certain path.

"Though to some it may appear odd, I count myself incredibly lucky to live the life I have created. Through it I have gained compassion, humor, resilience, generosity of spirit, and a delight in sharing possibilities and hope wherever I can.

"A thousand welcomes to you."

Staci Wells

"For as long as I can remember I have seen and heard spirits, seen auras, and had a telepathic rapport with animals, and a sense of knowingness about others.

"I have four spirit guides who work with me when I do readings and other metaphysical work. The one who worked with me in all the readings for *Your Soul's Plan* and now this book is my primary spirit guide. He has been with me all my life. He's never given me his name, so I simply call him Spirit. He appears to me as the very image one might imagine of an old and wise wizard. He always has a large, brown, apparently leather-bound book under one arm. The words *Book of Lives* are on the front in gold leaf letters. The *Book of Lives* is what most of us know as the Akashic Record, which Spirit aptly renamed long ago so that my young mind could understand its purpose. The name on that book's cover has remained the same even though I am no longer a child.

"I credit my relationship with Spirit with keeping me sane while growing up in a dysfunctional family. I would go into my room or outside to a quiet piece of grass, and my spirit guide would appear, ready to take me on an astral journey, talk to me, or simply stand or sit silently beside me. He taught me to meditate when I was quite young, around eleven or twelve. Nothing complicated, just a simple basic meditation for the purpose of connecting with my Inner Being and strengthening my connection to All That Is. Throughout junior high and high school, he would often appear to me, either standing beside me or outside the classroom window, and invite me to come outside and meditate. And so I did. I don't know why, but I was never admonished for cutting those classes.

"I clearly remember the first time I asked Spirit, 'What are the soul-level reasons why?' I was fourteen, and I had just made my first solo visit to a health food store. While waiting for the bus to arrive for my return trip home, I witnessed a car accident. In that moment I perceived the shockwave of psychic trauma coming from the cars' occupants and all who had observed the accident. I asked Spirit, 'Why do some things happen to some people and not others?' I have been asking this question ever since.

"I awoke one morning when I was twenty-one and saw Spirit standing at the foot of my bed, as though he had been waiting for me to awaken. Not a common occurrence for me, I assure you. He appeared to me in a way he never had before. Larger and brighter, whiter than ever, with blinding white rays of light emanating from him, a shocking site to see through sleepy eyes. 'Well,' he said, 'are you ready to do *The Work?*' In that instant I knew that I truly did pre-plan a life of Being of Service. I began putting aside my desire to become the next diva of popular song a la Barbara Streisand. I surrendered to becoming a professional psychic and to all the accompanying lifestyle and other personal changes inherent in that mission.

"The journey since that morning has had its ups and downs, its trials and tribulations, its challenges and rewards, all too numerous to mention here. Everything has served my soul's goals and the karmic lessons it chose for this lifetime. In working with Spirit over the course of my life, I have come to know compassion at a far greater level than ever before, and that compassion has enhanced my ability to serve the highest good of others. Also, I clearly see how my life's experiences have led me *here*. Along the way I've learned much about the soul-level reasons why we do some of the things we do, and much about the nature of the soul and the human evolutionary path.

"One day Robert Schwartz called and said he wanted to write a book that asked if we planned our lives before birth, and would I be interested in doing a reading that might be included in it. I felt the genuineness of Rob's intent. My heart and my spirit guide leapt with excitement, and *yes* immediately came out of my mouth. We quickly scheduled the first reading. Rob asked questions no one else had ever asked—and he asked *plenty* of them. The one question he asked most often was if I could I hear any conversation in, or otherwise describe, the pre-birth planning session. Yes, of course, I thought. I'd received flashes of awareness of pre-birth planning sessions previously, but I'd never been asked to focus so intently on them.

"I believe with every fiber of my being that Robert Schwartz and I made a pre-birth plan to collaborate on these books. The first time I read *Your Soul's Plan,* I became filled with the realization that the heart of the metaphysical awareness I had come to communicate in this life is pre-birth planning, and my heart chakra expanded in gratitude and joy with the knowing.

"Thank you, dear reader, for giving me this opportunity to fulfill my dharma—to be of service—and to communicate the message of pre-birth planning."

An Introduction from Staci's Spirit Guide

"I am the one who speaks with Staci. I am the one who stood before her long ago in the time in between lives and said, 'Do you want to work like this?' And she agreed, readily. Staci, like me, is on a quest to know and to teach. We bonded long ago. We were in the Library of Knowledge (on the Other Side, as you say), our quests for knowledge leading us to the same small area in the extensively large and grand Library. She recognized me because our soul groups had interacted occasionally. As her soul's passions became more and more about attaining higher knowledge and universal wisdom and about healing through the practice of universal compassion, her soul's energy and path became closer to mine. Since then we have walked together many a time in the time in between lives and sometimes in Life Form [body] itself. We walk together now in simple harmony even though just the one of us inhabits physical human form and human consciousness at this time.

"I am not of human primary origin, though I have played [embodied] in the human field more than once. Instead of choosing the human evolutionary path as most of you who are reading this book have done, I chose first to immerse myself in planetary systems where science and engineering are the prominent growth intentions expressed by those in the physical form.

"The more I learned while in those physical forms, the more I came to the awareness that everything is connected and that we are all interrelated. Once, when in the time of one of my own life-between-lives, I decided I wanted to explore this further and have the emotional experience of connectedness-to-all. I was then immediately drawn to Earth, and thus my entry into the human field of awareness.

"I have had four Earth lives, my first as a male during the sixth century AD. I was a quiet, inquisitive boy who learned to read early and who experimented with making healing elixirs from the things that came from or lived upon the Earth. As an adult I lived a nomadic existence. I wandered from small village to village, seeking to offer aid and healing wherever I could and relying on my knowledge of the plants and flowers to feed and sustain me between the kindnesses of others who took me in and offered me food and a roof over my head. I learned a great deal about human beings and human suffering during that life.

"Another of my human lives was as a priest in the tenth century in what became the order of St. Benedict. I had the freedom to read and to roam, and I did both.

"In another of my earthly sojourns, I intentionally lived a very short time, dying during the ninth year of that body's form. The purpose of that lifetime was to experience the rawness of basic emotions so that I could come to a clearer understanding of the basic texture of human life and human consciousness. That body acquired and contained within it so much emotional complexity in such a short time that it burned itself out quickly, and death came from an exploded aorta. The understanding I gained during that brief life remained in my consciousness and in my soul, and I have carried it within me ever since.

"The last of my Earth incarnations was in the eighteenth century, during the time of the great composers. This is the only lifetime in which I was present in physical form at the same time and place as she who is now Staci. In that life she had a passion for music, as she does now, and was among a small group of vocalists popular among the composers, often engaged in performance in the royal courts of Europe. I was about my business for the king (King George III) when I walked past the room in which a concert was taking place. The purity and complexity of both the music and her voice drew me to stand at the doorway and listen in appreciation. That day began a friendship that is somewhat similar to the one we have today, in that I was often sharing knowledge and information with her during many of our great and lengthy talks. I was an officer of the English royal court, a scribe, messenger, and humble servant to the king, rather like a modern-day secretary. This allowed me comfort, travel, access to personal libraries and other storehouses of written knowledge, and to observe the making of decisions that affected the lives of countless numbers of others. I held the confidence of the king and proved that I could be trusted. I witnessed much and learned a great deal once again.

"In the time-between-lives, when I am here in my true home (what you call the spirit world or heaven), I do many things and interact with many souls, corporeal and non-. Most of all I continue to study, to learn, to teach, and to heal. When Staci came to me in the time before her present life and form, she expressed a desire to work with me so that she could continue to explore knowledge and teach the concept of self-awareness through spiritual philosophy. As we spoke, her resolve clarified and her desire took form: *channelings* to speak with the deliberate intention of healing consciousness, mending wounds of soul and psyche through knowledge of self and soul. Her goal: to realize the great connection between her physical form and her indwelling soul, and to bring forth ideas that would stimulate much conversation and growth. She also intended that her awareness would include 'the other side of life' that is always there. Drawing upon the many lives of her own soul—lives of love, of service, of spiritual effort and growth—she gathered her own repository of knowledge and awareness and brought it with her into this present life form, much of it buried within her subconscious to be rediscovered or remembered through the process of her life's experience, the rest to be taught and communicated by me.

"The human form and field of consciousness fascinate me. There is so much to it—such richness, such vastness, so much emotional depth and texture, and so very much to be learned all in the one package of Humanity. When I am not actively participating in it, I am usually observing it or participating from where I am in the 'unseen world.' It is from this place that I interact with Staci, and with you through Staci, right now."

Pamela Kribbe and Jeshua

"I met Jeshua [Jesus's given Hebrew name, pronounced *Yeshua*] when I was thirty-three years of age. His appearance in my life was preceded by a deep personal transformation in which I let go of my academic career, my marriage, and my dwelling place. An astrologer once said to me that one of my life challenges is to continually let go of the old and embrace the new. This proved to be most difficult for me in the area of relationships. I had a tendency to become emotionally dependent on my partners and lose myself in a relationship to the extent that I had no healthy sense of boundaries anymore. My spiritual awakening, in fact, started when my heart was broken because of a romantic loss.

"At twenty-six years of age, I was pursuing an academic career and writing a PhD thesis on the modern philosophy of science. I was used to a very rational approach to life and was married to a scientist. Then I met a man who was a philosopher also and with whom I had amazing conversations about metaphysics and spirituality. I had always been interested in spirituality and the esoteric, but I had been suppressing this interest for quite awhile. I fell deeply in love with this man, and I thought he was the love of my life. He seemed to want to share his life with me, too, and so, the fairy tale could begin. But, the happy ending failed to occur.

"While I got divorced, he decided to go back to his girlfriend. I felt shattered by this experience, and suddenly my fascination with academic philosophy completely withered. I finished my thesis when I was twenty-nine, but I never pursued an academic career. I left the university, took on a variety of jobs, and started to read a lot of spiritual and esoteric literature. Then I met a woman who was a spiritual teacher and psychic reader. Meeting her was the beginning of a deep inner transformation. She helped me to become aware of old emotional pain that stemmed from my early childhood as well as multiple past lives, which I actually started to remember.

"This pain essentially had to do with facing my aloneness, by which I mean the kind of solitude that is unavoidable and part of life even if you are in a relationship. With her help I started to understand that it is only when you fully embrace that you are a being unto yourself, unique and independent, that you can connect deeply to someone else. I had a tendency to merge with and take in other people's energy. I had to learn to set boundaries and say no. I was also inclined to float above my body instead of being grounded and centered in my own being. She taught me that true spirituality is not about escaping or rising above our human emotions but rather about connecting with and having compassion for the most human parts of ourselves. I started to understand—with my heart rather than my head—what it's like to be grounded and true to myself. This was a revelation for me! I felt liberated and free for the first time in my life.

"Not long after I went through this catharsis, I met my husband, Gerrit. I stumbled upon his website on spirituality and reincarnation, and we started a lively correspondence. Connecting to him felt miraculous. There was a kinship between us that was unexplainable and yet so familiar. Unlike the devastating love affair in my past, our coming together was not surrounded by drama but by a deeply joyful, quiet knowing that we belonged together. Gerrit had always been very interested in the esoteric, and it was only natural for us to start working together as spiritual therapists. After our daughter was born, we built up our practice. At last I could do what my heart most longed to do: work as a psychic reader and teacher, and explore philosophical questions about life in a meaningful, practical way.

"One evening Gerrit and I were doing a personal session with a client when I noticed a presence near me that I had not felt before. I was used to speaking with my personal spirit guides, who I often felt around me and who would uplift me with their loving suggestions and sweet sense of humor. But when I felt Jeshua's presence, it was different. It felt like a solemn and deeply aware energy, very grounded and focused. At first it frightened me a bit. I asked the energy, 'Who are you?' and then I clearly saw the name 'Jeshua ben Joseph' spelled out in front of my inner eye. I instantly felt it was true; in a flash, my soul recognized Jeshua. My mind argued that it was extremely unlikely and presumptuous of me to believe that he would be next to me in my sitting room, but my heart reassured me that it is quite normal for Jeshua to be so close to us.

"Jeshua is not really an authority far and high above us. He means to be our friend, someone we can trust and be open with because he never judges us, although he is very direct and upfront. He asks of me to be truly honest with myself, to look my fears in the eye and not cover them up with self-serving theories. He is stern in a way, but it's a very loving way. It makes me realize what love is about. Love does not necessarily feel nice and comforting; often it asks of us to get out of our comfort zone, to be courageous and vulnerable.

"Expressing myself publicly as a channel for Jeshua raised a lot of fear and insecurity in me that have been very hard to overcome. My instinct (or survival mechanism) has long been to withdraw from the world, which I considered to be a very scary place. Jeshua is teaching me to feel safe in the world, to remain centered and self-aware while connecting to people instead of feeling fearful and fragmented. I'm still learning how to do this, but I think I've made some progress. And I have received so much from this work. Through channeling Jeshua, I have connected to my soul family across the word. I feel more at home on Earth. And most important: despite my fears, I have the deep fulfillment of doing what my soul really longs to do on Earth right now.

"With Jeshua's help, I now realize that we are on Earth to embrace our humanness, to go through the emotions we so persistently try to avoid, and to experience the deep fulfillment of becoming a fully grounded, human angel."

An Introduction from Jeshua

My Humanness

"I am Jeshua. I am the one you have come to know as Jesus. In speaking through Pamela, I call myself Jeshua to mark the difference between the real, living me and the artificial image that has been created of me in history. According to this image, I was a man with superhuman abilities, who had risen above human emotions such as fear and doubt. In truth, however, I was a human being, like you in many ways. I found a way to connect deeply to my soul and to follow my inner guidance in life, but I went through intense inner struggles just like you. Your cultural and religious tradition tends to deify me and push aside my human aspects. I tell you now that I *was* human. I am your brother, not far removed from the turmoil of earthly life but deeply familiar with the challenges you face. It is my wish to reach out to you and to tell you that you can overcome your challenges, that you are a strong and powerful being, and that you are needed at this time in history.

My Life Challenges

"When I started my human life on Earth, my soul knew that I was to bring in a new kind of consciousness, a consciousness to which many people—and certainly the political rulers of that day—were not open. It was my plan to be a public figure and to touch the hearts of like-minded souls.

"There was a group of people waiting to be awakened by my appearance on Earth at that time. This group was meant to create an opening for Christ consciousness on Earth. I could not fulfill the mission on my own; I depended on like-minded people to pick up my message and spread it across the world. Many of you reading this book are part of this group of souls. Many of you were alive around that time, and on the soul level you had made a vow to bring a new type of awareness to Earth.

"You may call it Christ consciousness or simply the awareness that we are One, connected by the same flow of Life that holds the Universe together and sustains All That Is. Human beings are essentially the same, and it is this sameness that, if recognized, brings us together and enables us to reach out to one another with a sense of compassion and fellowship.

"This notion of oneness and equality was very alien to the society I lived in two thousand years ago. People were strongly divided by race, religion, and social status. One of my greatest challenges was to face the injustices taking place around me and yet remain calm and focused. As a young man, I could easily get angry with the authorities. I had a passion inside me, a temper that could flare up like fire when faced with the unfair treatment of people. I had to learn to deal with that anger because it was central to my mission that I would awaken people's hearts. The heart is not awakened by anger, even if it is for a just cause. Behind anger there is always fear. Fear means that you do not trust the natural flow of Life and therefore feel vulnerable. When you become angry, you are really lashing out against your own vulnerability, which you do not want to face. More than anything else, the heart is awakened by forgiveness and trust—the opposites of anger and fear. To rise above my anger and fear, I had to go within, time and again, and feel that quiet place inside where all things are simple and clear.

"Your greatest challenges are never about what other people do, but rather about how you respond. They are about whether you can accept, understand, and thus rise above the emotions that others' actions cause inside you. Spiritual growth is not about you changing the world; it is about going within and changing yourself. This was the case for me, just as it is for you. In making peace with the difficult human emotions of fear and anger, you rise above them and become trusting and forgiving of others. You recognize their Oneness with you, and you release judgment. This is what I wanted to accomplish for myself, and in doing so, I touched the hearts of people who were also searching for love and compassion.

"Especially near the end of my life, I had to learn to trust and forgive in the midst of fear and hostility. My family and friends were fearful of what would happen to me. Some people were filled with hatred for me and were intent upon killing me. I had to remain calm amid this interplay of forces and keep the vibration of peace alive in my heart.

"In addition to dealing with anger, I had to face the challenge of loneliness in my life. Although I had a loving family and many dear friends, I had to face my most severe challenges alone. In my dying hour, I had to draw upon all my strength to remain focused on the energy of the heart so as not to be overwhelmed by either the hatred or deep sorrow that were present in the bystanders. I had to rise above my physical and emotional pain and feel the truth: that I was not dying on that cross (although my earthly body was); that my spirit had chosen this experience to evolve; and that by doing this, I would set an example for people who face the same challenges.

"You see, you are walking the same path I walked. You have been crucified in the sense that you have been faced with emotional extremes in your life—and in other lives as well. If you are drawn to this book and feel inspired by its message, you are aware that there is meaning behind the difficulties you experience. If you are open to the fact that you have chosen your life challenges, and if you are trying to find their meaning, then you have already gone beyond your initial reactions of fear, anger, and sorrow. You are now fulfilling your soul's mission.

Your Life Challenges

"Life challenges bring you to the core of your soul's mission, which is always to help you raise your awareness, release judgment, and create an ever wider space of compassion for yourself and others. The way in which the soul does this is different for each individual. Each soul creates the life path that offers the best possibility for experiencing the emotions it seeks to understand and make peace with.

"Life challenges generally run counter to your hopes and expectations. Although your soul planned them, they often do not feel like they are supposed to happen. On the contrary, they baffle and bewilder you. To the human part of you, who likes to stay in control of life, these challenges almost always feel like they are not meant to be. They seem to be unexpected, unjust, and too difficult to cope with. They generally evoke resistance, fear, confusion, and a sense of powerlessness.

"If you are in a deeply challenging situation right now and you feel confused, upset, or powerless, realize that this is the most fearful part of you speaking to you. The challenge makes you aware of fear that was already inside you in order for you to address it. The fear comes to you so that you can put an arm around it like you would with a frightened child. The purpose of life challenges is to heal your inner child, the part of you that responds emotionally to life challenges and easily feels betrayed, frightened, or alone. When you become aware that emotions are like children that need to be reassured and caressed, the challenge will bring out your true strength rather than your weakness. It will awaken the power to heal yourself.

"That life challenges are planned by your soul does not mean that you are destined to experience all the fear and pain they might cause. You have free will. You can choose to overcome them. Instead of becoming suffocated by negative emotions, you can heal and transform your challenges. Ultimately, they are there to remind you of your greatness, not your smallness.

"Just as you are not your physical body, you are also not your human emotions. You are instead the soul experiencing these emotional states. You are the conscious carrier of your emotions, and you can use your consciousness to approach the most difficult emotions with understanding and compassion rather than with fear and resistance.

"If you look at your challenges in this light, you may even become aware, generally after some time has passed, that they have been extremely valuable teachers for you. You may even thank your soul for putting them in your life path. The state of thankfulness in your heart shows that you have really understood the meaning of a particular life challenge. The peace you now feel in regard to the experience will enable you to help people who face similar challenges. You are teaching by example. This is your soul's mission as well.

"You are here on Earth not just to help yourself but also to make a contribution to humanity. Know that you are needed. Indeed, *I need you to complete my mission.* The purpose of my life was to introduce and pass on the Christ energy, which is larger than I, to people who would, in turn, pass it on to others. My arrival was meant to bring in the seeds of a new consciousness. You were meant to receive these seeds and let them blossom in your own heart so that others would be touched by them in the same way. You are becoming Christs yourselves. The rebirth of Christ is nothing more than the birthing of heart-based consciousness within you. You are part of my mission. I needed you then, and I need you now to fulfill our joint mission.

"How do you recognize your contribution to humanity? How do you know what you are supposed to contribute? Understand that your contribution is never separate from your personal goals. The life challenges you face always lead you to the specific areas in which you can serve others. For instance, someone who lost a child and has gone through the intense mourning process this evokes may, if this is the soul's mission, feel attracted to helping other parents deal with the loss of a child. The right people will cross their path to attract this kind of work to them, and as they do the work, they will feel joy and fulfillment even if they are among people who are dealing with intense grief, anger, or loneliness.

"Your contribution to humanity has to do with what you love doing and would do naturally even if you were not paid for it. This may change over the course of your life. There is a natural tendency in human beings to want to pass on to others the knowledge they have acquired at the level of the heart, because when your heart is awakened, you more easily feel the connection between yourself and others, even humanity at large. If there is love in your heart, you will want to share your knowledge with others, because this will make you feel even more joyful and loving.

"Often, the heart energy is awakened after going through a personal crisis. You have a saying, 'What does not kill you makes you stronger.' Life challenges as discussed in this book are like that. They seem to break you, but what they are actually intended to do is to break your self-created barriers of fear and judgment. If you allow crisis to purge these barriers, you invite a new consciousness into your life, one that will attract the right circumstances for you to fulfill your soul's mission.

"At this point in history, it is time for humanity to ascend to a new level of consciousness. It is time for humans to recognize their Oneness, even if they are of different races, genders, or cultural backgrounds. This time is a time of crisis and of opportunity. The crises your world faces in economics and ecology are due to a lack of heart-based awareness in these areas. Both the interactions among humans and the interaction with nature are often seen in terms of profit and personal gain. This is ego-based consciousness. I do not judge this type of consciousness. It has served a purpose, as all expressions of consciousness do. It is now time, however, to rise above ego-based consciousness. Earth is calling out for humans to reinstate the natural harmony between all that lives on the planet. The spirit of humanity is called upon to heal the wounds that centuries of fear, struggle, and separation have caused. The crises humanity is facing are to be solved, not by inventions of the mind like new technologies, but by the awakening of the heart, one human at a time.

"You are alive today because your soul wants to help humanity ascend to heart-based consciousness. It is by going through your own challenges and finding the opportunity within them that you contribute most to humanity's well-being. Your contribution is not so much what you do as who you are. It is your awareness that makes the difference. As more of you invite heart-based consciousness into your lives, it becomes easier for others to make the transition to a new way of being: at peace with themselves, humanity, and nature.

"I call upon you to have faith. I tell you that you are not alone. You can face your life challenges and overcome them. You can be a teacher of heart-based consciousness and reach out to others in a way that feels joyful and fulfilling. Your life has meaning, and you are needed to make your unique contribution to the larger whole of which you are part. Recognize me as your brother and next of kin. I am here to help you, but I need your help as well. Join me, and let us together fulfill the old promise of a new Earth."

CHAPTER 1

⚮

Healing

THE JOURNEY YOU TAKE AS you read this book will
be most meaningful and healing if you embark with a
certain conceptual framework in place. Let us begin,
then, with this most fundamental of questions: Why do we plan
before we are born to have certain experiences—including great
challenges—in our lives?

Karma

Karma is sometimes conceptualized as "cosmic debt," but in
my exploration of pre-birth planning, I have come to view it
more as a lack or absence of balanced experiences. For example,
if you have a disabled child and dedicate your life to caring for
and loving that child, after this lifetime either or both of you
may feel a sense of imbalanced experience. On the soul level, you
would likely seek to balance the experiences from that lifetime,
and if so, you may plan another incarnation together in which
you switch roles. You may therefore choose to be born with a
physical disability, and you may ask your former child to play
the role of your mother or father. Motivated both by great love
for you and by a desire to balance the experiences of that past
life, your former child would likely agree to your request. And so
another lifetime would be set in motion.

The soul's feeling of balance derives *not* from what it does for another soul, but rather from experiencing what it did not previously experience. For instance, the soul of your former child will feel a sense of balance after it experiences caregiving. Similarly, your soul will feel a sense of balance after you experience receiving care. The same principle would apply if you had abandoned your disabled child in the past life. Though you might very well choose to "make things up" to your former child in another lifetime, that act of doing so would not create a feeling of balance. Rather, the feeling of balance would come from experiencing abandonment yourself. "Hear me well," Jeshua said when speaking about this point. "Karma is not balanced by doing good to someone else as people like to think. It is not by doing something to someone that one balances one's karma, but by going through the experience oneself."

Too, there is a distinction between balancing and releasing karma. Karma is balanced when the soul feels it has experienced all sides of an issue. Karma is *released* when the underlying causes of the original imbalance are resolved. The distinction is significant; unless we heal the underlying causes of our karma, we will tend to create new karma even after the original karma was balanced.

Let us say, for example, that in a past life you held the false belief that the resources of the Universe are limited, that there is not enough to go around. Let us say, too, that this false belief generated great fear in you, so much so that you chose to steal food from your neighbor. At the end of that lifetime, when you transitioned back to the nonphysical realm and had your life review, you felt a desire to balance this experience. You therefore planned to experience material loss of some kind in your next lifetime. You also chose to carry both the energy of fear and the false belief in scarcity back into body for the purpose of healing them.

The experiences you plan for your next life would balance the karma, but they would not necessarily address the fear or false belief. If left unhealed, the fear and false belief would likely prompt you to take other actions that would generate more karma. The original karma is released only when the underlying fear and false belief are healed. On the soul level you would be aware of this fact and so might plan, for example, the experience of poverty or financial setback in your next incarnation, not as self-punishment for the act of theft in your past life, but rather as a means of mirroring to yourself those aspects of your consciousness (the fear and belief in lack) in need of healing. Though we dislike and resist suffering, it is a potent healing mechanism even if we have no conscious understanding of when or how it brings healing. A conscious awareness of its purpose, however, may empower us to learn the underlying lessons and create the needed healing in a much less arduous manner.

In one of our discussions, Jeshua described karma as "a set of false beliefs about oneself and the world ... the belief in fear and separation." I believe that at this pivotal time in humanity's evolution, we are returning to a state of unity consciousness in which our fears and belief in separation are healing. Contrary to popular concept, such healing can occur quite rapidly, even instantly. Said Jeshua:

> The releasing of karma can happen instantly when the soul realizes the true nature of its own being: pure Divinity, one with Spirit. From this realization springs deep peace. When the soul can hold this insight, it will liberate itself quite easily from the bonds of karma.
>
> There is a story in the Bible about a criminal who was put on the cross next to me. He was touched profoundly by the energy of compassion I radiated, and because of the deep surrender he experienced in his death process, I could tell him, "Today you shall be with me in paradise." There was a genuine release of karma in that moment, an awakening that he would remember in lifetimes to come.
>
> There is a paradox at work here that is inherent in duality [third-dimensional life]. Heavy karma can create great enlightenment; souls who have explored their dark side thoroughly

and carried heavy karma on their shoulders may become the greatest and most compassionate teachers for others. They may have taken a long time to become free, but they will all tell you that the difficulty was not in the amount of struggle and suffering they had to go through, but rather in seeing that the struggle was not real, that it was a result of their belief in fear and separation, and that in truth they were free from the very start.

Releasing karma is not difficult in the sense of having to go through a lot of suffering. It is difficult in that it goes against deeply seated illusions that have clouded humanity's consciousness for a long time. The key is to become aware of who you truly are [soul] and to remember that you are unconditionally loved by Spirit and that you are safe and free Now. Is it difficult to realize this? You surely *think* it is.

This book intends to help you remember who you really are: the vast, wise, loving, limitless, eternal, and Sacred Being who planned the life you are now living. As you come more fully into this remembrance, you will see ever more clearly that you can balance and release your karma and heal in the ways in which you need to heal. You are the powerful creator of all you experience, both the challenges you planned before you were born and the healing you create in this and in each Now moment.

Healing

We also plan challenges and other life experiences to heal various energies and aspects of our consciousness that may be unrelated to our karma. For example, in *Your Soul's Plan* I share the story of Penelope, a young woman who planned to be born completely deaf. When medium Staci Wells and I accessed Penelope's prebirth planning session, we discovered that in the lifetime prior to the current one, Penelope had the same mother she has now. In that past life, Penelope heard her mother shot to death by the mother's boyfriend. Penelope was psychologically traumatized by this event, so much so that it led her to commit suicide later in that lifetime. She therefore returned to Spirit with what could be termed an "energy of unresolved trauma," which now needs to be healed. In her pre-birth planning session, Penelope's spirit guide asks her if she would like to be born deaf so that no similar trauma will happen again and so that she may complete her healing from the previous lifetime. Penelope responds, "Yes, that is what I want and what I wish to do." So begins the planning of the life experience of complete deafness.

I also related the story of Pat, a gentleman who plans before birth to experience several decades of alcoholism. Pat forges this life plan in part because of the way in which he died in a previous lifetime. In that life Pat died in combat; he was the last man standing in a battlefield. As he roamed the battlefield looking at his fallen comrades, he felt intense fear. While in this state of extreme fear, he was shot and killed. The energy of fear was thus left lingering in his consciousness, very much in need of healing. Before he was born, Pat knew that a prolonged experience of alcoholism would be so emotionally painful that it would drive him to seek God, after which he would have a spiritual awakening that would heal the fear he had carried into body. Pat's healing began one day when he came home from work, drank literally every last ounce of alcohol left in his home, fell to his knees, and called out to God for help. In that moment Pat he felt God's presence. Several weeks later he checked into rehab and never drank again. Pat planned and brilliantly completed a circle of healing: he planned for the fear he carried into body to express as alcoholism, for the alcoholism to create emotional pain, for the emotional pain to drive him to discover his spirituality, and for his spirituality to heal the fear he carried into body.

Our life plans are designed to heal certain energies left unresolved from our prior lifetimes. These include judgment (of self or others), blame (of self or others), anger, guilt, and many other such negative emotions. If we complete lifetimes with these emotions still present in our consciousness, they become like residue on our souls. Our souls will then seek to transmute such emotions by planning (or in some cases, being almost reflexively drawn into) lives that reflect these emotions back to us so we may address them. That which remains unhealed from one lifetime must be healed in another.

Service to Others

On the soul level, the desire to be of service to others is a major motivation for planning certain life experiences. This desire is an organic expression of Oneness consciousness, which is our natural state of being in our nonphysical Home. By *Oneness* I mean that there is truly only one being in the Universe. You, I, and indeed every person are but individualized expressions of the One. It is for this reason that the term "service to others" really means "service to *seeming* others."

Let us say at the soul level you and I are planning a life together. When in a state of Oneness consciousness, you know that I am literally you. This knowledge is more than just an intellectual concept as it is for most of us when we are in body; rather, you actually *perceive* that I am you and that you are me. Naturally, then, you are inclined to be of service to me. Conversely, since I experience that you are literally me, I of course want to be of service to you.

Service to others is an accelerated path of spiritual evolution. What you give, you receive. What you teach, you learn. A common mistake—in truth there are no mistakes; all experience results in learning—of the spiritual aspirant is to focus overly on one's own growth, as though such growth is independent of service to others. Excessive focus on self, even when that focus is on spiritual advancement, actually slows one's evolution. We tend to forget this truth after we incarnate, but on the soul level we are acutely aware of it. We therefore plan to be of service to others in order to foster the expansion and evolution of the One of which we are all integral parts.

What does *service* mean? Certainly, service may refer to acts of lovingkindness.[2] One of the most common roles by which we serve through lovingkindness is as parents who nurture our children. Yet, it is also true that negative roles are sometimes planned upon before birth. Indeed, those who challenge us most in life may be doing so at our behest. Pat's children, for example, knew before birth that his alcoholism would prevent him from being as fully present or loving as he might otherwise be. They chose him as a parent not in spite of his planned alcoholism but rather *because* of it. They felt that the experience of having an alcoholic father would best foster their own evolution.

Those who play the most negative roles in our lives are not *always* doing so at our request. In the chapter on rape, for example, you will see that a higher part of the rapist's soul permitted the pre-birth planning of a rape so that a lower or darker part of the soul would have the opportunity to heal anger. Beverly, the woman who was raped, did not request such an experience, but she did know before birth that the rape was likely to occur. Her soul agreed to this plan for reasons I will explore in that chapter.

Three Layers of the Soul and Healing False Beliefs

That a higher part of a soul allows a lower part to carry out an act like rape was not something I had seen in the research for my first book, at least not in those terms. When I encountered it in subsequent research I was perplexed; my understanding had been that we as souls are Love. Jeshua clarified by explaining, "The soul is both love and nonlove. The soul is growing and evolving and is not all-knowing and all-love. The soul is the experiencing part of you, and through experience it moves from nonlove to love."

There are three "layers" to the soul: the Spirit-self, the Soul-self, and the earthly personality. The core of our being is the

2 Acts of kindness motivated by love. Similar to the Buddhist term *metta*.

Spirit-self, what some would refer to as Spirit, God, or the I Am presence. This part of the soul is all-wise and all-love. It is part of the realm of Being: ever-present, unchanging, One with all other beings, and All That Is.

The Soul-self is part of the realm of Becoming. This is the aspect of us that takes part in duality. The Soul-self evolves through experience. It can make what we could consider to be mistakes. It can forget its eternal connection to Spirit and feel cut off from the Love from which it was created and toward which it grows.

The earthly personality in each lifetime is one expression of the enormous and much larger energy that is the Soul-self. The personality is inspired by the Soul-self, and the Soul-self learns from the experiences of the personality, particularly the *feelings* experienced by the personality. Much healing can and does occur in our nonphysical Home when we return there between incarnations, but some healing can occur only through the experience of living through and surmounting a challenge while in body. In the nonphysical realm we have a greater knowingness, but life on Earth gives us the magnificent opportunity to transform that knowingness into a *felt experience*. It is the difference between having and being wisdom.

The Soul-self knows more than the earthly personality but is not necessarily completely aligned with Spirit. The Soul-self is multidimensional; it can express in several different dimensions or incarnations simultaneously. The healing that each of us does in our current lifetime brings healing to the other personalities that have been created by the Soul-self, and their healing brings healing to us. In the chapter on mental illness, you will see that Mikǽla agreed before she was born to experience several forms of extreme mental illness so that she could heal herself and in so doing bring healing to several of her Soul-self's other incarnations.

The question arises: Why would Spirit or God allow mental illness and other forms of suffering to occur? One answer is that Spirit is inherently unlimited. If Spirit were to prevent the

Soul-self from planning an incarnation and having certain experiences, then Spirit itself would become limited, which is contrary to the nature of Spirit. Spirit therefore allows the soul to experience all manifestations of ignorance, fear, and even darkness.

When the Soul-self plans an incarnation on Earth, the plan is created from both knowing and ignorance, love and fear. Ignorance includes false beliefs, some of the most common being "I am unworthy," "I am powerless," "I am alone," "Love is painful," "Life is untrustworthy," and "Life is suffering." The soul will attract life circumstances according to these beliefs. Over time, as the world mirrors these beliefs to the personality, they will come into conscious awareness. When the personality realizes the creative power of belief and the fact that one's outer world is but a reflection of one's inner world, then he or she may set about healing those false beliefs.

Doing so requires more than just intention and awareness; also necessary are experiences that disprove the false belief. We are better able to create such positive experiences when we act *as if*—as if we feel ourselves to be worthy, as if we know ourselves to be powerful, as if love is safe and life joyful. With the passage of time and repeated positive experiences, our false beliefs will be transformed. Perhaps most important, false beliefs cannot be changed by forcing ourselves to think different thoughts. False beliefs change when and because *feelings* change. Can you *feel* that you are worthy, powerful, and not alone? Can you *feel* the presence of Spirit and the Love the Universe has for you? Can you *feel* joy in and trust for life? To be truly released, beliefs must be addressed at the level of feeling. It can be the work of a lifetime.

If the outer world mirrors our beliefs to us, and if we therefore have repeat experiences and even entire lifetimes that provide evidence of those beliefs, how can we ever heal our false beliefs? To answer this question, we must understand that suffering results from the stories we tell ourselves. For example, the experience of having your romantic partner leave you is inherently neither good nor bad. If, however, you respond by thinking, "No one will ever love me" or "I will never be happy," you have created a story that in turn causes you to suffer. In the instant before your mind created the story, you had what Jeshua refers to as a *moment of choice*. In that moment you chose how to respond to the external event. There is a space within you from which you respond. When you become aware of this space, you also become aware of who you really are: not a victim, but a powerful creator. From this awareness healing is born.

Your soul uses challenges and crises to create a *need to choose*. If you never experienced challenge or crisis, if you were always surrounded by loving people and peaceful circumstances, you would have no need to choose. You, the earthly personality, would be happy, but you would not be motivated to go within, remember who you truly are, and consciously choose healing. Your soul, which longs to integrate its unhealed aspects, would feel that something were missing, and it would still feel clouded by the residue of unaddressed false beliefs. Your soul seeks to heal from within. Since you are an extension of your soul in physical form, you are "within" your soul and may therefore bring healing to it.

If there are unhealed aspects to your soul, you need not suffer continually until your healing is complete. As Pamela Kribbe points out, "The growth process is not linear. Lifetimes with a lot of negativity are alternated with more quiet and peaceful lifetimes, enabling the soul to recover from traumatic experiences and focus on other aspects of itself. The soul is not forced to pick bad circumstances until it 'gets it.'" Ultimately, and though it may appear otherwise, your soul wishes for you to heal until you are swimming in joy.

Contrast

Our nonphysical Home is very much as it is classically portrayed: a realm of great peace and love, joy and light. In such a realm we experience no contrast. We desire and plan lives on Earth because here there is ample contrast (duality): up and down, hot and cold, good and bad, love and not-love. As souls we learn through contrast. Contrast helps us to understand better who we are. Contrast also serves to generate intense feelings, and it is through feelings that we grow and learn. The feelings we experience are likely to be more intense if we forget that life on Earth is but a play on a stage, a play that we ourselves wrote. When we believe that the illusion of life on Earth is real, the stakes seem to be higher and so our emotions tend to be stronger. The intensity of the experience accelerates our evolution—*if* we feel our emotions and learn to work with them in loving ways. Nonphysical beings often speak of how wondrous the opportunities for spiritual advancement are on Earth and how humans may evolve more in one lifetime than they can in an infinitely longer period of "time."

Contrast is particularly stark in a learning-through-opposites life plan. In such a life blueprint, the soul plans to experience precisely the opposite of what it most wishes to learn. There are infinite shades and variations of learning-through-opposites plans. A common plan at this time in history is for souls who want to learn about unity consciousness—the Oneness of all beings—to incarnate into families in which they are very different from all other family members. The interpersonal frictions and even ostracism that result cause them to feel separate. The pain of feeling separation drives them inward and over time they come into a *feeling-knowing* of the Divinity that dwells within. When they sense Holiness within self, they are able to sense Holiness within everyone. They realize that Divinity permeates all things and all beings, that It is the very essence of all that exists. This awareness is the dawn of unity consciousness, a consciousness into which humanity is now rapidly moving.

Life Challenges Benefit the Personality

I am often asked, "Why must I suffer so that my soul can evolve and heal?" The answer to this fair and natural question is that life challenges benefit you, the incarnate personality, as well as your soul.

Noted psychic teacher, healer, and channel John Friedlander addresses this question with the following example. Let us say that for many years, and perhaps in several jobs, you have had to work with very difficult people. You have found the experience of working with these people to be tiresome and burdensome. At times you have felt it is more than you can bear. You have fantasized often about winning the lottery so that you can retire and, as you tell your friends, "never have to work with jerks again."

If your life plan is to learn kindness and generosity, you are very unlikely to fulfill your dream of winning the lottery. The predominant energy in your aura is that of the intended life lesson, and it is this energy that creates your experience. Because the egoic mind does not understand the link between "working with jerks" and learning kindness and generosity, you may feel your life circumstances to be unfair or even harsh. Yet, as you develop kindness and generosity, you are deeply enriched, as is your soul.

You and your soul are engaged in an exquisitely beautiful, meaningful, and mutually beneficial partnership.

The Pre-Birth Planning Process

After you complete a lifetime on Earth, you merge back into your soul.[3] The phrase "merge back into" is somewhat misleading in this context, because you are never separate from your soul. Nevertheless, your consciousness blends into that of your soul

---

3 Strictly speaking, the personality is eternal. A discussion of the eternality of the personality is beyond the scope of this book. Interested readers are referred to *Psychic Psychology: Energy Skills for Life and Relationships* by John Friedlander and Gloria Hemsher for an extensive and detailed explanation.

in a more complete way. An ocean wave is never separate from the ocean, but when the wave dies, it reunites with the ocean in the same way that you reunite with your soul. Your soul is enriched by all that you bring back, all that you experienced in your lifetime.

Eventually, your soul will long for a new physical life and the creation of a new personality begins. If it is time for you to reincarnate, your energy seeds—forms the core of—the new personality, which is whom you will be in your next life. This personality is genuinely new. Who you will be in your next life is not who you are now, just as who you are now is not who you were in another incarnation. The creation of a new personality is a sacred birthing that is accomplished not by your soul alone, but rather by your soul in partnership with Spirit. You—the new, emerging personality—have life and awareness. You feel connected to your soul like a child to its mother, and you are aware of your soul's greater wisdom.

At some point, when the desire for a new incarnation grows stronger, there will be a planning session in which the blueprint for your next life is forged. In the pre-birth planning sessions she sees, Staci Wells often describes this step as "the soul trying on the cloak of the personality." At this stage you receive input from various spirit guides who explain the purpose of the opportunities and challenges in the life-to-come. You are able to express any feelings, doubts, or questions. If you are concerned about any portion of the life plan, your guides and soul reach out to you in loving, compassionate support. You have free will and so must agree to the life plan before it is finalized. Though you can object and even say no, you will sense the great kindness and wisdom of your soul and your guides and so be likely to agree to the plan. Your soul feels grateful to you for your agreement and, indeed, for all you will do in your upcoming incarnation. Both your soul and your guides hold you in the utmost respect for the courage you show.

Spirit and your soul forge your life plan in an intuitive, not analytical, manner. Your soul has a knowingness about what it needs to work on, and it desires experience in these areas. Spirit responds to this desire by presenting your soul with various options for life plans. Your soul receives and absorbs these options as you would images on a movie screen. The planning process is difficult to measure in linear time, and the length of the process differs from soul to soul.

The language that is used in this book, and that must necessarily be used if we are to have any discussion of pre-birth planning, makes the process appear more analytical than it is. Here we use third-dimensional language and third-dimensional human brains to comprehend what is truly an interdimensional phenomenon. The language used to describe this phenomenon is therefore an approximation of what actually happens. Like other interdimensional phenomena, pre-birth planning is far more grand and magnificent than language can ever portray.

Free Will

Free will and pre-birth planning mesh in a rich, intricate tapestry. To understand how they work together, let us take the example of someone—I will arbitrarily call this soul George, even though the soul is androgynous—who has had many lives in which he made certain plans before birth but then deferred to the wishes of others when in body. In other words, George desires before he is born to learn and grow in certain ways, but when on Earth he tends to allow others to dictate how he lives his life. During the life review that occurs after each incarnation, George sees that he has this tendency and resolves to heal it. He therefore plans at the soul level to carry back into body energetically the tendency to defer to the wishes of others.

Let us say that there is another soul in George's soul group (a collection of souls who are at more or less the same evolutionary stage and who incarnate together repeatedly, playing every conceivable role for one another) who has precisely the opposite tendency. This soul, who I will arbitrarily call Sally, tends when in body to tell others what to do, imposing her will inappropriately on them. In her life reviews, Sue sees that she has this tendency and resolves to heal it. She therefore plans at the soul level to carry back into body energetically the tendency to dominate others.

George, who is aware of Sally's plan, goes to her and says, "I see that you are carrying into body the tendency to dominate others for the purpose of healing it. I am carrying into body the tendency to defer to the wishes of others for the purpose of healing it. Let us plan to marry when I am thirty. Though we know this will likely be a turbulent marriage, our hope will be that I learn to stand up for myself and that you learn to respect the wishes of others." Seeing great wisdom in this plan and the potential for much spiritual growth, Sally joyously agrees. Typically, there is a feeling of joyous collaboration among souls, even when difficult challenges are being planned.

Now, let us say that when George is twenty-five, he takes a job with an employer who runs roughshod over him, treating him with a profound lack of respect and kindness. George marshals his internal resources and makes a stand. He tells his employer, "Stop. You may not treat me this way. If you want me to continue working here, you must treat me with respect and kindness." In the moment George makes such a stand, there is a tremendous increase in his vibration. If he is able to maintain his increased vibration until he turns thirty, and if Sally does not raise her vibration to a similar degree, then by virtue of the Law of Attraction one of two things is likely to happen: either George and Sally never meet, or if they do meet, there is no attraction. In either case the planned marriage never occurs; their dissimilar vibrations prevent them from coming together. (Sally's soul would have taken this possibility into account in the pre-birth planning process and created a contingency plan. In that plan Sally will meet another partner who will provide her with the opportunity to learn the desired lesson.)

This hypothetical story illustrates how pre-birth planning and free will intersect in the most elegant of ways. Here, George used his free will to learn the planned lesson (standing up for and being true to himself), thus obviating the need for the planned challenge of the difficult marriage.

The New Human

Although life challenges produce tremendous growth for both the personality and the soul, suffering is not necessary for growth. As humans we have always had free reign in exploring our consciousness and using our creative power. Over thousands of years, we have made decisions that were increasingly based on fear and a belief in separation. Now, this process is beginning to reverse as we increasingly base our decisions on love and compassion. The human race is at the cusp of evolving into spiritual maturity. Said Jeshua:

> Even though the exploration of extremes is a viable process, it is now time to create a new balance and move beyond learning through suffering. Suffering can be a means of awakening, but that does not mean one shouldn't do everything to learn in different, more joyful ways. We do not judge suffering or negativity, but at the same time we will do everything we can to help you move beyond it.
>
> Humanity is evolving and recognizing ever more the Oneness behind all life forms. Humanity is now capable of breaking through the illusions of fear and separation and embracing its true destiny: to become the inspiration and the gateway to a New Earth that is the home of many different beings who live together in peace, joy, and creativity.

The new humans will move beyond the learning-through-suffering paradigm. Less driven by fear, we will find that curiosity, creativity, and love become our primary motivations to grow and learn. As fear diminishes and we feel safer, we will more fully indulge the natural curiosity we have about one another. We will give up unneeded boundaries and allow ourselves to feel what others feel, connecting with them in deeply empathetic ways.

Creativity will become a greater motivator as we feel free and safe to engage in uninhibited, joyous self-expression and sharing of ourselves and our abundance. Love—the surrendering of ourselves and the merging of ourselves with that which is greater—will expand human consciousness in ways we have not yet allowed ourselves to imagine.

"Beating" Life Challenges

Resistance to life and the challenges it offers often manifests in an attitude of "I am going to beat this thing." If you decree to the Universe that you are going to "beat" anything, you have just commanded the Universe to deliver to your doorstep more of what you do not want.

When you exude the energy of *beat* (or any of its variations, such as *fight, battle,* or *conquer*), the Universe feels you exuding beat energy and, like a tuning fork, brings it to you in obedient service. Regardless of your conscious intentions, the Universe manifests around you the vibrations to which you are resonating.

When you think "I want to beat this," the cells within your body respond and beat themselves into dis-ease, and healing of any kind is literally beaten out of your set of options. The harshness of the energy of wanting to beat something may also (and usually does) appear in other areas of your life, such as money, relationships, and personal circumstances.

You may feel that you have beaten a particular life challenge, say, cancer. If the cancer healed, it did so not because of the energy of beat, but rather in spite of it. The preponderance of the energy of your thoughts, words, and actions resonated to a frequency much higher than that of beating, even though your conscious mind may have believed that you were engaged in a so-called fight against the cancer.

For thousands of years, people the world over have unknowingly brought strife into their lives by trying to beat a life challenge. Peace, joy, prosperity, healing, and all the other blessings of the niverse are not created by beating anything; rather, they are created by embracing everything.

Why Ask Why

When you ask why something has happened or is now happening, you create a vortex of energy that attracts to you the answers you seek. Regardless of whether your conscious mind becomes aware of an answer, the energy that is drawn to you through the asking of why is deeply healing. I do not suggest you should obsess about why; on the contrary, the greatest healing is magnetized to you when you ask why and then release the question into the Universe as you would a helium-filled balloon into the sky. The balloon will find its proper destination, as will your question. When you ask why, the Universe responds, though not always in ways you can identify or in the time frame you may prefer.

If uncovering the deeper meaning of the events in our lives is beneficial, why do we not incarnate with full memory of our pre-birth plan? There are several reasons. As mentioned, our lack of memory of "the other side" makes life on Earth seem more real, and that perception causes us to experience intense feelings from which we learn much during an incarnation. In addition, if we were to reincarnate with full memory of the plan, it would be akin to taking an open-book test in school: less learning may occur if we are in some way handed the answers. Much greater learning may result when the test is closed book, when we search for, find, and integrate the answers on our own, just as you are doing now. Too, discovering the questions we want to ask and have answered is a valuable part of the journey. If we knew the answers, we would never look for the questions.

Ultimately, the intent in asking why is not for the mind to figure out the entirety of your pre-birth plan, but rather to prompt you to surrender to your heart. When you heed the call of your heart, you are fulfilling your life plan, even if your mind has no conscious awareness of that plan.

Victim Consciousness

A great shift in consciousness is now occurring on our planet. This shift depends completely upon those of us who are in body to raise our vibration, which means, quite simply, being the most loving people we can be. As we raise our vibration, Earth rises in vibration as well. Spirit guides, angels, loved ones, and others in the nonphysical realm can send love, wisdom, light, and inspiration to us, but we must receive and embody these gifts. The nonphysical beings who love and guide us cannot create a shift in human consciousness for us.

Victim consciousness—the belief that you have been victimized by a person, experience, or life in general—vibrates at a very low frequency. When we understand that we are the powerful creators of all we experience even if we may not know how or why we created something, we move out of victim consciousness, raise our vibration, and, in turn, raise the vibration of Earth. If your pre-birth intention was or your current intention is to contribute to the shift in human consciousness, know that moving out of victim mentality is a powerful and magnificent way to do so.

Victim consciousness is a false belief, one that has become part of our limited, habitual way of thinking. It has tempting secondary benefits: it is a way to obtain sympathy from others; it is a means of bonding with others who also believe themselves to be victims. Victim consciousness and its secondary benefits are not to be judged because it is easy to believe what we have been taught and natural to want support from and bonding with others. My intent is not to judge the choice to perceive ourselves as victims but rather to clarify that *it is a choice*. The alternate choice is to come into remembrance of our identity and power as expressions of the eternal souls that planned the lives we now live, to know ourselves as the creators, not the victims, of our experiences. This awareness uplifts the entire world.

Victim consciousness tends to be self-perpetuating. If you believe yourself to be a victim, you vibrate at the frequency of victim and energetically draw to yourself experiences that will confirm in your mind that you are a victim. One key to breaking this cycle is to release blame, for blame places you vibrationally at the frequency of victim consciousness. We may more easily release blame when we take responsibility for having agreed to our life plans. Such self-responsibility is the fertile ground in which expanded consciousness and self-knowledge blossom.

Judgment

Like victim consciousness, judgment resonates at a very low frequency. Judgment creates separation, separation creates fear, and fear creates most of the problems in our world. The current shift in human consciousness is in part a return to Oneness or unity consciousness, which is our natural state of being in our nonphysical Home. We cannot return to this of Oneness consciousness if we are in judgment of and therefore separate from one another. An awareness of pre-birth planning makes it easier to release judgment of others, for then we come to realize that every life plan is birthed in love and founded on wisdom.

Society reserves particularly harsh judgments for people who have certain experiences such as homelessness, alcoholism, drug addiction, and AIDS: "She needs to get her act together," "He isn't really trying," "She's weak," and "He needs to pull himself up by his bootstraps." The judgments of people who have AIDS are particularly harsh: "He must have been promiscuous," "She deserves it," and "AIDS is God's way of punishing homosexuals for being homosexuals." Yet, in truth these experiences are planned before birth, and they are plans of boldness, plans many would not dare to undertake. When we understand pre-birth planning, our judgments evaporate and are replaced by an abiding respect and admiration for the courageous souls who face such challenges.

Judgment may, however, be a useful tool for gaining insight into your life plan. Ask yourself, "What trait do I judge most harshly in the people who are in my life?" Then ask, "What is the opposite of that trait?" In all likelihood, before you were born you wanted to develop and express that opposite quality. In regard to the trait you have judged in someone else, it is likely you had that trait in a past life, and it is certain you have that trait (to some degree) now. All judgment of others is cloaked self-judgment. If you did not have the trait you judge, you would either be unable to recognize it in another or you would not judge it if you did see it.

Because what we experience outside ourselves is always a projection of our inner reality, it is not possible for us to be in nonjudgment of another until we are wholly in nonjudgment of ourselves. Speaking nonjudgmental words and engaging in non-judgmental actions are not indicators of being in nonjudgment. The one true indicator of nonjudgment is how we experience ourselves, for that is how we truly experience others.

Care must be taken here not to go into judgment of judgment. Although none of us enjoys being judged, we chose for good reason to incarnate in a time in human evolution in which judgment is commonplace. Simply put, judgment is a powerful teacher for us, and some of us learn best through the experience of being judged. That experience is an effective means by which to develop empathy, compassion, emotional independence, and many other divine virtues. The lives we plan before we are born are opportunities to develop and express such virtues.

Anger Toward Your Soul

If you have experienced trauma, and if you feel that the trau-matic experience was planned by your soul, you may feel anger toward your soul. If so, do not judge the anger as bad, and do not judge yourself for feeling anger. Your anger and indeed all your feelings, whatever they may be, are understandable and natural and right and true. Honor them. Respect them. Do not suppress them; instead, embrace them with love. Know that you are not your emotions; emotions are things you carry. Like all things that are carried, emotions may—when you are ready—be set down.

In my conversations with Jeshua, he addressed the anger you may feel toward your soul:

> Don't see the anger as a messenger of truth as in "my soul made the wrong choices"; see it as a messenger from the most hurt part of you. See it as a child who is in need of your attention and healing powers. Don't worry that the anger will alienate you from your soul or that your soul will be offended by it. *It is okay to feel the anger.*
>
> Hold the angry child within your arms and see what happens. You will see that not only is the child angry but also it is very lonely and sad. It longs for your company and guidance. Healing occurs the moment you connect to the child from your heart. If that happens, you are aligned with your soul: love flows through you and heals you from within.
>
> Work *with* the anger; do not fight it. Your hurt part needs to *feel* the energy of a wise, gentle, and compassionate parent from you.

Resistance

Suffering occurs when you resist emotions like fear and anger that may arise in response to the events in your life. The adage "What you resist, persists" is true: When you focus on something you give your energy to it, and resistance is a powerful form of focus. How then can you release resistance to negative emotions like fear and anger and so allow healing to flow in their stead?

To do so you must do what you would do if you had no such emotions. For instance, I felt much fear about revealing in the Preface that I experienced abuse as a child. (I also felt shame about the abuse itself.) For me this is an intensely personal matter. Before I wrote about it, I felt that doing so would be the equivalent of standing naked in front of the world. Had I allowed myself to be guided by my fear and shame, I would have chosen not to share this aspect of my life. Instead, I asked, "What would courage do now?" I made myself vulnerable by opening in this way—there is power in vulnerability—and I feel greater self-respect and self-esteem for having faced my fear and shame. Too, much of the fear and shame have now simply evaporated. In the same way, the mediums in this book spoke openly of some of the challenges they have experienced. We are no more courageous than you are. You will release your resistance to the circumstances and events of your life by doing what courage tells you to do.

If you believe you lack courage, remember that when your soul planned your life, you had the opportunity to succumb to fear and say no to the plan. Bravely, you agreed to it. Only the most courageous of souls choose to incarnate on Earth. You are one of these souls. The more difficult the life plan to which you agreed, the more courage you displayed in agreeing to it. If you have forgotten how courageous you are, this book will help you to remember.

When fear arises, remember this: You knew before you were born that fear would be a prominent component of your earthly experience. To know fear while in body is part of your plan. And so be very certain of this: *Only the courageous plan fear.* The courage it took to plan fear is the same courage it now takes to transform it. That you are in body is testament that you have the courage needed to transform your fears into love. Your desire to transform fear into love is one reason why you chose to incarnate at this special time of the shift in consciousness.

We Are Here to Heal

At the most basic level, the pre-birth contract is the same for everyone: embrace and transmute all discordant (unloving) energies. Energies we have not transmuted from any life will come to us in this life so that we may do so. We all requested this opportunity before we were born; indeed, it was a prerequisite for birth into the physical realm at this time. This lifetime is therefore of primary importance in the cosmic calendar. We are here to integrate into the whole of our Being and in so doing heal the remnants of all unintegrated energies from all our lives, both physical and nonphysical.

When we resist any aspect of life, we resist healing, too. When there is a block in one direction, there is a block in every direction. Ultimately, then, the purpose of every life challenge is the same: to grant us the opportunity to embrace that which we have so far resisted. As well, every life challenge is healed in the same way: through the realization of the power of what we think, say, and do. Our *experience* of life is not determined by our life plan but rather by how we respond to that plan. Our responses—our thoughts, words, and actions in every moment—create our experience and potentially our healing.

It is here that an awareness of pre-birth planning is profoundly helpful and healing. When we understand that we planned our lives, then we know there is deep meaning and purpose to all that occurs. When we know there is deep meaning and purpose to all that occurs, it becomes infinitely easier for us to think, speak, and act in loving ways. As we respond to life in loving ways, our previous resistance becomes acceptance, our acceptance turns into receptivity, our receptivity grows into embrace, and our embrace is transformed into gratitude for the experiences that open our hearts and expand us as souls.

You have embodied on Earth at this time to heal by awakening consciously to the memory of yourself as soul. Your healing comes and is completed when you see the light of your soul and know that light to be who you truly are.

CHAPTER 2

⚭

Spiritual Awakening

A
S SOULS WE CHOOSE BOTH the time period in which we will be born and the experiences we will have in the life-to-come. It is my belief that we live in a time of rapid and widespread spiritual awakening. If you incarnated in this time period, and particularly if you have come to these words, it is likely that you planned to awaken in this lifetime. By *awaken* I mean come to a deep, inner knowing that you are more than your body, more than your mind—that you are, in truth, an eternal being.

When we plan our lives, we often build into the blueprint major inflection points, catalysts or triggers that, depending upon our responses to them, can launch us in radically new directions. A spiritual awakening is one such point.

As sparks of our souls, we always have free will. When we reach a point in our lives at which the potential for an awakening was planned, we can accept the awakening or resist it. The repercussions of that decision, regardless of whether it is conscious or unconscious, will resound powerfully throughout the rest of our lives.

Seven years prior to the writing of this chapter, I experienced a profound spiritual awakening. When it began and as it was progressing, I did not know that I was awakening. In fact, had someone used the word *awakening* to describe what I was experiencing, I would not have understood what was meant. I knew only that dramatic, new vistas were opening rapidly before me, one after another. Suddenly, I was seeing facets of life I had never been aware of, though I sensed intuitively that they had been there all along. It was a time of exploration, excitement, and enchantment. I felt myself changing and expanding quickly, propelled by a powerful but invisible current. I did not know where the current would carry me, but I instinctively and joyfully surrendered to it. The thought of swimming to shore never entered my mind, and my life was never again the same.

What is a spiritual awakening? Why do some souls plan before birth to *give birth* to a new self within one lifetime? And how does one's life change after awakening?

My Life [4]

In May 2003 I was leading an unfulfilling life as a self-employed marketing and communications consultant. Although I enjoyed some of my work, I did not derive deep satisfaction from any of it. I often felt that if I were to fall off the face of the Earth, my clients would hardly notice; they would simply plug someone else into my role and carry right along. More important, my life was not a unique expression *of my soul.* A spiritual but not a religious person, I longed to make a contribution to the world that would be uniquely me, but I had no idea what that might be.

I come from a conventional background. I grew up in a conventional family in a conventional suburb of Cleveland, Ohio. I have a conventional education based on the scientific method. Coming as I did from such a background, my first attempts to discover the unique purpose of my life were also conventional. I began by telling friends and family that I felt there was a higher calling for me, and I asked them what they felt that calling might be. Generally, I received one of two answers. Some simply shrugged their shoulders and said, "I don't know." Others

---

4 Adapted from the prologue of my book *Your Soul's Plan: Discovering the Real Meaning of the Life You Planned Before You Were Born*

suggested I do whatever they were doing for a living. As you can imagine, neither of these responses was particularly helpful.

I then turned to another conventional approach: I spoke with a career counselor. I took the Meyers-Briggs Inventory and discovered my personality type. With due respect to the MBI, which can be a truly powerful tool, this information did me absolutely no good at all.

With conventional approaches proving fruitless, I decided to think outside the box. What could I do that would offer insight into my life purpose? With whom could I speak? A seemingly improbable inspiration came to me: consult a psychic medium. Knowing what I know now, I believe a spirit guide whispered that idea in my ear. At the time I did not know what a spirit guide was and believed that I came up with the idea on my own.

My session with the medium took place on May 7, 2003. I remember the exact date because that was the day my life changed. I told the medium very little about myself, describing my circumstances only in the most general terms. She explained that each of us has spirit guides, nonphysical beings with whom we plan our lives prior to incarnation. Through her I was able to speak with mine. They knew *everything* about me—not only what I had done but also what I had thought and felt. For example, they referred to a specific prayer I had said to God some five years earlier. At a particularly difficult time I had prayed, "*God, I can't do this alone. Please send help.*" My guides told me that additional nonphysical assistance had been provided. "*Your prayer was answered,*" they said. I was astounded.

Eager to understand the suffering I had experienced, I asked my guides about the major challenges I had faced. They explained that I had planned these challenges before birth—not for the purpose of suffering, but for the growth that would result. I was shaken by this information. My conscious mind knew nothing of pre-birth planning, yet intuitively I sensed truth in their words.

Although I did not realize it at the time, my session with the medium triggered a profound spiritual awakening for me. I would later understand that this awakening was really a *remembering*—a

remembering of who I am as an eternal soul and, more specifically, what I had planned to do on Earth.

For the next few weeks I continued with life as usual, although
the information from my guides was constantly on my mind. I
did not know what to do with it. Then, for the first time in my
life, I began to have metaphysical experiences of my own.

I awoke one morning at 3:00. Unable to fall back asleep, I
thought, I'll eat. I made my way down the hallway. Just as I was
crossing the threshold into the kitchen, I saw something moving
in the air around me. And this something was black, which made
it that much more frightening. I was terrified! I froze in the doorway, my heart pounding furiously in my chest. Without moving
a muscle, I scanned the room looking left … looking right … left
… right. I could not find whatever had been moving. I took a deep
breath, composed myself, and started into the kitchen once more.

Again there was movement in the air around me! And again,
whatever was moving was black. Again I froze in the doorway,
my heart racing. Slowly, deliberately, I scanned the room. I saw
nothing unusual. I stood motionless for a couple of minutes,
took another deep breath, and said to myself, "I don't know
what's happening here, but *I'm going to get my snack!*" I stepped
into the kitchen; again the black thing moved through the air
next to me.

By this time I had become aware of something important:
whatever it was, its movements were correlated with my own. So,
I began to play with it. I realized that I was seeing a thin black
line outlining my head, shoulders, arms—basically, the upper
half of my body. At each point the line was about six inches above
the surface of my skin. If I stood motionless, the line was also
motionless, which is why I couldn't see it when I was frozen in
the doorway. But if I moved my arm, for example, the line would
hover in the air for a few seconds, then flow very slowly until it
stopped six inches above my arm.

Eventually, I made my way to the refrigerator, where I discovered that the amount of light cast by the refrigerator bulb was

perfect for seeing the thin black line. So, at 3:10 in the morning I was standing in front of an open refrigerator, flapping my arms like a bird preparing for flight, watching a thin black line go up and down in the air!

When something inexplicable happens, I often have two reactions: intellectual and intuitive. These reactions are sometimes at odds with each other, and that was the case here. Intellectually, my mind said, "Okay, Rob, what's the differential diagnosis for an optical hallucination?" I thought, drugs—but I've never used any. Alcohol—but I rarely drink, and I hadn't had any that night. "Then I must have a brain tumor," my logical mind announced. Such was the absurd dialogue running through my head.

Meanwhile, my intuition said, "Rob, calm down. It's *not* a brain tumor. You may not know what it is, but for now just relax. You'll figure it out." Every day for the next week, whenever I had a free moment I Googled every term I could think of that might be related to what I had seen. After a week of searching the Internet, I stumbled across some arcane literature that referred to the "etheric fluidium"—*etheric* meaning nonphysical and *fluidium*, a Latin term meaning fluid-like. The literature explained that the etheric fluidium is the space between the physical body and the outer edge of the human aura, that the outer edge flows in a fluidlike manner, just as I had seen. I knew then that the thin black line was the outer edge of my own aura.

I believe my guides and Higher Self created this experience as a way of furthering my spiritual awakening and transitioning me into the new life that was to develop. Coming as I did from a conventional background, I could not have made an abrupt leap from the corporate sector to writing about pre-birth planning. In effect Spirit was opening me to that possibility by saying, "There is much more to the Universe than you have considered." I saw the outer edge of my aura many more times, though the experience occurred only when I awoke in the middle of the night. My understanding is that when I returned to my body after astral travel in the dream state, I was temporarily at a higher vibration and could therefore temporarily see things that are also at a higher vibration, like the outer edge of my own aura. (During sleep we leave our bodies for a variety of reasons, such as taking classes on "the other side," conferring with those with whom we share our lives, or whispering loving words of comfort to people in other parts of the world as they go about their day and face the challenges they planned before they were born.)

Just a few weeks later I had a much more profound experience, one that radically and permanently altered the way I look at myself, life, and the Universe. This experience is the touchstone of my spiritual awakening and the foundation of the work I do now.

One afternoon I was home in my apartment, having an average workday. I decided to take a break and go for a walk. As I walked down the sidewalk, *I suddenly felt overwhelming, unconditional love for every person I saw!* No words can adequately convey the power of this love. It was of an intensity and depth I had never experienced and had not known was possible. When I say "unconditional love," I do not mean the kind of love one might feel for a parent, child, or romantic partner; rather, this was an experience of Divine Love. It was a transcendent experience.

The first person I saw was a cab driver sitting behind the wheel of his cab, waiting for a fare to come along. I looked at this man, who was a complete stranger to me, and felt deep unconditional love for him.

Then I looked up and saw a barbershop on the street corner. I looked through the window and saw the barber cutting a client's hair. Again, two complete strangers—and I was overwhelmed with love for them.

Then I saw a young mother pushing an infant in a stroller down the sidewalk. As I looked at them, wave after wave of unconditional love washed over me.

As I looked around, every time I saw people I felt pure, limitless love for them!

Unlike the experience with my aura, no battle of interpretation occurred between my mind and heart. I knew intuitively and with absolute certainty what was happening: *I was in enhanced, immediate communion with my soul.* In effect my soul was saying to me, "*This love is who you are. This is your true nature.*" I believe my soul created this experience to facilitate the work I would soon begin.

After my session with the medium and the two spiritual experiences, I became obsessed with reading about spirituality and metaphysics. As I read I thought often about pre-birth planning. All my life I had viewed my challenges as nothing more than meaningless suffering and their occurrences as random and arbitrary. Had I known that I'd planned my challenges, I would have seen them rich with purpose. That knowledge alone would have greatly eased my suffering. Had I also known *why* I'd planned them, I could have consciously learned the lessons they offered. Feelings of fear, anger, resentment, blame, victimization, and self-pity would have been replaced by a focus on growth. Perhaps I might even have been grateful for the challenges.

During my intense study and inner exploration, I met a woman who is able to channel her soul and who agreed to let me speak with her soul about pre-birth planning. Apart from my one session with the medium, I had no knowledge of channeling. I was taken aback when this woman went into a trance and another consciousness, one that spoke quite differently than she and that had great knowledge of "the other side," began to speak through her. I spoke with her soul for fifteen hours over the course of five meetings.

These conversations were thrilling. They verified and complemented my reading and study. Her soul told me in detail about her own pre-birth planning: the various challenges that had been discussed, which had been selected and why, which had not been chosen and why not. Here I had direct, specific confirmation of a phenomenon of which very few people were aware. Because the pain in my life had made me extremely sensitive to—and intensely motivated to relieve—the suffering of others, I was excited by the potential healing an awareness of pre-birth planning could bring to them. I knew the information I had discovered could lighten their suffering and imbue their challenges with new meaning and purpose. As a result I resolved to write a book about the subject and to share its significance with others.

My enthusiasm for my new path was, however, tempered by the uncertainty of letting go of the old. Though unfulfilling, it was at least comfortable and familiar. Nevertheless, I was sustained—indeed, compelled to go forward—by the importance of the work, the opportunity finally to express myself in unique ways that would be of service to the world, and the certainty of knowing that came from directly experiencing my soul.

At first I thought the idea to write about pre-birth planning had originated in this lifetime. In truth, however, I had simply remembered my own plan. By working with several gifted mediums and channels, I discovered I had planned to write a series of books on this subject. In all I had dozens of sessions with mediums and channels, during which I spoke with many wise beings in spirit about my challenges and about pre-birth planning in general.

Because people across the world are awakening at this time, an understanding of the pre-birth planning of awakening is vitally important. In the early stages of awakening, you may feel lost or confused, unsure what to make of the experience. Even after the awakening has occurred and is understood, you may not know what steps to take next, how best to use your newly expanded awareness. This chapter offers a framework for understanding and building upon a spiritual awakening. I chose to explore my own awakening because I know it better and more intimately than I could another's.

My Session with Pamela and Jeshua

Many people assume that because of the work I do, I must know all the details of my pre-birth plan. Although I am aware of some, there is much more to discover. I was, therefore, excited to work with Pamela as she channeled Jeshua, one of the greatest teachers and most loving beings ever to incarnate on our planet. I sought to learn from Jeshua if and why I had planned a spiritual awakening in this lifetime. More broadly, I wanted to understand the role that such awakening plays in our lives; how we may best work with an awakening, particularly if it includes an awareness of pre-birth planning; and why so many are awakening at this time in evolution.

"There are a few things I'd like to say about spiritual awakening in general," Jeshua began. "You [incarnate souls] usually live within a veil or cloud of ideas about what's right and wrong, how you should live your life, and how to relate to your emotions. When awakening happens, a ray of sunlight pierces through that veil or cloud and opens you to an altogether new way of seeing things. It is a nonjudgmental, compassionate way of looking at yourself and all that goes on inside you. This is so new to most of you that to get acquainted with this perspective can be unsettling in the beginning. Spiritual awakening does not always feel good because it forces you out of your comfort zone.

"In *The Jeshua Channelings*[5] I described four stages of awakening in depth. I described what it is like to release ego-based consciousness and grow toward a heart-centered consciousness. Many people nowadays are in this process of transformation. The world is changing. I wish to say to all of you who are in this process that spiritual awakening is a journey within in which you release external certainties one by one until you get to the core of yourself. Within that core, you *are* Spirit. When you get there, you will experience a deep sense of relief, peace, and surrender. On the way there, you may meet with resistance, anger, and pain because your personality is not willing to give up its external certainties easily. It will usually put up a fight."

---

5 See References page for publisher information.

Jeshua's words resonated strongly with me. After my awakening, many of my old ways of looking at the Universe dissolved. Although logic and linear thinking once ruled my world, I became increasingly able to make heart-based decisions, even when they seemed illogical to me. Yet, the old limited and limiting ways of thinking and doing are habitual, and to this day I continue to shed an inner attachment to them, one my egoic mind does not relinquish easily. I feel myself gradually and eagerly embodying more of the wisdom and love of my soul, yet there is resistance that coexists with my eagerness. That resistance stems from my fear of the unknown. If the old me dissolves, who will I be?

"When you are in the middle of this," Jeshua continued, "you do not fit anymore in the old structures of your life. Jobs and relationships may fall away. You may feel lonely, not fitting in while not knowing where you are going. If you recognize this [is happening], please know that you are on your way, that you are not going crazy, and that you are tremendously courageous for taking this journey within. It is the world that is crazy to a large extent, persisting in maintaining this cloud of rigid notions of good and bad. You are liberating yourself from that. Have faith. We are right next to you. Guides and angels are constantly trying to remind you of your true nature, angelic and free. You are here to experience what it is like to be a human and also to enlarge the possibilities of humanity, to open human consciousness to a new horizon. You are doing this by going within and letting go of the false judgments you placed on yourself. You are a divine and pure being. Fix your attention on this inner core of light and beauty, and you will see that the pain and loneliness will diminish until your light shines out openly, attracting others and inspiring them to let their own light shine more brightly."

Jeshua's words were uplifting. "Can you say more," I asked him, "about what it means to spiritually awaken?"

"A spiritual awakening means that you become more aware of your soul, your greater Self, your divine essence. It means you realize there's more to you than your physical body and your present personality. You become aware of a dimension that transcends the realm of the visible, and you feel guided by that realm.

"Spiritual awakenings can happen in a variety of ways. Some people just catch a glimpse of the realm of their soul in certain moments. Others experience a shift in their experience that will cause them to make lasting changes in their lives. Generally, spiritual awakening means that one lets go of many preconceived ideas. There is a knowingness that there's more to life than can be grasped by the mind, that there's meaning behind the seemingly arbitrary events in your life, and that there is a greater force at work in the Universe that wants to guide you to achieve peace and joyful self-expression.

"Spiritual awakening is an ongoing process, not a one-time event," Jeshua concluded. "It is a gradual merging with your soul while you are in your earthly body."

"Jeshua, are people today more spiritually awake than people of previous generations?"

"Generally, yes. One might say that in this time *the need* for spiritual awakening is greater than ever before. This is a period of crisis. Evolution on Earth has reached a turning point. Humanity needs to make different choices if it wants to restore harmony. Many humans feel this need for change in their personal lives as a longing for purpose and meaning. They are not satisfied anymore by material wealth or worldly success alone. It may seem that a large part of humanity is still entranced by these goals; however, there is a large undercurrent now that points in another direction. Many, many people across the globe long to get in touch with their soul purpose, with their original intention for being on Earth at this time. This longing creates a new awareness in the collective consciousness of humanity.

"One sign is the rise of the feminine energy and the slow demise of the old, aggressive type of male energy. This energy still exists on the planet, of course; however, more and more people agree that it does not represent true leadership or strength. Humanity is gradually opening to a more balanced vision of leadership and power. The integration of the female energy is vital for this [to happen]. It means the feeling centers of humans, their hearts, are opening. They feel more connected to other humans and to living beings in general. They care more for the planet. And because you live in an age in which information is easily spread across the world, there is a growing sense of the oneness and interconnectedness of humans and life in general."

"Jeshua, if hearts are opening now, were people less awake during your lifetime?"

"They were less awake in general; however, there were individuals and even communities who were very evolved and in touch with their souls. There were different strands of consciousness. I knew there were enough humans present who would understand my message to plant seeds for the next generations to come. I also knew I would meet with resistance and that my teaching would be rejected by the ruling majority."

"Are there awakenings that are nonspiritual?"

"In my definition, awakenings are always spiritual in that they create a larger awareness of your true Self," Jeshua replied.

Finding Your Life Purpose

"Jeshua, I'd like to ask you about purpose and awakening. Many people write to me and ask how they can find their purpose in life. Many say they have felt a terrible sense of purposelessness for years. I felt that way for the first forty years of my life, until my awakening led to the work I do today. What would you say to people who feel that way? How would you advise them to find their purpose? What is the relationship between spiritual awakening and finding one's purpose?"

"Experiencing purposelessness means that you lost touch with the dimension of your soul," Jeshua explained. "However, it also means that you are truly seeking for meaning that goes beyond the physical. You are not satisfied by the more shallow goals one can pursue. In that sense you are awake when you experience purposelessness, for you know something is missing and that what you are missing is something inside rather than outside you. *You are longing for your soul.*

"I know the pain of missing your soul is hard to bear. Please realize, though, that when you sense purposelessness, you are sending a call to your soul to come closer to you, to merge more intimately with you. Your call will be answered, but you need to trust the process. This is when most people get stuck. They expect changes to happen quickly. If they don't they lose courage, and their minds get caught in negative thinking. For the soul to answer your call, many things need to happen first. Opening to the guidance of your soul means letting go of many preconceived ideas, emotional habits, and addictions that have become second nature to you."

By *addictions* I understood Jeshua to mean such things as fear, the more mild form of fear we call worry, and the continual and generally meaningless chatter in which our minds engage, much of which consists of judgments of ourselves, others, and life in general. Because these aspects of life are so common, and because most of us have experienced them for so long (usually since birth), we may mistakenly take them as natural and unavoidable.

"You are transformed by the connection with your soul," Jeshua continued. "In the beginning, allowing your soul in may mean you feel confused, uncertain, and afraid. This is not a bad thing; it means you are allowing change in your life. After some time you may feel dissatisfied with your life, job, or relationship. You may want to break free without knowing how and what to do next. This is a good thing. Do not get caught in fear at this point. Be aware of your feelings, and trust that the Universe will come up with a solution. You do not need to do anything right away. Just allow the change to take place on the inner level. Then you will draw external changes to you that will reflect your new desires.

"Finding a sense of purpose in your life that comes from within is tantamount to spiritual awakening, for the purpose that makes sense to you is the one that makes your soul sing. Whenever your creative acts, whatever they are, go together with a sense of joy and fulfillment, you are awake to the calling of your soul."

"Before my awakening in 2003," I said, "I did many things that did not resonate with me. Some of these were negative experiences. For example, I took jobs that did not speak to my soul, jobs in which I was just earning a living. Was this part of the plan for my life, and if so, why did my soul want me to spend so many years engaged in activities that were so unfulfilling?"

"You were searching for meaning," Jeshua told me. "Sometimes one first has to experience meaninglessness in several ways before one can open to what feels true to oneself. In your youth you were fed many ideas that did not resonate with your soul. For a long time, you tested these ideas against reality. This process was like peeling away the layers of an onion. You discovered you did not resonate with them. When you accepted this fact, you got to the core of your being, and this led to your spiritual awakening.

"It was part of your life plan to be born in the family you were and to be surrounded by the energies that were in your childhood," he added.

At the time of this conversation, I had not yet decided whether to discuss my childhood in this book. "I'm afraid to write about my childhood," I told Jeshua, "because it would be like standing naked and utterly vulnerable in front of the world."

"There is great power in vulnerability," he told me. "It takes courage. To be naked is also to be true.

"Breaking free from the influences of your childhood and finding your own path took a long time of preparation," Jeshua continued, "but this time was not in vain. You discovered important things along the way, and you developed valuable skills that are helpful to you now. You also developed a deep sense of compassion and spiritual wisdom because of the suffering you went through. All this waiting time has now made you ripe and wise beyond your years. You are the teacher you are not simply because of what happened to you in 2003; you are the teacher you are just as much because of all that happened before that date. The two parts of your life are not as separate as you think. The negative experiences, as you call them, paved the way for the spiritual breakthrough you experienced. They helped you become more aware of who you truly are."

Jeshua was right: I had divided my life into two parts, one that I was happy to leave behind, the other that I was eager to embrace. Yet, every step, even those I have long perceived as missteps, had brought me to this dialogue with him. As I took in his words, I thought of something I wrote in my first book: I am teaching what I most need to learn. For example, I suggested to others that they cultivate gratitude for their challenges. Jeshua was now lovingly pointing out to me that I could do more of that as well. I wanted to discuss the point further.

"Jeshua, when I look back on the many years in which I felt lost, I wish I had done something more meaningful. For example, I wonder if I should have joined the Peace Corps. What an amazing experience that would have been! Does my soul wish I had done something else? If other activities like the Peace Corps would have done more to foster my evolution, why did I not feel any impulse to travel those roads?"

"The experiences you had in the time you were lost were painful but not without meaning," Jeshua answered. "You needed them to find out who you really are. To say that you should have done more useful things with your time is to ignore the inner dynamics of the soul's growth process. The soul learns through opposites. By exploring what you do *not* want, you get clear about what you do want. You did not feel an impulse to join the Peace Corps because that did not resonate with who you were then. You did not make a mistake, and by and large your life ran the course it was supposed to run. Some things could have been different—there's always room for free choice—but you needed the experience to get to the point where you are now. Behind a powerful experience of awakening there always lies a whole development in the past that leads to this breakthrough. The past may seem meaningless in hindsight, but in truth it is the stepping-stone from which you leap into greater awareness."

The Pre-Birth Planning of Awakening

It was now time for the central questions. "Was my awakening planned before I was born, and if so, why?" I asked. "And was it planned to occur when I was forty years old?"

"The opportunity for the awakening was planned, yes. The awakening itself could not be fixed in time; it is the personality's choice to truly open to and go along with the soul's calling. But, circumstances around the age of forty made it likely that you would let go of the past and break through the veil of illusion that kept you imprisoned for a long while. The reason this opportunity was built into your life plan is that it was your soul's goal to shine its light on Earth from the heart, notwithstanding the pain of rejection you experienced early in life. You wanted to know what it is like to appreciate and love yourself independently of others, and you wanted to share this love with others as a teacher and writer.

"In your case forty was the right age. In general, around this age people are likely to pause and reflect on life, finding out what's really important to them and what goals they want to pursue in the second half of life. Also, in your early forties physical changes occur, especially in women—the start of menopause—that influence the psyche. So, around that age the likelihood of spiritual transformation through a crisis or awakening is certainly increased."

I then told Jeshua about my session with the medium in 2003. "That experience truly opened me to the nonphysical realm," I said, "and caused me to think about all sorts of things I had never considered, like the idea that we plan our lives before we're born. I feel that the session with the medium changed the course of my life and triggered my awakening."

"The session established a connection to your soul, and in that sense it certainly was vital to your awakening," Jeshua confirmed. "The meeting came at the right time. You were ready and open to get acquainted with the dimension of your soul. The Universe answered your call by putting this medium on your path."

"Was the session with the medium planned before I was born? If that session had not taken place, would I still have awakened?"

"The session had a high likelihood of occurring. Again, nothing is completely predetermined. It was a powerful tool. If it had not taken place, you would have awakened more gradually through various events. It would have been less spectacular. It was very likely that the session would take place, however, and it was almost only a matter of time before you would bump into this medium."

"Jeshua, not long after the session with the medium, I stopped doing corporate work and started to research and write my first book about pre-birth planning. Everything in my life has changed—for the better in my view—as a result of that decision. Now, my work is deeply fulfilling to me. I feel that I matter and that I am making a contribution to the world. I feel more alive, happier, closer to God. Could I have used my free will to refuse to awaken spiritually? If I had done that, what would my life be like now? Would my soul and guides have kept trying to awaken me? If so, how would they have done it?"

"After the session you started to feel your soul's inspiration, and this created joy and fulfillment in your life," Jeshua replied. "You could have refused to awaken spiritually in the sense of letting the opportunity go by, but at that point it was unlikely because you craved your soul's knowledge and light even if you weren't consciously aware of it. You were like the proverbial apple, ready to fall off the tree.

"If you had not awakened at that time, you soul and your guides would have kept stimulating you. They always do, at small or big junctures in your life. Life always offers new opportunities for change. The way guides help you is like whispering suggestions in your ear. Guides try to make you see things from a positive perspective. They send you the energy of healing and encouragement. You can pick up this energy even if you are not able intuitively to connect with your guides and receive messages or images from them. Guides will not force themselves upon you, but their energy is always available to you."

"If I had not awakened and gone on to write about pre-birth planning, would Spirit have found someone else to do what I now do?"

"Your contribution is uniquely yours. It fits who you are, your special interests and gifts. It is not a fixed assignment that would be passed on to someone else in case you did not want it. It has too much of your energy mark on it for that. And that is how it should be. Every soul has its own specific gift to give to this world, in accordance with its interests, capabilities, and energy. What attracts your audience is the energy of your soul, not the topic of pre-birth planning alone."

"Was my awakening planned by me, my soul, or both my soul and me?"

"Both. You are a part of your soul; you are not a separate being. However, the personality growing out of the soul with each incarnation has a kind of independence. It has its own say in the life plan, and therefore I say 'both.'"

"At what point in the pre-birth planning process did I come into existence?"

"To speak in terms of time is problematic here," said Jeshua. "The soul is eternal, and since you are part of the soul, not separate, so are you. The soul gives birth to you during the pre-birth planning process in the sense of a potentiality becoming realized. The potential is already there in a way that cannot be described in human terms. It's not important to grasp this with the mind. The personality is an aspect of the soul that is released by the soul at the time of incarnation. Although it remains connected to the soul, it is also independent of it in that it can make its own choices. This is necessary, for how else would the soul be able to learn and to experience new things through the personality? The personality is meant to explore life on its own and to have the choice to align with the soul or not. That is why it is meaningless to place judgments of right and wrong on the personality's behavior. The personality is the learning and growing part of the soul."

"Where was I before then, and what was I doing?" I asked.

"You, as the personality you are now, were dormant within your soul, not yet brought alive into material manifestation. You are like a seed carried within the womb of your soul."

"Is the soul already and always awake? If so, why does the soul need or want to create a personality that experiences a spiritual awakening?"

"The soul is not awake entirely," Jeshua explained. "It has a larger perspective than the human personality, but it is also growing and evolving. It longs to explore life and to enlarge its consciousness. It longs to experience creativity and joy and to continuously expand its boundaries in that regard. Life is endless and always moving.

"Also, the soul desires to be awake and manifest *while in human form.* It's easier to be awake if you are not in human form, not having to deal with the human limitations of ignorance and fear. So, the personality is, in fact, the most courageous part of the soul, the vessel through which the soul incarnates on Earth. To be awake and present in human form is deeply desirable for the soul, because it is only in matter that it can fully express its potential, its creativity. The soul wishes to enlighten material reality from the inside out and finds deep satisfaction in this."

"Jeshua, are there degrees of awakening?"

"Yes, there are. There are moments of alignment with the soul, which you experience as flashes of truth or guidance, and there are more lasting states of awakening. It is even possible to become more or less permanently aligned with the soul. This is what all of you aim for. It is wise, however, to accept that it is a gradual process in which you slowly open to your soul's reality."

Jeshua's Experience with Awakening

"Jeshua, respectfully, may I ask if you yourself are fully awake?" I felt somewhat uncomfortable asking this question, but it seemed both reasonable and important. "And were you fully awake in your incarnation as Jeshua? Did you experience degrees of awakening in that lifetime?"

"I am awake, but I am still learning and evolving. Even here we are transcending our boundaries always, expressing ourselves in new ways and thereby finding out more about who we are. In my lifetime as Jeshua, I was at times fully aligned with my soul, but there were also darker moments in which I lost faith and doubted my mission. I was a human being like you. I did experience a growth in awakening at the time prior to my death. At that time it required great clarity and persistence to keep my faith in the face of my oncoming death. I was visited by fear and doubt, but I also experienced grace and surrender toward the end. I was human in my life on Earth, not a god who had transcended all human emotion. I was born with a high sense of self-awareness, and this was part of my pre-birth plan. My personality was able to succumb to my soul's mission in that lifetime, but I did not achieve this without going through the very human emotions of fear, doubt, and anger."

"In that lifetime, how did you try to awaken people spiritually?"

"I tried to make them aware of their true strength, which lies beyond success, wealth, or gender. I tried to awaken their divine inner core by looking through the outer appearance and truly seeing them as divine, innocent beings. If you focus on this aspect of another, you bring it alive. By perceiving it, you make people more aware of it. To help awaken people is not about handing them theories or knowledge; it is an energy transmission foremost. It has to do with touching the divine energy in their hearts by listening to them without judgment and accepting them as they are, with all their doubts and fears and anger. To fully let them be and recognize their inner beauty, even if they don't see it themselves, may help people be lifted out of their state of self-denial or lack of self-appreciation."

"Do you feel you were successful?"

"I planted seeds, but it took time for them to blossom. Some people were immediately affected by the energy of my teaching.

Others needed to digest it slowly. Many people did not understand it. The people in power mostly rejected me because my teaching was about the equality of all men, and it ran against their doctrines of social hierarchy and separation."

By *separation* Jeshua meant the belief, widespread both then and now, that we are separate from God and one another. In fact there is no separation, only the illusion of it created by the limitations of the five senses. This is not a bad thing; the seeming separation from God and other people causes us to experience an intensity of emotion that we would otherwise not feel. On the Earth plane, growth comes through the experience of intense emotions and our reactions to them.

"In the long run, my mission succeeded," Jeshua continued, "but I am speaking of many centuries in time now. The Christ seed was planted in my lifetime, not just by me but also by my followers and companions at that time. Many courageous men and women tried to cherish and preserve those seeds. In this time [now] a broader awakening is taking place among humanity. Christ consciousness is gaining foothold slowly on Earth, as millions of people are reaching out for a way of living that is based on the heart rather than on fear and judgment."

How to Awaken

"Jeshua," I asked, "What can someone do to awaken?"

"Essentially, it is about looking at oneself with greater compassion and understanding. You frequently beat yourselves up for all the things you think you do wrong. But, you are not doing anything wrong; you are simply trying to make your life work as best as you can. Be kind to yourself. Recognize your innocence. You are an angel gaining experience in a human body on Earth. If you can recognize this fact, your suffering will be alleviated. Without the burden of self-judgment, your pain will be relieved, emotional or physical. You can let yourself be, and from that self-love, positive changes will occur in your life. You will begin to see that life does not want to punish you; it wants to liberate you and make you aware of the joy and freedom available to you. Awakening always starts with self-love."

"What can I do to awaken further?"

"You may start by congratulating yourself for all you have accomplished so far. You have had tremendous courage, facing the pain and grief of your childhood. You have accomplished a truly spiritual transformation inside yourself. Of course there are still emotions lingering inside that upset you, but you can transform these by allowing them to be, by not trying to chase them away, by seeing them as little children who turn to you for guidance. Awakening further is not so much about doing anything now; it's about allowing yourself to be who you are."

"Is everyone reading this awake? How would someone know?"

"People reading your book are longing to be awake," Jeshua answered, "and that is the beginning of awakening. The more you are aware of yourself, and the more you take responsibility for your own reality, the more awake you are. Again, awakening is a gradual process."

Using an Awareness of Pre-Birth Planning

Knowing that we plan our lives and our challenges before birth brings comfort and meaning, but it can be difficult to apply this awareness when in the middle of a great challenge. I asked Jeshua how people can use an awareness of pre-birth planning in a practical way when in difficult circumstances.

"The knowledge that you as a soul planned your challenges may help you see that it is not coincidental certain things take place in your life right now," Jeshua said. "It is not random or meaningless. This may help you accept what is happening, even though it is still very difficult to live with. Ultimately, it is not the emotions of fear, grief, or anger that really block you in life. Rather, it is your *resistance* to them that prevents life from flowing through you and bringing you healing. To know that your soul is allowing challenges in your life for a reason may help you let go of the resistance or the sense of anger and indignation you feel toward what is happening to you.

"Your soul is evolving just as much as you are. It wants to evolve *through* you. It is not standing by letting you suffer; it is right there with you. The soul knows, however, that the pain has meaning and leads to a new horizon, whereas the personality is generally less in touch with that awareness. So, to bring the soul's perspective to the attention of the personality can make the pain bearable because it is put in a larger, meaningful perspective.

"People can call upon their souls to explain to them why certain challenges are happening. If they open to that possibility, answers will come. It need not be through a psychic or any other person. They will get hunches or signs along the way showing them there is meaning behind their suffering. This can give them some relief and perhaps even a sense of peace with the situation. The relief or peace may not last long at first, but if they keep in touch with the soul's perspective, their suffering will be alleviated."

Jeshua's words reminded me of the great importance of meditation, which is a primary way of connecting with the soul. Prior to my awakening, I never meditated. Since awakening I have meditated regularly. In meditation there are literally filaments of light built from the Higher Self to the personality, thus creating a greater melding. On occasion I have also called upon my soul to communicate with me in dreams. Speaking aloud, I pose a particular question before going to sleep. I then ask to be sent a dream containing an answer to the question. I also ask to be awakened so I may write down the dream; otherwise, I know I will not recall it in the morning. (If you write slowly, you may prefer to keep a tape recorder by your bed.) On many occasions helpful insights were indeed provided.

"Jeshua, people often wonder if it is possible to avoid a challenge that was planned before birth."

"The question of whether you can avoid challenges is born from fear. This fear is very understandable, but it blocks your vision. If you make loving decisions to avoid challenges, there is an agenda behind those decisions that is tainted by fear. Truly loving decisions are born from trust, not the desire to avoid anything.

"It is possible to avoid challenges, but you cannot make it your aim. It is a negative aim; moreover, you will never know what challenges you avoided. There is no way to measure this. You are all invited to trust life, which requires that you surrender to life and let go of control. This is difficult for humans, but there is a Divine Guidance that is more wise and gentle than your human sense of control. Try to feel it, and count the blessings in your life, for they are testimony to this loving and guiding hand. You are not alone. Powers of love and kindness surround you and wish to help you live the most fulfilling life possible."

"Jeshua, when something bad happens, particularly if the same thing happens more than once in a person's life—for example, losing a loved one at a young age—a spiritually awake person will take some comfort in the fact that the experience may have been planned before birth, but still the person wonders, 'Why does this keep happening to me?'"

"If certain challenges happen again and again in someone's life, there is something there the soul deeply yearns to understand or live through. It's very courageous of the soul and the personality to decide to experience this challenge repeatedly. It's important the personality does not think it is doing something wrong or that it is being punished for something if the challenge repeats itself.

"It is not always possible to understand fully why certain challenges occur at the time they occur. The meaning will be clearer later, when you have gone through the most difficult stage. Often, when people reflect on their challenges later in life, they are thankful for them and feel they learned something very important and valuable through them. This knowledge is often not present at the time of the crisis itself, which is why a crisis is so challenging, but it will come in time.

"So, if you are wondering why certain challenges repeat themselves in your life, you can on the one hand ask what the challenge was teaching you the first time. This will give you a clue. Perhaps you want to learn or grasp this lesson at an even deeper level now. On the other hand, it is important simply to *know* there is meaning behind it, even if you do not understand yet what it is."

Jeshua's use of the word *know* struck me as significant. Trust is literally a carrier of light, and as light infuses our consciousness, we awaken. When we *believe* there is meaning in our challenges, we are demonstrating some trust in the goodness of life. Yet, when we choose to *know* there is meaning, we are deeply and truly trusting in that beneficence. It is then that we fully accept the light of our souls and awaken.

"Generally, crises bring you to a new way of living," Jeshua summarized. "They change you as a person, and it is you, the transformed person, who will really 'get' the meaning behind the crisis. You are growing toward a new you. This new you will understand what you do not yet understand or refuse to understand. The key is to trust that this new you is already alive in your being, waiting for you to embrace it. The new you can speak to you, encourage and reassure you. Connect to it by seeing yourself in the future, explaining to the present you the meaning of what you are going through and giving you advice about how to deal with your emotions from day to day." Here, Jeshua was offering a specific and practical meditation one can do to understand the deeper meaning of an experience.

"Jeshua, people who are awake and who are aware of pre-birth planning often wonder this: If the soul suffers the way the personality sometimes suffers, would the soul still make the same plans for the lifetime?"

"Again, your soul is right there with you. It is not up in Heaven looking down on you; it is not an outsider. Your soul is going through the experience with you but with the knowledge that this experience is meaningful and brings you to a place of beauty and joy. The soul shares your pain, but it does not condemn the pain like you do. That is the difference. The soul is in a deeper state of acceptance than the personality usually is. To be angry or upset with the soul for having put such difficult challenges along your path is to drive a wedge between you and your soul. The soul is a gentle force. It is the resistance the personality feels toward a challenge that can make it seem unbearable.

"If you connect to your soul, who dwells inside you, you may sense that the soul's plan is aligned with what you want, too. Often, personalities have certain dreams, longings, and visions they pursue. The Universe wants to fulfill these wishes, but that sometimes means challenges you did not expect will cross your path. Still, they are tied in with your deeper longings and desires. Those very crises you find so difficult to cope with will ultimately get you exactly where you as a personality want to be. But, because you do not see the end result yet, you think the soul is forcing you to go with a plan that is not yours. It *is* yours; you just do not have the overview yet. That is what being a human is about. That is what makes you the most courageous angels there are."

This seemed a good time to ask Jeshua about a topic that continued to puzzle me: the circumstances in which we agree to our soul's plan. In the nonphysical realm we call Home, where we are continuously bathed in Divine Love, are we making truly informed choices when we say, "Yes, I agree to the plan"? Do we genuinely understand what the Earth experience will be like?

"It is a leap of faith when you decide [before birth] to face certain challenges in your life," Jeshua told me. "The personality is aware of this. It may even resist the lifetime to come, and in that case the challenges will be more difficult to accept [when in body]. However, some part of the personality agrees to the plan, and the choice is not uninformed. Before birth it is explained to the personality that the challenges at hand are truly very valuable lessons the personality itself will want to learn for it to achieve its own goals. The personality may, for instance, long to experience a successful relationship in life, being happy with a spouse and raising a family. This is the personality's dream. It may also, however, have a tendency to become very dependent emotionally upon the partner, or it may have an overly idealized vision of what a romantic relationship is. So, although the vision of a loving relationship is a legitimate goal, the personality may have to learn first what it is like to be emotionally independent. It may need to experience a painful loss or breakup in the area of relationships before it will have the relationship it truly desires. The breakup may seem unbearable and cruel; however, the personality will, by going through the mourning process and spending time alone, grow a sense of emotional independence that will prepare it for a new, truly fulfilling relationship.

"The personality is not fooled by the soul, although it may seem that way when it experiences the challenges at an emotional level. The soul truly and deeply wants to comfort you. It does not want you to suffer unnecessarily. It has your best interest in mind. Simply trusting your soul may alleviate your pain.

"Every personality has a certain passion. The passion represents an aspect of the soul that wants to be expressed through that personality. The passion may be to paint, or to take care of children, or to be a spiritual teacher. The personality's challenges are always meant to connect them to their core passion and express it freely. If they want to become a spiritual teacher like you, they want to embody deeply the self-love and self-awareness they seek to teach others. They will need to embrace themselves with as much tenderness and compassion as they do others. This will bring them into the core of their passion and enable them to express it joyfully and without reserve."

Jeshua was now speaking to the heart of my own pre-birth plan: learning self-love. Mine is a classic learning-through-opposites plan. Earlier in life I felt much judgment and a lack of appreciation and acceptance. That experience was intended by my soul to serve twin purposes: to drive me inward, where I would discover and cultivate self-acceptance and self-love; and to create the passion necessary to write books about pre-birth planning, books that would help others to come to know and thus love themselves as sacred. Like everyone, my personal challenges and core passion are therefore inextricably intertwined, each nurturing and empowering the other.

"Jeshua, I said earlier that I feel happier, more alive, and closer to God as a result of my awakening and the work I now do. Yet, I still experience the so-called negative emotions that are so much a part of the human experience. What can I do to stay in that place of peace and joy?"

"Accept that peace and joy cannot be created through the will," he advised. "They will come about as a result of deeper acceptance of your painful emotions. As you embrace those emotions, just letting them be without wanting to change them, they will pass through you. It is in the nature of emotions to move and change, like the weather does. If you fix your attention too strongly on a negative emotion, it will not pass through you as quickly as it can. It will hang around, waiting for you to release it. It wants to move, like a dark cloud wants to dissolve by raining. There is a natural rhythm to your emotions. If you trust and try not to analyze negative emotions, the sky will become clearer.

"You are going into a next phase of awakening. During the first phase, you experienced a deep connection with your soul that truly fulfilled you. Now, a deeper layer of your soul wants to come to Earth, bringing in more love and wisdom to share with people and to give to yourself."

As we awaken spiritually, we see with increasing clarity that suffering is caused not by external circumstances but rather by our reactions to them, as Jeshua pointed out. This realization often brings with it a desire for healing so that we may respond more positively to the lives we planned. I asked Jeshua to speak to the topic of healing.

"True healing comes from within," he said. "It often takes more time than the personality expects, and that can make people desperate; however, your soul has provided you with the tools to heal yourself. It will create people and circumstances in your life that will in some way help you, even if you do not realize it. But foremost, you have incredible power available within you. God or Spirit is part of you. You are not alone. God seeks to enlighten you from within. To connect with this force of Light within, you have to trust. Trust that things happen for a reason, that there's guidance available through your feelings. Your feelings indicate what you need and want in your life. By this I do not mean your emotions, but your intuition. If you ask yourself honestly, from the heart, 'What is it I need right now?,' you will get an answer from within. You get answers like this all the time, but it takes courage to act upon them and remain true to your heart. It is possible, however, and it will lead you to greater self-awareness and then to greater healing.

"External healing modalities can be helpful if they remind people of their own inner power," Jeshua added. "It is often the vibration of the healers that makes the difference more so than the physical tools they use. It is when people recognize this vibration as healing and true that they can activate it within themselves."

Worldwide Awakening

"Jeshua, I'd like to talk with you about this time period on Earth, a time of widespread awakening. Many people talk about a major shift in consciousness. What is happening?"

"Many people nowadays are looking for a different kind of meaning in their lives. In the more wealthy countries, a large part of the population is aware that material goals do not truly bring fulfillment or self-realization. These people are awakening. Also, there is a sense among people that they are members of humanity in addition to being part of a nation or smaller community. In other words, people are starting to realize that they share their humanness with all other human beings across the world. This connectedness brings about a sense of oneness and responsibility for the planet. Awakening processes are hard to predict. It is better to focus on the present and your own process than on the future. There's nothing you need to know about the future to live a conscious life now. The best sense of security derives from being in the present and listening to your feelings rather than to theories and speculations about the future."

"People sometimes talk about the 'hundredth monkey,' a term used to describe the idea that when a certain number of people awaken—a critical mass, if you will—then very quickly many, many others will awaken. Is this how it works?"

"Yes, it does," Jeshua stated. "Although each awakening process is unique, when the vibration of humanity is raised as a whole, it becomes easier for people to pick up that vibration and be inspired by it. In the end more enlightened organizations will arise in areas like education and healthcare. There will be an influx of new energy into society that will provide humanity with more possibilities to raise awareness."

"Has there ever before been a period like this on Earth?"

"Every period is unique. There have been enlightened societies on Earth, very old ones that have not been recorded by history. This time is different in that the transformation process concerns all of humanity, and people are much more connected to one another globally than in the earlier days."

"How do people's souls benefit by having an incarnation during a time of widespread awakening?"

"People, or souls, choose to live in such times because they want to finish up their own unresolved business," Jeshua told me. "Living on Earth now are many evolved souls who want to clear old pain and trauma from past lives on Earth. Living in a time of awakening has many benefits, but it can also make life quite intense at times.

"It can be challenging to let go of much of your old identity and open to a new, heart-centered way of living," Jeshua added. "Yet, this is the soul's truest desire, and it therefore took the opportunity to incarnate at this time."

"Is everyone going to awaken? If not, what will happen to those who don't?"

"It's not possible to make predictions about that. There is no deadline of any kind. The house of my Father has many mansions. Each soul will find a mansion that is in accordance with its vibration at a certain point in time."

"Do beings on other planets or in other dimensions experience spiritual awakenings? Are there beings who have no need of such an experience?"

"There's a unique quality to life on Earth in that it covers such a wide variety of beings and experiences," Jeshua observed. "However, the Universe is teeming with life, and all life seeks greater self-awareness and self-expression. All life is geared toward further, unending awakening."

∽

You are alive at what may well be the most exciting and important time in human history. As Jeshua said, the Earth has seen enlightened societies, but the spiritual awakening that is now occurring is a global phenomenon. Pause for a moment to give thanks that you are here. Regardless of your circumstances, simply offer thanks for the honor and blessing of being in body here, now.

Let me share with you what spiritual awakening means to me.

I have come to *know* to the very core of my being that we live forever. I have no fear of death, for I know there is no death.

As I write these words, my father is very ill. I do not know when he will choose to return to Spirit—perhaps this year, perhaps next. When he transitions, my grief will be eased by my awareness that he has, in effect, simply walked out of one room of a very large house and into another. Though I will no longer be able to talk with him in body, I will most certainly talk with him, and I *know* that I will be heard.

My father is suffering. Every moment he is short of breath. He has great difficulty walking. On occasion he experiences intense physical pain. He cannot recall conversations we had just one day, and sometimes hours, earlier. He is confused, no longer able to manage on his own, and in his confusion is deeply fearful of what will become of him. He has no particular beliefs about an afterlife.

Though my father does not think so, I know his experience is profoundly meaningful. Without this knowing, I would be furious with God. I would ask angrily, "Why do you allow my father to suffer like this?" It is still hard for me to see him suffer, but I believe that he planned this portion of his life to teach him how to accept caregiving—love—from others. And as he does so, he is in service *to* others. He has made it possible for me to open my heart. For most of my life I could not tell him I loved him. Now the words come easily.

I have come to know, too, that each of us is loved beyond anything we can conceive of as love. This love is unfathomable to the human mind. When I was younger, I sensed it as an ineffable sweetness that seemed to be everywhere. Now I know that it *was* everywhere. And always will be.

I have come to know that God/Source permeates—indeed, *is*—every insect, leaf, caressing breeze, ray of sunlight, atom and molecule, and person. Each person is a vital thread within this tapestry. If just one thread were removed, the entire tapestry would unravel. In our seeming separation from one another, we often cannot see that we are essential; instead, we feel small, insignificant, even meaningless. Yet, the full beauty of the whole is contained in every part, and the whole is as beautiful as it is *because of* every part.

I have come to know that we who incarnate on Earth are among the most courageous beings in existence. We are revered throughout the Universe for having the bravery to assume physical form on one of the most challenging of planets. Consider for a moment what you did in coming here. In the nonphysical realm you knew yourself to be limitless. You created instantly with thought. You were able to see literally in all directions. You communicated telepathically. You were in perfect health and did not age. You were in a state of unity with All That Is, knowing yourself to be one with God and every other being. You were awash in a vibration of all-encompassing love, peace, and joy.

You then chose to place yourself in a physical body and confine your perceptions to those of the five senses. You removed yourself (seemingly) from all-enveloping Love in order to experience an environment in which fear often predominates. You planned great challenges. You then chose to forget both your true identity and every aspect of the realm from which you came. You did all this to foster the evolution of your soul.

To veil yourself from your own grandeur and magnificence is an act of extraordinary courage.

Now, as you awaken, you recall yourself as Divinity Incarnate.

CHAPTER 3

೧ல

Miscarriage

T HE EXPERIENCE OF MISCARRIAGE IS often a
combination of shock, grief, anger, and guilt. For a parent to lose a child at any age is excruciatingly painful,
but when that loss occurs *before* the child is born, when parents
have not even had a chance to cradle the infant in their arms,
they feel an intense and unique type of sadness. How do parents
say goodbye to a child they do not yet know? Too, the bereaved
parents are often angry with themselves, each other, and the
Universe. How, they wonder, could their unborn child be taken
from them? What could they have done to prevent it? Were their
genes defective? Who is to blame?

To understand, I spoke with Rebecca Valentine, who was
thirty-four years old when she miscarried at sixteen weeks ges-
tation. (The miscarriage had occurred seven years prior to our
conversation.) Although she had moved through the phase of
acute grief long ago, I knew from our previous contact that
Rebecca still carried some unresolved grief as well as guilt and
self-blame. I later learned that self-forgiveness had been a lesson
with which Rebecca had struggled in past lives. She had brought
this lesson forward into the current lifetime for healing and was
now struggling with it once more.

When I discovered that Rebecca had not completely forgiven
herself seven years after the miscarriage, I saw her story as all the

more important to this book. At this time in human evolution, we as souls desire to heal, once and for all, those longstanding issues with which we have wrestled over millennia. Like Rebecca, many people have a particular lesson they were not able to learn in multiple past lives and seek, therefore, to resolve in this lifetime. When we see such lessons in our lives or in the lives of others, it is helpful to view them with compassion, love, patience, and respect, remembering that only the most valiant agree before birth to face and heal the wounds of the soul.

Rebecca

Rebecca is the mother of four children: Max, 13; Tucker, 10; Tavia, 7; and Isabella, 5. She and her partner, Wes, are raising their family in a small town in northern Colorado. Rebecca's ex-husband is the father of the boys; Wes is the girls' father. Calvin, the infant who died, would have been born after Tavia and before Isabella.

The miscarriage occurred on June 11, 1999. Rebecca's pregnancy had gone smoothly until that morning, when suddenly her water broke. "*We're going to lose this baby,*" she yelled to Wes. Wes quickly called a friend of the family, who took all the children.

"I went into the bathroom," Rebecca said, "and Calvin came out. He was in my hand, very tiny, and his thumb was in his mouth. It was like having a live baby, only a mini version. I wrapped him in a hand towel and took him into bed with me. I was dazed; I felt like I was moving in water. I was sitting there holding Calvin, just looking at him. Even knowing he was dead, I still had this incredible need to protect him. I was trying to get the blood off him, taking care of him as if he were alive. But, your brain doesn't think logically. It really doesn't think at all."

Rebecca returned to the bedroom, where she started to bleed heavily. She ran into the bathroom again and passed out so violently that she knocked off the top of the toilet.

"The next thing I knew," she recalled, "I woke up on the floor of the bathroom with eight EMTs around me, trying to get a vein.

I remember them saying, *'Don't let her eyes close. Keep her awake or we're going to lose her.'* What was so strange was I could see the tops of their heads, and I could see me lying on the ground. I remember feeling so cold, like I couldn't feel my arms or my legs anymore. And I remember having this feeling of wanting to be still and let go. I was conscious of the fact the baby had died."

Rebecca watched the EMTs from her vantage point at the bathroom ceiling. Then she saw Wes standing in the doorway, looking terrified. "What will happen to my kids?" she thought. "They'll split up my family." And with that thought, she suddenly found herself back in her body.

"From that point on, I wasn't looking down on these people anymore; I was on the ground looking up. I remember telling them to get a butterfly needle because I have small veins. I knew that using a large needle, they weren't going to be able to find any vein at all since they were collapsed. Nobody would listen to me. The next thing I heard was, 'Get Flight for Life.' They started to take me downstairs to get me into the ambulance.

"When we went downstairs, there was a man sitting in my living room who I had never seen before. He had dark brown hair with a beard and very dark brown eyes. He looked remarkably like a guy I used to date years ago, someone very gentle and kind. I looked at him and thought, He really looks like Donny.

"We got into the ambulance. This same guy came out—he was dressed in a white polo shirt and khaki shorts; he wasn't in any sort of uniform—and onto the ambulance. He took my hand and said 'Sweetie, you're going to be okay.' I got this great feeling of peace. I believed him. I absolutely, 100 percent believed him.

"I said, 'I need a pediatric needle.' He said, 'I know.' He found a vein on the first try and hooked me up [to the IV]. Then he told the ambulance driver, 'She doesn't need Flight for Life. She'll make it. Just get her to the hospital.' Then he got off the ambulance.

"There were two people in the front seat of the ambulance and me and one EMT in the back. One of them asked, 'Who was that?' Another said, 'I thought he was on the Flight for Life team.' And the first person said, 'No, I thought he was part of your team.' From what I understand, there had been three different teams there: the volunteer fire department, Flight for Life, and the EMTs from the hospital. Everybody thought he was with another team. Then he left the ambulance. No one ever saw him again."

The ambulance rushed Rebecca to the hospital, where an emergency procedure was performed. After doctors stabilized Rebecca, they informed her that her baby had died of an encephalocele, an anomaly at the top of the neck that prevents the spine from connecting with the brain stem. They later told Rebecca that her placenta had torn and she had been in the process of bleeding to death.

"The doctor told me, 'He died awhile ago,' Rebecca recalled. "I said, 'Three weeks ago.' 'How did you know that?' he asked. 'Because I felt it.' I had been in the boys' bedroom painting and had picked up a cement block. I felt something happen, and I got this horrible feeling of dread. I thought, 'My baby just died.'"

Rebecca brought Calvin home from the hospital and kept his body on ice until she could make arrangements for a cremation. I asked her to talk more about the feelings she experienced that day.

"The first thought I had [as I held Calvin] was, Oh my God, I'm so sorry! I remember feeling incredibly shocked. Here I was looking at a baby that was so formed … he looked like, if I could blow him up into a bigger size, he would have survived. I felt horrified that I could not keep him safe, and along with that a huge sensation of guilt. And just feeling the most tremendous loss I've ever felt in my life."

"Rebecca, after you came home from the hospital, how did you explain the miscarriage to the kids?" "I said, 'The baby's gone. He had an illness that didn't let him live. But we know that he never suffered.' We cried. Tucker was stroking my hand. He said, 'Can I sit with you?' He was afraid of hurting my belly. I said, 'Yeah, you can sit with me.' I had Tavia and Max on one side of me and Tucker on the other. We snuggled in bed for a very long time."

A few days later, Rebecca and Wes held a ceremony to help their children understand what had happened. With the Carly Simon song *Life is Eternal* playing in the background, they planted ivy as a memorial. Rebecca and Wes asked the kids if they had anything they wanted to say to Calvin. Tucker answered, "I just want him to know I love him." Together they created a mural; the kids were asked to draw or post things they hoped Calvin would find in Heaven. They drew rainbows and dinosaurs, and they posted *Barney* decals and photos of themselves.

"In the days that followed," Rebecca said, "Wes and I went over what happened. 'Donny' had come up to Wes and said, 'Wes, is there anything I can do?' Wes said no. Then the guy just sat down. Never said who he was. Just sat there waiting. Then, after he got off the ambulance, he just walked down the street. He didn't get in a car and drive away. He just disappeared.

"Since that time I have tried to piece together exactly who that guy was. I'm convinced he was someone sent here to help me. That he looked so remarkably like someone I already knew just made be believe that all the more."

"Rebecca," I asked, "do you know if Donny was alive then?"

"He's alive now. He's a teacher in New Jersey."

"How was he able to get in the ambulance without a uniform?"

"That's what I wondered."

"There are stories of angels temporarily taking human form in emergency situations," I offered. "Do you think he was an angel?"

"That's all I could chalk it up to," she replied. "The fact that this person appeared as someone I trusted … that makes sense to me."

As I considered what had happened to Rebecca, it seemed to me that a miracle had taken place. I asked Rebecca if she believed she would have died had the unidentified man not intervened.

"I would imagine, yes," she said solemnly. "Because they still had not found a vein, and I was bleeding profusely." Then she shared an important detail. "When I said to him, 'I need a pediatric needle,' it was already in his hand. That's the thing that has stayed with me all these years. I never saw him, like, look for a needle. I never saw him ask for one."

I could accept that an angel or other nonphysical being had taken human form and saved Rebecca's life, but one part of the story still baffled me.

"And then this man," I said, "who was not in medical attire, who had no credentials, and who was unknown to everyone there, told three different medical teams, none of which he was actually on, that they should take you to the hospital by ambulance rather than by helicopter, *and no one questioned him?*"

"Exactly," Rebecca said.

We were silent for a moment, Rebecca allowing me to digest the events of that day. Not knowing what else to say about "Donny," and feeling there was nothing else I *could* say, I asked Rebecca to talk about how she felt in the weeks and months after the miscarriage.

"I was incredibly depressed," she said sadly. "It was all I could do to wake up in the morning. I didn't want to face anybody or anything. I blamed myself. *'What did I do wrong? What didn't I eat?'* I got real brutal with myself and had a self-loathing period that lasted well over a year. I gained weight because I didn't want anyone looking at me and thinking anything nice."

Gradually, life returned to normal for Rebecca and her family. Then, two years after the miscarriage, Calvin began to visit them. On one occasion, as Rebecca lay in bed she felt the sensation of a child sitting on her, and the room light went on and off. Soon thereafter Rebecca read in a book that the deceased can work through electricity to signal their presence. One day she asked Tucker if he had noticed anything unusual in his bedroom.

"Oh yeah," Tucker answered nonchalantly. "Calvin comes in here."

"What do you mean?" Rebecca asked, startled.

"Well, the door opens, and I feel him come in."

"What do you guys do?"

"Nothing. He just crawls in [to bed], and we spoon. When I wake up in the morning, he's not here anymore."

Rebecca told me that Calvin's visits were deeply comforting and an important step along the healing path for her and her family.

"Rebecca, do you think that's why he came back?" I asked. "To help you get over the grief?"

"I do. I think he came back to let me know I am okay and he is okay."

Rebecca's Session with Staci

Rebecca's poignant story had raised many questions for me. In addition to the central question about whether she had planned her miscarriage, I sought to understand Calvin's pre-birth blueprint. Would a soul knowingly place its energy in a fetus that would not be born? What would a soul learn or how would a soul grow by doing so? And what of the mysterious "Donny"? Who was he, and how had he been able to save Rebecca's life?

Rebecca, Staci, and I began with a moment of silence as we waited for Spirit to present to us what we needed to understand. "Calvin is here with us," Staci suddenly announced. I was startled but delighted by his appearance.

"I forgive you," he immediately said to Rebecca. "There is no blame."

That Calvin would begin our time together in this way told me he was acutely aware Rebecca still blamed herself for the miscarriage. We often assume our loved ones are so busy with their new lives in Spirit that they are not aware of how we feel or what is happening in our lives. To the contrary, they know our feelings with an intimacy that often goes well beyond what was experienced on the Earth plane. They check on us often, guiding us with intuitive promptings, loving us through images planted in our nighttime dreams.

As we were about to discover, Calvin's words were relevant not only to the miscarriage but also to another lifetime in which he and Rebecca had been together.

"Now I see images from a past life," Staci announced. "I see a fort, a military installation in some territory in the United States in the 1800s. I see men in uniform. Calvin is a soldier in that lifetime, and Rebecca, you were also a solider. You were his superior. There was an officer higher up than you at this fort, but he was often traveling, so you were left to run the fort. You liked to manage the men, and you developed a close bond with many of them. You had a good relationship with Calvin and felt like he was a son to you.

"I see a situation developing just outside the fort, fighting, and I see the soldiers trying to keep the gate closed. It's being invaded; the men are trying to prevent Indians from coming in. I see you inside the fort, Rebecca, at your desk because of your natural reluctance to get involved in combat. You were very good with words, but you didn't like physical fighting.

"You're looking out the window at the men trying to prevent the Indians from coming into the fort. Calvin is standing behind you; you're seated at your desk. You are discussing what you're watching. You send him out to join the men in the battle. And he took—*oh my goodness!*—an arrow right to his heart and was killed in just a couple of minutes.

"You felt responsible, and you did not forgive yourself. Calvin is showing me this. I see you kneeling on the ground beside him, crying and crying. You cried for about three days, and it took you a month to see the light of day again.

"You died in that lifetime of an aortic aneurysm around the age of forty-nine, about ten years after the incident where Calvin died. All that time you carried him in your heart. You always felt you never should have sent him out. He was special to you. You had a deep bond and affection for each other.

"When you died, Calvin was one of the many who greeted you. It was a big relief for you to see him again. I see you in your spirit bodies, your lightbodies—an oval shape of white light—melding together. Where our arms would be, I see the edges of the light-bodies reach out and blend into each other. You are talking very intimately. He's telling you that sending him out did not cause his death in an untimely manner. He would have died in a few months anyway in some other battle, where you would not have been around to protect him. This was how it was meant to be.

"You're not accepting it. You keep saying, 'I can't forgive myself. I can't forgive myself.' At this point, two people who love you very much, a spirit guide and your mother from another lifetime, pull you away and bring you to a place where you can rest. It's a place where I've seen many people after they cross over. It looks almost like a hospital room, except not so clinical. It's a small bedroom area, and there is a window you look through when you are lying in bed that looks onto beautiful gardens. It's a very restful place with lots of light coming in.

"You spend what we would call a couple of weeks just resting. Spirit tells me that this is 'resetting time.' You adjust to being out of physical life and back in spirit form again, getting your bearings. Very few interact with you in your resting phase. I see a spirit guide. I see again that motherly figure. I don't see Calvin coming to you. I see two others, a father figure and somebody you consider a brother. They visit only one at a time, and the visits are very brief, like a touch for reassurance.

"I'm asking to be taken to the pre-birth planning session now. The first thing I see is a small, green rug in the middle of a wood floor. On one wall there's a rectangular window. Against another wall there's a table with an arrangement of flowers. There are two other walls that contain, for lack of a better word, monitors. Flashing on the screens are images from your most recent past life and other past lives. You were alone there with your spirit guides before the rest of your soul group came in, and you viewed your past lives on these screens with your guides. You talked over karmic themes you had been working on in these previous lifetimes.

"Now the room is filled with members of your soul group. Some have a keen interest in healing, but a large portion of them are artistic. I am told that about a third of your soul group were in physical embodiment at the time you were doing your pre-birth planning. That third of your soul group are primarily teachers. So, your soul group is made up of healers, artists, and teachers.

"You are talking about what you'd like to work on in this lifetime. You feel that in your last life you progressed along the path of emotional independence. You didn't conquer it, but you certainly spent enough time alone to learn to be a better resource for yourself. You want to continue that. You're speaking with a spirit guide who looks male in appearance. He is taller than you and wearing a creamy white robe. He has dark hair and a dark beard but light skin. He lets you do the talking and just nods his head and says a few words.

"I'm not seeing you as the spirit body I saw when you crossed out of that lifetime. Now, I see you with two legs and arms, wearing the cloak of personality you will be in your current lifetime. You've already selected parents, and you know what you will look like. You tell your spirit guide that there are elements from some past lives that you like very much and want to incorporate into this life. One of these is a love of nature. You want to be somewhere where there is lots of open country.

"You walk over to the green rug and sit at one end of it. A second spirit guide comes over and puts down what looks like a game board. It's mostly blank at this point—there are just a couple of lines on it—but it fills in as you start planning your life. I see someone who appears older, like a father figure, sitting down across from you. He looks like he's around forty-five or fifty years of age. Dark hair, but silver at the temple. Caucasian. At times he's totally occupying the cloak of the personality, and at other times that dissolves and I see the spirit body underneath. Especially the lower half of his body tends to do that, as if he's having trouble hanging on to the physical representation of his form. I am told this happens because this soul is already in corporeal form.

"So, he's not there in the time between lives as you are; he's there astrally while his physical form sleeps. This is somebody who is a teacher to you, somebody you knew around five years of age. He was like an uncle at that time."

"You're describing Ted Roter, who was a next-door neighbor in the home I moved to when I was three and a half," Rebecca explained. "My father was a very distant, cold man, didn't have a whole lot to do with the kids. Mr. Roter and his wife were the most loving people. He would always come over to our house, pick me up and take me out in his truck, and buy me candy. Whenever we had parties at our house, he would sneak upstairs to bring my sister and me food, because we had been banned to the bedroom. He was always looking out for me. To the day we left, when I was in sixth grade, he was just like a father to me. He was this big, burly guy with dark hair and graying temples, just as you were describing."

"When you moved in, I'm sure on some subconscious level there was recognition," Staci added. "You got some nurturing, before it was too late, from a father figure.

"Let me continue. Calvin is in the background in this room. He's waiting for you to plan other, lengthier aspects before he feels it's appropriate to come forward and talk with you. But as he does, he moves across the back of the group and around to the side, turning to approach you. His spirit body changes and takes on the form of the body he had in that past lifetime.

"You have mixed feelings when you see him. You are happy but still filled with sadness and a lack of forgiveness for yourself. He sits down and reaches for your hand.

Calvin:	I want you to forgive yourself. Once again, my death was not of your making. It was simply time for something that was meant to be. Let go of that life and the heavy, negative connection you still hold to it. Go back in your mind and look at that lifetime again, at the positive things you did before and after you met me.
Rebecca:	I want to repay you for what I took from you.

Calvin:	It was only a short time, and time is meaningless.
Rebecca:	No, no, I can't forgive myself this way. I can't let it go. I must do something to make up for this. Our relationship—it was like father and son.
Calvin:	Would you like to continue that relationship in the lifetime you're planning?
Rebecca:	But I do not want to be a man. I will be a woman.

"You both come at the same time to the idea of you carrying him in your womb. I see him put his hand on your belly.

Calvin:	Will you be safe knowing that you will only carry my body for a short time?

"At this point you're crying because you feel the sadness, the pain from losing him in that previous lifetime and the grief at knowing that you will carry him for such a short time in this life.

Calvin:	That is all the time I had left in that lifetime. I will give you the gift of my life for that period of time if it will help you.
Rebecca:	It doesn't matter how much time, I just want you with me. I will feel better knowing that I can make up for what I stole from you. I cannot forgive myself any other way.

"This is one manifestation of your karmic challenge of finding balance within yourself. This is a part of yourself that is very out of balance, even during the time between lives. Calvin doesn't seem to believe that this is going to work for you.

Calvin:	Are you sure this is going to be enough?
Rebecca:	After I carry you in my body for this short period of time, I will be able to let you go and release this emotional burden.

"He shakes his head, because he doesn't believe you're going to be able to do it. Now one of your spirit guides steps forward. He doesn't sit down with you and Calvin; he bends over and talks to you face to face.

Spirit Guide: Are you sure you'll be able to let this go?

Rebecca: Yes, I still want to do this.

"You're very upset and still crying. The soul group in the room is silent at this time. I sense their loving support of you, their wishes for you to become well and whole emotionally, but also their skepticism. You consult with a few more people in that session, then go into a meditative state prior to entering the body of your mother."

Staci's remarkable glimpse into Rebecca's planning session had gone right to the heart of the matter: Rebecca had been unable to forgive herself for "causing" Calvin's death in a past lifetime. In her pre-birth planning, she had decided to challenge herself in the same way, this time hopeful of rising above the guilt and self-blame that would be created by the miscarriage. On a subconscious level, she would also carry into body the guilt from the past life with Calvin. It is subconscious memories of this kind that often make the healing of a particular issue much more difficult for one person than for another. If Rebecca is able to forgive herself for the miscarriage, she would then heal the guilt and blame from *both* the past and current lifetimes

"A couple of decades ago," Staci continued, "my spirit guide taught me a meditative ritual for letting go of emotional burden. I want to pass this information along to you, Rebecca. Get a candle at least six inches tall. Scratch Calvin's name into it with a pen or knife. This tells your mind who the candle represents. Then take a piece of paper and write on it, 'I release this and let it go to God.' The first time, you light the candle and burn the paper in the flame. Symbolically, this tells your mind that you are releasing the emotional burden into the ethers. Then for ten or fifteen minutes you simply repeat, silently or out loud, 'I release this and let it go to God.' Then extinguish the candle. The next day you do the same thing, except you never write that sentence on the paper again. You just light the candle, repeat the mantra, and then extinguish the flame. Most people feel their burden lightening within a few days to a few weeks. By the time the candle has burned down to a little stub, the heavy problem is not there anymore. It's literally a way to reprogram your mind to release this."

Staci's suggestion struck me as potentially very healing for Rebecca, but I knew the most healing thing we could offer Rebecca in that moment would be the opportunity to talk with her beloved Calvin.

"Staci," I said, "can Rebecca talk to Calvin?" The instant the words left my mouth, Calvin came through to Staci.

"He wants me to tell you that he is not coming back into physical life during your present lifetime. He was going to come back about five years later to a different set of parents, but he changed those plans because you were not able to let him go, really. He has no regrets about this and is very confident. He says, 'You did not handle my passing like you thought you would. I can't let you go until you do. I want to be around you to comfort you. We have been friends too long for me to leave you now.'

"And he wants to be there for you in the afterlife when you make your crossing out of this life. He says that he knows what it means to you to see him, to be with him, after you pass out of your lifetime, and he wants to be there to see the look on your face again when you see him.

"He also says that your guilt has prevented you from sensing him at times."

"I just want Calvin to know how much I love him," Rebecca said softly.

"He knows. He says he's a part of your family, almost as if he had been born."

"Calvin," I said, "at the beginning of the session you told Rebecca that you wanted her to know you forgave her. Could you say more about forgiveness and how she can forgive herself for the miscarriage?"

"Lack of forgiveness is like a ball and chain attached to you," Calvin answered. "The ball precedes you as you enter a room, hovers above you as you sit or stand, and can even occupy the same space as your body, extending front and back as if centered within your abdomen. It insulates you while carrying it and prevents you from experiencing total happiness, total joy, even total grief. It acts like a wall."

"People become comfortable with it," Staci added, "just as people become comfortable with unsatisfying marriages and stay in them because it's better than facing the unknown. Calvin is telling me that this has become a thought pattern for Rebecca, a habitual way of thinking and feeling, and that it needs to be released."

Staci's insight reminded me of something I had learned on my spiritual path: it is best not to argue with our thoughts or feelings. Rather than strengthen them with our attention, we may observe them and let them drift by gently without judgment, as one learns to do in meditation.

"It sounds easy, but it's obviously not, or I wouldn't have kept it around for so long." Rebecca laughed as she spoke, but her underlying pain was palpable.

"Do you want to let it go?" Staci asked directly.

"I'd love to let it go. Love to. The mantra ... I believe in the power of those, but I'm wondering if there's anything else that might help, because, my God, it's so ingrained in me."

"You're trying to complicate what is simple," Calvin offered.

"It all starts with a decision, and you never made the decision at your core." Staci said. "The decision to let it go."

"That understanding is the key to helping you unlock your heart," Calvin told Rebecca. "Letting go is never easy, but life is truly a gift, and having been alive for any amount of time is a wonderful thing. In my case, I may not have lived outside the womb, but in the time you carried me inside you, I was both in the body and outside, but very near. There were delights, many delights, to my eyes and ears and heart during that time. I fully enjoyed even the little time I had in the existence you now enjoy.

"In helping to release grief, all I can say is that life is a celebration, and there is always time for more life. People should understand that life continues, whether they see it or sense it or not. There will always be existence, and there will always be the opportunity to inhabit physical body in the future, whether in human form or another form on some other world. We come to physical life to experience ourselves, to experience the challenges through which we evolve. We love that process, and we all crave it from time to time. This returns us to physical life again and again.

"Know that though you may not see us, we are still very much alive. We often visit those we love, place our hands on their heart, and surround them with our form so that they may feel our love, so they may grasp that life is eternal. Just because they can't see us does not mean we do not exist. Life never ends. It is All That Is. It is the stuff of which we are made, whether we are in spirit form or physical body. Life is truly everywhere, and just as I am but a step away from my mother, so are we all literally just a few steps away from those we love. The speed of thought is a powerful connection, and thinking of the loved ones who are no longer with you brings us to your side immediately, whether you sense us there or not."

We paused for a moment to take in the beauty of Calvin's words. I could feel his great love for Rebecca and for all who would eventually hear him.

"May I ask him one more thing?" Rebecca said. "The doctors told me he never suffered."

"That's right," Staci confirmed. "He's saying he was long gone from the body."

"And did he visit Tucker?"

"He says he visits Tucker all the time. He says he's turned lights on and off in the house and that this is his way of saying hello to his family."

It now seemed time for us to discuss the most extraordinary aspect of Rebecca's experience, the presence of the unknown man in her home. I listened quietly as Rebecca shared the story with Staci. Immediately, Staci solved the mystery.

"That spirit guide [from the pre-birth planning session]—that's exactly who it was," Staci said. "The one who said, 'Are you sure you'll be able to let this go?'"

"Can we bring him in and ask him why he assumed physical human form?" I suggested. No sooner had I asked than Staci began relaying to us the words she heard from this spirit guide.

"We do this from time to time," he informed us, "when, as in the case with Rebecca and Calvin, the soul is not able to accomplish something it deeply wishes to accomplish. Had Rebecca died, she would not have completed all the karmic challenge of this life situation. We were highly aware that Rebecca had another child coming, more responsibilities and more accomplishments in this life, and how important this is to her. It was not her time. We process into corporeal form on a case-by-case basis as needed. A clairvoyant would have seen a peculiar glow in my aura compared to everyone else. But no one did, and that is often the case."

I asked why he had chosen to present himself in a casual white shirt and khaki shorts.

"He wanted to have a casual appearance," Staci answered, "so as to be more accepted by all, so as to produce a relaxing energy that Rebecca and others would sense. And he's telling me that some of them saw him dressed differently. Some of them saw him in white."

"In medical attire?" I inquired.

"Yes."

"Is that how he was able to get into the ambulance?"

"Yes, but he did not need to present that form to Rebecca. His purpose for being with Rebecca was not just to save her life, but also to calm her."

"Did he purposely choose to look like her old boyfriend Donny in order to comfort her?"

"The familiar form helped induce subconscious, soul-level recognition between him and Rebecca," Staci explained. "The recognition of a trusted advisor and friend."

"There was a critical moment," I pointed out, "when this man made a medical decision. He told them to take her to the hospital in the ambulance, not to the helicopter. Everybody listened to him, even though nobody knew who he was. Can you ask him how he managed to have that kind of effect on people, especially with such a critical decision?"

"A manipulation of energies. He says it's a wave of energy he put out through his auric field. He likens this to two different things: the way a hypnotist can formulate a suggestion and deliver it in a way where people suspend disbelief and it's accepted, and what we've come to know in our culture through *Star Wars* as the Jedi technique. He says that's what the Jedi technique was based on. It's simply a wave of energy they send out through their auric fields, and people accept it.

"In the case of a mother who gives birth to a child who lives six hours or six days or a month, it is not that the child had an incomplete life. It simply wanted for whatever reason—and there are usually two or three reasons—to have a little more experience, a refresher course, a bit more time with mom, a bit more time seeing through eyes that perhaps in a previous life it did not see through. In every one of those cases, the soul of that child is thankful to the mother for giving it the experience. No matter how short a time it seemed to the mother, it was enough for the child. The mother served in a compassionate way as bearer and caretaker of that infant soul."

⮟

Rebecca's session with Staci was conducted as part of the research for my first book. I later decided to hold her story for this book. Because Rebecca had a long time in which to work with the information provided by Staci, I asked Rebecca to comment on how it had affected her life.

"By the time I spoke with Staci regarding the loss of my little boy, I had become a different person, somehow less than I once was in many ways. Where once I was happy and optimistic, I was now sad and defeated. My self-confidence had given way to doubt and self-loathing. After all, if I couldn't sustain a life inside me, how on earth could I possibly deserve the glory of what I already had—three healthy, vibrant children?

"By learning about my life plan, I was able to let go of the self-inflicted guilt. I could look upon my experience with miscarriage as one of learning. I had closure, because it no longer held for me the poisonous mystery of all those what ifs. Which isn't to say it doesn't still sadden me sometimes or cause me to wonder what he would have looked like, which sibling he would have been most like. That still happens. But, it happens within the bounds of acceptance, and so it doesn't carry with it the grief it once did.

"My session changed my life and allowed me to get back to the business of living and nurturing my other children. It brought me home to myself. That's a journey I could not have made on my own."

Corbie Channels Rebecca's Soul

To gain additional insight into Rebecca's pre-birth plan, I asked Corbie to channel Rebecca's soul. In particular, I hoped her soul would offer words of healing to parents who have lost a child to miscarriage. How would our souls encourage us to respond? How does the soul itself view such an experience?

"Mother/Father God," Corbie prayed, "surround us with Your unconditional white light of love, compassion, wisdom, service, and truth. Let only truth be spoken, let only truth be heard. Allow me to be a clear channel to bring Rebecca Valentine's Higher Self to speak with us today, and as always may I be head, hands, and heart completely in Your service. In the name of the Christ this is asked, and in the name of the Christ this is done. Amen."

"Amen," I repeated.

"Good afternoon," came the greeting through Corbie. "You have asked for the soul of Rebecca Valentine. I am pleased to be here." Corbie's speech had slowed considerably, indicating that she had slipped into a trance state.

"Thank you for joining us today," I said. "I would like to ask if the miscarriage with Calvin was planned by you prior to Rebecca's incarnation, and if so, why?"

"Rebecca, the personality, asked [before birth] to be allowed to feel motherhood in all its forms," answered the soul. "She is a beautiful volunteer, a vessel who understood that in this instance the gift was the conception, not the life led.

"When the soul is enfleshed, even should it not experience the world as a human being separate from the mother, there is still the understanding of the world through the mother. The soul who perhaps has had difficulties in other lives wants to 'stick just a toe in the water.' Perhaps a soul who has not been on Earth before but is used to other forms wants to try something on briefly, the way you try on one hat and, like it or not, choose another. Rebecca, because of her strength of motherhood, understood and was willing to open herself up to the possibilities. The other children were indeed planned, for should she have been a woman who had miscarriage after miscarriage, that in itself would have been a complex karma. This was not required."

"Why did Calvin's soul want to have the experience of being conceived but not born?" I asked.

"Even in a rape," Rebecca's soul replied, "even in intercourse in anger, there is no denying that when the sperm meets the egg, it is the ultimate expression of God's love for life and creation. Calvin wanted to feel that love but not forget it. When one is born, one forgets much of what one knows in the womb. Calvin asked for the benevolence and the blessing of feeling the love of creation and then being able to take it back and let it heal some of his own karma. Calvin asked that this be his gift to give him strength to come back in a full pregnancy and birth [in a future lifetime] with more faith in humanity and the love that is in the world."

"You mentioned that the experience of being conceived, but not born, could bring healing to Calvin. Can you explain how that happens?"

"The feeling of the little, physical body being completely and totally nourished, encompassed, held, and kept within the mother is the greatest totality of love a human being can feel physically. What is sought as humans grow older—a hug from a child, a lovemaking session, a giggling pile in front of a fireplace with all your friends—are attempts to recreate that all-encompassing physical love. When the soul is out of the body, it is in touch with the Love of God. But, if a soul has had difficulties in perceiving love when in a body, sometimes this [being conceived but not born] is a way of reminding the soul—and so preparing the personality for its next incarnation—that humans are capable of incredible, beautiful, all-encompassing love for one another. As the mother holds the unborn child, so we are cupped in the Hands of God. We are all in the Womb."

This was an important revelation. I had seen examples of people who had carried negative energies like fear from one incarnation into the next for the purpose of healing the fear, but this was the first reference I had heard of bringing back into body an energy like love. Apparently, Calvin had difficulty feeling loved in past lives. In the womb he had been awash in Rebecca's love, intimately aware of her every thought and feeling about him. His intent was to return to Spirit with that awareness, then carry that feeling-memory into his next lifetime.

"It was a way of extending love to another, an act of service," continued Rebecca's soul. "It has created a bond of love between Calvin and Rebecca that will be served beautifully in another life when both are enfleshed. It takes a great heart to do what Rebecca has done and not lose all faith in the world.

"Calvin will, when he is next enfleshed, spend his life reaching back to that misty feeling of love that when born he forgot but still retained a sense of. When he meets Rebecca in that life, their meeting will open the door within him to express to the world that love and therefore bring the world that much closer to understanding the profound gift that is a life born of [love founded in a previous] life. It will enrich both. Rebecca, who will have the faint shadowing from the lifetime with the miscarriage, will suddenly feel healed and will most likely see that as Calvin's effect. It will also give that personality [Rebecca] a deeper understanding of humanity, of love. The two of them will bear a child who will be the culmination of truly unconditional, unselfish love. It will be something spectacular."

"We've talked about why Calvin wanted to have this experience of the miscarriage. Why did you want Rebecca to have it?"

"Motherhood, children, the passing on of beliefs and faith have been a theme for some few lifetimes recently. I say *recently* in that in the near past the life was most always female. There was one life where there was a miscarriage. The husband blamed the wife [Rebecca], who saw it as a great failing of hers. She was not able to have children after that and spent her life with an empty womb in place of her heart. She tasted the bitter side of motherhood, but motherhood is bitter and sweet. She had a particular devotion in that life to the Virgin Mary. She volunteered her womb to God and wished many times she would have been given that opportunity, not because it would have raised her, not because her child would be God, but because the thought of being in service to God, such a simple surrender, seemed like the answer to everything. She has, in effect, done that this time."

"But wasn't the miscarriage in a previous life also an act of service to God in some way?"

"Yes, but it was not understood in that way," said Rebecca's soul. "Also, not all miscarriages are specifically and only in service to God. Some miscarriages are a return emotional impact for emotional impact. Some are simply that the soul coming in finds that the vessel is not forming correctly, and it wishes to come in fully structured. There is not one logical, emotional, or spiritual reason for things that happen, whether miscarriages, murders, starvation, marriages, or love; otherwise, a soul would come back three or four times and have completion. There is too much to learn on Earth, too many facets."

"You said that sometimes a miscarriage is planned as an exchange of emotional impact for emotional impact. Can you say more about that?"

"If there is a couple and one deserts the other, there does not have to be that [same situation in order] to balance. There is a desertion when both are enfleshed. A mother who wants a child desperately can feel somewhat of a desertion if the fetus can't hold on for birth."

"So, if I understand correctly, sometimes if one partner abandons another in a lifetime, then the one who was abandoned may be ..."

"The miscarried child," the soul answered, finishing my sentence. "The one who did the abandoning is the bereft mother. That is correct."

In such a pre-birth plan, the mother is not being punished for having abandoned a partner in a previous lifetime. There is no punishment. The mother would have chosen to feel the feelings of desertion she had caused in another. On the soul level, we seek to understand, and therefore to experience, all aspects of situations and feelings. In so doing we develop compassion and empathy. From our limited vantage point while in body, we often focus only on the suffering that is engendered, but upon our return to Spirit we discover to our delight that we have opened our hearts and expanded our souls.

"Can you tell me for what other reasons might a soul plan a miscarriage?" I inquired.

"To teach itself hope. To feel what motherhood would be like without necessarily going through an entire life as a mother. If a soul has a majority of male lives, it may be that the first few times it is female there is a pregnancy but not a birth so the vibration of female can be settled into. The difference in male and female lives when it comes to what one eats, what one does for a living, how one reacts in the world, is less different than might be thought, but there is nothing that marks the experience man versus woman so profoundly as the bearing of a child. A man carries life within him, but it cannot be enfleshed save by the woman."

"You mentioned hope. How does a miscarriage help a soul to teach itself hope?"

"When a woman wants a child and tries and tries and miscarries, why does she not shrug her shoulders and say, 'Oh well, I suppose not'? How many times does the woman go through fertilization and rounds with the doctor and everything she can to call the soul to her with her husband? A miscarriage can teach resilience, hope, belief in the Self, and eternal forgiveness. The woman who has miscarriages and does not blame herself can model that for others. Always, if you have five women, all of whom have had miscarriages, one will have done it more often in other lives than the others, and she may be able to model hope and resilience to those who are less used to it. All of us, if we have had an experience in our life cycles more than others, use that to teach."

"You mentioned forgiveness," I said. "Was part of your motivation for planning this so that Rebecca would learn how to forgive herself for the miscarriage?"

"Exactly so. To understand that there is nothing to forgive. She did nothing wrong. On the contrary, she gave a gift. If any lesson could be learned from this and through your work told to others, it is that even when a woman holds a life in her for only four days after conception, she has gifted that soul those cells. She has, in her way, had the faintest touch of God through her womb. It is always something that will bless her. What I would hope for Rebecca is the recognition of her perfection, the recognition that she was as profoundly serving of Calvin as she is of those children who lived. Every fruit of her womb was a perfect, unblemished blossom, no matter what it looked like on Earth."

"There may be people who read your words," I observed, "women who have had miscarriages, who say, 'I have done everything I can to work on self-forgiveness, and still I have not been able to forgive myself. How do I do it?'"

"No hand can be forced. Be gentle. If you had a child who was constantly saying, 'I'm not good enough' or 'I'm so stupid,' what would you do? You would hold that child. You would direct into it as much love and belief as you could and then let go, knowing that you've done what you could. Rebecca must love herself that much. When love is created within the womb, that love is encapsulated in the egg of the mother. That is the love we hold for ourselves [as souls] brought down to pinpoint. Why do people love to see children of their own flesh with their eyes, their thoughts, their actions, their habits? It is because it seems to be a permissible way to love themselves, but they don't need to have children to do that. You are your own children. Just as Rebecca would forgive her sons, her daughters, just as she would do all she could to comfort them and assure them of their worth, she must do that for herself. That is part of the lesson and the gift of Calvin's very short stay with her."

"How do you as Rebecca's soul evolve as a result of her learning self-forgiveness?"

"When souls learn self-forgiveness, it strengthens later incarnations. It is harder for the world to tell them they are not worthy, to tell them they are wrong. There are those souls who have a profound belief in why they are on Earth and what they are meant to do. Those are souls who have learned self-forgiveness. Forgiveness erases a blackboard; there is more room to write poetry or scientific formulas or draw beautiful pictures on a clean board than one that is scribbled with *not worthy, foolish, not good enough*. Most lessons on Earth come down to, 'I am not sufficient in and of myself.' The soul knows that it is always, even in the most difficult lives, self-sufficient. Personalities forget that. It is part of being whole. It is part of being connected to All That Is, to the Single Instant of Love in the Universe. Love is always sufficient. When you think you are not [sufficient], it is because you think you are not loved or lovable or that you do not have enough love in you."

"Let's talk about the grieving process. For people reading your words who are still grieving miscarriage, how would you advise them to heal?"

"It is important they understand who they are grieving for. They do not grieve the child; they grieve the [child's] lost potential. They grieve their lost hopes. If they knew the child bore them no ill will, that nothing they did was wrong, and that they are not at fault, it would be easier. Some people grieve the death of their parents because so much was left unsaid. If those who lose parents, even parents they loved enormously, said all that needed to be said and look with gratitude on what was given to them, then they enfold within their hearts the memory of the parent. They rejoice that the parent is now out of what may have been a difficult body or life, and they know that there is no loss of love. So, for those who grieve, this is not to say you have no right or are foolish to do so. No emotion is foolish if it helps you purge yourself of regret or lost hope, but then let it go. Grief should not define a life. You are on Earth not to grieve constantly for what you do not have, but to rejoice in what you do, and to share those gifts with others. That is how things multiply."

"Let's talk for a moment," I requested, "about the grief of the father, because sometimes fathers are overlooked when a miscarriage occurs."

"Their energy is very different. They do not feel the emptiness inside their own bodies. They do not feel the echoing chamber. For men it is, 'Was my seed imperfect?' It is how men are constructed. For them the same answer applies: There is no loss. The soul that agreed to touch yours still does. The child's potential has still affected your life, and you can take that and work it into the world in ways of beauty and strength. Perhaps you will be able to take those feelings and turn them to another child who is enfleshed and does not have a father.

"When a child is conceived," continued Rebecca's soul, "whether or not that child is born, that man is now a father. That imprint is on him; he will always have the energy of being a father. He can express it either by trying again to have his own child or by sharing it with those who are already on Earth. That gift is never taken away. The energy of being a parent is something that informs a life. It is very potent medicine."

"You said there is no loss. I know what you mean, but a mother or father who has just experienced a miscarriage may have difficulty with that statement. Could you say more?"

"It feels like a loss—no one would deny that—but I would encourage the grieving parents to realize that the child is still yours. People grieve a death, thinking that the person is lost to them. When someone moves across the world, you may never see them again, but you have not lost them. It is as if the child has moved across the world. Know that you have added to the love the world contains. Nothing is for naught. Nothing is ever for naught when it comes to creating a life and expressing the Love of God in another human being.

"You have, for the time you had that child within you, cradled your own soul and the soul of the child. Their love for you remains with you. Do not look at it in a small frame of reference. Take your energy, your love, everything you would have given to that child, and give it elsewhere. If you are all truly of one flesh, then by loving another child, you love the child you lost, and its soul will know. It will not feel less loved, because when the child is outside the body, the child knows there is no more or less love, there is only Love. Love another child. The child you lost will feel it. People do not understand how profound this is. If they did, they could all plug into that Love that has no separation. Your book would not be necessary."

I asked Rebecca's soul if there was anything else it wished to say.

"The energy of motherhood and fatherhood ... please treat it as one of the most profound gifts you can bring to the world. It is the touch of God in humanity. Do not waste the gift by believing that if you have a miscarriage or an abortion you are bad. Honor your wish to be a mother or a father, either through your flesh or in service, for the energy is always complete. The energy is never a miscarriage or an abortion; the energy is your opportunity to reach out and be as the Finger of God touching another in love. The love that you give another is what knits the wounds of the world. You all have it."

❧

Love, forgiveness, and healing. These are themes of Rebecca's life, and they are inextricably interwoven.

Rebecca loved herself enough before she was born to take on one of the greatest challenges one can face: being a mother whose child dies. She did so because she knew that she had not forgiven herself for Calvin's death in a previous lifetime. And so out of love she gifted herself with the opportunity to learn self-forgiveness. This self-forgiveness *is* the healing she sought in this lifetime.

In my conversations with Spirit, I am often told, "Nothing is as it appears." Here on the Earth plane from our human vantage point, the death of an unborn child would appear to be an unmitigated tragedy. Yet, Rebecca knew in her planning session that Calvin's death could be her rebirth. She knew that she would blame herself for the miscarriage and that guilt would ensue. As Calvin told us, that lack of self-forgiveness insulated Rebecca, sealing within her the grief she needed to express in order to heal.

Emotions are energy in motion, and energy seeks to flow and express itself. It is for this reason that expression heals while suppression intensifies. Like a dam holding back a mighty river, Rebecca's lack of self-forgiveness blocked the flow of grief, leaving it to churn and grow.

The difficulty Rebecca experienced in forgiving herself was built on a foundation of false beliefs, beliefs that she as a mother had done something wrong, not eaten the right foods, somehow not adequately cared for her unborn child. In her willingness to consider the *possibility* that the miscarriage had been planned, she illuminated those beliefs and found them to be hollow. No belief in pre-birth planning is necessary for healing; all that is required is a simple willingness to consider that there may be a deeper spiritual purpose to all we experience.

One might then ask: How can the death of an unborn be in Divine Order? In its infinite wisdom, the Universe gifted incarnating souls with a trial period we call pregnancy, a time in which the souls of the parents and unborn child may intimately experience one another to decide if a life together would truly be a blessing to all. The greatest good is always served, regardless of the decision made. If the intertwining of lives will foster the expansion of all souls involved but the fetus is not viable, then the incarnating soul will return to those parents in a subsequent pregnancy. This awareness alone is deeply healing.

Why else do souls seek the experience of miscarriage? Beyond the desire to cultivate self-forgiveness, many souls plan a miscarriage to develop compassion. When hearts are broken open through grief, profound compassion may emerge. The soul of the miscarried child is in loving service to the parents, gifting them with the opportunity to choose compassion over anger, bitterness, and blame. When they choose compassion for themselves and each other, the bereaved parents literally raise the vibration of the entire planet. Those parents chose courageously before they were born to serve the world in this way, and Spirit reveres them for that choice.

At times a soul who has had difficulty in past lives feeling her feelings may plan a miscarriage to push herself *to feel* deeply to the very core of her being. At the level of the soul, a miscarriage planned for this purpose is not a punishment but rather an opportunity for transformation. If this person permits the experience of the pain, it forever enlivens the capacity to feel love, peace, and joy more profoundly. The heart comes alive and, after the pain is healed, pulses with an expanded ability to revel in the beauty and pleasure of life.

Some souls, particularly those intent upon experiencing and thus knowing themselves as compassion, build miscarriage into their pre-birth plans as a safeguard, a means of redirecting themselves if they go "off track." For example, if a couple becomes diverted by the pursuit of money, power, or status, the miscarriage option in their pre-birth contracts may be activated. Years after the miscarriage, those parents will often speak of how they grew closer and refocused themselves on what really matters, building rich, purposeful, and compassion-based lives not in spite of the miscarriage, but because of it.

Spirit has shared with me that some souls can completely balance and release their karma simply by touching the Earth through a fetus; they need not be born. Those souls are then liberated to move on to higher dimensions. Here again we see that conception can be an extraordinary gift. To bless another soul in this way is one of the highest forms of service anyone can perform. If you grieve the loss of an unborn child, consider that you may have given another soul one of the greatest gifts imaginable.

On Earth and throughout the Universe, Divine Order is created and Divine Will expressed through service. Rebecca's life is a radiant example of service to self and to others. Rebecca is in service to herself when she grants herself the magnificent possibility of healing what was left unhealed from her previous life with Calvin. She also serves Calvin beautifully, gifting him with the feeling-memory of a mother's unconditional love that he carried back into Spirit and will later take back into body. Calvin, in turn, loves Rebecca enough to serve her by associating his energy with the fetus and by changing his plans to reincarnate quickly. Out of love for and in service to Rebecca, he chooses instead to remain in spirit so that he may guide her through her life and then greet her when she returns Home.

Also in service to Rebecca is her spirit guide, who lovingly assumes the physical form of her former boyfriend, Donny. Knowing that this appearance will generate feelings of trust and peace in her, the spirit guide stages a rare and miraculous intervention in a human life. When we as souls choose to confine a portion of our energy to a physical body, we create a sense of separation from Spirit, a perception that we are on our own. Yet, our guides and loved ones walk hand-in-hand with us, ever aware of our thoughts, feelings, and circumstances. Never do we go forth alone.

Assisted by the love and wisdom of Calvin, her spirit guide, and others in the nonphysical realm, Rebecca emerged from years of self-torment to forgive herself. That self-forgiveness paves an energetic pathway for other mothers and fathers to forgive themselves; indeed, it makes self-forgiveness easier for all on Earth, regardless of circumstance. And as Rebecca's soul told us, it strengthens her in future incarnations while in this lifetime erasing a blackboard on which had been scrawled *not worthy*. Now she has written in its place the words *loved, loving, and lovable*.

That is the remembrance for which Rebecca's soul had hoped: Rebecca's remembrance of her own perfection.

Abortion

A chapter about the pre-birth planning of miscarriage would be incomplete without a consideration of abortion. Whereas the mother, father, and others affected by a miscarriage do not knowingly choose (after incarnating) for the miscarriage to occur, an abortion requires the conscious decision of at least the mother. When a woman makes the decision to abort a pregnancy, is she fulfilling a pre-birth plan? Is her decision made in conjunction with the soul of the unborn child? If a soul knew that a pregnancy were going to be aborted, why would that soul associate its energy with the fetus?

To answer these and other questions, I asked Staci to channel her spirit guide speaking on the topic of abortion.

"I sense a collection of others with him [my guide]," Staci began. "He wants to express something for a grander number of entities than just himself." I was surprised by Staci's announcement. In the many sessions we had done together, she had never opened with such a statement. The presence of other beings indicated to me that Spirit considers the topic of abortion to be an important one for humanity.

"What would you like to say about abortion?" I asked. I wanted to give Staci's guide and the others who were present a platform and an invitation to convey all the wisdom they could offer. Staci was silent for a few moments as she centered in her guide's presence and awaited his words.

"Greetings, Robert," came his salutation. "We are aligned today in much anticipation of the forthcoming product [book], which is the output of a great collaboration. When I use the term *we*, I am speaking for myself as Staci's spirit guide and also for the Council of Elders, the ones who form a supportive ring around all the soul groups in existence and who in particular pay attention to the human vehicle as format for education and learning. We are with you today to tell you about the choices for individual incarnation, the repetitive experience of physical form through the educational system that is schoolhouse Earth.

"Abortion is never because of one and only one universal reason. The reasons for abortion are many and varied, both within the individuated [incarnate] personalities and within the souls of mother and baby. Know that the fetal body is not fully occupied by the soul upon conception. There are many instances in which the fetal body is not occupied at all during the first trimester. Often, the souls of mother and child will meet in the pre-birth planning area during the first trimester so that final arrangements and agreements can be made, or if made previously, cemented at that time. This experience occurs so often it could be said that it is the norm; however, be aware that many mothers experience connection with the spirit of their unborn child from the moment of conception. We would say that in 20 percent of all human pregnancies, particularly in modern times, this is the case. Many women, however, experience a gradual knowingness of connection with the spirit of the baby within. We see this occurring anywhere from the fourth or fifth month to the eighth month of pregnancy, that is, anywhere in the second or third trimester. In some instances this is because of the mother's anxiety. In other instances it is because the spirit of the child has not attached itself yet to the fetal body in any significant fashion or has spent any significant time in the mother's presence.

"We say this to illustrate that Spirit does not occupy the fetal body on a full-time basis during the first trimester, when most abortions occur, and we add, when most spontaneous abortions occur. Because they are spontaneous, they are judged to be natural and of God or God's making. We say to you that you are all of God; therefore, how could you do anything that is not of God? We encourage you to step outside the limited thoughts humanity has held about the nature of life and the nature of the beginning of life—the origination point where soul and body, that which is matter, meet.

"When the fetal body is birthed into the light of life surrounding it [the physical plane], there is often a rush of the soul entering the body, fully seeking and anchoring into it in those final moments. This intensification of the connection between the soul and physical body usually causes a great deal of confusion and disorientation to the soul occupying the body of the baby.

"We say this so you will come to a greater awareness and understanding of when the soul makes its connection with the physical and neurological system within the baby's body and of when the kundalini [life force energy stored at the base of the spine] becomes energized, as the multiple doorways of connection between body and soul are so rapidly and intensely exercised.

"Understand, too, that during the process of abortion, whether it is induced by mother, doctor, or assistant of any kind, or whether it is a naturally occurring, spontaneous abortion commonly called a miscarriage, the soul is not attached to the fetal body at the time of the body's death. There is no pain, save for that the mother carries as a burden of guilt.

"We would like for your readers to see this, come to a greater understanding of their own experience, and forgive themselves for what they thought was murder or for what they may have judged someone else to be doing as murder. There are multiple vehicles—in other words, bodies—that can be utilized for the growth experience of the individuated soul. There are those souls who form strong attachments to a few of the souls in their soul group, form a sense of family with them, and often choose to incarnate together as family or friends. There are times in cases such as this when a soul who has been miscarried or aborted will not choose another vehicle in which to incarnate until one comes up within that soul family. That is the choice of that child's soul. We want mothers to know that their experience is their own. They can choose to feel miserable and guilty and think they were responsible for ruining someone's chance at life, or they can see from a greater awareness and know that there will simply be another opportunity for that child's soul, whether it is with that same mother or somebody else. We want mothers to see that they have not caused any harm to the child; they have not killed a soul. The soul continues to exist, and when the soul is ready, it will put a portion of itself into physical form. It will choose the best parents for the kind of experiential opportunity it desires.

"Like humans, souls can change their minds. So, while a soul may choose a family and the mother may then become pregnant, if the body is not viable and a miscarriage occurs, or if the mother terminates the pregnancy, then the soul of the child may choose to see if the mother gets pregnant again or may choose to have a different experience. The council will then review the options available and present to the soul through its spirit guide the best opportunities for the experience and growth desired.

"There is no need for the protocol of judgment surrounding any woman's choice to terminate a pregnancy or for the natural termination of any pregnancy. Yes, there is grief because of the hopes and dreams that will go unfulfilled, but there should be no grief, no mourning of the death of a soul, because there is no such thing. There is only a blending, and it is this blending that many mothers feel most often in the second and third trimesters. But even then the soul occupies the fetal body in only a part-time manner, anywhere from a few minutes to a few hours, sometimes even a few days at a time. Just as when the human is approaching death and the soul of that human tends to be in and out of the body but still connected to it, so, too, during pregnancy does the soul come and go. The soul is not around much of the time until and particularly during the seventh, eighth, and ninth months. We again emphasize that the soul fully seats itself into the fetal body during the process of delivery, entwining itself in the neural net of fibers that enables the soul to animate the body. It is during that process where the veil so often given reference to is drawn. The soul feels that confusion during those first few moments of birth, because the connection to the life-in-between-lives is now behind it. It does not see it anymore. It sees only what is in front of it, what is surrounding it. In many cases that is the mother's womb or birth canal. Birth, whether natural or caesarean, is truly for the soul like waking up and not knowing who or where it is."

Staci became silent. I knew that Spirit had finished presenting the information they wanted us to have. Now it was time for questions. I asked Staci to clarify the increased connection the soul makes with the fetus during the second and third trimesters.

"What I'm seeing here, Rob," she replied, "is a soul forming something that looks like a tail that wraps around the spine of the fetal body. That's something I'm seeing in the fifth month. It's like claiming it. Even though the spirit may not reside entirely in the physical body, the energetic connection has been made."

"Are all abortions done with the consent of the soul associated with the fetus?" I inquired.

In that moment Staci's consciousness stepped aside, and her spirit guide began to speak through her again.

"Yes, always," he stated. "Sometimes the mother has to do a bit of explaining or convincing. Invariably the soul of the child always agrees once it comes to the understanding that this is the best decision. We cannot say that every soul is happy about this. There are some, occasionally, who express disappointment. This is just part of the adaptability soul growth encourages."

"Why would a soul associate its energy with a fetus that's going to be aborted?"

"For some of these souls, the experience of that type of shortened pregnancy is like window shopping: looking through a window to see what's on the other side, what it might like to choose. For some souls that is enough. It is enough simply to have a look around, a glimpse, a sense of connection, no matter how small or for how short of a time period. Let us remember that it is the human form that makes the value judgment associated with time. For us in spiritual form, it is all as one. There is no relative value placed upon the experience weighted by the passage of time or not. It just is."

"Thank you," I replied. "As you know we have a number of dramas that play out here on the Earth plane among doctors and nurses who perform abortions and people who protest in front of or bomb abortion clinics, or who sometimes murder those who perform the abortions. Please speak to this."

"These souls are working through issues of anger, fear, and all the behaviors generated. And so, one person may, for example, lose her husband in a raid on an abortion clinic, but on the soul level there was an understanding in the pre-birth plan of that woman that her husband would be taken from her in death in a sudden way." Here, I understood Staci's guide to mean that losing the husband specifically as the result of a raid on an abortion clinic would have been a *potential* in the wife's pre-birth plan. At a soul level, she would have agreed to experience her husband's early death through some means. Whether or not the husband's death occurred in such a raid would depend on whether the potential murderer were able to heal the anger or fear that was carried into body.

"Although there would be great pain," the guide concluded, "on the soul level there would be an understanding of the greater purpose, an understanding that those who are moved or affected by the event would make significant growth in their process of accomplishing connection with their souls. The complex web of energetic threads between each individual life is like a resonant musical instrument: the plucking or strumming of one thread causes a vibrational response through the rest of the instrument. [On the soul level] there is a greater understanding as to why that event occurs and the growth that it will foster in each individual who observed or was affected by it. There is a great resonance of never-ending love, compassion, and understanding. It is all absorbed by the greater whole. No one being needs to carry the burden alone, because no one being ever does."

CHAPTER 4

⚬⚭⚭

Caregiving

WELL BEFORE I BEGAN THE research for this book, I knew that one of the topics I wanted to address was the pre-birth planning of caregiving. My interest in that subject was strong even before my father became ill. Now, as he struggles daily with a host of serious physical ailments as well as confusion and fear, and as my family and I look after him, I search for meaning in our experience. This chapter is part of the search.

As medical science finds ways to extend our lives, and as illnesses like Alzheimer's become increasingly common, more and more people find themselves being cared for or caring for loved ones, often on a long-term basis. As souls we can incarnate in any location and at any point in linear time. We choose the circumstances that will best foster our evolution. Those selecting the current period in human history knew before birth that it would afford many opportunities for caregiving. Regardless of whether the caregiving is offered to one who is elderly or young, physically or mentally disabled, it creates an enormous impetus for growth.

Why would someone plan to take on the hard work and intense emotional demands of caregiving? Why would a soul want to be in a position in which care was required from another? To answer these questions, I spoke with Bob Barrett. Age seventy at the time of our conversation, Bob had been caring for his wife, Kathryn, for fourteen years, an experience that began one month after he retired. Both the length of the caregiving and the seemingly improbable timing of its beginning strongly suggested to me that it was part of a larger plan.

Prior to our conversation, Bob said that the caregiving had propelled him on a personal spiritual journey in which he had come to believe that he and Kathryn were now fulfilling a pre-birth agreement. That new perspective had allowed him to persevere through some exceptionally difficult moments in which he felt like giving up. How, I wondered, had Bob's understanding of his plan strengthened his resolve and changed the caregiving experience for him?

Bob

"I met Kathryn in April 1958," Bob recalled, "when we were juniors at Michigan State University. She was beautiful, intelligent, and confident. Kathryn was a flirt and enjoyed every minute of it; she bragged that she dated almost every night of her sophomore year. She would tell confidants that she had more than six marriage proposals, one of which was after mine!

"I fell in love with her the first night we met. It was a blind date for a party at my fraternity. We clicked immediately. We told each other outrageous stories about ourselves, joked and laughed constantly. When I kissed her goodnight, she reared back and said I didn't know how to kiss. When I asked her to teach me, she said I should practice on a mirror. But, on our next date she taught me for an hour how to kiss. From that time on we were inseparable."

Bob and Kathryn got engaged during their senior year and married right after graduation. Their only material possessions were their clothes, a car Bob's parents gave them as a wedding present, and one hundred dollars from Bob's grandparents. Over time, the absence of material wealth would forge a strong bond between them as they worked together to build the life of their dreams.

After marrying, Bob and Kathryn stayed at MSU for the next school year. Kathryn taught fifth grade and paid the bills while Bob earned his MBA.

"She was a great teacher," Bob said proudly, "because she had three years of summer teaching experience with inner-city kids. Kathryn was a very active, energetic, accomplished person, full of self-confidence and the determination to live a better life than she had as a child growing up in a working-class family. Her father initially discouraged her from attending college, but she borrowed the money and accomplished her goals. I loved and admired her for that determination and what she accomplished on her own."

Bob and Kathryn had a son, Christopher, and two daughters, Wendy and Holly. Because Bob's career in management with Mobil Chemical required frequent travel, Kathryn had primary responsibility for taking care of the children. In her free time, she volunteered in religious activities, was active in book clubs, and became a gourmet cook.

"Kathryn took pride in her appearance for the first thirty-five years of our marriage," Bob told me. "She used her good looks to flirt on an occasional basis, but we had a strong, loving relationship. Neither of us would let anything or anyone come between us."

Following a successful career, Bob retired in April 1994. In May he and Kathryn traveled to California to attend a wedding. Afterward, as they shared a quiet dinner in an airport hotel before their flight home, something happened that would forever alter the course of their lives.

"Kathryn said, 'Oh gosh, I forgot to take my allergy medication,'" Bob recounted, his voice suddenly grave. "'Would you mind going up to the room and getting those for me?' I went and got them. She took six or seven different medications, then we ordered our meal. We were eating and talking back and forth normally.

"Then all of a sudden I realized I was doing all the talking. I looked at her, and she was staring at me. I said, 'Kathryn.' No response. 'Kathryn, are you all right?' No response. I reached across, took hold of her arm, and shook it a little bit. 'What's the matter, dear?' No response."

Bob called for an ambulance, and Kathryn was rushed to the hospital. She was kept in observation for several hours and then released when doctors could find nothing wrong.

After they returned home, Kathryn was a different person. She no longer took care of the household; those responsibilities fell to Bob. She lost interest in her friends and usual activities. A longstanding but previously mild problem with scoliosis suddenly became extremely painful. Her doctors suspected a stroke but could not confirm one.

"I could not communicate with her," Bob said sadly. "She was sinking deeper and deeper into this culture of pain. She would get one medication after the other, from codeine to morphine to Valium.

"Since the incident in California, Kathryn has undergone a dramatic change. I no longer know who she is. The last time we made love was on that trip in 1994. She would like to retain the intimacy we enjoyed, but I find it impossible because she seems like a complete stranger to me."

Bob explained that Kathryn now sleeps eighteen hours a day. She suffers chronic pain from polymyalgia rheumatica and osteoarthritis. She has not cooked a meal in fifteen years and shows none of her previous interest in food or nutrition. "She gets little exercise and has gone from looking young and attractive for her age to looking older than her age. She is smaller and stooped over compared to before."

Bob and Kathryn share a frustrating morning ritual. When Kathryn wakes up, Bob asks if she needs to use the bathroom. Usually she does not respond. Bob repeats the question. If Kathryn says yes, he escorts her. Afterward, he asks if she would like to return to bed. Again there is no response. Bob then goes to the kitchen for a cup of coffee. When he returns, he asks Kathryn if she is finished in the bathroom. Again he receives no reply. He then waits ten minutes, helps her from the toilet, and slowly walks her back to bed.

"Then I give her the morning medications. After giving her Valium, I spoon-feed her other meds in applesauce. She'll ask me what's in the applesauce. For the thousandth time I will tell her. After taking the meds in applesauce, she will ask where her Valium is. For the thousandth time I will explain that she took that fifteen minutes ago. This will start an argument where she insists that I withheld the Valium. Finally, I will say that I don't care if she believes me or not, but she is not getting a second Valium.

"When that settles down, I will ask if she is hungry. No answer. After a few minutes I'll ask again. She will say 'Why, are you hungry?' 'Please,' I'll say, 'just answer the question. ARE YOU HUNGRY—YES OR NO?' Then she will say, 'What have you got to eat?' I won't answer because she won't remember what I say.

"So I will go to the kitchen, get the assortment of options, and show them to her. She will ask what this is and what that is. Then she will go through a period of tasting the various options without giving an indication of what she would like. This process can take thirty minutes. Out of frustration I'll insist that she make a decision. Finally she does, but she thinks I'm angry with her."

Their conversations later in the day are not much more fulfilling. "Because of her lack of involvement in life, she has no basis for conversation with me," Bob observed. "Our time together is either me telling her what I have been doing, what I have read or seen on television, or reminding her about appointments. I will read to her from books, but she has trouble remembering what she heard a few minutes before."

Bob has faced other challenges that fall outside the daily routine. For many years he and Kathryn enjoyed trips to their second home on Martha's Vineyard. Now, Kathryn will often cancel their travel plans at the last minute, saying she is unable to go because she can't find her eyeglasses or false teeth. Recently, when Kathryn did join Bob on a trip to the Vineyard, she did not dress or leave the house during their two-week stay.

Too, Kathryn has occasional delusions. Once Bob was awakened in the middle of the night by police officers shining flashlights in his face. Kathryn had called them, claiming that Bob had imprisoned a woman in the attic and asking them to search the house. When the officers informed Kathryn that no one was in the attic, she told them that the woman must have escaped via a secret stairway constructed by Bob. To this day Kathryn believes that someone is living in the attic. If a piece of clothing or jewelry is missing, she believes the woman has stolen it.

Bob was in tears after some of these experiences, and years ago he considered leaving Kathryn. In part he felt overwhelmed because his children left the vast majority of the caregiving to him. Though he was not serious about it, he had thoughts of suicide from time to time. Yet, rather than leave Kathryn or harm himself, Bob chose instead to embark on a path of deep spiritual exploration. "I had a lot of questions but not answers," he said. "So I started reading."

Bob began by reading about physical pain, studying the works of Norman Cousins and John Sarno. He learned about the strong link between mind and body, emotions and health. Then one day his older brother sent him a copy of *Conversations with God.* It led to a breakthrough.

"I read the book, and everything in it was significant to me," Bob exclaimed. "So I read his [Neale Donald Walsch's] other books. I read his nine books each a half-dozen times. And through that I *remembered* reincarnation. That led me to believe that what I was experiencing was not happening by accident." Eager to expand his awareness, Bob went on to explore the writings of Brian Weiss, Gary Zukav, and many others. He read ... and read ... and read. He also started meditating on the changes he saw in Kathryn, thus further deepening his insights.

"I began to feel that Kathryn was doing this to produce the effect of my becoming more spiritual, less involved with control, and more involved with taking life as it comes," he explained. "That led to the belief that Kathryn has agreed to do this for me out of love. Once I began to understand that this is all part of a plan, that changed everything. That made something that was intolerably frustrating, first of all tolerable, and second of all desirable."

"Bob," I asked, "what would you say to those who don't believe in reincarnation or pre-birth plans?"

"Whether you know there's a plan or not, the plan is going to unfold—to your benefit. What sustains me is knowing that reincarnation exists and that Kathryn agreed, before we came to this incarnation, to become dysfunctional and thereby allow me to become a full-time caregiver and learn the lessons of kindness, patience, compassion, and love.

"I believe if we stick to it, we will progress our souls."

Bob's Session with Barbara and Aaron

Clearly, Bob had come to see deep meaning and purpose in his experience with Kathryn. Yet, Bob and Kathryn could have chosen to work on any number of life themes and to do so with many other souls. Why had they selected each other, and why these particular lessons? I hoped that Aaron would be able to answer these questions. I also hoped he would provide us with wisdom for the many people who struggle with caregiving. What can they do to find purpose in, and perhaps even transform, that struggle?

Our session began with a few moments of silence as Barbara's consciousness stepped aside and Aaron entered the body.

"My blessings and love to you both. I am Aaron." Immediately I sensed great warmth coming from him. "What I offer you is my own personal perspective. I do not guarantee it as an absolute truth, but what I see as truth. If it does not resonate as truth for you, please simply lay it aside."

Aaron asked Bob for the years of his and Kathryn's births so he could access the Akashic Record. By tapping into the records, Aaron would learn all the thoughts, words, and actions, both from this lifetime and past lives, that are relevant to Bob and Kathryn. We paused for several seconds as Aaron absorbed the details. Then, even though this totality of information was now his, Aaron asked Bob a series of questions about Kathryn's health and his life with her. He sought to build trust with Bob and to gain additional insight by sensing the feelings underlying Bob's replies. When ready, Aaron offered us his impressions.

"This has been very hard on you," Aaron said to Bob. "You have really lost your wife. You find yourself tied down to a woman who has become in many ways a stranger. You must at times feel lonely, angry, bewildered, and frustrated. So, I want to direct attention to in what ways it was planned before the incarnation.

"But, I also want to bring some attention to Kathryn's situation, because I think some healing is possible for her. Barbara, through whose body I am speaking, has been to a healing center in Brazil to see a man affectionately called John of God. Many different healing entities incorporate into John's body and work through him.

"Each human being is that which is positive and that which is negative, for most humans about a 50/50 balance. People are attempting to become more positive, to let go of some of the old negative attributes. This is part of what you are doing in caring for Kathryn. A person does not have to be highly negative to open the door to external negativity. I dislike the word *possession*, but I don't know any other English word for it. I see clearly in Kathryn the presence of an entity cohabiting the body, and this is where work with John of God could be very helpful. There would be help to release that spirit, which is a service not only to Kathryn but also to the spirit that shares the body and needs to let go."

I was shocked by this revelation. I had never encountered anyone who was unwillingly or unknowingly sharing the body with another consciousness. A discussion of negative entities is beyond the scope of this book, but it is perhaps helpful to mention that possession may occur when an individual's auric field is weakened through illness or the use of drugs or alcohol. Someone with a healthy energy body is unlikely to encounter this phenomenon.

Fear, however, is a powerful magnet, and to fear such entities is to issue a call to them. It is for this reason that all our fears are best dealt with in the manner in which we park our cars. That is, we remove the ignition keys, lock the doors, and then go about our lives without giving another thought to the possibility of the car being stolen. We deal realistically with the potential problem, but we do not call it into our experience by fearing it or dwelling on it.

Fear is also alleviated when we are able to feel compassion for the negative entity, and we may find compassion in such circumstances by reminding ourselves that any such entity is itself suffering. In its suffering it seeks the distraction or relief of attaching itself to another being. Indeed, we might substitute the phrase "suffering being" for "negative entity."

"Let us come back to you and Kathryn, to past-life karma," Aaron continued. "You each have certain karma, and you resolve to come into a lifetime with certain challenges, but the nature of the challenges may not be specifically spelled out. There are different possibilities. For example, rather than the illness, Kathryn could have been hit by a truck. She could have had a genetic disorder that surfaced at this time in her life. This is almost irrelevant in your situation. In some situations it's relevant. For example, Barbara's experience of deafness came for a specific reason. There was a pre-life choice to be deaf.[6] For Kathryn there was only the

---

6 Readers are referred to the Introduction for information about Barbara's pre-birth plan.

choice to be incapacitated, not how that incapacitation would come, and for you the choice to take care of her. Why? Why would you have chosen this?

"You do not come into the incarnation for comfort or convenience. Your primary reasons for coming into the incarnation are to love, to release and balance old karma, and to form new and more wholesome patterns."

Here, Aaron had drawn an important distinction between balancing karma and releasing karma. We balance karma when we take actions that offset things we did in past lives. We release karma when we correct the underlying beliefs, attitudes, or character traits that first caused us to create the karma. Without doing the latter, we are likely to repeat old patterns of behavior and thus create more of the same karma.

"There are two past lives I'm going to talk about," Aaron said. "In the earlier of the two lifetimes, you and Kathryn were married and in opposite-sexed bodies. You were female [the mother], and she was male [the father]. You had a child who was beautiful and healthy until age five. This girl child contracted a disease similar to polio. She was paralyzed, and you provided total care. You had two younger children. The children were sent away at first so as not to catch the disease. They came back some months later. Your whole life seemed to be about taking care of this sick child. You loved the child. You could not bear to see the child in this situation. So, you took the two younger children and left, leaving the sick child to the father, who was Kathryn in that lifetime. In your heart you were not happy with your choice. Part of your pre-life planning in this lifetime was to stay to take care of her. It really is as simple as that.

"What you are learning is not to be stoic, Bob, but to deal with this with love. And I see that you are doing it with love. You care for her, and she knows that. At this point you have released and balanced much of the karma. You are not going to desert her."

I was delighted to hear Aaron say this. Through his love of and service to Kathryn, Bob had not only balanced much of the karma incurred during the past life but also had healed the underlying tendency to flee from difficult situations. In his current lifetime he had made a different choice.

"Your situation does not need to be as challenging as it is," Aaron offered. "I'll talk more about this. I also want to explain the second lifetime. In that lifetime Kathryn was the mother, and you, Bob, were her son. She was a very loving and beautiful woman. Your father had died a few years earlier. There were no siblings. When you were sixteen, your mother was injured in a carriage accident. She became partially paralyzed.

"You already were doing the chores of your father, and now you had on top of that the commitment to take care of your mother, the one who was Kathryn. You did it, Bob. In fact, as years went on, finally you married, but your mother went to your home. You shared your attention between your wife and mother. But, there was an undertone of resentment. You did fulfill the part of the life plan to take care of your mother, but you were not able to do it with love. Simply put, in your current lifetime you were to do it with love. Love does not mean that there will never be resentment or pain. And the love must be extended to the self as well as to the other, caring for yourself as you care for Kathryn. Much of your plan in this lifetime was to be in a situation in which there was challenge and to meet that challenge with love."

"Aaron, what part did Kathryn have in these plans?" I asked. "Did she agree to be disabled to give Bob the opportunity to practice this challenge with love?"

"Yes," Aaron replied. "Basically, yes. In this current lifetime, under the same type of agreement, something would create disablement for Kathryn so that Bob would have the opportunity to practice. This may seem like a great burden for Kathryn, but remember that in an ultimate sense a lifetime is as brief as a snap of the fingers.

"Kathryn is also learning. In the first lifetime I mentioned, the father [Kathryn] was very angry, feeling himself abandoned. In the second lifetime, as the mother who became injured, she felt unworthy to ask for care and love. She wanted to disappear. She did not want to be a burden to her son. And because you experienced resentment, Bob, she felt resentment. She used that negative energy from the one you were to feed into her anger over being disabled.

"In this lifetime it would seem that Kathryn is again moving into a dark place. You are not feeding that, yet there are ways in which you can help her to come out of the dark place. Constantly talk to the old Kathryn, even though you don't see much of her. Keep trying to bring her out from this place of darkness. Keep inviting her out."

"I have this strong feeling," Bob said, "that I am supposed to be accepting of her choices. I wonder how much I should insist or talk her into doing some of the things that would leave the darkness."

"This is a very important question," Aaron acknowledged. "You cannot force her, but love holds the door open. It's okay two or three times a day when she's awake to say, 'It's beautiful. Please come for a ride in the car with me.' This kind of persistent, loving response helps to take energy away from the negativity that is within her. We have to think of it not as a possessing external entity, just negativity. The more you feed negativity with negativity and contraction, the more energy you give to it. The more you feed negativity with kindness, the more it loses its energy."

Aaron's point was well taken. Negative earthbound spirits may be driven from a person's home by sending love to them; their discomfort with the high vibration of love prompts them to leave. Moreover, when someone we love is ill, it is important not to feed any negative emotions the loved one may have in regard to the illness.

"Remember," Aaron said to Bob, "there is that which is positive in Kathryn. It is as though she is a window so smudged with dirt that you could not see through. You keep washing the streaks off the window, but the nature of the window is clear and radiant. Let her know that you see that clarity and radiance in her. Be her mirror. Help her to see it in herself." Aaron was reminding Bob that Kathryn, like each of us, is a being literally made of light, sacred in nature. He was also reminding us that we call forth in others those traits to which we give our attention. When we focus on someone's light, we magnify it.

"Aaron," I said, "were there any other past lives that played a meaningful role in the pre-birth plan for Bob to take care of Kathryn?"

"There are many past lives. Let us use your computer search engines as example. You type in a word, and it gives you 327,000 possibilities with the ones that are most relevant at the top. What I've done is to pick what is most relevant. A year from now, or even in a different week, a different past life might come to the surface. If something changed in the relationship between Bob and Kathryn, that might bring a different past life to the top."

"You mentioned that the specific challenge was not spelled out ahead of time. Why did it end up being an illness and not, say, a car accident?"

"It was not completely arbitrary," Aaron replied. "There are many factors. In that second past life with Bob, Kathryn had a bad accident and became crippled. She had so much body pain from the accident that, as she planned this current lifetime, there was a strong movement in her that said, 'I see the need to become incapacitated, but this time without as much excruciating body pain.' Also, Kathryn was a wife in a lifetime in which Bob was not present. The husband had a stroke and lost function of half of his body. Kathryn did indeed take care of the husband, but there was a lot of impatience of the husband's inability to move himself easily and of his general neediness. So, she needed to come into an incapacitated lifetime in order to develop compassion for herself and for this husband she had in a past life."

"Can you say more," I asked, "about how the experience of illness and requiring the care of another helps Kathryn to grow?"

"In the lifetime in which the mother [Bob] left, leaving the father [Kathryn] with a child with polio, Kathryn wanted to leave but had enough of a sense of responsibility to stay. Yet, there was much resentment and sometimes a brusqueness with the sick one. There was awareness [on the part of Kathryn's soul] of the need to experience impairment and to fear another's brusqueness. And she did in the next lifetime I related, when she had the accident. Because she experienced resentment, she was adrift. She allowed herself to move into feelings of unworthiness and various unwholesome traits, and to blame others. So, she needed to come back into this relationship with Bob, choosing a less but still highly painful and debilitating impairment. She does not know what Bob is going to give, whether he is going to give resentment again or whether he is going to transcend it this time. Whatever she receives, her work is to not move into a place of self-pity or feelings of unworthiness or despair."

Here we had come to a theme I would see again and again in pre-birth planning: a soul who had responded to a challenge in a past life by developing feelings or beliefs of unworthiness would then seek a similar type of experience in another lifetime in order to rise above it and come into a knowing of one's infinite worth. Regardless of the circumstances or challenges of an incarnation, we as souls desire before we are born to remember our inherent magnificence while in body.

"Why did Kathryn's illness begin just one month after Bob retired?" I inquired. "Certainly it was not just chance."

"It began at that point because the decision was not to cut into the earlier part of their life, not to impact Bob's work and the opportunity to earn money, not to impact the family life and the children. Rob, as you would perhaps put it, the candy was pulled out of the mouth—the suddenness of it, the anticipation of retirement—that was part of the plan. Bob felt before the incarnation a fear that if this happened too early in their lives, he would abandon Kathryn. It needed to come at a point where it was very clear he would not and could not abandon her.

"The caregiving contract was with Kathryn and not the children," Aaron added. "In a different karmic situation, it could have been with one of the children."

"Some people may judge Bob's children for not taking a more active role in Kathryn's care."

"Since you may not know the pre-birth plans with any accuracy, then the question is simply, Where is compassion here? When one finds oneself in a situation where one is judging of others, one can almost always assume that part of the pre-birth plan was to be pushed into a situation in which judgment would arise in order to work skillfully with the judgment, release the judgment, and offer a deeper unconditional love for the self and the others involved."

"Aaron," I said, "please speak to those who are caregivers and feel burdened, angry, or overwhelmed, or simply can't understand why it's happened."

"My dear ones, it is not surprising that you feel angry, not surprising that there is resentment. Please remember that life is always teaching. There is always something you are offered to learn, and that something almost always has to do with learning a deeper love for yourself and others. When resentment arises, watch how you relate to the resentment. Is there a desire to blame the other for the illness? Is there then an attacking of the self, saying, 'It's not their fault, I shouldn't blame them?' Watch how the mind wants to attack, whether it's the other or the self. You can be certain you are in the situation because you have chosen to learn how to relate to anger and resentment in a more wholesome way. Can you open your heart to yourself and your own being and to others and their pain? Can you enter the spaciousness of compassion and begin to watch with more spaciousness the mind that moves into judgment? Begin to know, 'I do not have to believe everything I think. Just because the mind thinks this thought of resentment or self-anger doesn't mean I have to get caught up in the story.' As you do that, there is more compassion."

"Aaron," I said, "many people take care of people with Alzheimer's. What can you say to them? And, why is Alzheimer's so common at this time?"

"The primary reason why Alzheimer's is prevalent today is simply because people are living long enough to develop the disease,"

Aaron answered. "When one moves into an incarnation, there is a contract, but each being has free will. So, when the contract is to become a caregiver, the caregiver can make the decision to leave. The movement into Alzheimer's is more gradual than the sudden debilitation of a stroke or accident. If it becomes clear that the other is going to withdraw as caregiver, the one who is developing Alzheimer's may simply pull back and not develop it, or not nearly as severely."

Aaron's insight echoed my understanding of pre-birth planning. If a soul wanted the experience of relying on another for care but was unsure before birth of the future response of the caregiver, or if the caregiver were unsure whether he or she would choose to stay, then the gradual onset of Alzheimer's would provide a safe "testing ground" in which to discover if the desired experience could be created.

"Many people agreed before birth to experience Alzheimer's because it simplifies life to a certain degree," Aaron continued. "There's no longer a lot of planning. There's not so much a past or future; one doesn't fret so much about yesterday or tomorrow. For many people this is a useful catalyst. The intention may have been to learn to live in the moment.

"You asked what advice I have for one who is caring for a loved one with Alzheimer's. Simply, to remember this is a beautiful soul for whom you are caring. The gift to the caregiver is that you watch your own resentment, your own grief, your own anger come up again and again and again, and you have the opportunity to make the commitment not to allow that pain, grief, and anger to interfere with wholesome, loving words and actions. This will not always change the behavior of the one with Alzheimer's, but sometimes it will. The more the caregiver is able to respond in a skillful, kind, and predictable way, the more the fear is resolved for the one with Alzheimer's. The more the caregiver responds with fear, the more negative the one with Alzheimer's becomes. They are a barometer to some degree. Yet, sometimes their reaction is strong no matter what you do. Then you have the opportunity to remember not to take it personally."

"Aaron, how would Bob know when he has balanced and released all the karma he has with Kathryn, and more generally, how would we know we have balanced and released the karma we have with the one we're caring for?"

"Rob, when there is fear or stress, the body contracts. It shows up sometimes as ailments like heart problems, high blood pressure, fibromyalgia, and immune system diseases. When there is the ability to work skillfully with stress, you can feel the openness of, the lack of contraction in, the body. One can learn to read this body barometer. The question is, 'Am I reactive to stress, or am I able to be with stress without the mind becoming obsessive, wanting to attack, contracting with fear?' It becomes quite clear when one is simply moving along day to day with as much kindness as possible, with love, with graciousness, with ease. When you have helped the ill one through for a period of time, and when the mind has ceased to obsess about the situation, ceased to attack the other or self, then you can be reasonably certain the karma has been resolved and balanced."

Aaron now turned his attention directly to Bob, who had been quietly taking in his words.

"Bob, let me add one thought here. At a time when Kathryn is more clear, you might remind her, 'Sometimes you become angry, frightened, and hostile. I would like to decide now, while we are more clear, what I can do when that happens to help you find your true, loving center.' Perhaps it would work for you just to sit beside her and talk to her, stroke her hair, hold her, and say 'I love you.' If, when you do that, she lashes out, then of course you do not sit there and allow yourself to be hit. But, if you practice this enough, she may be able to relax. You need to explain when she is calm what you intend to do when she is agitated."

"As I look into the future," Bob replied, "I hope that Kathryn will transition to the other side before I do so that I can take care of her until her ending. Does the plan say anything about that?"

"I hear your question, Bob," Aaron said gently, "and I am sorry, but there is no specific decision in this regard. There are too many possibilities. Your intention is to stay with her. It's vital for you to develop trust once you've set that as a loving intention. If it doesn't play out that way, there will be a reason.

"Bob, you are working hard to release and balance old karma. You're to be honored for that. Please honor yourself.

"I thank you, Rob, my brother. My blessings and love to you. If you have no further questions, I will release the body to Barbara."

Bob's Session with Staci

With love and compassion, Aaron had helped us to understand Bob and Kathryn's pre-birth plan. To see what else we might learn about caregiving, Bob and I asked Staci and her spirit guide to access the conversation that took place among Bob and the members of his family prior to birth. Staci and her guide did so on two occasions: a lengthy first reading followed by a shorter, supplemental reading. The two sessions are presented separately.

What karmic themes, I wondered, would Staci discern in Bob's life? What would Bob's pre-birth planning session reveal to us? In particular, since we had not discussed Bob and Kathryn's children in any detail with Aaron, I wanted Staci to listen to some of their words in the planning session. Why would they agree before birth to have a disabled elderly parent? And what would Staci's spirit guide tell us about the way caregiving is viewed from our nonphysical Home?

"Bob," Staci began, "you are going to hear about the karmic lessons your soul chose to focus on in this life and aspects of your personality that your soul wanted to change in some way or maybe just experience for the enjoyment of it. Think about your life and past lives as the plot of a book and your karma as the theme of that book. Your karma is the reason behind what you experience, the simple truth behind it all. There are two phrases I use interchangeably: karmic lesson and karmic challenge.

"Remember, Bob, this is something you decided for yourself. We decide what we want to experience and why.

"Your most important karmic lesson I describe with the key phrase, 'personality maturation through responsibility to family.' In other lives being there for your family and making sure they are cared for, clothed, and fed has been a huge challenge for you, one you didn't feel very good about and wanted to master. You felt it would mature you. You also felt it would enable you to obtain a more compassionate aspect to your personality. In some of your other lives, as in this one, you've also been working on leadership. As a leader you have a history of being arrogant and self-serving. You'd had enough of that aspect of personality. You wanted to build more compassion, and you wanted to be of compassionate service to your family."

"That resonates with me," Bob told Staci. "Beyond Kathryn's caregiving, I was the sole caregiver to her mother. That wasn't what I had in mind when I retired, but I was glad to do it and found it over time to be a very rewarding experience."

"Your plan," Staci said, "was that this last phase of your life would be intensely focused on that particular karmic challenge. You wanted to experience yourself as patient, cooperative, diplomatic, understanding, and able to compromise. I hear you talking about it in your pre-birth planning session. I keep hearing over and over again about going it alone and that you wouldn't have the help in this phase of your life that you were used to in the rest of your life."

"I do relate to the going-it-alone aspect," Bob replied, "because my children, as loving as they are, are almost completely uninvolved. But, I don't experience self-pity. What I experience more than anything is frustration. And frustration can easily lead to anger, particularly if I'm tired. I have to regularly remind myself that I'm choosing the anger and that there are other paths to choose."

"This makes you a more mature personality," Staci offered. "There were also some other karmic lessons you wanted to master, two primarily, and I would call them your second and third most important challenges. Your second most important challenge is learning to control overly impulsive tendencies. You like personal freedom. In many of your other lives, you've had dominion over yourself; no one else has been in authority over you except your parents. Sometimes, however, you do your best learning when your personal freedom is limited. You learn from the restriction and limitation.

"I've never seen people with the karmic lesson of learning to control overly impulsive tendencies who were not extremely intelligent and quick witted, sometimes to their own detriment. There is a high degree of mental ability that is brought in as part of this lesson and that is conducive to great leaps and bounds. But, remember that leaping to conclusions is not good, and that is what you're trying to learn not to do.

"Something else associated with this karmic lesson that I see in a lot of people is escapism," Staci continued, "whether through the use or misuse of mood-altering substances, infidelity, or even exercise. Most people with this karmic challenge will, instead of doing the very tough work within themselves, reach for a quick fix. Here, I do not sense these more negative aspects of it. Your desire from the soul level to express love was so strong, and you seek balance in so much of what you do, that I don't feel you going there. You're more self-aware, evolved.

"Your third most important karmic lesson is emotional independence. Why was emotional independence so important to you? You have an arc of lives where you have been a leader who was not very kind. You've killed people, maimed them, manipulated them for your goals and desires. As you were planning, you began to expect much more of yourself, a higher form of leadership. You began to see that when you sank into self-involvement, you were not an effective leader. So, now you're trying to be a leader of a kinder, gentler, more persuasive, and less manipulative type. You decided on emotional independence as one of your karmic challenges because when you have mastered emotional independence you are a better leader. You're no longer dominating people to get them to fulfill your needs or do what you should do yourself.

"Most people who have the karmic lesson of emotional independence spend a lot of time in relationships where they are actually dependent on the other person for their well-being," she added. "Emotional independence is about learning that you are the only source of your own happiness."

Having addressed Bob's major karmic lessons, Staci shifted her focus to Kathryn.

"Kathryn spends a lot of time with family and friends on the other side when she's sleeping," Staci told us. "There is a lot of happiness there for her. She is free of the confinement of the body. She feels the lightness of being she doesn't have here. She feels joy and love.

"Kathryn is primarily working on becoming more self-referencing, looking to herself as the source of all things. Her most important karmic challenge in this life is spiritual growth and evolvement through first enriching the relationship with herself. She is learning to nurture herself, and she is working on emotional independence. And like you, Kathryn is working on building a more compassionate nature through responsibility to family. She's done a good job of that in this lifetime. I don't feel that is an issue for her in this current phase of her life."

Now that Staci had provided the major karmic themes for Bob and Kathryn's lives, it was time to listen to their pre-birth planning session. I asked Staci to include some of the conversation with Bob's children, particularly Wendy, who Bob had told me is the child most strongly affected by Kathryn's illness. Bob and I waited in silence for a couple of minutes as Staci entered a meditative state. When she was ready, she began to tell us what she was seeing and hearing.

"Bob, as you're building the personality for the life and making your plans, there's a sense of fun, enjoyment, and looking forward to being in physical form," said Staci. "There is delight." This comment did not surprise me. Though we as incarnate personalities often do not view our lives with delight, the predominant feeling among souls during the pre-birth planning process is truly one of joyous collaboration.

"I'm right alongside Bob," Staci said. "I see a dark, wooden floor, partially carpeted, a table off to one side, and a window that looks out on the gardens. This room is two stories up in the building. Yes, there are buildings on the other side, Bob, and we create them with our thoughts. Large buildings like this we create through consensus of thought.

"On one side of the room are a few members of Bob's soul group. On the other side is an anteroom. There's a half-wall between this little room and the larger room that Bob and the soul group occupy, like a wall between a living room and a kitchen. This anteroom gives the spirit guides a place to talk amongst themselves while Bob is planning his life.

"I see Bob's main spirit guide, who says he's been both a buddy and a servant to Bob [in past lives together]. He has quite a sense of humor. He's behind me; I'm sitting between him and Bob's planning board. Bob is starting to take on the cloak of the personality. The form of his lightbody has become larger and angular. I see dark places where our eyes would be. I see facial features begin to form. I have a sense of a male energy with Bob by this point in his planning session. Opposite him I see Kathryn in a similar state of transformation into the cloak of the personality. There is a softness and feminine quality, a roundness to her form.

"I'm coming in on the middle on the conversation.

Kathryn:	In this life you'll have the benefit of my giving birth to and mothering your children, and mothering you as well.
Bob:	I know, and I appreciate it. I regard you so highly for your ability to do that. I've never been the kind of mother you are. I've never developed that ability to nurture others.

Kathryn:	Would you like the opportunity to do that now?
Bob:	What do you mean?
Kathryn:	It would fulfill my karma to once again go down the path of incapacity with you. It would take me back to an internal frame of reference, where I could once again learn who I am, to manifest my being, and to comfort myself. It is a strength I have been developing for some lives now.
Bob:	Yes, I know.
Kathryn:	I am committed to continuing to do this.
Bob:	But what about being a baby [helpless] again?
Kathryn:	That is a natural process of physical form on Earth. What I choose to experience is the loss of full personal independence.
Bob:	I would gladly repeat this process with you to test myself, to see what I have learned, and to make amends to you. I have felt bad for neglecting you [in certain past lives]. I've come to realize that my neglect of you was a result of my own self-centeredness and arrogance. I expected you to be something you could not. I expected you to always be the strong one, to always be there for me. I was unable to be fully available to you with the same love and compassion you've shown to me. I would love the opportunity to make this up to you.

"The conversation moves toward planning children. There is talk about incorporating Bob's son, Christopher. Bob, he is somebody you've had other lives with and that you want very much to go through this life with as a buddy more than anything else. He's never been a child to you in any other life until this one.

| Kathryn: | He will be long gone [from our home] by the time this happens. |

"As she says that, she references a particular area of Bob's pre-birth planning chart. It's like a flow chart. It's got a line to something, and that something can look like a house or a building, or it can be a word that represents whatever the event is. Then the line continues beyond that to the next thing and the next and the next. Very often there are forks in the road, where we've built in the possibility that we may make a decision that might carry us in another direction.

"The part of Bob's chart I'm looking at has to do with Kathryn's illness. It's like a big blob of white light. I'm asking Spirit, 'What does that mean?' I hear Bob's spirit guide saying, 'This is a protected time.' The white light serves as a shield covering that time so that nothing else impacts it. It looks like a blob because it was not known that Bob would react in any particular way. Bob knew on the soul level his propensity toward self-centeredness. The test was in making the choice not to react from selfishness. That phase of Bob's life was not specifically planned beyond the experience itself; it was left open and uncharted. How Bob reacted to it was his choice in this life.

"Let me get back to the conversation. They go on to the next child, Wendy. Kathryn is sitting opposite Bob, and Wendy is now sitting on Bob's left side, Kathryn's right. Wendy is a bright, shiny bubble of sunlight, joy, enthusiasm, curiosity, and fun. She loves this soul who is her mother very much. I see them link their lightbodies together for a moment; it looks like one person slips an arm through the arm of another. It's a greeting and an intimate, familiar sort of touch.

"Wendy expresses that she's glad Kathryn has consented to be her mother in this life. She has an 'Oh boy!' attitude about it. Kathryn brings up the subject.

Kathryn: (to Wendy)	One of my greatest joys in life has been my strength, my ability to persevere in the worst of times.
Wendy:	Yes, I know. I've been with you through some of that.
Kathryn:	Yes, you have. This time I have planned, and your father and I have agreed, that I will suffer a severe, permanent, life-altering, consciousness-affecting, physical condition at this stage of my life. [Points to a specific place on the planning chart.]
Wendy:	I see.
Kathryn:	This is as much for my development as it is for your father's. I don't want you to feel personally responsible for it, and I don't want you to feel responsible for me.
Wendy:	But Mother, you know I care about you, and you know I hate to see you weaker than you really are.

"As Wendy talks about this, I see a life in Scotland in the 1500s. Kathryn and Wendy were husband and wife. Wendy was the husband. Wendy is talking about that past life because there was a time when Kathryn, as Wendy's wife, had given birth to a male child and had to take quite a bit of time recuperating in bed afterward. The baby was very big and tore her up inside but did not kill her. Wendy thought she was going to lose her. This past life is a holographic image that plays to the side of Wendy's lightbody. I, and everybody there, can see it very clearly. You can see through it, and it can be seen from all angles.

| Wendy: | You know I'll be afraid of losing you, Mother. |
| Kathryn: | And you know there will come a time when you *will* lose me, but it won't be at the time of the onset of this condition, whatever it may be. |

| Wendy: | Yes, Mother. |

"There is a feeling of being reassured. She's quiet for a moment.

Wendy:	But what if you fall silent and can't communicate?
Kathryn:	We'll still be able to communicate through touch and the words spoken in silence. You know that.
Wendy:	Yes, yes. But what if Father is unable to care for you?
Kathryn:	That won't happen, my dear. Your father and I have already planned this. It will serve your father's purposes to stay and to see to my daily needs. This is our agreement. You have no reason to doubt it.
Wendy:	Yes, I know. But Mother, I'm afraid of being alone without you.
Kathryn: (laughing)	Then why agree to be my daughter?
Wendy:	So that I may enjoy you once more. So that I may try on this role of being your daughter instead of your son or your husband.
Kathryn:	Why do you choose to be a daughter and not a son?
Wendy:	So that I may become more nurturing and sensitive, and so that I will have the opportunity to raise children of my own and to nurture others in a capacity that the female form will give me and that is not available to the male form.
Kathryn:	Then why are you afraid of that which you know is an eventuality?
Wendy:	It is my own problem. It is my own avoidance of learning this hard lesson that I am all right on my

own and within myself, that I can continue to exist in health, wisdom, faith, and hope without your being there.

Kathryn: So now I give you the opportunity to care about me. I do this for you lovingly, willingly."

Staci's Supplemental Reading for Bob

In hearing Staci's first reading for Bob, I had been struck by how seemingly quickly Bob and Kathryn had arrived at the decision for her to experience some form of incapacitation. In subsequent discussion, Staci's spirit guide said that Kathryn's and Bob's planning sessions "were both in process together, though not occupying the same room. They were energetically able to pop in and out of each other's sessions as plans would formulate." Thus, some of the discussion about Kathryn's illness had taken place in *her* pre-birth planning session and so was unnecessary in Bob's. In a supplemental reading, Staci heard the following from Kathryn's planning session. Here, Staci's guide took her to the end and most important part of a discussion between Bob and Kathryn.

"Kathryn: The heart of the matter is that I need a greater experience to move me toward consciousness, toward a greater understanding of myself. I have seen you in other lives realize the process of growth in yourself. I seek to emulate this in living with you during so much of my life and particularly the last thirty years of life.

Bob: I will act as your safety net and surround and hold you while you find yourself. I do this because I know it will reinforce trust in me, in the personality I seek to create and mold for this lifetime and the generations to come. I am well aware that the influence I will have will be with many people. Our life together will teach me how to help and teach others.

In so many lives you have been supportive of me. You have allowed me to take the lead, to do what I felt I must. You have enabled me many times to help others, but you have done so quietly. I know and understand now the resentments you've harbored in the past in our efforts to bring to light the best of what we have to offer.

In this life-to-come I will feel denied. I will feel mistreated by your form. I will feel ignored. But, I will also feel my purpose and place by your side. It is my greatest hope that the love we have shared together in the past will keep me connected to you. I believe there will be resistance within me, resistance to the loss of my personal freedom, but this I can bear. I realize you have given up so much in other lives for me. In this life you are planning, I will serve you by taking care of you, which really is taking care of me."

When Staci's vision of Kathryn's planning session stopped here, indicating to me that that dialogue is all her guide wished to present to us from that session, I asked Staci if she could return to Bob's planning session and perhaps hear something that would shed further light on his intentions and motivations. Spirit responded to my request by presenting Staci with images from one of Bob's past lives.

"Spirit is showing me a lifetime," Staci said, "where Bob experienced himself as a learned man, teacher and healer, his first lifetime as a doctor. I hear this was in Greece during Roman times. I am being shown Bob walking down a street, smiling and being greeted, knowing he had touched the lives of so many people. The feeling of warmth and generosity of his soul that he got in touch with was overwhelming and fulfilling. He was at his most compassionate self in that life.

"Bob decided he wanted to deepen that experience for himself, and thus his quest in this current life is to further develop compassion, to further his ability to see others as they are rather than judge how they could or should be. Bob understands that this awareness and acceptance will enable him to enjoy a greater level of compassionate service to others, which, in turn, gives him other experiences he enjoys—greater intellectual capacity and influence in life. Bob consistently has chosen to be a learned man in his lives of male identity, which are the majority of his lives on the human plane.

"Bob's soul has heightened his awareness and thus his experience of how service to others increases joy within the self. So, he seeks to be of great service to Kathryn; however, the handling of emotionality without manipulation is still something he seeks to learn, and thus we have Kathryn as his greatest challenge.

"Now I'm being drawn back into Bob's pre-birth planning session. I see one of the other souls gathered there to be of support come out of the gallery area and give Bob a gift, a bouquet of flowers.

"Next, I am seeing Bob conversing with the entity who's chosen to be his father.

Bob:	Teach me what I need to know. Bring me back to myself. Remind me who I am. You've always been good at seeing the real me, brother.
	This time I need you to father me. I need to learn about me through you in the early stages of my life. I need you to ground me in greater understanding of the role of purpose in life, so that I may continue on, even when taking each step is the hardest thing I could possibly do.
Father:	Why do you seek this?
Bob:	I have planned a life of tremendous growth. The path before me is a steep incline to walk, but it is,

I feel, a necessary road to further self-determination and wisdom within my being, and to greater strength.

To love is the greatest gift of all. I know this now. I understand it in a way I could not possibly have before. I want to demonstrate this understanding to those I know and to those who have helped me in other lives. The primary focus of my heart's desire is Kathryn, who has agreed to become my wife.

For you to do me this favor, this great favor of consenting to be my father, will allow me to come in [incarnate] on a vibration whereby I can quickly develop trust, trust in my family as well as trust in myself. This is paramount to what I must do. All that I have thoughts of doing in the world is all and always for the purpose of better serving others.

Within me lie great joy and humbleness, but I have forgotten what humbleness feels like. I must remind myself of this so that I may be more of who I am.

Having Kathryn in my life will help me be at my best ability to serve others, and it will ground me in circumstances that allow for greater understanding, awareness, and growth. I will, I believe, go back again shortly after this life is over, having benefited from the experience with greater knowledge and understanding, hungry and thirsty once again to get out into the world with my hands and help others to heal.

"Spirit is telling me," Staci added, "that Bob had withdrawn from service to others as a healer and authority."

Then, abruptly, Staci's speech patterned changed. Her guide was now speaking directly through her.

"There was once a life experience," said Staci's spirit guide, "where the entity [Bob] created a personality that became hampered and bogged down and lost sight of the true essence of Self and the awareness and joy that come through serving the needs of others. This personality became outraged, annoyed, and insolent, and remained fixed in that attitude for the rest of its life. This was destructive to others and self-destructive as well. This personality died in a round of gunfire in a battle he had started. Ever since that life, this entity has pulled back, unsure of its ability to be of genuine service to others, fearful of getting lost along the way, of reincarnating and losing that connection with Self and thus feeling prideful, boastful, and yet soulless in that the personality forgets there is a soul. This has affected him significantly, and yet through the process [of reincarnating in lifetimes in which he refrained from serving others] he has created greater coherence in his ability to express his true passions and to be compassionate. Kathryn's presence is the last 'notch.'"

Talking with Staci and Her Spirit Guide

The information provided by Staci and her guide had raised several questions for me. "Staci," I asked, "why did Bob and Kathryn not plan something less extreme?"

"Because Bob and Kathryn knew they wouldn't be able to produce a less extreme experience. Both are impassioned and have been given to extremes in their emotional character. They haven't mastered the middle path."

I then asked why Kathryn's health had suddenly deteriorated just one month after Bob had retired.

"Bob wanted to retire at that point because part of him knew the next part of his life would be completely taken up with this," Staci answered. "It was a planned shift. He was acting in accordance with guidance he was feeling but wasn't consciously aware of."

Staci paused. When she began speaking again, her speech had slowed considerably. Her spirit guide was now speaking through her once more.

"The entity known as Kathryn has been of such a compassionate and understanding intelligence in so much of what you would refer to as her other lives that she knew better than to burden Bob with this extreme and dramatic change before he was ready," said the spirit guide. "And to Kathryn, this [Bob's] retirement was like the flip of the switch: it started an energy in her neurological pathways that cascaded toward the event mentioned. The event was planned for a dramatic, sudden alteration of the status quo for two purposes. One, Bob and Kathryn prefer to have dramatically expressive personalities when in physical form. Two, it would open the corridor, the energetic connection, so that resonance with the challenges would be immediate, unconscious, and not recognized. That way Bob could take care of her and be in and of the moment. The rest would happen automatically, and Bob and Kathryn's great intellects would not step in the way of allowing events to play themselves out."

"Staci, we've touched on this, but I'd like to learn more. Did Bob's children agree before birth not to be part of the caregiving so that Bob could do it?"

"Let me see what comes to me … The children were told that this was not their challenge, that this was primarily for Bob. Wendy and Holly felt a sense of being needed and a desire to help. I don't get that sense with Christopher. But, Bob raised an arm [in the pre-birth planning session], saying, 'This is my role to fulfill. This is my responsibility. It is my duty and honor to do this for someone whom I so love and cherish.' I hear both Wendy and Holly saying yes and pulling back in involvement. When I look at the pre-birth planning chart and that white blob, I don't see kids pulled into that. It's just Bob and Kathryn."

"Staci, Bob could have planned caregiving in any other time period or location. Why the United States at this time in history?"

Again Staci's guide stepped to the forefront. "You are looking at this from a historical frame of reference. For Bob and Kathryn this is merely an extension [of other lives together]. This time and place is conducive to Bob experiencing himself as a successful man, providing him with an opportunity to assume roles of responsibility and leadership. For both Bob and Kathryn there was the certain knowledge that at this point in humanity's evolution, and given the culture and technology of North America, their needs would be provided for in a level of social order and physical comfort. The money earned by Bob, in particular, would provide both accommodations—their home environment—and medical technologies and care. It was not important that this occur in a time, historically speaking, where medical care was better than in a previous life, because it was the experience of the disorder and the caregiving that was desired. This could have been fulfilled in any time and place, but to enjoy the comforts of life and to live a longer life, it was necessary that this couple be located within the North American continent."

"Please speak to those who are caregivers and who feel burdened, resentful, or angry."

"Come from the heart, and all else will drop away," offered the guide. "The impetuous responses of blame, frustration, and anger are childlike; they come from outside heart space. Since the greater purpose of all Earthly incarnations is learning to drop fear and love unconditionally, we would remind caregivers that they have plenty of love to go around. See yourself in similar circumstances. When you identify with the person you are taking care of, your present-day needs of ego gratification will drop away and you will realize your connection with that entity for whom you are entrusted the care, keeping, and feeding. You will open the compassionate side of your nature as you come to the understanding and realization that we are all One. What happens to them can happen to you. We would ask that you, the caregiver, place yourself in the other person's position and feel the powerlessness, helplessness, and frustration of being in a physical form that no longer is fully functional. It is simply another opportunity to learn unconditional love in all forms of expression. We would ask all caregivers to turn away from their own ego and fear and turn instead toward the heart, the heart of love and compassion, no matter what."

"What about people who are being taken care of and who feel guilty about imposing?"

"Be gentle with yourself. Understand that although you may not realize the greater good being served by your physical incapacitation, that greater good *is* being served. There is a harmony that exists in your situation, like a single note that connects all of you. By 'all of you' we mean you and those who care for you, whether it be family, friends, or hired help. You are providing each of them with a special opportunity to express love, to perhaps make right something that individual feels was handled poorly or did incorrectly in another life.

"Understand that what may be required from you is forgiveness—forgiveness of yourself so that you may begin to accept your situation and gain from it all you can. Then the people who serve you may gain from the experience all they can. Be certain you are providing those who care for you with an opportunity so great and grand that it could not be achieved any other way.

"Love yourself enough to accept your situation with a kind heart.

"And for some of you," concluded the guide, "who have held the false assumption that the only people worthwhile to occupy space on your planet are those who are so-called productive members of family and society, you get to learn that all individuals have a right to exist as they desire and are able to be held by the physical body. There is no such thing as being deserving of life. We, you, all of us choose whether to have physical life. No one decides for us; thus, no one judges whether it is our right to occupy physical form or space on the planet. Use your time to come to a greater understanding and acceptance of your fellow human beings, and seek to understand the common thread that binds us all."

∿

In our quest to love unconditionally, we assume bodily form in order to gift ourselves with the unique joy of expressing and thus experiencing love on the physical plane. Through giving and receiving, the caregiver and the one who receives care bless each other with the expression and experience of love. In this holy relationship, they bestow upon each other the opportunity to know themselves as loving, eternal souls.

Often, the challenge for the one needing care is to believe that he or she is worthy of such love. As Aaron told us, Kathryn had a past life in which she, as Bob's disabled mother, felt unworthy of his care. Feelings or beliefs of unworthiness are one of the primary reasons why we as souls plan pre-birth to need the care of another. We seek to discover while in body our inherent, limitless worth and so place ourselves in a position in which we will require care so we may learn we are worthy of it. Like a candle in a dark room, our inner light may be most visible to us in the darkness of illness or incapacitation. When we come to know our infinite value—that is, when we *feel* it—then the caregiving may come to an end or it may continue as a form of service to the caregiver.

How then is the caregiver served? Caregivers may cultivate empathy and express love, often in ways they could not in previous lives. As Bob told us, Kathryn has given him both opportunity and motivation to learn kindness, patience, and compassion. These divine virtues are inherent in the soul and so are not learned anew; rather, we discover them within ourselves when we express them. (*Discover* begins with the Latin prefix *dis-*, meaning "away." As we express our divine traits on the Earth plane, we move away the cover, the veil of forgetfulness that conceals our true nature from us.) Just as the keys of a piano already exist but require human touch to create music, so, too, are the qualities of the soul within each of us, awaiting our decision to bring them forth.

The caregiver is called upon to express kindness, patience, and compassion for self as much as for the one in need of care. As Aaron wisely said, "Love does not mean there will never be resentment." This awareness engenders profound self-forgiveness and thus self-compassion. If you care for a loved one and judge yourself for feeling resentment or anger, ask yourself what you would say to a dear friend in similar circumstances. Surely, you would tell your friend that he is a deeply loving person who is giving much of himself. You would tell her that she is devotedly doing her best. You would remind your friend that he is human. We can give to others only what we give to ourselves. If you seek to give kindness, patience, and compassion to a loved one who requires caregiving, give these things to yourself first. Then will they easily and truly flow from you.

Caregiving lends itself to judgment. Apart from judging themselves, caregivers often judge the one they take care of for not responding as they would like, just as Bob at times judges Kathryn's behavior. Often, both the primary caregiver and people outside the family judge various family members for not doing enough. Someone unaware of the pre-birth agreements made by Bob and Kathryn's children might well judge them for leaving most of the caregiving to Bob. Then, too, those receiving care may stand in judgment of their caregivers for not expressing sufficient patience or understanding, or they may judge themselves for being too needy or demanding.

We cannot cease to judge others until we no longer judge ourselves. When we are aware of our self-judgments, we may heal them. When we deny that we judge aspects of ourselves, we ensure that we will stand in judgment of others, for what is denied cannot be healed but most surely will be projected. If you judge another, rest assured that you carry that same judgment of yourself.

The profusion of judgment inherent in the caregiving experience is one of its primary attractions for an incarnating soul. I have said that healing is a major motivation for planning a life challenge. If in other lifetimes you stood in judgment of yourself or others, and if you desired before being born to heal your judgments, then you would see caregiving as a clear mirror with which to show your judgments to yourself. It may appear that your role is to be a caregiver like Bob, one receiving care like Kathryn, or one called upon to step away like Wendy, but your true role at this time in human evolution is to release judgment and embrace unconditional love of self and thus all others. The ancient call to love your neighbor as yourself was in fact a call to self-love. Truly, regardless of our degree of self-love, we always love our neighbors as ourselves. Nothing else is possible.

Self-love emerges and blooms in the soil of self-awareness and self-forgiveness. When we are aware of our innate goodness, as Bob is increasingly becoming aware of his, then we can rejoice in who we are. When we forgive ourselves for our perceived faults and wrongs, as Bob forgives himself for feeling frustration, then discernment replaces self-judgment, creating a safe space in which to choose another way. Bob and Kathryn's experience of caregiving is, therefore, a potent impetus toward self-awareness, self-forgiveness, and ultimately self-love.

Pity is a subtle form of judgment. All pity implies the judgment, "You are weak, perhaps even powerless." Although it is true that a need for care may engender pity, it is equally true that pity may engender a need for care. All who are pitied sense the pity, whether consciously or not. If they are not sufficiently awake, they will unknowingly internalize the pity by believing themselves to be the weak and perhaps powerless victims of forces beyond their control. This false belief may then require healing in another life in which they plan to experience circumstances seemingly beyond their control so as to afford themselves the opportunity to reclaim their power. If you pity yourself or another for having to give or receive care, know this: We live in a benevolent, deeply loving Universe in which all change is both for the better and called to us *by us*. To deny the former is to deny the fundamental nature of the Universe. To deny the latter is to deny our limitless power to create.

Ultimately, seeing a loved one incapacitated and in need of care can be a heartbreaking experience. It is intended to be so. Only that which is brittle can break. As souls who wish to love unconditionally, we *want* life to crack open the brittle parts of our hearts. Only then does our love, like Bob's love for Kathryn, pour forth more freely.

CHAPTER 5

⤸⤷

𝒫ets

ONE OF THE QUESTIONS I am most often asked
is, "Are pets part of our pre-birth planning?" Millions
of people love their pets dearly, and it is only natural
for those who are aware of life blueprints to wonder. Intuitively,
I have long sensed that our pets are indeed an important aspect
of planning at the soul level. The Universe is much too finely
ordered for our animal friends to come into our lives at random.
Yet, until I explored the subject closely, I was unsure of the role
of pets in our plans.

Marcia deRousse, who describes herself as "middle-aged,"
stands four feet six inches tall, but her height belies her forceful
presence. As a medium and an actress, she is poised, self-confi-
dent, and charismatic. One of her psychic gifts is the ability to
communicate with animals. I first met Marcia at a talk I gave
in Los Angeles when she asked what role cats play in our lives.
(I replied that cats are our teachers, modeling for us the ability to find contentment in being as opposed to doing.) Some
time later Marcia and I became better acquainted by e-mail. I
was struck by her depth, wisdom, humor, strength, and open
heart, a heart so open that she was easily moved to tears when she
spoke of her pets. When I later learned that pets had been such
a key part of her life, I wondered if they had played a role in her
spiritual growth. Moreover, I felt certain Marcia had planned her

dwarfism. What, I asked myself, was the connection between her dwarfism and the animals that had been or were now in her life?

Marcia

"I was born in Pontiac, Michigan, but we moved to a farm in Missouri," Marcia told me as I settled in to listen. "I lived a great deal of my life in the Ozarks. I am a psychic, a medium, an empath, and an actress. I have a degree in theater, and it's always been a great love. In this life I wanted to prove that I could be an actress in spite of appearances. I have physical challenges that have made that very difficult." Marcia explained that the term *dwarf* refers to anyone shorter than four feet ten inches. There are more than two hundred forms of dwarfism, but regardless of type, dwarves typically experience problems with bones and joints.

"Marcia, what was it like to grow up as a dwarf?" I wondered.

"I was nicknamed Bridget the Midget," she laughed, "and never chosen for any of the games because they all said, 'She's too little. She can't do it.' I'd come home from school and cry. I began to pray literally every day that I would be blessed with a sense of humor so I could have people laugh with instead of at me. So, I started studying drama and speech, and I really excelled. I felt like this gift had been given to me. I always manage to bring out the funny."

I asked Marcia what dating had been like for her in her youth.

"I had guys that were my friends," she explained, "but dating wasn't that important to me. I know I selected this time [life] to be okay on my own. The reason I know that is because I was so afraid of being by myself. When my mother died, I didn't think I could do it. And if I hadn't had my cat Snowflake"—Marcia began to cry gently—"I don't think I could have."

"Let's talk about your pets. What kinds of animals did you have? What did you learn from them?"

"When I had a near-death experience in 2003, I saw them after I went through the tunnel and got to the light. It looked like a veritable Noah's Ark! It made me really happy to see them.

"The first pet I had was a little cockapoo [dog] named Dusty. Dusty was there to teach me to love myself because he was so loving." I heard the fondness in Marcia's voice. "Dusty looked dusty. He was white with little reddish-brown tips on the end of his curly fur. He had big, soulful brown eyes. When the kids would tease me, I would come home, put my arms around Dusty, and tell him all the mean things they said." Marcia started to cry again. "He would lean into me and lick my chin. I thought, If he can love me this much, I have to love myself, too. I remember thinking that as a kid.

"He was truly my friend that was always, always there," she added. "When I couldn't talk to people, I could talk to him. That was the beginning of my pet communication, because I heard him talking back and telling me, 'It's okay. To me you're perfect.'"

Ever since then Marcia communicates with animals. Sometimes she hears words; other times her pets create images in her mind. Marcia said that animals love to talk with us and that they are not shy about letting us know how they feel. "If they're upset with me, I'll get their back," she said, referring to the way a pet may physically turn away from its human.

I asked Marcia to talk about another pet that had made a difference in her childhood.

"My palomino, Cheetah. She was fifteen-and-a-half-hands high. That's a tall horse!" she exclaimed. "I wanted a big horse so I could learn to be fearless. She was so gentle and kind. I would find something I could get up on, jump up on her, grab her mane, and let her run.

"Many times I'd go to her after a bad day at school. She'd take that velvety nose and rub it up against my head. I could hear her: 'It doesn't matter what they say. Look what you and I can do together! Get on! Let's go!' That's what I would do—ride and feel the wind. My mother would be screaming, *'You're gonna break your neck!'* But when Cheetah and I were together, we were soulmates. She taught me not to be afraid.

"When I went to college, we had to sell her. That was one of the most heartbreaking days of my life, to watch her being driven away. Just before she got in the trailer to go, she turned, looked at me, and said, 'It's okay. I forgive you, because I'll be okay, and I'll always love you.'" Marcia was now sobbing, and I was tearful as well. "It was time for me to spread my wings and fly. She knew she had helped me do that. She was an amazing soul."

"That's a beautiful story," I said. "Were there other pets?"

"When I was a teenager, there was a little chicken that came to us. His mother and all the other chickens had been killed by a fox, but he had survived. His beak was twisted, and he couldn't eat with our chickens because they'd push him aside. He became my buddy. I'd take a handful of grain, and he'd eat out of my hand."

"What was his name?"

"I named him Crooked Beak," Marcia replied. I burst out laughing. "I learned from him compassion as well as it was okay to be different. You didn't have to let it get you down. He didn't. It never bothered him. He felt like he was special."

A few years later, just before she finished college, Marcia brought home a mixed terrier-poodle that eventually had puppies with her sister's terrier. One of those puppies was Brutus, whom Marcia described as a great teacher to her. He would be part of her life for the next sixteen years.

"I watched him be born," she recalled. "He was black, but then he turned white with a pearl-gray overlay. He wasn't beautiful; in fact, he looked like Yoda from *Star Wars*." Marcia and I laughed. "He looked like this wise little man. He had big ears that would go up and down. When he was listening to people, you'd see the expressions change on his face. He never got to be more than twelve pounds, but he was going to protect me.

"There were times I would think, Gosh, if I didn't have a dog to look after, I could go do things. And he would say, 'It's okay. If you want to go, go.' Of course I didn't, because I wasn't going to leave him. I was responsible for him at a time when being irresponsible was easy. He taught me responsibility.

"He talked to me a lot. He taught me to listen. He taught me about unconditional love. He was so unconditionally in love with me. Completely, no matter what I did. I tended to be a little selfish then, and he taught me that's not the best way. He taught me to be a servant to humanity and to animals."

When Marcia's mother became ill, she lived with Marcia for several years. She always knew when Marcia was coming home from work because Brutus would go to the door and stand there, wagging his tail. He did this not as Marcia was driving up, but when she turned off the highway exit—five miles away. He sensed her energy.

"By the time he was fifteen," Marcia continued, "he developed lung disease, went blind, and got cancer. There were many times he could have made it easy on himself and just gone Home, but he waited until he thought I could handle it. Finally, one day he was gasping for air. I took him to the vet. The vet said, 'I think he's ready.' Brutus looked at me and said, 'I am ready, Mom, but I won't go until you're ready.' I brought him home, but he was still gasping for breath. So, I took him back to the vet to be euthanized. All the way there he snuggled close to me. He said, 'Always remember how much I love you. I'll come back to you if you want me to.' He started coming to me right away, the next night. I could feel him on the foot of my bed, saying 'Look, I'm healthy again! I'm happy!'"

Marcia was heartbroken over Brutus's death and told herself she would never get another pet. Yet, a short time later a feral cat gave birth to kittens on the roof of a friend's home. One of the kittens fell off the roof and into a trashcan, where Marcia's friend found her mewing pitifully. Soon thereafter Marcia had a new companion.

"She was a white Siamese, with reddish-orange tips in the Siamese spots, and these big blue eyes," Marcia remembered. When the Siamese first saw Marcia, "she hissed. And in that hiss I heard her say clear as a bell, 'What took you so long?' I fell hard in love with her." Marcia named her Snowflake, Snowy for short.

Snowflake proved to be a loving caretaker of Marcia's mother, who had developed dementia. One day, as her mother was resting on the sofa with Snowflake next to her, Marcia walked by and heard Snowflake say, "I'm a good nurse, huh? I've got the white uniform and everything!" When Marcia's mother eventually returned to Spirit, Marcia saw small flecks of light radiate from her mother's body, and she could tell that Snowflake saw them, too. Snowflake then walked over to Marcia and said, "My job with her is done. Now I need to take care of you." And that is exactly what she did.

Snowflake formed a strong bond with Twinky, one of Marcia's other cats. When Twinky passed away, a friend of Marcia's had a premonition that a black cat, a new companion for Snowflake, would come to Marcia's house. Sure enough, a few weeks later a very large black cat appeared at Marcia's door.

"Hello, how are you?" Marcia greeted him. "Aren't you the goofiest-looking cat?"

"I like that name," replied the strange black cat. And so, in that moment he became known as Goofy.

Goofy started to visit Marcia and Snowflake regularly. Marcia soon discovered that a neighbor owned Goofy. One day the neighbor came by to retrieve him, calling him by his given name, Asahi. Goofy looked at Marcia and said, "Is that the dumbest name you've ever heard?" Goofy continued coming to Marcia's for visits until the neighbor gave him to Marcia. "I think he's chosen to stay with you," the neighbor said graciously.

"Goofy worshiped Snowflake," Marcia said. "It was totally unrequited love. He would follow her, and she would turn around and box his jaws." Marcia told me that when Snowflake died, Goofy would poke his head under various pieces of furniture looking for her. "I'd go up and say, 'Goof, she's not under there.' He'd say, 'She's got to be here somewhere.' I realized that he was grieving along with me."

Marcia added that Goofy is stubborn, opinionated, and wants everything his way. "I am an opinionated person, but I hold back a lot," she confided. "But he says, 'Just make whatever you want to be known, known.' So, I'm learning."

Goofy has made it known that he does not care to go to the vet. Since he weighs twenty-two pounds and Marcia, eighty, getting him there isn't easy for her. She puts Goofy in a cat carrier and slides the carrier across the floor and porch and down the front steps into a child's toy wagon. Then she pulls the wagon to her car and slides in the carrier. The sight is so comical that Marcia's friends have said they would like to film it.

A month after Snowflake died, Marcia brought home a new pet, a gray Siamese kitten named Willie. Marcia described the relationship between Goofy and Willie as "hate at first sight," but said they have since become close friends. Willie sometimes breaks things around the home, then looks at Marcia and says, "But I love you." She knows he is there to teach her patience.

Marcia Speaks with Her Pets

Marcia had shared her feelings about why these loving animals came into her life. Aware of her ability to communicate with animals, both living and deceased, I asked if we could speak briefly with her pets. I wanted to know why *they* thought they had come into Marcia's life. We began by talking with Willie.

"Of course I was part of the [pre-birth] plan," Willie informed us. "My job at this point is to remind you [Marcia] to have fun."

"He's showing me an image of children, the youthful spirit," Marcia said. "He wants to bring out childlike qualities in me."

"It may change as I get older," continued Willie, "but at this time I am here to remind you to enjoy yourself and that it's okay to go on living. Snowflake is okay. Snowflake is happy. I'm not replacing her. I'm teaching you to have fun again and to laugh."

"Thank you, sweetie," Marcia said softly.

Next, we talked with Goofy.

"I came here because I wanted to be with Snowflake. She and I have a long history together. So do you and I. You needed me to be here when she died. You needed me to protect you from you. You were so lonely and grief-stricken. I'm a boy, and boys take care of girls." Marcia and I laughed. "When Snowflake died, you didn't want to go on. But I was here, and I needed you. I still need you. I need you every day." And with that, Goofy ran off.

"Marcia," I asked, "can we talk with your pets who have returned to Spirit?"

Immediately, her dog Brutus began to communicate.

"On the other side, I am a teacher of other animals who aren't quite oriented when they come back," Brutus told us.

"I was your first real teacher on those important things," he said to Marcia. "I came to teach you to be more giving, loving, compassionate, and kind. I did a darn good job! Also, I came to you because your mother had remarried your step-dad, and if you hadn't had me, you would have felt abandoned by your mother. I came to be your kid."

"I believe that," Marcia agreed. "He and Snowflake were like children to me."

Then Snowflake spoke to Marcia.

"When I came into your life, you were in so much pain. I knew what was going to happen with your mom. I taught you how to be independent and to know you were okay, that you were enough."

"That's the truth," Marcia explained, "because we had so many hospital stays with my mother. I'd come home, and there would be that beautiful, little Siamese face looking at me, needing me, wanting me. I was very emotionally dependent on my mother. I felt so alone and inadequate when she died."

Then Dusty made an appearance.

"You were a little child who didn't have any friends," Dusty reminded her. "I taught you that you could make friends, that people would like you, and that even if people made fun of you, you could always come home and I would be there, and I would love you."

"Thank you, Dusty," Marcia said lovingly to him. "I'll never forget you." We were quiet for a few moments as Marcia savored the connection with her cherished cockapoo.

The silence was abruptly broken. "Oh, Cheetah!" Marcia exclaimed. I started. Evidently Marcia's childhood palomino had appeared in her mind's eye. Marcia was thrilled and surprised to see her. "I haven't seen you in so long!"

"Your soul already knew," Cheetah said, "but I helped you understand just how brave you really are. I was so honored to teach that to you. Your time with me was for you to learn not to give up."

There was only one pet who had not yet spoken to Marcia. "Can we talk with Crooked Beak?" I requested.

Marcia paused for a moment as she tuned into his energy.

"Oh, he looks so beautiful now!" she announced joyfully. "He's a big beautiful rooster now! And his beak's not crooked anymore." We both laughed.

"I allowed myself to be deformed," Crooked Beak told Marcia, "so I could see that it doesn't matter what the body looks like; it only matters what's inside. You loved me even though I had a crooked beak and looked funny. I'll always love and appreciate you for that."

Marcia's Session with Staci

Marcia had shown great insight into the deeper spiritual meaning of her experiences with the pets in her life. And, not surprisingly to me, so had the animals themselves. Still, there were many unanswered questions swirling through my mind. Had these animals been with her in past lives, and if so, in what sorts of relationships? Does the pre-birth planning we do with pets differ from the planning we do with souls incarnating as humans? More generally, what is the nature of an animal soul, and why do animals choose to share our human voyage with us?

As you will read, Marcia's pets speak very differently in Marcia's pre-birth planning session than they did through Marcia herself. Marcia spoke with the personality created by the animal soul whereas Staci hears the planning conducted at the soul level.

"Marcia," Staci said as information began flowing to her, "in so many of your other lives, you lived with a sense of being separate from others. It is a sense of separation that you usually use to propel yourself forward on a path of leadership. In these lives you adopted an attitude of judgment, of 'I hold myself as separate and higher than others around me.' In this current life, your soul is trying to balance that attitude, to move away from judgment about others and still be a leader. Your soul is very passionate about this goal.

"Now, here's something else I see. You have a karmic lesson of spiritual growth and evolvement through the enrichment of the relationship with yourself. My spirit guide told me that this is the 'course' the Earth school offers. Other courses in spirituality are offered in other planetary systems. The lives of somebody who chooses this karmic lesson have built into those lives times of aloneness, a sense of separation until the personality comes to enjoy its own company and takes pleasure and sustenance in it. The challenge is to come into connection with your inner being, and thus your soul, and thus the God-stuff that runs through us and connects us all."

"When my mother got sick, one of my deepest, most horrifying fears was being by myself," Marcia replied. "When she did go Home, it took me awhile to realize that I was okay, and not only okay but also happy and productive. I don't know if I would have gotten to the place where I am if I hadn't had the rug pulled out from under me."

Marcia had just described a classic learning-through-opposites experience. For Marcia, inner connection had been achieved through outer disconnection from her beloved mother. It is in this way that our souls evolve.

"I will now go to past lives," Staci said. "I see a lifetime in a circus, an older sort of circus in the Northwest [United States], around the year 1870. The circus began in the South and traveled west to where the money was. The animals were imported from outside the country. The ports in the South, especially around New Orleans, are where the animals came through."

Marcia later confirmed that she already knew about the circus life. Through conversation with both Marcia and Staci, I learned that Marcia had been the beautiful daughter of the circus owner.

In that lifetime she had an affinity for animals, just as she does now. They were her great love and the focus of her existence. Interestingly, as a child in that past life she often pretended to be a mermaid—half human, half animal.

I learned, too, that Cheetah had been Marcia's horse in the circus lifetime, during which they had done trick riding together. Marcia's feline companions from her modern-day life, Snowflake and Willie, were both felines in the circus: Snowflake a lion, Willie a tiger. Crooked Beak was there as a macaw. Dusty, Brutus, and Goofy were present in the circus life as well, but in markedly different form—as elephants.

"In that past life, the animals were the ones you bonded to," Staci told Marcia. "They were the ones you chose to spend your time with, the ones whom you understood and who understood you. The macaw was your friend for twenty years. It would sit on your shoulder while you worked with the animals. The bird became your constant companion in that life; that relationship outlasted all others. That animal lived with you; it wasn't stabled somewhere. This was your buddy and the one you occasionally argued with, too. The bird's personality appears to have had quite a sense of humor.

"He came back to you in this lifetime specifically to ground you in the message that size and one's body appearance don't matter in the grand scheme of things and to bring you the gift of humor, that you may always possess it and use it as your great strength."

"That's exactly what he did," said Marcia.

"I am now starting to see conversation from your pre-birth planning session," Staci said. "I am going to be quiet as I follow this energetic thread." There was a very long pause. I waited eagerly to see if Marcia's pets would be present.

"I see the pre-birth planning room. I see Marcia. My viewpoint is as if I am standing on the same side as the spirit guides in the anteroom. The opening from the pre-birth planning room to this anteroom is very, very wide, not like a usual doorway. Marcia is on one side of the pre-birth planning chart, which to me looks like a small rug on the ground. Marcia is in her lightbody. Across from her is the spirit of this macaw who came back as Crooked Beak. I see this head and beak that start out as macaw and then transform into what I can only guess is Crooked Beak, because there is a dip in the ridge of the beak. He has been many birds. He likes being a flightless wonder." All three of us burst into laughter. "That is what I hear from my guide," Staci said.

"I am coming in on the middle of this conversation.

Crooked Beak: In an instant [the instant I come into your life], that twenty-year history [from our life together in the circus] will flash into your mind, and all the joy and comfort we brought to each other then will be with us again. I bring this to you as a gift, as I have no particular desire to incarnate again in this form so soon. I do this to repay you for the nurturing and kindness you showed me.

"And in that moment, I see his thoughts of how scrawny he looked and how large his beak was in that life as a macaw, and of how he was taken as a baby out of the nest while his mother looked on from about three hundred feet away. He was taken by men and handled roughly, thrown into a cloth sack where it was dark.

"He remained with them and struggled with captivity until he was handed to you, Marcia, when he was approximately one year old. The first thing you did was bathe him. To him this was like his mother would treat him. From that moment his experience with you was different than his experience with other humans. He experienced your kindness and healed emotionally. That began a most valuable friendship. You healed this bird heart and soul." Marcia was now weeping. "I see all this, but it's not spoken in the conversation. He is thinking about it, and everyone in the room knows he's thinking about it and can see it as well.

"At this point I pull back and broaden my focus. I see a gallery area sectioned off. I see a small group of souls there, maybe ten.

Something unusual is that they are all huddled close together. I have not seen this before. There is a lot of light and energy. Something is coming to me about this. My spirit guide is speaking." Then, suddenly, Staci's guide began to talk through her.

"The light in the room," he explained, "is the energetic frequency generated by these individuals, who walk a higher [vibrational] path than some. This soul [Marcia] has taken this soul group purpose of walking a higher path and has experienced a going off track, a walk along the side rather than in the middle of the path and so has had a kind of detour. Some of the other individuals in her soul group have gone on to achieve in the scientific community and others among the lay community of large, organizational churches. This soul's unique propensity toward individualism has shifted its path and guided it along somewhat parallel lines, yet still walking its own journey. This soul, of high mind and high-minded purpose, recognized that the shifts it had made in some of its more recent lives were not entirely conducive to the higher ideals to which it applies itself. In one of this soul's former lives it lived a life of asceticism, again as a loner, as a personality that separated itself from others and held itself to a higher purpose. That life is looked upon by this soul as the achievement of a certain level of mastery, but the achievement was without emotional connection, and thus the soul dedicated its next evolutionary goal to the achievement of a richer emotional expression of its depth. That is part of, and present upon, the path this soul walks to this day."

"Wow!" Marcia declared.

Staci and her guide had just offered important insight into Marcia's pre-birth plan. I took the word *detour* to refer, perhaps in part, to that period of Marcia's life when by her own description she had been selfish. That focus on self was in some ways a continuation of her earlier lifetime as an ascetic. Through the selfless love and devotion of her pets—in effect, through the example they had set—Marcia healed that pattern and reached the goal of rich emotional expression with both animals and people. Truly, her pets had been, and still are, her teachers.

"Let's talk about Brutus," Staci suggested. "I am once again seeing Marcia's pre-birth planning session. Across from her is the soul of Brutus. Although Marcia is seated just above the floor, Brutus's soul is floating three feet off the ground. I hear this deep, broad-chested laughter coming from this entity. I hear him talk about being one of your elephants in that circus life, Marcia, reminding you of the good times together. You understood each other; he knew what you were thinking all the time. All of this was brought with him into the present life in the personality of Brutus. This soul is effusive, bubbling over with joy and good humor.

Brutus: I will teach you to know who loves you. My presence in your life will remind you always to pick the positive path, the path of joy, the path of least resistance. Let me lead the way. I will show you how.

"There is an undercurrent of bright-eyed optimism and humor. It's infectious to you, and you're chuckling," Staci said.

"Oh, yeah," Marcia replied, "and I felt that way when he was here, too. I couldn't be sad around him."

Brutus: When I was your beast [elephant], you were sad many times over. Did I not come to you and lift your spirits then? Elevate your mood?

Marcia: Yes, you did.

"Together," Staci continued, "you think of a time in the circus life when you were sitting, and he was standing behind you. You were lost in thought until this trunk reached around your shoulder and took the food you had in your hand!" Marcia chuckled. "Which made you laugh, just like it does now. You're both thinking about this when you say,

Marcia:　　　I accept your love and joy in my life with grace and humility. I accept your comfort.

"Together, you bend forward and look down at your pre-birth planning chart. You point to two places on your chart.

Marcia:　　　I see you and hear you, here and here. Here [points to the first place] you will guide me, hold me up, and lift my spirits. And here [points to the second place] is where I am most open and receptive to your buoyance.

"Buoyance; that's a word even I don't use, and I use some four-syllable words," Staci said.

"Both Marcia and her pets have very large vocabularies," I offered. Marcia was laughing even harder now.

Marcia would later share with me that, through her psychic gifts, she had come to know that Dusty had sent some of his energies into Brutus as a type of partial walk-in. This was the first time I had heard of a walk-in occurring among animals, though I was already well aware of the phenomenon among humans. The term *walk-in* is used to describe a situation in which one soul leaves or "walks out" of a body and another soul then enters or "walks in." A soul will choose to walk out of a body either when it has completed all it came to do or when it concludes that it will not be able to do what it had planned. Typically, the physical body would die at this time; however, the walk-in soul keeps the body alive. The soul choosing to enter the body feels it can accomplish its learning without going through infancy and perhaps childhood as well. Thus, the walk-in opts to begin an incarnation by entering a mature rather than a fetal body.

Occasionally, a soul walks into a body and "braids" its energy with the soul already present. In such instances, the incarnate soul does not walk out; rather, the two souls blend into one coherent personality in order to combine their gifts (generally in some form of service to the world) and share the experiences of the lifetime. Evidently, some of Dusty's energy had been combined with Brutus's, suggesting that Dusty and Brutus had shared similar intentions: to guide Marcia, to lift her spirits, and to be a source of buoyancy in her life.

"I am going to focus now on Snowflake," Staci said. "I'm hearing that Snowflake was one of the big cats in that circus life. She tells me that she has been with you, Marcia, in almost all of your lives and that she sees herself mostly as support and somebody to hold your hand. In the former life as the large cat, she taught you about womanhood, how a woman holds herself erect, how you can be a woman and still be self-possessed and powerful. In that life, as in so many other lives, she also felt herself to be in a motherly role to you and was in this current life, also."

"Yes, she was," Marcia agreed.

"Snowflake came into your present life because she wanted to subject herself to change. She wanted an environment that would cause her to have to adapt, because she herself has been on a several-lives journey of learning to become more flexible, which one can do when one is centered within one's own power. She taught you this by her example. I hear that you were receptive to these lessons, that you understood and even acknowledged her and what she was trying to show you.

"I slip into seeing the pre-birth conversation.

Snowflake: I feel the most compassion for you above all humans, as I have seen you in your human history as a soul full of conflict, full of humanity's principle journey of wrestling with lower self and giving way to Higher Self and higher truth and the recognition that life works better congruent with it.

"I need to describe what this soul looks like, because it's different. I have a sense of something unique here. This cat's soul has been on a different journey than what we humans have gone through in terms of the soul's evolutionary path. She looks—wow! I can't get over how tall, how large the soul's lightbody is! Both this cat's soul and the dog we focused on before—the bodies are larger, I am told, because they experience themselves as large beings. This has come after the passage of what we might call time, but also after the accumulation of much knowledge and experience.

"Snowflake says in the pre-birth planning that she has been in human form before, did not like it, and so chooses not to incarnate in that form ever again," Staci told us, concluding her vision of that portion of Marci's planning session. It was now time for questions.

"Staci," I asked, "do the souls of animals usually incarnate as people at some point?"

Staci's consciousness stepped aside, and her guide spoke through her again. "The souls of animals do at times choose to incarnate as individualized humans," he answered, "sometimes for support of a human partner, sometimes simply 'to try the experience on for size,' as you say. The difference between the souls who incarnate only as animals and the souls who inhabit animal form and then enter into human form and the human evolutionary cycle—sometimes repeatedly so, living the cycle over and over—is that they [the former] do not become attached to the human experience.

"Many of these animal souls stay out of the framework of human incarnation because they choose not to get into the emotional depths, the emotional extremes that are the human experience. The individualized souls that inhabit animal forms do feel emotions at various levels, usually on a species-to-species differentiation, but sometimes differentiated within the same species according to their own evolutionary process and their desire to experience emotionality in all its forms and extremes.

"The human experience is one of duality and extremes," the guide continued, "and thus extreme duality. The animal souls are centered and focused more than human nature normally allows. Many of these souls are of a higher order who choose not to become caught up in human conflict. Many think of themselves as friends to humans. Some do not. We have encouraged rapport between humanity and these creatures, great and small, for many reasons, all of which serve the purpose of enriching lives, as has been experienced by this soul we call Marcia.

"The companionship of animals is a gift to be treasured, to be tended and nurtured, to be encouraged, vitalized, and maintained. They are always trying to teach you something in some way, from the simple act of loving unconditionally to the higher forms of thought to even lessons of self-possession, self-worth, and self-esteem, which have been part of the relationship between Marcia and her companions.

"These little beasties, whether they be inside your homes or outside in nature, are equal forms and go through similar processes as your own. They may be for a time a little wiser, because they choose not to enter into the human evolutionary experience. This gives them the opportunity to see life from perspectives most humans do not reach, and thus they should always be acknowledged as special and looked up to, for there is always some sort of guidance given to you [by them] to guide you through the human experience, whether they are on two legs or four or possess wings.

"The lower, slower form of dinosaur that remains on the Earth today as reptile is of a soul level different from other two- or four-footed creatures with hair or feathers. They are an offshoot of a third race of soul beings who, early in their evolutionary path, encouraged domination of others, control and manipulation, and the use of fear and intimidation. These souls are on an evolutionary path of walking slowly toward gentleness and kindness, but their path is different from yours, the human one, and different from the creatures such as those we talk of today."

Marcia then asked Staci about her pre-birth plan with Cheetah.

"I am told by my guide," Staci responded, "that this horse was able to demonstrate to you, with full intent and purpose, the karmic lesson of emotional independence. She was both wise and crazy, which was indicative of the balance you achieved in yourself and your life at that time.

"I am at the pre-birth planning session. Cheetah has just come into the room, and there is a wave of laughter through the soul group because she comes in wearing the cloak of the personality of a horse, and her attitude is, 'Ain't I something!'

"You had thought about her, Marcia, but she wasn't in the gallery section with the rest of your soul group. She knew what was going on and wanted to make an entrance.

Marcia: (delighted)	I knew you would come!
Cheetah:	Of course! You don't think I could let you go another round without me?"

"She comes over to the other side of the pre-birth planning chart. She lies down on her belly and chest and crosses her front legs.

Cheetah:	I'm very happy with this body. I've spoken with my mother; I know this is the body I will have. This is what self-possessed looks like.
	This is the manner in which I shall instruct you. I am your friend. I am also your confidant and your guide.

"With that, she rolls over on her side and kicks her feet up, then rolls back to a sitting position, like a little celebration.

Marcia:	I welcome you in my life.

"You reach out your arms, Marcia, throw them around her neck, and hug her. Her feet are doing another happy dance, and there's joy in her expression. That hug takes place for some time. That's a deep hug. I see heart chakras connecting.

Marcia:	All of my heart will happily and with pleasure accept your company on this journey.
Cheetah:	I am with you as mother, guide, confidant, and playmate, but always I want you to see that I hold my head high, that I hold myself proudly. I want you to see this, because there will be times when you need to *be* this, when you need to be strong like me. It is through our unspoken communication that I can best exemplify this to you. Will you allow me to be a strong, steady, and supportive guide in your life this time, closer than before?
Marcia:	Yes, most certainly I will! My heart is open to you. I am full of joy knowing that I will share at least some part of this journey with you and be with my old, wise friend again.
Cheetah:	That's right.

We laughed at Cheetah's comment.

"Oh yes, that was my Cheetah," Marcia said. "She had no self-esteem problems whatsoever."

"Let's move on to Willie," Staci suggested. "I hear him say,

Willie:	I remind you to know yourself. I shall be the living, breathing example of fortitude, courage, balance and loyalty, self-possessed and strong within myself and my own character.

"As I see him saying that to you, Marcia, there is this other part of his personality that pops out, almost like a second head. It's a crazy, laughing, maniacal kind of personality. I've never seen that. It's a remarkable example of how we manipulate ourselves and show our thoughts on the soul level. He is communicating to you that he's got a crazy side that is going to pop out from time to time.

"Let me see what else this little guy says to you. I don't know how to communicate this to you the way he does, because it's in pictures, mostly. He sees himself as a butler, one who is of taste, breeding, and culture, and who serves you well. So, he is matched to you in vibration in that he holds himself to a higher code. I hear him talking about a life in which you two inhabited physical form at the same time. You were both human.

Willie: When we were little boys together, I let you run all over the countryside, and I chased after you. In this life don't expect me ever to chase you. My role is not brother. It is not even necessarily as friend all the time, although I am your friend. In this role [as Willie], I see myself as your gentle guide.

I will serve as an example to you of small but mighty, a reminder to you of what you hold yourself to and how you can achieve it. For you desire that innermost quality of secret strength, do you not?

Marcia: I do. I wish to possess that which I have long sought, not as one who pushes others away through distaste and distrust, but rather as one who can handle anything and anyone, if I so choose.

Willie: Yes, but getting that strength of mind into your little body will be an achievement for you, simply because those around you will give you the opposite message: that you are little and thus can achieve only little things.

I come forth at this time to volunteer once again to be a part of your life during a time when a shift in your evolution will take place, a shift in your personality's ability to express soul. My energy will add to yours and increase the sureness of self

within you so that you are able to fulfill the purposes of your life: the achievement of an affinity
within yourself based on soul-level love; and the
recognition of your worth as a soul, as a possessor
of human form, combined with the recognition
that you are much stronger than you believed.

Putting those together brings you to the point of
shifting your life from internal-based satisfaction
of individual needs to a more externalized expression of what you have recognized in yourself. You
will be able to reach out to others and model the
truth and trust within yourself in a way you've
not been able to in other lives, because you will
have ceased to judge yourself. In other lives you
judged yourself as you judged others.

Marcia: I know.

Willie: In this life, as I understand you, here, now, you
wish to go beyond that and achieve the recognition of affinity with others in spite of the
appearance of difference.

Marcia: So true. Yes. Yes.

"You spread your arms wide.

Marcia: I welcome you into my heart and my life once
again. Know that I trust and treasure you always.

"That's beautiful," Marcia said softly.
The conversation with Willie concluded, I asked Staci if she
would now listen to Marcia's pre-birth dialogue with Goofy.
"Immediately, I am taken to the planning session," Staci said.

Goofy: I am like you, similar in form. I will be much
smaller for you in this life than I have been before.

"In his mind he goes back to when he was one of your elephants in that circus life, Marcia. All of a sudden, I also see another past life. In this other life, you are in a structure where there are bars on the windows. This is where you live. You are looking out a window, across an African plain, and there is a female lion outside the window. You are the wife of an explorer at the turn of the sixteenth or seventeenth century. The lion raised her cubs near your house. You set out food, water, and goat's milk for her and her cubs every day.

Goofy:	Like you, I have had to put up with being isolated, being put places I would rather not be, and being excluded. I have lived with these circumstances, some of which were due to the callous nature of humans and their disregard for anyone but themselves.
Marcia:	I know. I'm so sorry.
Goofy:	No apology is necessary. I know that in all of these circumstances my own best intentions were served, even though I may not have liked the circumstances much.
Marcia:	In this life I will strive to be of greater service to you.
Goofy:	In lives gone by, I have lived with restriction, just as you must live with restriction in this life yet to come. While it is not my desire to inhabit the world of humans again so soon, I would enjoy being mated with you for a time. And so I shift my being into feline consciousness once again.
Marcia:	In a smaller package, please, or you will not be able to live with me.
Goofy:	I know.

"The soul body with its cloak of personality starts getting smaller until I see a little kitten, black and fuzzy.

| Goofy: | Is this small enough? |
| Marcia: (laughing) | Wonderful! |

"Then he swells back up to what he looked like before.

Goofy:	I see myself holding your hand as we go through life together, being your companion, your protector, and your friend, and always, always showing you that sometimes life is better off lived in a smaller package. Can you not see this truth in me?
Marcia:	This I will strive to learn. And I find your energy completes mine, and complements it as well.
Goofy:	Thank you. Just remember that I may move more slowly and with more deliberate intent than you are used to with me. I have been happy-go-lucky before, haven't I?
Marcia:	Yes, often.
Goofy:	I still have that within me, but in this life I will choose to exercise caution more than the happy-go-lucky nature that has been so strong within me. I will try to balance myself with caution and so show you the strength that can be achieved when one is in reserve.

"And at the same time he breaks into this little dance. Then he composes himself.

| Goofy: (laughing) | But with a primarily serious nature. |

"Marcia, at that point your attitude was, 'I dare you to be serious.' So, although there is a little bit of teaching you by example, there is also some friendship and play here, and some recognition on the part of the cat's soul that it, too, is growing."

Staci's Spirit Guide Discusses Animals

The pre-birth planning portion of the reading complete, it was now time to talk more generally about pets with Staci's spirit guide.

"Do pets generally incarnate to help people with their life challenges?" I asked.

"Not always so," he responded in his usual halting style of speech. "Those who are open to sharing their lives with pets are usually of a gentler form of communication and persuasion. Not all souls who reside in human form are resonant with animal souls, and thus the experience is not planned [by those souls]. If it should happen in their lives, there can be reactions that run from fear to simple fascination to a 'so what?' kind of attitude."

"In the pre-birth planning session, the animals sound just as intelligent as people do," I observed. "Are they, and if so, why do they choose to be so-called less intelligent on Earth?"

"The animals you heard speak today might be said to possess a higher intelligence," answered the guide, "because they have not allowed themselves to get caught up in the evolutionary wheel and the emotional depths to which human souls subject themselves. For the most part, animals are able to learn more quickly from their experiences than those in human form. Those in human form who have occasionally inhabited the form of animals possess two common qualities: a reverence for all things and the innate knowingness that all living things possess intelligence. Not all animals express the same level of intelligence, just as not all humans express the same level of emotional growth. This is why you will find some animals to be akin to juvenile delinquents and why some animals will sometimes allow themselves to be swept up into a highly emotional expression of anger or fear. But, they learn more rapidly from the experience."

I asked Staci's guide to clarify the difference between an animal and a human soul.

"As best I can describe to you through this vessel, the difference is in how the soul perceives itself. It is not a difference you would recognize if you saw a human body inhabited by a soul who has primarily inhabited animal form in most of its other lives. We will say, however, that animal souls tend to have a sensitivity, a clarity of their beingness, that is undeniable to themselves. Many human souls will spend many lives learning to allow themselves to truly be and not chase after accomplishment as it is judged by others. Animal souls who incarnate into human form usually do so to understand the human experience at a greater, more purposeful level, so that when they regain their prior forms as animal life, they can be of better service to their human companions who are caught up in the evolutionary cycle and process."

"What percentage of souls have incarnations as both animals and people?" I inquired.

"Just five percent of all souls choose to inhabit animal form. What percentage of these also choose, while remaining primarily on the animal wheel, to take forays into the human life form? Two to three percent. So, it is very rare. I say to you again that the human path is not an easy one. There are not many who will purposely volunteer if they start from a higher perspective than the one most human souls start from. The animals, the souls who inhabit them as best we can describe to you, are of higher intelligence, a higher sense of order, and a higher sense of purpose, unique and different from the human experience." From previous conversations with Staci's guide, I knew that his use of the word *higher* was not intended to imply better. Here, *higher* was a neutral, nonjudgmental term used in regard to frequency.

I then shared with Staci's guide my understanding that after a human lifetime ends, the person sets up a home in the nonphysical realm, has a life review, conducts a social life, and attends classes. Where, I asked him, do animals go, and what do they do?

"Animals inhabit the same spaces," he explained. "Their life review is short and purposeful. They, in your terms, 'get it' much quicker than most humans do. They do not agonize over mistakes. They do not continue to despair over what they once despaired of. They move on. The time after review is most often spent playing. They play very quickly, very easily.

"Many animals choose to go into the garden area, which brings them comfort and where they are able to socialize with others of like resonance and get their bearings again. Many choose to remain in or repeatedly visit the gardens. There are other souls who, rather than remain in the garden, move quickly toward their animal and human companions from other lives. They seek out those with whom they have been in other lives through the energetic threads of connection that run through them and remain.

"As for classes, not all animal souls are intent upon learning and educating themselves in the same way as souls who come through human form. They do not go into the library. They do not necessarily converse with the souls of those who once occupied the personalities of Socrates or Plato, for example. They tend to congregate among themselves to discuss and review that which they have learned. They are most comfortable, just as you are, with those of like mind, of similar frequency, of harmonic resonance, and so will gravitate to them unless and until a companion who has been human arrives or otherwise comes into their awareness. Then they will bring themselves to that individual's side, at least for a time.

"There is definitely a bond between a human soul and its animal companions. No matter how many feet they possessed, no matter if they were footed or winged, hairy or hairless, the animals are drawn to that human soul when it crosses over. Those who have near-death experiences report seeing their beloved pets who died some years before. This does indeed happen, but it does not happen in every case because not every human has valued and enjoyed the companionship of an animal."

"Did God or Source," I asked, "plan for certain animals to be pets to humans, and if so, why?

"The plan was for souls to be whatever they desire to be. There is no 'why' other than The Great Experience."

"What role do pets and other animals play in the shift now occurring in human consciousness?"

"It can best be described as a two-fold intent on the part of the animals. One is to guide humankind through this energetic

shift in consciousness, thought, and behavior as if they were ushers at a theater, standing at the doorway, waving you in with a
flashlight saying, 'This is the way.'

"There is another purpose: some of the animals have agreed
to serve as vessels to hold you through the journey. They are the
'basket' that carries your humanity, your human soul and personality, through this river of change. It is rather like the animals
hold the best and worst attributes of humanity—the emotions,
the compassion, the anger, the thirst for revenge, the 'what's mine
is mine and I'm not sharing'—including and up to the highest
forms of awareness exhibited by humanity.

"In humanity's less-than-best moments, the animals hold what
is the best of you. There are times when you lose the connection
to yourselves and a temporary form of so-called insanity devel-
ops and envelops the consciousness, such as that generated by an
extreme fear response or being in extreme survival mode. When
you come out of the insanity into the moment, the here and
now, all you need do is see an animal in its natural state or look
into an animal's eyes, whether this is your pet and beloved one
or a creature in the wild. By looking at the animal and making
that energetic connection, you open the door within you, behind
which were hidden the emotions of your being. All the pieces and
portions of human consciousness then return to the individual,
sometimes flooding the more sensitive of you with emotionality
to an overwhelming extent, often producing a barrage of tears.

"Not every individual animal holds all that is within human
emotionality," concluded Staci's spirit guide. "Some animals,
like some humans, hold only a tiny portion of the soul's awareness. And so the consciousness within the animal has only the
simplest and least complex of emotions, because the animal's
physical form cannot contain the whole of the complexity of that
emotionality that some humans see as belonging to humankind
only. Some souls make the choice to place a bit of themselves
in an animal in order to enjoy that physical form's complex
abilities. Some souls desire a simple emotional experience. Some

souls desire to experience Earth close up and so choose the life of an animal for that advantage—the viewing of Earth life through the animal's eyes."

"What can you tell us about dolphins and whales?" I wondered.

"Dolphins and whales do not come from the same place [as other animal souls]. Dolphins and whales house what this channel has come to term 'other.' They arise from a subtype of soul that is ancient, whose history is beyond that of the Earth. Both species were brought, though separately, to Earth as part of a seeding project from other planetary systems.

"You might say that whales are the elephants of the sea; in fact, there is an energetic resonance between the two. In another planetary system, Sirius, where the life of all creatures was looked at with value and purpose, there was a race of beings that inhabited the only inhabitable planet in that system. The race of this planet knew that its sun was going to go nova, that what was becoming brighter and brighter in their sky would soon explode and go dark. The intelligence and self-perception of this race of two-legged humanoids was evolved to the point where all made peace with the ending of that race's existence. Not a single soul desired to outlive the others. All accepted their so-called fate with humility, knowing that there is a beginning and ending to all, that life as constant energy will always ebb and flow, and that the energy on the planet was simply ebbing. There was no further judgment. They did, however, want to preserve the species they regarded as the most intelligent, in their thinking, of God's greatest creations. They recognized the intelligence, the emotionality, of these creatures. They recognized also a greater purpose in their continued existence.

"And so a project was created that lasted several generations, a project of selecting the creatures they would save, selecting the right home for them, and transporting them off the planet. These are the creatures you know of as whales today. There were other marine mammals brought along with them, most notably sharks and octopi. There are some amongst you in human form this day who are of the souls that resided on that planet at that time. Many of these souls are the ones who seek out the whales, work with them, care for them.

"The whales are great beings. This race simply felt that they should not be brought to the same fate as their own. The whales are one of the most ancient of races on your planet. We know of no soul who has inhabited the body of the whale and also human form."

"Thank you," I said. "And the dolphins?"

"I hear laughter," Staci responded. "I feel like I am touching joy." Then her guide continued to speak through her.

"The dolphins bring joy and laughter, harmony and lightness of being. The dolphins and the souls that reside in them are enjoying lives of higher purpose as expressed through high frequency. Many of their thoughts and communications are outside their own pods, broadcast to the Universe, broadcast at times to humanity as a group. At other times dolphins are pulled inter-dimensionally and energetically along a thread of connection to individuals of human soul and body who are able to resonate to this strong, high frequency of joy. Yes, the dolphins bring great joy into their being.

"When dolphins were saved and brought to Earth by those of a planet outside this galaxy, it was at a time when humans were new upon the Earth, and so it was felt that humans would not be a threat to the dolphins. Just as the whales, the dolphins were brought to Earth because of the preponderance of water on the planet. Their unique quality is the joy they hold. They come from joy. They resonate in joy.

"They are helpers and enlighteners, but they will not interfere in the lives of humans unless asked. This is not necessarily in regard to physically being in the life of a human, but rather their energetic presence. Whether recognized by the human or not, dolphins often bring joy to those who are sick and in need of healing and to those who are depressed. If you could get them to wear a clown suit, they would, as they truly enjoy fulfilling the role of bringing joy to all creatures. This may be seen as a gift to humanity, but it was not intended for that purpose. It was intended to enable the creatures, the dolphins themselves, to prosper.

"There are dolphins on other water-bound planets in other places in the Universe. There is great intelligence in these mammals. They are not possessive by nature; they share. Theirs is a life of freedom and joy, and as such their energy brings balance to this planet.

"We would suggest encouraging the support and energetic activity of dolphins by reaching out to them in one's mind telepathically in a prayerful moment. Reach out from heart space. To call upon the dolphins is to bring joy into your life, your heart, the lives of others, and the world globally. They appear to swim in the ocean, but when they are asleep, they swim in the ether all around you. There are not many of them on the Earth at this time, fewer than before. They are to be appreciated. It is a cause of sadness to us when humanity persists in the wholesale slaughter of this species, as they were not meant for food. They were meant to be and to enjoy, and their wonderful byproduct is the joy and harmony they bring."

I asked the spirit guide if beings on other planets have pets.

"Some do. Not all planets house or encourage the mentality that appreciates pets."

"What kinds of pets do they have?"

"The equivalent mostly of your cats and dogs and some small monkeys. Birds are not considered pets on all worlds. Many worlds do not have small birds, only large birds that are not conducive to the formation of pet relationships."

"What kinds of worlds don't have the mentality for having pets?"

"The hominid [human] form," he said, "is not necessarily prevalent or in existence at all on some of these planets. There is no form [body type] a pet could occupy, nor is there a desire for pets. Turning our gaze to some other planets and races, there are some that are engaged actively and solely in the pursuit of intelligence. The sharing of one's life with an animal companion is very occasional, bordering on rare, on those worlds."

"How are pets thought of and treated in civilizations much more evolved than human civilization?"

"There is a sense of equality that permeates the relationships. There is the expression of genuine care and affection from one to the other and back again, and this is much more accepted than it is on Earth. There is a nurturing and caretaking of each other, primarily from hominid to pet, that is much greater and more reverent than what we see in so many human-pet relationships on Earth. It is all a result of a different understanding, a different awareness."

"Is there anything else you would like to say about pre-birth planning with pets or animals in general?" I asked.

"We hope people will see that the enlightened viewpoint toward animals is one of equality. So much of humanity devalues that which is in animal form. We would say to you that while human and animal may be different, human and animal are also made of the same matter, with the same God-stuff running throughout. We would also say that humanity would be well served by adopting more humility in its attitude toward animals. Although the animals may be silent for the most part, they are not without knowledge or wisdom. If humans could disengage themselves from arrogance and its inappropriate display and be quiet among and within themselves, they would be better able to match frequency with that of the animal soul and would then come into a place of understanding the animal, respecting it, and seeing it in a whole new light, with value, purpose, and meaning. Too often humans move through their lives in a self-centered way and only occasionally can be brought outside themselves through the love of their animal companions. We only can say that more of this should be indulged in. Animal souls are good for humanity."

～

We who are Love can never be anything else, but we can most surely forget our true, eternal nature. Hidden from ourselves by ourselves when we cross the veil of forgetfulness to assume human form, we have created the most remarkable of opportunities: to remember ourselves as Love and so know ever more deeply, ever more intimately, and from the soul's perspective ever more sweetly who we really are. From the forgetting and remembering a more profound self-knowing is birthed, one that would not be possible without the self-selected, self-induced amnesia of the physical plane.

The process of placing our energy within a body, and in so doing forgetting that we are vast, majestic, Divine Beings made literally from the energy of Unconditional Love, is akin to being struck on the head by a heavy tree branch and rendered unconscious, only to awaken with no memory whatsoever. What would happen if you actually had such an experience? All who love you, each member of your family, every dear friend, would come to your side and express great love for you. Though you would recognize none of them, their powerful outpouring of concern and affection would touch you deeply. You would conclude that only a truly loving person could be so beloved. And in that instant of realization, you would know, beyond any doubt, your true nature.

Such is the role pets play in our lives. Just as people with amnesia do not remember those who were in their lives before the forgetting, so, too, do we not recall the pets who were with us before we were born. Yet, our pets come to our side and express their great love for us, reminding us daily that only we who are Love could be so beloved.

And they remind us not only that we are loved but also that we are *worthy* of love. When Marcia came home from school and cried over the cruel words from the other children, her dog Dusty was there to tell her she was perfect, that she "could always come home, and I would be there, and I would love you." Cheetah, her faithful and adoring palomino, also reminded Marcia that she was worthy of love: "It doesn't matter what they say. Look what you and I can do together! Get on! Let's go!" And so they would ride like the wind, the smallest of children on the largest of horses, both free and safe, in love with life and each other.

Too, pets bring healing. Indeed, our animal companions are master healers, in part because they embody love in an entirely nonthreatening form. The clear absence of threat creates within us a willingness to receive healing. We may fear accepting love from another person, but Marcia had no such fear with Brutus or Snowflake. When Marcia's mother lay ill in the hospital, Brutus, tail wagging and big ears flopping, was a healing balm for Marcia's heavy heart. When Marcia's mother returned Home, it was Snowflake who healed Marcia's grief, saying, "My job with her is done. Now I need to take care of you."

How do pets heal us? There is no greater healing power in the Universe than that of unconditional love. Yet, beyond unconditional love, pets heal by transmuting energies. Even when we feel weak and small, our pets still come to us for care and so remind us that we are strong enough, capable enough to provide it. Even when we are enmeshed in anger or blame, they sit joyfully at our side, radiating contentment and instilling peace within us. When we feel shame, guilt, or unworthiness, they look at us and see only perfection. Our pets see us as *light,* the light of which we are literally made, the light we knew ourselves to be before we were born. When we lose sight of our magnificence, they remind us of it.

Author and channel Hannah Beaconsfield writes that when a family is steeped in conflict, a pet will sometimes choose to return to Spirit. Instead of the family dying, the pet dies, taking with it the disharmonious energies that were "killing" the family. Similarly, she says, pets often act out and thus release emotions a human has repressed. At times pets develop symptoms in order to "share" an illness a human is experiencing; it is their way of showing unconditional support. Beaconsfield has also learned of another type of support expressed through pets: our deceased loved ones may place a portion of their energies in the body of a pet in order to remain physically present and so continue to love, protect, and guide us. In like fashion, a deceased pet may choose to return to its human either through reincarnation—say, a cat reincarnating as a kitten—or as a walk-in. In the latter case, a cat who had returned to Spirit could, for example, enter into a soul-level agreement to trade places with the human's new cat. The soul of the new cat walks out of the body; the soul of the former, cherished companion returns to the human it loves by walking in.

Sometimes a loved one, even a spirit guide, will incarnate *as* a pet because it is the best, and perhaps only, way to share a lifetime with us. I have a close friend who planned not to have children in this lifetime. A soul she loves and who loves her dearly incarnated as her dog so they could complete the mother-daughter relationship they shared in a past life as Native Americans. Both had been healers in other past lives, and they continued their healing work together in the current lifetime. My friend often brought her dog into healing sessions with clients, many of whom commented that they felt healed by the animal's presence.

Ultimately, whether it's Willie reminding Marcia to have fun, Goofy caring for Marcia and so healing her grief after Snowflake's death, Brutus teaching compassion and kindness, Snowflake modeling independence, or Dusty, Cheetah, and Crooked Beak loving a little girl who just needed acceptance and friendship, each of these animals came to Marcia to love her and to receive her love. When we choose to take human form on the physical plane, our primary intent is to learn how to give and receive love. We select Earth as the school in which we will learn this lesson because here there are teachers who have mastered it. We call them dogs and birds, cats and horses. Yet, Love by any other name is still Love.

CHAPTER 6

∽◌∽

Abusive Relationships

I N THIS CHAPTER YOU WILL meet Kathryn, a fifty-three-year-old author, speaker and life skills instructor who works with women who have left abusive relationships and who now seek healing. Kathryn was abused by her ex-husband, Tim, to whom she was married for twelve years and with whom she has a son and a daughter.

In the United States, approximately four million women have been physically abused by a partner, and almost twenty-one million have experienced verbal abuse. Of course, men, too, suffer abuse within the context of intimate relationships.

Statistics about abuse are compiled in a way that creates a false dichotomy. In truth, all verbal abuse *is* physical abuse. Largely unaware of how energy works, modern society draws an arbitrary and inaccurate distinction between the two. Words are energy, and the energy of abusive words penetrates the chakras or energy centers, pounding the body as hard as any fist might. There can be no verbal abuse without corresponding physical abuse, even if the effects of the words do not manifest in the body in identifiable ways.

Yet, Kathryn's story is about much more than abuse. It's about the external struggle to make a relationship work and the internal battle over whether to walk away. It's about emotional intimacy: what creates it, what tears at its fabric, and what ultimately destroys it.

As souls we seek the experience of giving and receiving love on the physical plane. If we desire to receive love, would we plan to be abused? If we wish to give love, would we plan to be abusive? Or are abusive relationships not part of a pre-birth blueprint but rather are indicative of a plan gone awry? Kathryn and I sought to answer these questions both through a session with medium Staci Wells and, because Kathryn is clairaudient, through a direct conversation with her spirit guides.

Kathryn

Kathryn remembers that when she was a child, her father was controlling and a perfectionist.

"He definitely wanted it done his way," she told me. "Dad had me under his thumb. I was fearful of my father, although he did not abuse me ever. I wanted him to be pleased with me. I wanted him to love me."

During their teen years, Kathryn and her friends frequently congregated at a park downtown. Often, her father showed up unannounced to check on her activities. A strict curfew was in place, and Kathryn was required to tell her father both where she was going and if she was leaving that location.

Kathryn enjoyed a feeling of liberation when she eventually left home to attend college. There, she started dating Tim. Though they were the same age, Tim was already in the workforce. Kathryn was attracted to his ruggedly masculine appearance and the affection he showered upon her.

"I don't remember ever seeing my parents kiss or hug," Kathryn told me. "This was all new to me, and it felt good!"

It was also new to Tim, who, as Kathryn would learn, had not received much love from his parents.

"Tim was raised by an overpowering abusive mother and a father who taught him to be macho without accepting responsibility for his actions," Kathryn explained. "He was taught that his problems in life were always because of other people."

In her second year of college, Kathryn was one of a handful of students selected for the ski team. She was proud and excited. Tim, however, was threatened by the prospect of her new friendships with others on the team and by the ski trips that would take her away from him. He forbade her to participate; Kathryn joined the team anyway but felt guilty for doing so. In retrospect, Kathryn believes Tim's reaction was a clear danger sign, one she should have heeded.

Soon thereafter a friend asked Kathryn to be the maid of honor in her wedding. The night before the wedding, Tim broke a date with Kathryn to go drinking with his friends. Later that night he came to Kathryn's home, where he was angered to discover that she had been out with her friends.

"He asked why I had gone out," Kathryn recalled. "I wasn't supposed to do that. He'd ask a question, and if he didn't like the answer, he'd punch me. As I cried he would say, 'Oh, this doesn't hurt,' and then he'd punch me again."

At the wedding the next day, "I had this massive bruise on my arm the size of a softball. It was black and purple and blue and throbbed terribly. I pulled the sleeve of my dress down to cover it, but it was a windy day, and the sleeve blew up. A friend said, 'Did Tim do that?' I lied, 'No.' He said, 'I think he did. You don't have to put up with that.' It went in one ear and out the other. I was so ashamed. I thought I was responsible for Tim hitting me."

"Kathryn," I said, "you continued to see Tim after that incident, so there must have been much you liked about him. You mentioned that Tim was affectionate. What other qualities did you see in him? What were the other good parts of the relationship?"

"Ninety percent of the time, he was a nice person," she answered. "He was kind and caring. He was very huggy-kissy. We'd spend hours at dinner. We'd talk all night about our lives, our childhoods, things we were dreaming about in the future. I was so in love with him. He made me feel so ..." She sighed wistfully. "I never loved anybody that much."

Kathryn and Tim dated on and off for many years. Incidents of abuse occurred periodically, but for Kathryn they were more than offset by the happy times. When Kathryn was in her early thirties, she and Tim married.

Two years later after giving birth to their first child, Kathryn experienced post-partum depression. Tim was unable to understand her depression and became angry whenever she talked about it. He also showed little interest in taking care of their child. "I had all of the responsibility, and he had none," she said sadly. Kathryn's comment would later take on much greater meaning when we delved into her pre-birth planning.

I asked Kathryn to describe how Tim spoke to her.

"Tim would say, 'Are you dumb? What's wrong with your head? You don't think.' He'd also say, 'If you think you're going to find somebody that's better, think again. You will never find anybody that treats you as good. You will never find anybody as good-looking as me.' He would tell me I wasn't smart enough, pretty enough, skinny enough. If I had a piece of cake, he'd say, 'You want to look like your sister? Stop eating that.'

"Once," she continued, "I read an article about how women in Pakistan aren't free. I said, 'I wish I could do something to help them.' Tim said, 'Who are *you*? What the hell do you want to help them for?' I had to be very careful. He didn't like me being compassionate to anybody."

Kathryn then described a particularly terrifying episode when she and Tim were talking in the bathroom and something she said caused him to fly into a rage.

"I thought he was going to kill me. Tim grabbed my shoulders and pounded me against the bathtub. The children came into the bathroom screaming, '*Daddy! Daddy! Stop! Stop!*' He was so angry—past the point of knowing what he was doing. Finally, the kids got his attention and he stopped. There was water all over. I was crying and hyperventilating, and the kids were yelling, '*Mommy! Mommy! Are you okay?*'"

Kathryn and Tim's marriage continued along the same rocky path for some time. It was only when Kathryn's brother died unexpectedly from heart failure that a shift occurred in her relationship with Tim.

"I didn't allow any of the feelings about my brother to surface because I was busy taking care of my kids and my parents, totally ignoring my own needs," Kathryn said. As a result she had anxiety attacks. In the counseling Kathryn received for her anxiety, she talked about her relationship with Tim.

"By the time I got through with counseling, I realized I should be treated better," Kathryn told me. "So I started to stand up to him."

"Is that when you began to think about leaving?"

"Yes. I was fighting with myself. It was an internal war. The more I learned to respect myself, the more I was falling out of love with him. I was fighting it because I thought, I've got two children. I married this man 'til death do us part.

"We had long stopped talking of our emotions," she added. "One day Tim said, 'You're not going to leave me, are you?' And out of my mouth, before I even thought about it, I said, 'Yes, I am.' I told him our marriage was over."

Kathryn divorced Tim and over time built a new life for herself. "Day by day, one step at a time, I slowly took back my life," she said. Today her daughter lives with her, and Kathryn devotedly helps to raise her daughter's son. Kathryn's son lived with Tim for a number of years and is now enrolled in college.

I asked Kathryn how she has grown as a result of her experience.

"I've done a lot of healing over the years, a lot of looking in the mirror and accepting responsibility for my part in all this. I've learned that fear is only within myself. As soon as I feel fear, I face it and it goes away. I feel my emotions more than I ever used to. I used to pretend they weren't there. Now, I allow myself to feel."

Kathryn's Session with Staci

Given the scope and intricacy of pre-birth planning, I had no doubt that Kathryn and Tim had planned to be together. The important relationships in our lives, and even those that are seemingly less important, do not form randomly, no matter how coincidental an initial meeting on the physical plane may appear. What I did not know was if Kathryn had anticipated the abuse, had she foreseen this possibility, and had she understood just how emotionally searing it would be. If so, why had she placed herself in this position? And what had Tim hoped would happen? Had he understood there was the potential for him to become abusive?

With these questions in mind, I listened as Staci used her psychic gifts to see and to hear Kathryn and Tim's pre-birth planning. Although I did not know it at the time, she was about to provide some of the most extensive and startling pre-birth conversation we would hear in the course of our work together.

"I am seeing something I haven't seen before in any pre-birth planning session," Staci announced at the beginning of the reading. "I see Kathryn, Tim, and two other souls in male form lined up to talk to her. They also want to be a spouse or in her life as a romantic partner. What is unusual here is that I see her pushing those two aside and allowing Tim into her space. That tells us right away her relationship with Tim was intentional. Now, let's see what else I can find out as I circle us in.

"In this planning session, Tim has not yet taken on the cloak of the personality in the coming lifetime. He still wears the cloak from a previous lifetime, but not the most recent. It is a lifetime in Italy in the 1400s. That is the last lifetime he felt good about himself, so he wears that personality."

When we are in spirit, we may assume any form we like. When people see deceased loved ones who look just as they did during their time on Earth, it is because those souls choose to present themselves in familiar form. In many planning sessions Staci has seen, souls had assumed, either entirely or partially, the appearance they would have in the upcoming lifetime. In a few instances souls had assumed no human form at all, preferring instead to remain in lightbody or spirit form. In this case, Tim had chosen the form he had in a more distant past life in which he felt a sense of self-worth. As we would soon learn, this choice reflected what he intended to work on with Kathryn.

"Kathryn talks about how there is a great hunger and thirst for him, that in previous lifetimes she wanted him but could never have him," Staci continued. "She was never able to catch his attention in that way. In those previous lifetimes, he was already taken by someone else.

"Kathryn has always recognized Tim's need for self-approval. She observed him in other lifetimes and saw that he never felt assured. She wanted to love him. She talks about feeling a great empty vessel inside him. She has seen that in him for centuries. She would like to fill it. It was her agreement to show him the good that she sees in him and to get him to see that good as well.

Tim:	I don't want to depend on another for good feelings about myself. I have lashed out for so long. The emptiness you have seen inside me in Earth life is a reflection of that. I don't want to feed off you, but neither do I know that I can trust myself not to, particularly when you offer me so much of yourself. I am concerned that I will forget to honor you and cherish the love you bestow on me. I have forgotten this before with others. It would not be fair.
Kathryn:	My desire is to love you, to experience the feeling of being in your arms and being loved by you.
Tim:	But I may hurt you, and I don't feel ready to rush back into life so soon. I'm not sure.

"Tim pauses as he considers Kathryn's request.

Tim:	I will go. There are many I could choose to live with [choose as parents], and this will serve my purpose on my path toward wholeness."

As I heard Staci relay Tim's decision, I was surprised; he seemed to have come to his decision very quickly. Then I reminded myself of something important I had learned about pre-birth planning: decisions are not always or entirely made in what we would consider to be an analytical manner. Rather, there is a *feeling* of rightness about the decision, and the plans are based upon that feeling. And then I reminded myself of another equally important fact: time as we know it does not exist in the nonphysical realm. Tim's "pause," though seemingly quite brief, would have provided more than ample opportunity for him and Kathryn to communicate through feeling.

Kathryn: I will accept most of the responsibility for raising a family. I am not perfect. There may be times I strike out in anger, too, but we both want to learn the power of self-control.

In you I will see myself. In me I hope you will see yourself. That is all I want. I see such beauty in you. I always have. I want to show that beauty to you. Your gentleness, your compassion—they could become so much stronger with me.

Tim: I am working on all these things, but I cannot promise always to be gentle. I hope that I may be as much help to you as you will be to me.

Kathryn: I am strong. I know who I am. I have courage. I have the compassion to understand and accept. Be with me for this time.

Tim: Yes.

"A quiet hush comes over the room," Staci said, referring to the members of the soul group and to the spirit guides who were present. "I see Kathryn and Tim put their heads together where the third eye is. It's a moment where the souls meld. My spirit guide tells me that this was their way of sealing their promise and showing devotion to each other."

An energy center located between the eyebrows, the third eye is considered the site of psychic vision. This gesture by Kathryn and Tim, although clearly an expression of affection, may also symbolize looking ahead to the coming lifetime and sharing a common vision for it.

I now saw part of Kathryn's motivation for planning an incarnation with Tim, but I did not fully understand how she had hoped to grow in this lifetime or how abuse by Tim might further that growth. I asked Staci if Kathryn had any conversation with her spirit guides in that regard.

"She is talking to a female spirit guide about this," Staci replied as she visualized another scene from Kathryn's pre-birth planning. "This guide embodies compassion. Everything about her is soft and yet strong at the same time. A gentle strength. They talked before Kathryn went into the Room of Souls, where they do the actual pre-birth planning session. That name—Room of Souls—was just given to me by my spirit guide. That's one of the terms they use to describe it.

"I see Kathryn and this spirit guide leave the building where the Room of Souls is and walk into a garden. I see Kathryn's guide transform from a light being into a humanoid form. They are talking about compassion. This spirit guide has been with Kathryn for—the words I am given are 'many generations.'

Spirit Guide: I have reviewed some of the talks we have had. I am aware of your desire to have Tim as your spouse. You want to proceed? You want to take on the challenge of this relationship?

Kathryn: Yes. Yes, I do.

Spirit Guide: All that I see shows me this may not turn out as you expect. Are you going to have compassion for someone who may speak harshly and raise a hand to you, someone who will go to emotional extremes with or without provocation?

Kathryn:

His desire for self-perfection is as great as my own. He has remained a quest for me for so long that I am ready to take on this challenge no matter what the cost. I feel in my heart that I can offer him love when others turn away. I feel in my heart that he needs this kind of strength, this backbone of support, so that he can take from me and add that to his self. The strength I have will be enough for both of us.

"Kathryn's spirit guide shakes her head no.

Spirit Guide:

I fear you are confused. I am concerned that you are not seeing all possible ramifications.

"Kathryn stops walking and places her hand on her guide's arm.

Kathryn:

No, I know what this could lead to. In my heart this will fulfill the promise I made to him when he was my son, my baby boy whom I could not protect.

"I am seeing the image of a very old past life in caves," said Staci. "This boy of hers was killed by a man who crushed the child's skull with a rock. This man was somebody who roamed [the countryside], who was not related. He was angry and wild. Kathryn has a need to make up for not being able to protect Tim. She still has so much love to give to him. That is part of her motivation.

"They talk and walk some more. Then they sit down on the grass by some bushes. The spirit guide takes out that board [the planning diagram] with the black and white squares on it and points to a particular place on the board.

Spirit Guide: In this lifetime you were a woman in Rome. You had very little say in your own affairs. You lived meekly, depending on the goodwill of first your father and then your husband in a time when women were both revered and scorned. Do you want to repeat that—to be both revered and scorned, uplifted and batted down? Ask yourself, Will this foster positive development in you?

Kathryn: I have strong feelings, though wise they may not always be.

Spirit Guide: This is a life where your very foundation, your heart and soul, will be called into question time and time again. You will have to learn to deflect what you are told you are and to be mindful always of your truth. Are you strong enough?

Kathryn: If I am not, won't this surely make me strong?

Spirit Guide: No, it will not surely make you strong. That is your choice. You can choose just as you did in previous lifetimes to look down and never see another face again. You can choose to see your hands and feet and become powerless.[7]

Kathryn: No, that is not what I want. I was powerless in a lifetime where I lost him to a beating. I know that my love for him will be the strongest thing.

Spirit Guide: But what about your love for yourself? Isn't this your greatest goal for this lifetime? Not just to show love to others, not just to be loved, but to love yourself?

---

7 A reference to several past lives, including the one as a woman in ancient Rome. In that lifetime Kathryn was so disempowered by her experiences that she literally spent her life walking with her gaze averted, looking down at her own hands and feet.

Kathryn: Yes. I understand it is all these things and more.

Spirit Guide: It is not more; this is the very core, the very thing from which all else you want will come. Your love for yourself, your joy that comes from within, and your ability to share that love and joy with others all come from this one lesson. As you grow and go on to have a family of your own, it is the love within that you will share with them.

      Are you willing to suffer what might happen with this individual, who has a history of striking out, impulsiveness, and not looking to himself as the source of his problems and answers? Are you willing to suffer the possible consequences?

Kathryn: I want to raise him up like I was not able to [in the previous life].

Spirit Guide: Then why not choose to be his mother instead?

Kathryn: That will not give me the joy I am looking for. I want to try a romantic relationship. Perhaps it is the longing to feel him in that way. I have already given birth to him. This way I will have him when he is grown. He will come to me as a man and I as a woman with our attitudes already in place. The joy we share will be more than enough to make up for any loss that may happen. I am ready. Let me go in [to the Room of Souls] now."

I was mesmerized by the power of this pre-birth dialogue and the remarkable detail in which Staci heard it. When Kathryn and I later discussed the reading, she told me, "This poor man had his skull crushed when he was my child, and I wanted to love him like nobody else had ever loved him. I did do that. I showed him that." In regard to not having heeded the advice of her spirit guide, she said, "I always jump in the water and then look for my life jacket. So, I'm even like that on the other side. I get it honestly, then."

Staci's spirit guide had facilitated the reading, directing her to exactly those visual images and pieces of conversation that would best address our questions. Aware that he had played a critical role, I asked him for concluding comments regarding Kathryn's pre-birth planning or her life with Tim.

"The personality bounces between extremes of behavior before becoming grounded in a sense of self," replied the spirit guide. Staci's speech had slowed, as it generally does when her guide speaks through her, but now there was also an unusual solemnity in his tone. "You start as children as loving individuals. As various karmic energies activate in your lives, you begin to view your experiences through these karmic filters. Some people are able to stay in the present. Most people filter their present experiences through old conversations in which they were told how bad they are. In Tim's case he was told he was bad at a very early age. We do not judge the woman who is Tim's mother and who gave him these messages. It was Tim's challenge to rise above those messages utilizing unconditional love of self.

"Kathryn and Tim are working on similar karmic issues," he continued. "Neither can be judged. Matters of the heart, matters of impetuousness and impulsiveness, are indicated in both lives. Kathryn came into this lifetime more emotionally evolved and stable, with a great desire to receive love and to give love to Tim and many others. She cannot be judged for that. Both individuals were aware that this [abuse] could happen and yet chose to go forward with this relationship."

Kathryn Channels Her Spirit Guides

To gain additional insight into Kathryn's life plan, I asked her if I could speak with her spirit guides. At this time in human evolution, most people do not hear their guides consciously. That Kathryn is able to do so presented a rare and exciting opportunity to talk directly with those involved in her pre-birth planning.

Intuitively, I felt that Kathryn's choice of Tim as a partner was linked with her choice of a father in this lifetime. I began there.

"Why did Kathryn choose a controlling father?" I asked.

"Kathryn chose a controlling father because this would teach her as a child to do as she was told, especially when a dominant male figure appeared in her life," replied the spirit guides. "Although Kathryn was born with intelligence, she would learn to have difficulty using her mind when a male figure entered the scenario.

"Kathryn's childhood was of such that she became fearful of her father, the most dominant male figure in her life at that time. The fear she felt would shut her mind off. When she met Tim, she felt the same fear with his aggression and until she began to heal would do as he wanted. Her mind was not capable of thinking until long after the scenario had passed. This gave Tim the edge he needed to abuse Kathryn to the degree he did. Had Kathryn not experienced this mind alteration, she would have challenged Tim, and his aggression and the relationship would have taken an entirely different path."

"My sense," I said, "is that Kathryn wanted an experience in which she would break free from someone and stand on her own. Since she did not do that with her father, she then brought in a controlling boyfriend/husband to continue learning lessons in independence."

"True," confirmed the guides. "In previous lives Kathryn had been controlled. When you feel unworthy, you're very easily controlled by other people. You don't feel worthy to please yourself; you want to please everybody else. The issues are freedom and worthiness.

"Kathryn and Tim wanted so much to help each other. Kathryn wanted to gain strength, to find worthiness, to learn to walk with her head held high. She wanted to help Tim open his heart to love, to help him with his own worthiness. It was agreed that if Tim did not learn what he desired, Kathryn would leave the marriage and shake his entire foundation."

"If one of Kathryn's objectives was to be strong and independent," I asked, "why choose a controlling father instead of loving parents who would teach her to stand on her own?"

"Although her father was demanding and controlling, he also was an example of strength. Her mother was gentle, kind, and giving. This gave Kathryn the potential of a very good mixture of character. As Kathryn worked through her personal growth, she would learn to mix the strength of her father with the kindness of her mother and mold herself into the person she needs to be to fulfill her life path."

"Was Kathryn's plan to marry Tim only if she didn't gain strength and find worthiness when she was younger?"

"No, she would have married Tim regardless. She had to live through the experience to know truly what it was like so she could help others gain strength through their experiences."

"If Tim had chosen not to be so controlling and abusive," I wondered, "how would Kathryn have then gone on to do the kind of healing and teaching she now does?"

"She wouldn't. She would be a leader in building strength in people, but she wouldn't center her vision on people living with abuse. She would reach out to a different group."

"When Kathryn and Tim were planning this lifetime, was it understood that he would likely behave the way he did?"

"It was always believed Tim would abuse Kathryn to a degree, but not to the degree he actually did," replied the spirit guides. "It was a possibility that healing would be found later in the relationship. With healing, Tim and Kathryn's relationship would have taken a much different path."

"My understanding is that often souls are drawn together vibrationally in the pre-birth planning based on their emotional wounds. For example, it sounds as though both Kathryn and Tim had feelings or beliefs of low self-worth and that this drew them to each other. Is this an accurate understanding?"

"Souls are drawn together for many reasons. Sometimes it is emotional wounds. Sometimes it is the experiences and lessons the souls want in order to achieve mastery in their soul growth. There is always a win-win scenario in pre-birth planning. One would not enter a contract selfishly, only for himself. Souls want to give and receive. Such is the case with Kathryn and Tim.

Kathryn wanted so much to give love to Tim, and Tim wanted so much to help Kathryn with her worthiness. At the same time, Tim did hesitate, worried that he would hurt Kathryn too much. It was Kathryn who was insistent upon sharing her life with Tim this time around."

"Is it correct to say that if people heal their emotional wounds while in body—for example, they learn to love themselves, they come to feel their true worth—then they would not choose in future lifetimes to be with someone who is likely to be abusive?"

"Yes, this is true to a degree," answered the guides. "For example, Kathryn has certainly healed her wounds and found her true self-worth. Her worthiness is now engraved deep in her soul. It is likely she would never choose a future lifetime with someone who is likely to be abusive; however, we never say never. Perhaps she would choose a future lifetime with someone likely to be abusive to help that soul with its lesson. If Kathryn would enter into such an agreement, she would not suffer with her worthiness the way she has suffered in this lifetime because there would be no wounds open to suffer with."

"Please speak to those people who want to heal themselves so they never again plan to be with an abusive partner."

"For those wanting to heal themselves from abusive partners, we first want to help them recognize that they are indeed courageous to have entered into such an agreement in pre-birth planning. If they can open their minds and hearts to believe they have the strength to heal, then healing will begin. It is as easy as summoning the desire in the heart. We ask them to have faith that there is a better life waiting for them, not only while they walk the Earth but also far beyond the veils. Have faith, and trust in the Universe and in your own pre-birth plan.

"There are many souls walking the Earth now who are ready to help all who yearn for knowledge, all those seeking growth. It is your personal growth here on this Earth that will transcend into your timeless soul growth. There are many avenues for your healing; the modalities are too numerous to mention. Ask and ye shall receive.

"We extend our deepest love and gratitude to you and your work. Namaste."

∽

In large part Kathryn and Tim's is the story of two souls who each chose parents and a romantic partner based on emotional wounds. Their history of past lives and their pre-birth choices parallel each other.

Tim had several past lives in which he was unaware of his value and felt a great emptiness inside. He therefore chose a controlling, abusive mother who mirrored his feelings of unworthiness to him, telling him from an early age that he was bad. It is likely that Tim's mother herself lacked a sense of self-worth and so was energetically drawn to Tim in the same way he was drawn to her. Moreover, as Kathryn's spirit guide said during her pre-birth planning, Tim had a history of not looking to himself as the source of his problems and answers. He then chose parents for his current lifetime who, as Kathryn told us, taught him that others are to blame for his problems. Tim's pre-birth choices are vibrational resonance in action.

Similarly, Kathryn had several past lives in which she felt herself to be lacking in worth and so allowed others to control her. Determined to master lessons of worthiness and freedom, she therefore chose a controlling, domineering father who mirrored her feelings of unworthiness to her. Like Tim's mother, Kathryn's father did not know his worth and so was energetically drawn to Kathryn in the same way she was drawn to him.

In her excellent book *How People Heal*, Diane Goldner quotes gifted healer Rosalyn Bruyere:

> [Your parents] are limited in exactly the way you were in your last incarnation. Our chakras are pre-matrixed at birth. They reflect all you have accomplished in your previous lifetimes. Getting to where you were before is relatively easy. Getting beyond it—that's the work of a lifetime.

Tim's choice of parents and Kathryn's choice of her father reflect where they left off in past lives. This is their starting point. Their choice of each other as romantic partners reflects their shared desire to evolve beyond that point and foster healing in each other and in themselves.

Just as feelings of unworthiness drew Tim to his mother and Kathryn to her father, so, too, did those feelings draw them to each other in their pre-birth planning. Kathryn's words to Tim, "In you I will see myself. In me I hope you will see yourself," speak of a desired future in which they have discovered their infinite worth as Divine Beings and now see that grandeur in each other. Yet, their choice of each other as partners indicates that they *already* saw themselves in each other prior to birth: Kathryn glimpsed her feelings of unworthiness in Tim, and Tim viewed his feelings of unworthiness in Kathryn. Indeed, Kathryn's statement, "I am ready to take on this challenge no matter what the cost" suggests that her choice of Tim is founded in part on a lack of self-worth, for no soul aware of her magnificence would plan an experience with such disregard.

Even so, the life blueprint was also based on deep, mutual love and an intent to heal. Kathryn sought both to show Tim his gentleness and compassion and to help him strengthen those soul qualities. She desired to show him his own beauty, beauty that had long been evident to her but hidden from him. Tim wanted to help Kathryn discover her worthiness and so "be as much help to you as you will be to me."

That the relationship did not achieve what was sought is not a failure. That Kathryn planned an incarnation with Tim against the recommendation of her spirit guide is not a mistake. From the perspective of the soul, there are no failures or mistakes, only experience. Experience is never bad. Our souls do not judge us; instead, they welcome the wisdom, feelings, growth, and deeper self-knowing that result from all experience.

When a soul reaches a certain stage of evolution, decisions regarding future incarnations are based in large part on compassion. Kathryn's compassion for Tim was so great that she was willing to assume the risks of planning another lifetime with him. Such compassion is to be celebrated, not viewed with regret. The depth of compassion Kathryn demonstrated in her pre-birth planning is cultivated over hundreds and sometimes thousands of lifetimes. Yet, beyond this stage of evolution lay another in which the compassion remains but wisdom and self-love lead to different pre-birth choices. At this level one says, "I feel great compassion for you, but I will not agree to be abused by you."

Kathryn has now reached this point in her evolution. By stepping away from Tim, Kathryn fulfilled her spirit guide's wish for her: that she learn to love herself. Her love of self is now so strong that, as her guides said, she would be very unlikely to agree to a similar pre-birth plan. Vibrationally, she would not be drawn to a potentially abusive partner, and should such a soul approach her in its own planning process, she would be more inclined to be of service as a guide rather than as an incarnate partner. For you who seek this stage of evolution, for you who were or are in an abusive relationship and wish never to repeat the experience, be assured of this: While in body your primary task is to heal the emotional wounds that led to planning the abuse or the potential for it before you were born.

Like all who have been in so-called failed relationships, Kathryn has at times blamed herself. She has wondered if she could have done more, if she tried hard enough, if she loved well enough. Friends and family may have asked similar questions about her life or they may have viewed her as someone who made poor decisions. They may have asked why she entered into a relationship with Tim, tolerated his abuse, didn't leave sooner. These are natural questions to ask from the level of the personality.

In his wisdom Staci's guide knew that such questions would be asked. Of all the subjects on which he might have spoken, he therefore chose that of judgment. When we realize that others have pre-birth agreements to enter into potentially abusive relationships for the purpose of healing themselves or helping a loved one to heal, we may look upon their lives with compassion and understanding. When those who have been abused come to the same realization, they may embrace themselves with compassion and forgiveness. Judgment against others or self has no merit and is an anchor to the soul, blocking light, creating separation, and damming the flow of love in the world.

While in body the suffering we experience in intimate relationships often makes us regret giving our love. By contrast, when we review our lives after returning to the nonphysical, we are much more concerned with the times when we *did not* give love to others and to ourselves. In the life review, we see and feel holographically, in exquisite detail, what would have happened had we made more loving decisions. (However, because we are supported by the unconditional love of our guides and the sense of Oneness we experience in our nonphysical Home, we do not judge ourselves.) In all likelihood Kathryn will emerge from her life review with a profound sense of a life well lived. At one time she gave love to Tim; at another her focus shifted to self-love. Had she turned away quickly from Tim, neither of them ever would have known if he might eventually discover his inherent worth. Had she never turned away from him, she would have duplicated her life in Rome. These expressions of love and self-love are opportunities seized, not missed, and are therefore cause to rejoice.

Kathryn's repeated use of the word *heart* in the pre-birth planning session reflects the way she intended to and did love Tim in this lifetime. She tells her spirit guide, "I feel in my heart that I can offer him love when others turn away. I feel in my heart that he needs this kind of strength." Kathryn also says, "In my heart this will fulfill the promise I made to him." Many spiritual traditions view the heart as the seat of the soul in the human body, the channel through which we receive and express Divine Love in the world. The phrase "harden the heart" is more than a colloquialism; it refers to the literal stagnation of energy that occurs when a person refuses to give or to accept love. Remaining open in the heart means giving love freely and unconditionally, just as Kathryn and Tim did in their pre-birth planning and just as each of us did in our own pre-birth planning.

We come, then, to the essence of Kathryn's life and every life that is lived on Earth. We are here to remember Love and then express and thus concretize it on the physical plane. This is the experience the soul seeks. If you were or are in an abusive relationship, your soul asks you now to recognize the great courage and deep compassion it took to plan such an experience so you might bring healing to yourself or another. As you acknowledge your courage and compassion, and as you remember that your life plan was created in and with love despite all outward appearances, self-judgment is replaced by self-forgiveness, and unworthiness gives way to an abiding self-respect and self-love. Therein lies the healing you sought before you were born.

Your healing is your soul's crowning achievement on the physical plane. It is the work of your lifetime.

CHAPTER 7

⌘

Sexuality

MOST OF US TAKE OUR sexuality as a given and are completely identified with it. That is, we believe we *are* the straight woman or the gay man. At the soul level, however, we have no gender; rather, we are a beautiful meshing of both masculine and feminine energies. Before we incarnate we choose a particular sexuality wisely with love for ourselves and for those who will be in our lives, because we know the experience will best foster our and their evolution.

Typically, when in body souls who have chosen heterosexuality do not struggle with or even question their sexual orientation. Rarely do they wonder, "Why am I heterosexual?" Moreover, society generally does not judge or discriminate against heterosexuals. Thus, although it is certainly reasonable to ask why a soul would plan to be heterosexual, this chapter endeavors primarily to explore the pre-birth choice to be homosexual so as to offer a perspective that may increase understanding and nonjudgment among people regardless of their sexual orientation.

Though society has made great strides in its acceptance of the many ways in which people express sexuality, homosexuals are still treated very differently from those who are straight. To take but one simple example, gay and lesbian marriage is for the most part illegal in the United States at this time. In an infinite number of smaller, less obvious ways, a life of being gay or other orientation affords a soul a uniquely challenging context in which to experience and thus know itself. The difficulty of the challenge is evident in suicide statistics among youth: lesbian, gay, bisexual, and transgender youth are up to four times more likely to attempt suicide than their straight peers and up to nine times more likely if they come from a rejecting family. Individuals who question their sexuality later in life may face a different set of challenges, including the shock or outrage of their heterosexual partners and the possible need to change and adapt to a new way of living.

Why do souls plan lives in which they will be different from the majority in this way? Why do they risk or even seek moments of judgment by others? And what of their likely challenges to self-acceptance and self-love?

Jim

"About a year after I married, I was very suddenly aware that I had been attracted to men all my life," Jim Ashburn said.

Jim was born in 1946 in a town of 1700 people in western Pennsylvania. His father was a commercial kitchen contractor. When Jim was in his teens, he discovered "racy, gay novels," as he called them, hidden in his father's closet and was shocked to learn that his father had such fantasies. (As Jim told me of his discovery, I considered that Jim had chosen his parents and thus the predisposition to be gay before birth. I wondered if his father had ever wanted to leave his marriage to be with a male partner.) A grandmother, great aunt, and two great uncles lived with Jim, his parents, and Jim's younger brother. Jim described their household as having an "Irish Catholic culture ... *very* Catholic." The parish was the primary focus of family life.

"I completely shut out anything that didn't fit into what middle-class white people were supposed to be," Jim recalled. "That certainly included any attraction to boys. I just liked to be around them. This was pre-sexual. I remember catty-corner from my house there was a hardware store. The guy that ran the hardware store was just fascinating to me! I didn't know why. Somehow I knew this was not something to talk about."

During his childhood Jim received mixed messages about sexuality. In Catholic school "they taught us that masturbation was a mortal sin," Jim said. "You would go to hell if you did it. I remember being almost in tears at times about wanting to.

"My grandmother added to that dynamic. She would say, 'Your body is filthy.' My dad, who was a very loving father, never contradicted her, but he would take me aside and say, 'Your body is a gift of God. Your body is beautiful.' It saved me from some tremendous scarring."

When Jim was seven, he and his father were gardening in front of their home. As a boy named Bobby Weir walked by, Jim, without understanding what it meant, yelled something he had heard at school: "Bobby Weir is a queer." Jim's father laid down his shovel, looked at Jim, and said very seriously, "Don't ever use that kind of language about another person." Years later when Jim came out, that memory served as a powerful support for him.

Jim had one close friend, Mike, throughout childhood. Mike joined Jim and his family on many of their outings. Often, Jim and Mike would take long walks along the railroad tracks, picking elderberries that Jim's grandmother made into jam.

"Once we were playing in an empty lot with some other guys, and Mike took us into this little clubhouse and told us about sex," Jim said with a laugh. "He told us the way babies are made is that men pee in women's bodies. My reaction was, 'That can't be true, because my parents would never do that!'" Jim was now laughing harder. "But, that set me on a course of exploration. I found books in the public library. I knew I wasn't supposed to be reading these, but I took them to a corner and sat there on Saturday afternoons. Mike and I would spend long days talking about what I was discovering."

In high school Jim became close friends with Sue, a woman in his class. Mike and Sue were also good friends, and the three of them shared much together. Jim's friendship with Sue blossomed into love when he was in college, and he and Sue married after their sophomore year. Because Sue was infertile, Jim knew they would never have children.

"It was just amazing to make love with Sue," Jim remembered. "I wanted to pleasure her. I was curious about her body, because I had never been with anybody else. We were sexually very compatible. We really loved each other. I wasn't allowing myself to feel anything about other men's bodies, so I didn't have any of that to compete with or compare."

"You weren't thinking about men at all at that time?" I asked.

"Consciously, no. Underneath, yes. The ability of the mind to repress is amazing."

"So, early in the marriage neither you nor Sue had any indication that you were attracted to men?"

"No, not at all," Jim replied. "This was 1967. Gay liberation was starting, but it wasn't widely known. It wasn't in the culture to even question your sexuality. At that time the only personality who was out was Liberace. There was just no role model for being gay and something other than Liberace," he said with a hearty laugh.

"Jim, at what point in the marriage did your interest in men begin?"

"I'm a little shy about this story," he chuckled. "About a year after Sue and I married, a buddy and I occasionally would go to a [straight] porno film. One time *Deep Throat* was showing. I came out of that theater realizing I had no idea what any of those women looked like!" Jim and I laughed. "But, I knew every hair on Harry Reems's body. This experience flooded me with the awareness that I was attracted to men and always had been.

"I walked out of that theater onto Liberty Avenue, Pittsburgh, PA. It was *Liberty* Avenue quite literally. I thought, 'Oh my God, I'm gay!' I stood there for quite awhile."

Shortly thereafter Jim realized that he was attracted not only to men in general, but also to his friend Mike in particular. He confided his interest to Mike, who, though he had never been with another man, was open and curious.

"We had sex," Jim told me, "and it was wonderful! It was amazing to hold another man's body in my hands. Every part of me was alive. I was easily able to make love with Sue because I loved her, but the real electricity was around another man's body.

"Mike and I had been together twice only, but it was affecting me deeply. Sue said one night, 'Jim, something is going on and you're not telling me about it.' I remember breaking down, crying. I said, 'I'm aware that I'm gay, or at least that I have this strong feeling.' She was totally shocked. She wasn't very sophisticated in the ways of the world.

"I remember her sadness and fear. She was insecure—this would lead rapidly to the disillusion of our marriage, but I didn't see it that way. I saw myself being committed to her. There was never a period of, 'You are doing a bad thing.' It was more, 'How are we going to accommodate this in our marriage?'"

Because Mike was sexually active only with Jim, neither Sue nor Jim was concerned about the transmission of a sexual disease. As Sue came to see that Jim was not going to leave her, she no longer felt threatened; in fact, she even maintained her friendship with Mike. Jim and Sue communicated openly and deeply about his sexuality and in many ways grew closer during the seven years in which he was involved with Mike. Then, not long after the relationship with Mike ended, Jim and Sue moved to California.

"When we got there," Jim recalled, "Sue got out of the car, walked to an overlook, and started to cry. She said, 'I just know you're going to fall in love with a guy here in California and leave me.' I didn't want to hurt her, so I decided I was not going to have sex with men. I totally repressed that part of me. It was terrible, horrific. I became obsessive. I couldn't think of anything but having sex with men."

Jim repressed his urges for the next two years, during which time he became an activist, campaigning for an ordinance to protect sexual orientation as a human right. While campaigning he met a man with whom he became involved. Later, Jim founded and ran a gay and lesbian support hotline. He began seeing a different man, and his relationship with Sue grew strained. To cope with the strain, Jim and Sue founded a support group for married lesbian and gay people.

"It was supporting one after another couple in splitting up and doing it with more openness, love, and communication than would have normally been the case," Jim said. As Jim and Sue watched other couples separate, they gradually realized that they, too, needed to part. "We came to accept that," he told me. "We were best of friends all the way through."

Several years later Jim met and fell in love with Zachary, the man with whom he now shares his life. Sue remarried and eventually severed contact with Jim, something Jim attributes to the influence of her husband. Jim said he is deeply pained by Sue's refusal to stay in touch because he considers her a soulmate. Today Jim runs a nonprofit foundation in northern California that brings gay men together in heart circles—groups for close sharing and support—and he is active in HIV prevention.

"Jim," I said, "how would you counsel someone who came to you and said, 'I think I may be gay but I just don't know'?"

"Before I had sex with a man or a woman, I had already gone through a process of self-acceptance so I didn't feel guilt," Jim answered. "With Sue it was an expression of love. With Mike it was with the idea that it was an okay thing to explore. Many people have sexual encounters before they feel fine about it. They end up with guilt, and guilt is hard to get rid of. So, I would say to any sexual being, go through a period of self-acceptance first before you express it."

"And those aware of their sexuality but who have not yet told family or friends?"

"Find a few core people you can talk to," he advised. "Come out to them first, then to others. Generally, people love you. And generally, people intuitively already know and are just waiting for you to say the word. If you encounter homophobia, it's important not to take it personally. It's not about you; it's about the other person's internalized fears and things taken on from mainstream culture."

"Jim, as you look back on your journey, what have you learned about yourself and life?"

"Repression does not work," he said firmly. "There is no way one can live a lie and have a good life. If you can express only a part of yourself, then you are going to be only part of a person in the world. Self-expression adds to life. It's the beginning of happiness."

Jim's Session with Staci

If Jim had wanted the experience of being a gay man, why, I wondered after our conversation, had he chosen to be born in a time and location in which his sexuality was neither understood nor accepted? If his intent had been to challenge himself, why had he chosen such a loving and understanding father? And what of Sue? Had she known before birth that she and Jim would marry and that he would become aware of his attraction to men during the course of their marriage? If so, why had Sue sought such a painful experience? And what role had Mike played in their pre-birth planning?

"I'm going to start our session," Staci began, "by telling you, Jim, about your karma and specifically about the life challenge of discovering and coming to terms with your homosexuality after you'd already been married and living a straight life.

"I have been picking up glimpses of past lives having to do with Sue and Mike. I keep picking up a tremendous sense of love from Mike to you. This love seems bigger and broader than just human sexuality. I'd almost say *agape*. In fact, as I say that, my spirit guide says, 'Unconditional love in all its expressions.'

"I have the sense that Mike is a more evolved soul than most. He has a thread running through his lives of being a priest, monk, or somebody who spends a lot of time in quiet and solitude, nurturing his relationship with himself and his connection to All That Is. In those lives there has been a theme of loving service to others. In many of them, you and he had some kind of relationship.

"The one that's important here is one in which he was a priest. I'm hearing 'Rome' and 'Vatican.' You were younger than him, an acolyte. He knew you in the two years prior to when you committed yourself to that path. My spirit guide tells me you were part of his family, a cousin. You approached him about going into the priesthood and about your sense of a calling. He became your counselor, your mentor. He loved that, and you loved that, too.

"Spirit is telling me there have been two lives in which Mike was your father. One comes to me strongly now. I see a gem mine. You two just finished your work. I see him putting down a shovel, wiping sweat from his brow, and saying, 'We've done it! This is what we've been working for!' He's holding some kind of rock in his hand. It's very dark and black, like raw gemstone. As he's talking, I feel this tremendous outpouring of love, love that spans generations and time. Though he's speaking to you from his heart and his beliefs in that life, it's not big enough to contain this huge amount and history of love between you. Again, I need to state that this goes way beyond human-defined love to something much grander, something we hold ourselves up to and aspire to.

"Now I am going to get to karma. My spirit guide says your most important karmic challenge is 'learning to know your truth and how best to use it by experiencing changes in your emotional family and learning to adapt to those changes.'"

By "emotional family," I understood Staci's guide to mean those people with whom Jim has important relationships in this lifetime, not solely his birth family.

Staci continued. "I often see this lesson expressing through a divorce, a death, a huge illness, or literal craziness. Jim, you chose to go through change in the family you created in order to understand your truth and also to give Sue a hand in learning a lesson that has been very tough for her. I'm going to put her aside for a bit. We'll get back to her later.

"In your relationship with Sue, you were working on some issues that were first presented to you by an older, female family member when you were a child. I hear the word *berate*. Do you know who I'm talking about?"

"Yes, I definitely do," Jim replied. "It's my grandmother. She shamed me about my body. She was just anti-body. I would get tan from sun exposure during the summer. She would scrub me with a washcloth, saying, 'You're dirty, you're dirty.'"

"The message about shame," Staci explained, "was intended to contrast with your inner experience of yourself [as a child] and also with your relationship with Sue, who so graciously blessed you with an experience more loving. Part of your soul-level quest in this life is to become a more adaptive and flexible personality. The chosen experience—and I do hear this is chosen—of placing oneself on one path and waking up to self while on that path is a contrasting experience. Learning to embrace that truth is like jumping tracks. Your choice [before birth] was to do this in order to make significant progress within one lifetime."

When in body we motivate ourselves with contrast and also learn from it. Early in Jim's life, the shaming words of his grandmother contrasted with his innocent, childlike knowing that there was nothing wrong with either a suntan or his body. Later in life Sue's appreciation of Jim's body contrasted with his grandmother's shaming. Both contrasts were intended to serve as fuel for his possible future acceptance of his sexuality.

"Your second most important karmic challenge," Staci continued, "is emotional independence. Emotional independence means recognizing that you and you alone are your source of happiness and well-being. Along with emotional independence, you are also working on the karmic challenge of relationship issues and skills."

"I have been building community for gay men in northern California for twenty-one years," Jim told her. "We have heart circles as the core ritual, a deep way for gay men to connect."

"Through my brother's soul-level choice to be gay in this life," Staci said, "I came to the understanding that some men are still traumatized from a past life where they were women and savagely abused. They still want to work with a woman's sensitive nature but are too afraid to come in as female.

"Jim, you're working on bridging understanding and bringing out a nurturing quality in these men you reach out to. This is exactly what Mike did for you in this life. It's the same expression of nurturing, compassion and love, even beyond sexuality, that Mike has expressed to you in several other lives. I'm told now that you came in with the baby boomers because you excitedly anticipated the experience of love in physical form in a much broader, more unconditionally accepting space than you had experienced in prior lives.

"This brings me to the next karmic lesson, being of compassionate service to others. Your compassion is so strong and your loving nature so huge that it feels to me like your body can barely contain it. Part of the path of being of compassionate service to others is that you have an experience early in life to remind your consciousness of compassion. There was probably somebody who made you very angry or disappointed, or who broke your heart. What you were meant to have from that experience was an Ah ha! moment in which you come to understand that maybe the person was conditioned to have that kind of response, maybe abused early in life. Suddenly you embrace compassion toward that person who was pivotal in your life for starting this process. Am I talking about your grandmother?"

"Absolutely," Jim stated. "You are helping me to contextualize her, because I did exactly what you are saying. I saw that she couldn't help herself, and I learned compassion that way. I've never entirely seen her purpose, but I do in what you are saying here."

"There is one negative side to wanting to be of compassionate service," Staci pointed out. "That is the tendency to think you know what's best for others, that if they would only do it your way, they'd be fine. It's really an expression of a desire to dominate others. But, I don't feel this in your energy.

"Everything I sense about you shows me your greatest passion is bringing others into balance the way you have brought yourself into balance. That brings me to your last karmic lesson: balance. This is usually about emotional balance. I'm told that part of the expression of this lesson is that you wanted to separate love and sex by conscious choice. I think you came to the realization that although your heart was passionate about sexual relationships with men, it never meant that you loved Sue any less."

"Yes, yes!" Jim affirmed.

"I want to explain what Sue sought to gain and maybe dispel any lingering guilt you may have," continued Staci. "Sue is also working on the lesson of balance. You gave her an experience in which she could have gone off the deep end. She had to come from a place of balance within herself to maintain the marriage. Also, she has a history through a number of lives of seeking to be loved by others instead of loving herself. She wanted to learn to nurture herself so she could form her own sense of self-worth. So, she probably chose a less than fully functional family to be born into. That is the process one goes through.

"You loved her in a way she had not been loved before in this life, and that love was very healing to her. That was part of your contract with each other. But, it was not your contract to be lifemates. You had to back out at some point for your own self. In my meditation [before today's session] I saw and heard the pre-birth planning discussion. Sue agreed to this experience. She said, 'You will be an example for me.' By seeing you go through the process of discovering your truth and then declaring that to her and to the world, you served as a living example to her. She's not been able to do that for herself yet, but she really wants to."

Staci paused for a moment. "I am now seeing *Sue's* pre-birth planning session."

This was a surprise; I had expected her to tune into Jim's planning session. Yet, I knew that Spirit was presenting to us exactly what we most needed to hear.

"There is, as I've so often seen in these rooms, a wood floor and wood furniture on her side of the room. There's a banister that separates the pre-birth planning area from where the soul group gathers and observes. There is a window on the wall to the left of Sue. Through that window there is more light coming in than I've ever seen in one of these sessions.

"This light is not coming just from the window. I focus my attention to where the wall and ceiling meet behind Sue. This is a first for me, and I hope Jim will be able to tell us why this is significant. I am looking up at a lightbody in the form of a large ball. I am told this is the soul of Sue's father, who is observing the session. Jim, is there a special relationship between Sue and her father?"

"No," Jim told her. "He was an Archie Bunker type. Not quite as openly prejudiced, but a very simple man. We used to laugh that her mom was Edith and her dad was Archie."

"Sometimes, the most prejudiced personalities are simply living a life of experience and actually come from a higher place of knowing this," Staci said. "I feel emanating from this spirit a tremendous excitement and love. Sue's spirit is one he enjoys spending time with. They have been lovers. They are best friends. There is joy because once again she's chosen to share life with him.

"Jim is seated in front of Sue. He is wearing the cloak of the personality, much more detailed than Sue's. Sue is still quite a bit in her lightbody. I'm beginning to see [traces of] the personality across her chest, shoulders, abdomen. I'm coming in in the middle of a discussion.

Sue: I will harbor and hold you.

"As she says this—this is hard to describe—I see her referencing another life in which she was your mother, Jim. Part of her lightbody comes out, like a second set of arms overlaying her lightbody, holding the baby [Jim]. I see a visual image at her head level. It's memories of two lives. The first was in the western prairie of the United States. She was your mother. You lived a very short time, just a few months. In the second life, you were her son's friend. This was in ancient Greece. So, there is a motherly resonance that was expressed in your relationships with her. She wanted to nurture you [in those past lives and in this current lifetime]. And you wanted to nurture her.

Jim: I will repay you with kindness. I want to hold you and give you the love and nurturing I was unable to and prevented from giving in other lives.

"You reach out, palms facing her. You are very excited.

Jim: Perfect! That would be perfect! You know I love and adore you.

Sue: (laughing)   Yes.

Jim: But, I will also betray you as I come to know myself.

Sue: Yes.

Jim: Can you coexist with me through that experience? The harmony between us during that time will have a ripple through it. Are you sure you can agree to this?

"Sue tilts her head forward and down a bit as she contemplates this.

Sue: It is my gift to love you. It is that which I give to you in unconditional embrace that feeds and enriches me. Do you understand this?

Jim: Yes, I do.

Sue: Can you conform to this?

"I see that visual image again; it's like a TV screen. Her thoughts make a visual representation of your life together. I see the two of you standing in your [future] living room, having a conversation. She's thinking about when you come out to her.

"'Can you conform to this?' she's asking. 'Are you sure you can go through with a straight marriage? And are you sure you can come to grips with this [your sexuality] during this marriage?' She knew how hard it was going to be for you.

Jim:	Yes, yes, yes!
Sue:	This is what I truly desire: knowing myself and experiencing a greater gift of love and a more eternal sense of the presence of unconditional love.

"She's delighted you're going to be in her life in this way. There is a joining of hands.

Sue:	This is a gift we share with each other through the years. We will know and come to understand each other.
Jim:	But, what do you get from me? What will this do for you? How will you use it? What will you accomplish?

"*This* is the announcing of your sexuality and what that will eventually do to the relationship.

Sue:	I will use it as a means of self-discovery, my own process of coming to an enlightened viewpoint of myself when in physical form. There has been many a lifetime where I skipped along my path instead of applying myself to the goals I had created. Having you in my life in this way is both a treat and a challenge. It will serve me well, as both the giving and receiving of unconditional love enables me to feel better about me. Your

eventual realization of your truth will cause me in the long run to turn around and face myself with a new level of self-reliance and self-realization that I hope will make me whole again.

"Jim, you reach out to her face—it doesn't look like a physical face; it's soft, round, and not well-defined—in a gesture of love and appreciation.

Jim:	It is not my desire to hurt you.
Sue:	I know.
Jim:	It is only my desire to love you and in so doing, love myself.
Sue:	I will help you do so.
Jim:	This is a kind and loving gesture. I've always thought you were one of the kindest women I've ever known.

"Sue chuckles. I see her having thoughts, memories of lives as a woman and lives as a man. The lives as a woman are on the left side of the visual representation of her head; the lives as a male are on the right. She's chuckling because when she's been in male form she's been less than nice—raping, pillaging, abusing small insects and animals. On the soul level she's come to a place of absolute understanding of the purpose of those lives and so doesn't feel bad about herself or the things she did. But, when in physical form as a female, she wrestles with issues of self-love, unconditional love, and emotional balance.

Sue:	Your love will be a gift through which I may better know myself. I will observe you learning your truth. You will be an example for me. And by providing me with exactly the opposite of that which I crave, to be loved and adored [in

a lifelong marriage], you will force me to look at myself and recognize that I have long been dependent on another's need for me.

To have you, hold you, and let you go is an experience in love that I may use in learning to love me. You will give me cause to learn to nurture myself, which will aid me in what has been a struggle in so many lives: to value myself and become richly independent.

Jim: I know.

Sue: In this you will reward me, for the love I have given to you over   the centuries will be returned to me in this relationship, in this one time. And it will satisfy me in that it will complete the cycle. Every way I could possibly come to know and love you I will have experienced by the time this life is complete.

Jim: Isn't that marvelous?

"The circle is complete with this relationship in this lifetime," Staci concluded.

We paused for a few moments to take in everything that had been said. We now knew Sue's excellent reasons for choosing such a difficult experience. Then a particular question came to mind.

"Staci," I said, "Sue is infertile. Can your guide tell us if that was part of the pre-birth plan?"

Immediately, Staci's speech slowed and her guide began to speak through her. "Although for a brief time in her life there was a desire for conceiving and bearing children, it was not meant nor planned to be a theme of her life," he answered. "She never felt capable of bearing the responsibility for a full-term pregnancy. There was another light [memory] still resonant within this soul of a pregnancy of multiples that never reached a successful conclusion. Indeed, it had the effect of tearing apart her uterus. And so, there was an aversion to having that experience of pregnancy again in this life. It was felt by this individuated soul that she would be able to have experiences to promote the increase of adaptiveness in her personality through other familial individuals, not necessarily those born to her womb."

This was important information. When we plan our lives with one another, we do so for mutual growth and learning, and each soul is given the experience it seeks. In this instance, since neither Jim nor Sue had planned to have children, his sexuality and her infertility dovetailed perfectly. Neither would deprive the other of a desired experience. In a fundamentally different type of life plan, Sue could have elected to bring into body a strong desire to have children and contract with Jim prior to birth for him to interfere with, or perhaps even thwart, that desire. In that case there would be rich opportunities to practice and master forgiveness.

We had learned that Jim planned his sexuality and his discovery of it later in life as a form of service to Sue. Yet, what had been Jim's objectives for himself? What had he sought to learn, and how had he hoped he would grow as a result of this experience? Sensing that the conversation between Jim and Mike would answer these questions, I asked Staci to take us to that portion of Jim's planning session.

Staci was silent for several seconds. "I'm starting to see Jim's pre-birth planning session. The first thing I notice is that instead of sitting in front of the banister that separates the planning area from the soul group observing and supporting the session, Jim is closer to the side wall, directly in front of the window. I've never seen this before. He's making room for more souls from his soul group to be part of the planning. My spirit guide tells me that Jim's placement in the room indicates that he is utilizing the role of the observer in his life this time around. At first the purpose was to observe the family around him and the contrast between himself and his family, then later in life to observe himself and others, many of whom are members of his soul group. He is observing, helping, and learning from them all at the same time.

"I see Jim in front of his pre-birth planning chart. It looks a bit larger than other charts I've seen. There's a lot to do! I see Mike approaching the chart and becoming seated. I never see the individual souls at the pre-birth planning chart seated in chairs. They are always floating an inch or two above the floor, usually in a kneeling or cross-legged position. As Mike sits down, I see him as he was in two other lives. It's like these [personages] come out from and then go back into his body, as if I were seeing it on a film as two translucent overlays. These lives are those most strongly connected to his involvement with Jim in this life, so he brings the memory and personality remnants from those lives to this.

"Mike is obviously feeling joy, love, and happiness. It seems that you, Jim, have asked for him. It's not a case of you looking for this kind of individual to interact with; you actually requested *him*. You called him out from your soul group and asked him to play a part in your life. He is eager and glad to do so.

Mike:	What would you have me do?
Jim:	I would have you accompany me early on in life so that we may continue our long walks and talks.

"Jim, you are referring to that life in the Vatican, when you pursued the priesthood and he mentored you.

Jim:	It would comfort me to play with you in my childhood. It would strengthen me to know you are there. Your support and guidance have consistently been of great value to me.
Mike: (laughing)	I know.
Jim:	I am not ready to relinquish that so easily or so quickly in this life. I wonder if you might do me a favor.

Mike:	What is that?
Jim:	If you might agree to be my partner and allow me to explore my sexuality with you in a way that would be loving, emotionally supportive, and tremendously freeing for me.
Mike:	What do you mean?
Jim:	It is my hope that we can frame this great trust and love we have into a relationship—two men loving each other. In this exploration you would give me a tremendous gift that will help me use my inner strength and enable me to come to the full comprehension of my personal truth. You see, I have chosen to experience this life as a gay male ...

"I didn't know we used the word *gay* on the soul level," Staci interjected. "This may be my conscious representation of the word that was used.

Jim:	... because I believe this will bring me to the point of having to love myself with an unconditional acceptance I intend to use to strengthen me and to give me the gift of compassion, so I may bring what I have learned and embraced about myself to others.
	It is my quest to bring self-acceptance and self-love into the hearts of many. Since I am comfortable in the presence of men, and since I strengthened my understanding of the male experience of emotions and spirituality through my sojourn as a priest, I feel I must embrace those men and even women who are learning to come to a place of comfort about themselves but who have not reached it yet. I will bring together those seeking

wholeness and show them possible paths to their own heart, their own soul, their own wisdom.

You will give me a tremendous gift if you will allow this to happen in our relationship in this life.

Mike: Of course I will! Although it is not my plan to embrace this kind of sexuality or life expression, I want you to succeed. In the times we have been in human form, I have tried to instill in you a respect and reverence for that which is in your being. There were times when this had to be presented to you in terms of a greater love, the love of God, for example.

Jim: Yes, I know.

Mike: You have experienced that love as more than a concept.

Jim: Yes.

Mike: You have experienced the love of All That Is and the humbling that comes from recognizing you are but one of so much that is beyond you, the humbleness that comes from your recognition of your small place in the Universe and the recognition that each place in the Universe is beautiful, warm, and purposeful.

Jim: Yes, this I know.

Mike: Why wouldn't I want to give you this gift? If this is what you require in your next step toward the embracing of loving wholeness, I welcome the opportunity to give it to you.

Jim: Are you sure? What if we don't spend all of our lives together?

Mike: There has always been a portion of one or the other of our lives that has not been lived completely with the other. This would not be startling

	to me. It would not be new. I can embrace and agree to that. I do not need you to be in my life to experience completeness or loving wholeness, nor do I need you to be my loving companion. I would like you to be my friend.
Jim:	A solid foundation of loving friendship, kindness, and trust will be firmly established in our first twenty years, if we can keep to this plan.
Mike:	Yes.
Jim:	After which our relationship can be as deep as you want or any expression of love and kindness you may want. I do not need you to love me in this way my entire life. I've always come to you for guidance and instruction, and so it is this I seek from you, in addition to friendship.
Mike:	You have it. This will work according to my plans for this life as well, in that it will give me something to remember and reflect upon for a long time. It will redirect my focus toward certain relational issues I continue to challenge myself with, honesty being one of them, and also transform the way I see myself, giving me an experience through which I, too, may embrace unconditional love and self-acceptance.

"Mike's hands had been together palm-to-palm or sometimes just one resting on top of the other. Now they go palm up.

Mike:	Why not?

"There is laughter between you and Mike and a hug. Then Mike gets up and floats away from the pre-birth chart, back into the soul group area."

Staci concluded her glimpse into Jim's pre-birth planning session. It was now time to talk with Staci's spirit guide. I asked him to tell us more about why Jim had planned his life as he had.

"This individual soul's solace has always been found through hard-won battles," came the guide's reply, "such as in the life when this individual declared its renunciation of the life its parents expected and instead went into the priesthood as a process of knowing itself, of communing with its being and thus All That Is and the God-consciousness beyond it. In other lives he advocated for others in various forms, from the holding of a sword and shield in more ancient Earth lives to the present day in which this soul advocates for others in terms of discourse—what it speaks, how it listens, how it perceives, and in the gentle guidance and directing of individual forms toward wholeness.

"Through many lifetimes and all the times in between, this soul has often superceded the needs of its own self and personality with the needs of others. There has been an acknowledgment that there has been overlooked the necessary focus on the nurturing of oneself and the utilization of certain principles of unconditional love for and acceptance of self. It took many lives for this soul to come to certain knowledge of and embrace the fact that all love must first come from self-love and then to learn to love itself, whole and pure, in the way it perceives God loves it, in the way we all sense our connectedness with what you term the Divine.

"In this life, as part of its quest toward self-mastery and the integration of self so as to form a more complete and perfect whole and be of better service to others, this soul chose finally to embrace self and to create an environment through which it would experience the contrast of love with a body type that is not considered the normal expression of love in the culture. This soul essentially had no choice but to come face-to-face with itself and with desires that were so strong they could not be ignored, so as to put this soul on a perfect path for itself and to cause it to have a recognition of its truth, requiring this individuated personality to embrace itself with an aspect of self-love that has not been experienced before. By doing this it completes the whole picture of what love is."

These stirring words indicated to me that Jim had magnificently forged a degree of self-love unlike that attained in any of his previous lives. Yet, had Jim's gradual awakening to his true nature and then painful separation from Sue truly been necessary? I asked Staci's guide why Jim hadn't planned simply to accept his sexuality earlier in life.

"It was very important for the individual [Jim] to embrace the norms of society," answered the spirit guide. "It wanted to experience life in the mainstream. It felt it had taken itself out of mainstream life in some previous lives, particularly so in one lifetime with the entity Mike, which has been discussed, where there was a priesthood in common between the two of them.

"In this life, the present one, this individual wanted to experience the wholeness and completion of relationship with Sue, but beyond that it felt that its road, its best path to discovery of love of self, would be to walk through the norm in your society, to experience the thoughts of a heterosexual man. This individuated soul wanted to walk the path of acceptance, and at this time and place the frame of acceptance was within your straight society, one man married to one woman.

"This soul has in many lives walked the path so many others have walked, something that is not outside the norm, not outside what is acceptable. It has remained within the limits of acceptable behavior and finds a great sense of stability and self-worth through this process. It did not want to go back over previous lessons. The soul of James has already in your terms 'been there, done that,' and so it sought to walk the normal path through the time it set for itself. Then it would begin to experience the difference, the imbalance, and access exactly what this soul intended to access: finding the balance within itself instead of experiencing the emotional rollercoaster it could have experienced as it tried to please all at the same time.

"This individual remained true to what pleased itself and to the experience of love as it was felt within. And so, by following the course of love through the normal marriage to a woman, it found its worth, value, strength, and self-identification as a man. This individual embraced and thus utilized it [heterosexuality] as a platform, very strongly built, upon which it could base itself and then move forward. It was simply, you might say, a jumping-off platform. It gave this soul a more balanced perspective from which to pursue life than any other path or lifestyle would have."

I then asked Staci's guide to speak more broadly about homosexuality.

"Sometimes this experience is just sexual; sometimes it is a wholehearted embrace of love of the same sex. Most often, when experienced once or twice, the soul will continue along a path in physical form of what you call heterosexual love. About twenty percent of all souls enjoy playing in self-expression as homosexuals, whether male or female. For them it offers a safe journey through the experiences they desire. They become more and more comfortable in embracing that form and play in it for many more lives—five, ten, fifteen, twenty. Remember, please, that this is just a part of life experience. It is experienced not only in your planetary system, but also in others, though the male/female expression is a bit different. Your planetary system is more for the experience of certain emotional concepts, such as love and fear, desire and longing.

"It [experiencing homosexuality] is a desire. When felt, it is acted upon. There are many of us who have not had that experience, yet we have experienced many more lives in many other places than you [humans]. You would say that we are wise. We do not lack understanding of the experience, nor is it an aversion. It is, rather, a total and complete understanding of it through service to those who have gone through it. And so, the experience is complete within ourselves without ever having to embody and embrace homosexuality."

"For what other reasons do souls choose to be homosexual?"

"An experience in a prior life, where, because of its sexual role, the soul was enslaved, injured, or killed and does not wish to experience that again. So, it comes back as the opposite sex but is not yet ready to love the opposite sex and so loves the same. For example, if one has been a woman abused by a man, one may choose to incarnate very quickly again as a man so as not to be in a less than fully powerful position. But, one will not be ready to make the switch to love a woman. So, one will contract with another soul, also in male form, so that there is a feeling of safety, closeness, and rapport, and so that experiences can be gained. There would be a lack of comfort in having a relationship with a woman, and so one continues to be in relationships with the male."

Jim then asked why a soul would choose to incarnate as a heterosexual.

"There is the interaction, the playing with the opposite sex in terms of heterosexuality, that provides unique experiences," the guide told us. "In your planetary system there is a school of opposites, defined often as 'contrasting experience.' When male is in relationship with female, there are many opportunities to embrace various learning concepts that would not occur in conscious thought or be observed by the individual without the contrast of the opposite sex. Being in concert with the opposite sex puts you in concert with opposites [in general]; it is part and parcel of the experience of this schoolhouse. In some other planetary systems, there are different forms of procreation, different personality structures, greater and lesser expressions of duo-sexuality."

"I understand that in other planetary systems there are more than two genders and that some actually have five," I commented.

"These other planetary systems extend some of the lessons gained in your planetary system and also give access to many other lessons that are not able to be experienced or contained in your system. A large part is not describable to you because you do not have the words and because this channel does not have imagination capable of it." Staci's guide was referring in general to the human mind, which cannot conceive of much of what exists in the Universe. "We hope this is enough to satisfy your need at this time."

"Jim chose to be Catholic," I said to the guide. "He was taught growing up that masturbation is a sin. Why was that planned? He could have chosen another religion."

"This induced into the personality the necessary message, both subliminal and conscious, that self-love and love of the penis were wrong. Remember that this soul chose to embrace the experience of opposites. Although these messages were induced in this current life, they were never harbored in the life in which this soul journeyed through the Vatican. And so, these messages—the sin of self-love, the sin of masturbation, the sin of the body—were an affront to this personality, one this personality would look at and reflect upon for some time and come to reject in its process of embracing unconditional love of self in all forms. It was simply a concept that needed to be presented and induced into this personality's life to set up the struggle of contrasts that would result in unconditional love and acceptance."

"One last question. Jim's grandmother told him his body was filthy and embarrassing, and she scrubbed his body clean. What role does she play in Jim's evolution?"

"She embodied an experience that James contracted to have in this life." This individual [the grandmother] has portrayed the role of mother and father in two of his [Jim's] other lives. In this life, this soul was working with concepts and challenges of her own that had nothing to do with James's presence in her life. Her soul-level agreement with James was to provide a certain sense of physical care and thus extend a set of circumstances that would nurture his physical form in the role of family, but more important, she was to provide for him the messages and contrasting experience about one's own body. In addition, her own imbalance would serve as a living example to James of where he did not want to go within his own conscious personality.

"James has long been on a path of a kinder, gentler, less extreme expression of his inner nature. His grandmother, on the other hand, has not, and they have not experienced a friendship in any of their lives together. In this life her role was to be antagonist, to provide the input of contrasting messages, messages that were opposite to the experience this soul desired to have in physical form."

Jim's Session with Corbie

To add to the wisdom that Staci and her guide had shared with us, I asked Corbie to peer into Jim's past lives. Corbie opened with her customary prayer, which served both to establish a link with the nonphysical beings who would guide us and to set a clear intent—that we be granted an understanding of Jim's pre-birth plan.

"The first pivotal life I see," Corbie said after finishing her prayer, "was in sixth-century Kenya. Jim, you were a little aberrant in your behavior, but you were considered a shaman, madman, or wise man, depending on who was looking at you. You dressed in androgynous clothing. You did not want the 'I am a guy, I hunt, I procreate' [lifestyle]. You talked to things [etheric beings] that were 'out there.' You said it was your way of enticing God to come and dance with your people and that you were given this instruction by the sun. Your people had a very basic religion: God *was* the sun. That's where everybody thought God lived.

"When you began to give prophecies, everyone thought you were crazy. But, you had a sense of nature, a very deep one. You could sense eclipses, celestial movements, and when droughts would happen. One day you said, 'The moon will bleed with fury at their mockery, and the sun will turn his wrath on them.' Sure enough, after that there was a lunar eclipse—the moon had this reddish tinge—and then a drought. You predicted the end of the drought correctly. So, as far as your people were concerned, nothing was too good for you because you held their lives in your hands. When they said, 'What do you want?' you said a husband, not because of the sexuality but because in that civilization husbands hunted and fed people.

"Sue was a heterosexual male who was told by the tribal elders, 'You're it.' He was gifted to you. There wasn't any sexual intercourse, and the husband/wife duties were very delineated. When there had to be the planting of the fields, there was 'sexual magic'—ritual—but it wasn't carnal. This is where sexuality was first pulled away from the idea of lust.

"The next life I see was where you and Mike were serving as priests. You acknowledged that there were feelings for each other, but you ignored them in order to stay true to your vows. Mike said to you, 'In Heaven, where there is no body and no carnal lust, our feelings will be more appropriate and understood by God. It is our broken forms here that mistranslate this deep affection.' This was apparently something he wrote to you, because I see these words on parchment.

"In the next life I pick up," Corbie continued, "Mike is your father. Mike says to you, 'It's never enough for a father just to raise his son to have more kids. It's a father's duty to provide for the rest of the generations.' With that [in mind] you married, and here again it was Sue. You got her pregnant, but sex was a duty for you because your father had said to provide for the generations. So, you've got to *make* generations. You had a very passionate nature and couldn't understand why you were ignoring her sexually. When she was pregnant—great!—you were off duty for nine months. She was well fed, clothed, and respected in the community, but there was no big love for her. Your love was for the idea of Family—capital F, the next generation—and the populating of the community. After this life was over, Sue said she wanted a life where you really loved her for herself.

"Now, here is a pivotal life for Mike. I see him as a rabbi pouring over scrolls. This is during World War II. He is marked [as Jewish] and taken to a concentration camp. He was not homosexual in that life, but he ministered to the pink triangles [gay men] when not even the other camp victims would. Understand that homosexuals in a concentration camp were given the worst treatment. Even other prisoners were allowed to steal their food.

"Mike saw gay men who truly loved one another. They were diseased, exhausted, and starved, but love was still there. That woke him up to something greater than self. The rabbi's personality was so moved by the love these homosexual men had for one another that he decided to come back with you this time, saying 'I want to prove that to myself.'"

As I took in Corbie's words, I realized that Mike had been motivated by the simple desire to experience something he had observed in a prior life, not an unusual motivation in pre-birth planning. As souls we seek to experience everything. Indeed, there is nothing to do in the Universe other than gift ourselves with different types of experiences.

"The sexuality between you and Sue," Corbie summarized, "always goes south no matter which life it is, because you always need to think bigger. You and Mike always tried to ignore any kind of sexual connection and still have a heart connection. That is why you came into the father-son life. You always come to create something that is 'a baby not of the flesh.' When Sue chooses to go through some of her toughest lessons, it's usually with Mike there, either as a spirit guide or in the flesh, to help her make sense of it. He's the most evolved of the three of you."

"Corbie," I asked, "earlier you said 'the next life.' I know there's a sequence to lives, and yet I also know that from the soul's perspective all lives happen concurrently. Can you explain?"

"It's like a banquet," Corbie offered. "A really fine chef can do the soufflé, the salad, the turkey, and the hors d'oeuvres at the same time, but when you dine, you dine in courses. Or, it's like having all the chess pieces on the board at once. Which ones are we moving? Which ones are we looking at? A chess player has to think six moves ahead. Whatever he does with this move at this time, four moves later it's going to affect the queen. If we can do something like chess with our limited minds, then surely we can do it when we are out of body."

"Corbie, Jim told me that Sue is infertile. Did Jim and Sue plan her infertility, and if so, why?"

"Yes," Corbie replied, certainty in her voice. "Sue wanted to be loved for herself, not for what she could provide. Often if a woman has children much of her individuality gets stuck in a corner until the kids are out of the nest. She came in female, able to be loved by and married to you, Jim, but not having children meant that she would have your full attention for as long as she could."

"Corbie, Jim also told me he grew up Catholic and, more specifically, was taught that masturbation is a sin. Why was that chosen?"

"What I am hearing [from Spirit] is that it kept him at least outwardly heterosexual, 'straight lined' until he was mature enough to have the relationship with Mike. Also, if your best understanding is that heterosexual life is right and you marry, and then the homosexuality comes in full force anyway, it's less diluted." In other words, I thought, Jim had wanted not simply *an* experience of himself as gay, but rather a particularly *intense* experience of all that meant.

"Jim," Corbie added, "if you had come in with a gay orientation and had spent your life thinking of yourself as gay, you would be a different person. You wouldn't be able to understand viscerally what it is to live a straight life and then what it is to discover the life of a homosexual man and be fulfilled."

I then asked Corbie to explain the difference between a soul who plans a lifetime in which it realizes and accepts its sexuality early and a soul who plans a later discovery, as Jim had.

"Going from a straight to a gay self-recognition," Corbie answered, "is like people who have been lifelong Catholics and then convert to Judaism. It is like someone who is a racist and then discovers what it is to be on the progressive end of the civil rights movement. I am getting a picture [from Spirit]. It's the difference between rolling hills and mountains. With rolling hills you are walking and eventually you get tired, but you are not aware of the ups and downs. When you climb a mountain, it is a heightened experience. You have the cleats digging into the rock and the pitons making sure you don't fall."

"Corbie, what are the lessons for Jim in this lifetime?"

"Being able to see love as something bigger than the people involved. Being able to see himself as something bigger than just this one particular incarnation. For Sue the lesson is, I am hearing, to love and let go. Mike is here to start things rolling but then to step back.

"Jim," Corbie went on, "there is something about you when I connect with your energy. There is the sense that I can allow myself to cry, not out of pain but out of relief and gratitude because *somebody sees me.* That's all any of us truly wants—to be seen for who we are. People like you who see us for who we are instead of what we've been told we are or ought to be are the generous angels in ordinary clothing who hold out a golden key and say, 'Here's the key to you. Do you want it? I see where it fits. I will stay here until you do.' There is an incredible trust that the other person, even if not seeing it at that moment, will get it right. This, I think, is why on the soul level Mike loves working with you. It's not going to be long before you have evolved to where he is. You are one of his star pupils.

"If you get quiet, you can sense the heartbeat of the world, slow and deep and resonant. There is a peace there that is also within you, Jim. Because you have anchored that, you can hold it out to other people in big ways and small. You can believe in them when they don't believe in themselves. Whether you say that to them out loud or there is just that little bit of knowing in you that holds the pilot light for them, that's where you are."

"This is exactly what I do with people!" Jim exclaimed. "I get this feedback all the time. It's a mysterious thing. I don't exactly understand it in myself, but it's what I gift to the world, absolutely.

"My gayness was terrific for the struggle around self-acceptance. That has informed my ability to support others in finding self-acceptance, whether it is around sexuality, race, or whatever."

"Corbie," I said, "please speak to people reading these words who know or believe they are gay but are having difficulty accepting it."

"You don't say, 'I wish I had a hand there, but it's a foot,'" Corbie replied. "If there were no morals, no right or wrong, you would not judge it. When you judge your own sexual orientation as wanting, void of purity, or the only way to be, you are seeing limits. You are looking at how the world views it, not what is. Try looking at what you are as neutral. That's when 'gay' is simply who you are. People who are born with a heterosexual bent don't keep looking at themselves and asking, 'Why am I straight?' It's simply what they accept about themselves. So to those who are still wrestling, please believe that what you are wrestling with is not your own rightness or wrongness; it is simply how you are reacting to you within the context of the world.

"After all, when we are out of the body, we are everything and nothing."

～

Self-love.

As souls incarnating on the Earth plane, our pre-birth planning in general, and the planning of challenges in particular, is often based on an intent to cultivate self-love. To love ourselves we must first accept ourselves, for only what is accepted can be loved. To accept ourselves we must first know who we are. With wisdom Jim crafted a majestic pre-birth plan that was intended to, and did, lead to self-discovery, then self-acceptance, and ultimately self-love.

Jim's self-discovery occurred when he stepped onto Liberty Street that remarkable day. Before he was born, he wisely designed the circumstances—the strict Catholic upbringing, the shaming grandmother—that prevented such self-realization from taking place earlier in his life. As Staci's guide told us, these elements of Jim's background kept him on the path accepted by society, the path he needed to construct a solid platform from which to launch a new way of living. Jim's life plan also included an essential component that would facilitate that launch: a loving, nonjudgmental father. In selecting his father, Jim chose someone who provided the openhearted acceptance of homosexuality that would later make his self-discovery possible. Without that nonjudgment Jim might well have repressed an awareness of his sexuality much longer, perhaps even for a lifetime.

I am often asked how one may come into a knowing of one's pre-birth plan. If you seek to understand your plan, look closely at the circumstances in which you were born—the historical time period; its culture, norms, and mores; your race, religion, and economic status—as well as the attitudes and beliefs of those who played key roles in your formative years. Often you will see a scripting of opposing forces that causes a powerful and unavoidable dynamic tension. Look particularly closely at these forces, for the tension they generate is imbued with deep purpose. Before birth each of us desires to experience such tension because it both triggers and fosters our spiritual evolution. In Jim's life the dynamic tension was between an inner voice that urged repression—the echoes of his judging grandmother and the religious figures who taught that masturbation was a sin—and an opposing inner voice that urged compassion, a compassion derived from his father's loving acceptance of others.

Within that inner tension lies choice, and the choice is always between love and fear. From the perspective of the soul, it is the choice, the exercising of our free will that makes life a grand adventure, one to be sought again and again. As souls we hope we will make the choice for love. When we do we raise our vibration, imbue ourselves with light, and cultivate divine virtues like courage that become part of us literally for all eternity.

In the time between his self-discovery on Liberty Street and the moment he disclosed his new self-awareness to Sue, Jim battled with the choice between love and fear. Though a relatively brief two weeks, this time was an *inflection point* in his life, a period in which a key choice would be made that could well determine his direction for much of this incarnation. Jim could have succumbed to fear—fear of hurting Sue, fear of her possible judgments, fear of the internalized voice of repression he still carried—and decide to conceal his sexuality from Sue. Yet, this is not the choice he

...ade. Bravely, he summoned his inner strength and told Sue that he was attracted to men. His choice was profoundly meaningful because it required him to rise above much of the conditioning of his childhood and the fear it had fostered.

Jim's life is, therefore, about much more than experiencing himself as a gay man. It is about choosing courageously to be true to himself. In the moment Jim chose to be honest with Sue, he raised the frequency of his consciousness. Too, he experienced and thus knew himself as courage, a powerful experience for the soul and one that makes life on the physical plane exquisitely desirable. Had fear not been present, courage would have been neither required nor experienced. For you who resent or resist the people or circumstances in your life that give rise to fear, know this: They are there at your behest so that you may make the choice to be courageous. This realization will engender gratitude for their presence. The high vibration of gratitude is incompatible with the low vibration of fear and so utterly transforms it.

In this beautiful way, fear is turned upon itself as it generates the consciousness that heals the fear. Such is the pre-birth plan of many souls incarnating today. Because you are reading these words, you sought before birth to heal fear on this planet and knew that you would be given ample opportunity to do so. Every soul in body at this time has the capacity to heal fear in some way; you could not be present if you lacked this capacity. Every choice of love over fear cultivates the quality of courage within our souls and brings healing to both the individual and the Earth as a whole. Each such decision ushers in the Golden Age, an age you came to create and be part of, and renders a dramatic upliftment of human consciousness unlike any the planet has ever seen.

Jim's courageous choice to accept his sexuality and the choice of love over fear formed the touchstone of the self-love he now enjoys. All who experience themselves as courage grow in self-love. Many wonder why, after making a courageous decision, the feeling of self-love later fades and difficult circumstances recur.

The Universe always supports a courageous decision, but it also requires the individual *to continue to make courageous decisions, one after another.* Many are not able to do so. When they do not, their light quite literally dims, and their diminished vibration remagnetizes challenges into their lives. These challenges are planned as potentials prior to birth, and they constitute some of the timelines Staci sees in the pre-birth planning charts. When Jim and Sue moved to California and Jim chose a "return to repression," that is, when he reversed some of his previously courageous decisions by choosing fear over love, he drew to himself a period of difficulty that was intended to allow him to choose again. Ultimately, Jim grew in self-love, not because he made one brave decision to disclose his sexuality to Sue but because he made many courageous choices over a period of years. His road to self-love was steep, long, and made longer by a detour into repression, yet courageously did he continue.

Because teaching *is* learning, pre-birth plans are designed to afford us the opportunity to teach what we most need to learn. At times the teacher is recognized as such in a formal sense, but more often we plan to teach others through what we live— through example, struggle, and even what appears to be failure. Jim sought to learn to love himself in this lifetime and so planned the potential, activated and realized by his free will, for coming to terms with his attraction to men within the context of a marriage to a woman. Sue had the identical intention for this lifetime—to learn to love herself—and so planned the experience of being married to a gay man, an experience she hoped would break open her heart and deliver her to a place of self-love. Both she and Jim hoped he would serve as her example and teacher, and he did so with love. Similarly, in her struggle to love herself, Sue served as example and teacher to Jim. Their pre-birth plans and their lives when in body mirrored each other in these fundamental ways. It is here that we see a central tenet of pre-birth planning: families, both those into which we are born and those we later create, often choose to be together because the members are teaching and learning the same lessons. Commonly, that lesson is self-love. If Sue someday understands that Jim loves her and chose with love to be her example and teacher, she may forgive him. If you were or are the partner of someone who hurt you by coming into an awareness of sexuality, consider that this person may have done so at your request, in service to you, out of love for you.

What then of parents who struggle to accept their child's sexuality? If you are such a parent, your child knew before birth that you would have this struggle and chose you not in spite of it but because of it. Your struggle is both an opportunity to learn to love and a form of service to your child. Remember, in the physical realm nothing is as it appears. Had your child wanted a parent who would experience no such difficulty, a different choice would have been made. The pre-birth choice of a parent is always made with love and wisdom.

Why would a child choose a parent who will struggle with that child's sexuality? For the same reason Jim planned the challenges he faced: as a profound impetus to self-love. This awareness permits parents to forgive themselves for any judgments of the child. Parents' self-forgiveness is the beginning of both greater self-love and a healing of the relationship with the child. If you have judged your child, gently embrace your judgments and yourself with forgiveness and compassion rather than judgment of judgment. Be at peace in the understanding that your child's choice of you as parent was perfect. Nothing less is possible.

And if you experienced or contend now with self-judgment or the judgments of others in regard to your sexuality, know that you are among the most courageous of souls. Your journey toward self-acceptance and self-love blazes an energetic trail that makes it easier for all persons, even those who will never meet or know of you, to accept and love not only their sexuality but also all aspects of their being. What you gift to yourself, you extend to everyone.

You are the world's teacher, a blessing to one and all.

CHAPTER 8

∞∞

Incest

DURING THE WRITING OF MY first book, I came
into contact with a woman—I will call her Paula—who
had been sexually abused by her father. Both Paula's
father and mother died years ago. Through a medium we were
able to speak with them. They explained that the potential for
incest had been agreed upon by all prior to their birth. Paula's
father told us that he and Paula's mother had past lives in which
both of them had sexually abused their children. They had carried
this "energy of incest" into body not for the purpose of expressing
it, but rather with the intention of healing it. What we hoped,
Paula's father said, was that incest would not happen and that
the "energy of incest" would be healed if and when he controlled
his impulses. Because it was unclear before birth whether Paula's
father would be able to do so, Paula's mother created a contract
with Paula in which she agreed to protect Paula from her father.
Unfortunately, Paula's mother failed to protect her, and Paula's
father did commit incest.

The conversation with Paula's parents was deeply moving.
Both her father and mother were profoundly remorseful. Both
apologized repeatedly. Both begged for Paula's forgiveness. And
in a moment of extraordinary poignancy, Paula's mother said to
her, "I always loved you. I even loved the smell of your hair."
Paula, the medium, and I were in tears. Paula later told me that

the conversation healed wounds that had been with her for her entire life. It was then I realized that an exploration of the pre-birth planning of incest could bring a similar kind of healing to others.

As I considered the subject of incest for this book, I alternated between viewing it through the lens of the soul and the human lens. From the soul perspective I saw once again an opportunity to offer healing, and I felt hopeful as well as humbled and honored to do this work. From the human perspective, however, I felt fear. How could I possibly suggest to the world, and in particular to people who have experienced incest, that something so traumatic would, or even could, be planned by a soul? If the Universe were indeed asking me to put forth this awareness, how could I do so with love and compassion? In particular, I was concerned that those who have experienced incest might feel blamed, even though at the soul level we feel no blame, judgment, or guilt in regard to the planning of any experience. I prayed, asked for guidance, and moved forward knowing that my path would be illuminated.

In this chapter you will meet Debbie, whose story differs from Paula's in a fundamental way. Although Paula and her parents hoped that incest would not occur, Debbie and the members of her family felt before birth that incest was highly likely. Out of deep love and in service to her parents, Paula was willing to assume the risk and decided before birth that if it happens she would use incest as a catalyst to growth. Debbie, by contrast, knew that incest was the most probable path and so designed a life plan based upon that probability.

Paula's story was offered as an alternative to the story you are about to read. If you have experienced incest, please allow your intuition, not your logical mind, to guide you in discerning whether your life plan is more like Paula's or Debbie's. *Feel* your way into that question. As you do, be gentle and loving with yourself. Bathe yourself in compassion, and allow any thoughts or emotions of blame of others, self-blame, anger, or anything else that may arise to move through you without judgment. Remember, you are *not* your thoughts or emotions; rather, these are things you have. Jeshua advises viewing these thoughts and feelings as tender, young children calling out for understanding and love. Be the wise and gentle parent to them, embracing them as you would embrace your own child. Healing comes through loving all and not rejecting any parts of ourselves.

Debbie is someone who might be referred to as an incest survivor. Yet, Debbie has done much more than survive incest; she has created for herself a life in which she thrives. In my conversations with her, it was clear she had healed herself in quite profound ways. A skilled psychotherapist, Debbie now devotes her life to guiding clients along the healing path she knows so well. Debbie's healing emerged from an intensive process that included conversations with her guides, angels, and family members in Spirit who spoke to her of her pre-birth plan to experience incest. For Debbie, these conversations were blessings that empowered her to understand and heal the pain of her childhood. It is rare for me to meet someone who has been gifted with such insight into her life plan. I felt I had been guided to Debbie so that I might share her experience and her healing with the world.

Debbie

"I noticed around age thirty-five that I had a lot of behaviors, thoughts, and feelings that didn't make sense," Debbie told me. Age fifty-four at the time of our conversation, Debbie radiates warmth and kindness. "I didn't understand why I turned out that way and how come I had so many problems through my life.

"I started looking at myself and realized I could hardly remember anything about my childhood. This was before I became a therapist. I didn't trust anyone. On the surface I was friendly and open, but I never let anyone too close. I behaved seductively toward men, but when they got close, I would run away. I cried every time I had sex."

In addition to difficulties with men, Debbie was troubled for many years by a need to exercise rigid control over her daily schedule and home environment. She battled insomnia, particularly if guests were sleeping in her home. She drank a great deal of alcohol. She felt worthless, unlovable, and undeserving and was plagued by guilt and shame, all without knowing why.

Debbie described her father as an alcoholic who was weak and afraid of her mother. For most of her life, she remembered little about him.

As a child, Debbie suffered from intense anxiety and was given tranquilizers. She displayed obsessive-compulsive behavior, washing her hands again and again often to the point of making her skin raw. She feared being abandoned and frequently hid in the closet of her bedroom.

Problems in relationships with boys first surfaced in high school. "I'd go out on one date," she recalled, "and then I'd get repelled, for what reason I didn't know, and then never speak to the boy again. It was nothing he did.

"I did have one boyfriend through college. Finally, he broke up with me and started dating other girls, but I would still go over to his apartment to have sex with him. I thought I'd always have a piece of him that way. He kept calling me back, so I thought there was something about me that was special."

Through much of college, Debbie battled severe depression. After a suicide attempt, she left school and returned home, eventually becoming a flight attendant.

"That's when I started one-night stands," she said. "They were all the wrong men, and all for the wrong reasons. I could have been killed, but I didn't care. I thought this was the only way I could get men to like me. I hated myself. I was miserable and lost." As Debbie spoke, there was no trace of shame or self-judgment in her voice but simply a compassionate understanding of who she had been at that time in her life.

Debbie met and married her first husband, an older man who made her feel safe and secure. "But, I still had me and my problems there," she acknowledged. During the first years of their marriage, Debbie miscarried, then later had an ectopic pregnancy. She was diagnosed with severe endometriosis. "These reproductive problems were signs of what had happened, trying to get my attention, but I didn't connect the dots," she observed.

Depressed, unhappy, and convinced that her husband was the cause of her unhappiness, Debbie left her marriage and moved in with her father. Soon thereafter more clues to her childhood emerged.

"I woke up in panic attacks, where I couldn't breathe," she recalled. "I felt like someone was choking me. Just intense fear. I never slept though a night."

Over the next few years and following her divorce, Debbie remarried and completed a graduate degree in psychology. She became a counselor at a domestic violence shelter, working with people who had been sexually assaulted or molested.

"I noticed that some of the things they were experiencing, like anxiety, I also did," she said. "That was part of the [pre-birth] plan. There were opportunities for me to remember, but I wasn't ready to listen."

A subsequent position at a community mental health center provided Debbie with further insight.

"I'm sitting there across from the client," she recalled, "listening to their story, thinking how similar their symptoms are to mine. One day I thought, I wonder if I was molested?" Debbie also began to feel inexplicably angry with her father, her anger increasing the longer she worked at the health center. Soon circumstances intervened to answer the question she had posed to herself.

"My in-laws had to move in with us. I quit my job to take care of them. As soon as I quit, I had the time to fall apart, and so it all came flooding back. I finally realized the truth. And it wasn't just in my head that I knew; I knew in my whole body. I knew in my heart. I realized my whole life had been a lie, that everything I thought was true was not, and that I was going to have to work really hard to make sense of everything."

Debbie began to experience flashbacks to her childhood, some of which were so frightening that she spent nights sleeping on the floor with her back against the wall. That way, she felt, no one could sneak up on her.

"My bed was against the wall," Debbie said, her voice suddenly tense as she recalled one of the flashbacks. "I remember trying to be so still and so quiet. Maybe if I don't move, nothing bad will happen. I remember feeling nausea and fear. My heart starts to pound. My body feels hot; there is heat running up and down my arms and legs. I know something is going to happen. There is nothing I can do to stop it. I'm powerless.

"I look at the door. It's dark, but there's some light coming from the hallway. I see his [her father's] shadow moving toward me. He just keeps moving toward me. He gets close. I smell the gin. I feel the roughness of his beard against me. I don't like it. *I'm really scared!* I want to scream, but I don't.

"It feels so wrong! But I don't know it's wrong, because I can't talk to anybody about it. My mother knows and doesn't do anything. So, I think maybe something's wrong with me. Nobody seems to care."

After that flashback Debbie understood something that had long puzzled her: though she had consumed much alcohol over the years, she had never been able to tolerate the taste of gin. Now she knew why.

As memories from childhood surfaced, Debbie began to suffer from nightmares as well.

"There was one I had over and over. I'm an adult in the dream. I'm in a public bathroom. There's blood everywhere. I knew it would be really bad if anybody saw that, so I was frantically trying to clean the bathroom. I got it done just as I heard people entering the next room. I went into the next room; it was a therapy group. Everybody was taking their seats. I looked across the circle. My father was sitting there next to a psychologist I worked with who treated people who had been molested.

"I couldn't sleep for months," she added. "I cried. I wailed. There were times my husband would take his parents out of the house so I could let myself go. *It hurt so deep inside me.* I would crawl around on the floor like some kind of wounded, helpless animal. That was releasing part of the hurt I couldn't get to any other way. Thankfully, I allowed myself to do whatever I needed to do to heal."

Debbie purchased *The Courage to Heal* and worked through the exercises. At times she sat on her patio and screamed furiously at her parents—*'How dare you! How could you!'*—letting out the pent-up anger. She tried not to leave home unless necessary. Even a trip to the post office was almost more than she could bear.

"I remember walking into the post office, thinking that on my back were big letters that said, *'I was molested.'* I thought everybody could see it. I wanted to crawl out of there. I was so ashamed and embarrassed."

Despite the pain it entailed, Debbie continued to look within, giving free expression to whatever arose.

"As the emotions came through me, I allowed myself to sit with them versus stuffing them as I had done all my life and which made all the problems I had lived with.

"Then one day I made it for a few hours without crying. As time went on, I made it a few days without crying. And then, finally, I felt a sense of relief, because everything made sense. All my life I thought I was crazy, worthless, and a bad person. It took me awhile to forgive myself for some of the behaviors I engaged in, some of the people I hurt, but now I could move in a direction that was right for me because now I knew the truth."

"Debbie," I asked, "was the incest with only your father?"

"My grandfather, also," she replied. "The reason that's important is because I remembered about him first. To keep sane our minds protect us from how much we know at a time. I let that come into my awareness before I could move on to my father and process the big, painful memory."

"Let's talk more about healing. How did you do it?"

"This is the happy part of the story," Debbie answered, her tone now noticeably brighter. "It took intense symptoms and processes. I started moving back—I call it traveling back to my

Self [soul] with a big S—and I realized that all the things that had happened to me I chose [before birth]. So, it was also in my power what I thought about them and to change the meaning they had in my life.

"That healing process was torturous, but I couldn't stop or I would never come out the other side. Knowing that I had chosen the experience put it all in place. It was for my own growth, what I wanted to do and get out of this lifetime."

"Debbie, it sounds as though your healing consisted of spending time alone, allowing the memories to come back, and then crying and grieving as much was as needed."

"It did," she confirmed. "And also finding a safe place. I found a meditation group and sat in that group for a whole year. I found that supportive place of unconditional love. There was nothing I could say, feel, or do that was so awful they would not continue loving me. Also, during that time I was really deepening my connection with Spirit, realizing who I really am, that other part of me."

I asked Debbie to tell me how she knew she had planned the incest before birth and why she had made those plans.

"I was in meditation on a beach," she told me. "All the members of my family who had died came to me." Debbie later explained that she saw them in her third eye, considered by many the seat of psychic vision. The clarity and quality of the vision was such that Debbie *knew* her loved ones were there with her. "They stood in front of me and said that all that had happened between us was done in love and service. They were pointing to me, saying,

> You wanted to heal the world this time. Your life had to have sorrow, pain, grief, and hurt in enough measure to invoke personal healing. If you had been comfortable, the impetus for personal healing would not be as great. If the hurt were not enough for personal upliftment, your contribution to the world would have been less passionate and significant.
>
> You helped from a safe distance before [in past lives], but when it became your story, too, you had to get involved in a

much deeper, committed way. Through personal healing, you know what it [healing] feels like. You can guide people through their pain in steadfastness and love, because you came through it yourself. Thus, you can be more energetically impactful in the world. You reach more people in healing by the healing of yourself and by your prayers and meditations.

"I thanked each one of them for the part they played in my life," Debbie said. "If they hadn't played their parts so well, I wouldn't be where I am now, in touch with my Spirit. I was able to bless them for helping me find my way back to myself. You take your power back and realize that I planned it all. I was in charge. They were just doing what I asked."

"Did your father and grandfather come to you?"

"My grandfather, my mother, all of my mother's side of the family. My father's still alive. I work with him at the soul level now, because he still denies that anything happened."

This was an essential point. Each of us can communicate directly with the soul of another person. In these communications we may ask that our love for or forgiveness of the person be conveyed for the purpose of healing a relationship. It is then up to that person, the incarnate personality, to decide whether to accept the love and forgiveness. At the soul level, though, every such message is joyfully received. It is well to open and conclude such communications with an expression of gratitude to the person's soul for listening and caring. Gratitude is the equivalent of a static-free interdimensional phone line to the soul.

"In another meditation," Debbie continued, "I was in contact with my mother. I said, 'Why, Mom? Why did we have to do all this?' She said, 'Because you asked.' And she said, 'I'm still working with your father. Just because I'm not in physical form anymore doesn't mean the connection is broken.'"

"Did anyone else in spirit explain to you why you had requested these experiences?" I asked.

"My maternal grandmother said, 'This was laid out a long time ago. The plan was multilayered. You were to heal yourself, your family, and then help the planet to heal. This was a very specific plan and would not have happened without a carefully planned order of events.'

"So, I wanted to do this," added Debbie. "Everything had to fall into place as it did for me to do my work here. I think the incest was the best possible thing that could happen. I've been given information from Spirit that to the depths of pain and grief I felt, that's also as far as I can go in joy and love. And if I don't know the difference, then I wouldn't be able to love as much as I do now."

"Debbie, do you believe your mother's pre-birth plan was *not* to protect you from your father?"

"I think that's true."

"Please speak to those who have experienced incest, are wondering whether it was part of their life plan, and are saying, 'I can't believe I would have planned this.'"

"Honor yourself like no one has honored you before," she advised. "If that means not understanding for right now, then honor that. But sit with it long enough and often enough to allow some higher light into that space. That comes with time and from dedication to yourself and your worth. Whatever your truth is, that's okay.

"And listen to your feelings. Let those feelings move through you, even though they're scary and they hurt and sometimes you feel like you're going crazy. As you release them, it does get easier. Then at the end there may be a different perspective."

"What thoughts would you like to leave people with, Debbie?"

"Start with honoring your feelings and allowing a little space for a miracle to happen. It's out there. It's just a matter of looking for it and allowing it into your life."

After my conversation with Debbie, her guides offered the following message:

> Healing yourself changes the vibrational frequency of your generational line: your past, present, and future selves.

Forgiveness also changes the vibration, which affects all involved. By healing yourself you help uplift the entire planet because you are contributing love, peace, and forgiveness rather than lower vibrational emotions. Stop fighting yourself; surrender and allow. Healing will occur naturally if allowed.

You on Earth in human bodies are to be the channels for healing to pass through to others on Earth. Be still and listen. You are powerful and creative beyond your understanding.

Debbie's Session with Pamela and Jeshua

Debbie's feelings of certainty in regard to her pre-birth plan, as well as the many confirmations she had received from Spirit, were meaningful to me. There is no better indicator of a pre-birth plan than a person's own resonance. Still, I felt myself struggling with the notion that a soul—any soul—would plan incest. I hoped that Pamela and Jeshua would help me and all who read this book to better understand the pre-birth planning of such a difficult life challenge. I also hoped they would offer words of healing to those who have experienced incest.

Prior to the session, I asked Pamela to address specifically the karmic origin of the incest and also the question of why Debbie had not remembered the incest for such a long time.

"Debbie, I will first give you my impressions of your auric field and what I feel about the challenge of incest in your life," Pamela began. "I see a warm cobalt blue in your aura, around your shoulders and head. Through this color I sense that you have deep inner wisdom and that you have achieved a breakthrough in your inner evolution this lifetime. I can feel that in daily life you are always seeking to stay attuned to your inner guidance, your soul's mission. You have surrendered to a higher wisdom. You have connected to your own greater Being, your soul. This radiates a sense of peace and balance to me.

"What helps to fully heal is to stay attuned to negative emotions that may come up inside you and *allow them full expression.*

By that I mean allow yourself to fully feel them in your body. Ask them what message they have for you. I feel that sometimes you so dearly want peace and harmony to pervade your life that you neglect the negative emotions a bit. There's a little girl hiding inside these emotions, one who still has some anger and sadness about the past, not just the abuse but also for not having been taken seriously as the beautiful and wise child you were. I sense that as a child you had a gift to offer to the world, and you felt this gift was not truly recognized and appreciated by your environment. At the same time, at a deep level you have healed yourself and have genuinely forgiven the people around you. You have moved beyond feeling a victim; the emotional pain I see is only remnants."

Here Pamela was echoing an important point Debbie had made in her conversation with me: that emotions need expression. In midlife Debbie realized that her habit of repressing pain, though understandable, had led directly to many of her difficulties. It was only when Debbie gave expression to those emotions, when she angrily cursed her parents and howled like a wounded animal, that healing came. Evidently, though, even deeper healing was possible.

"It's important to address this [the remnants of anger and sadness]," Pamela continued. "Your energy will become more firm and grounded. By staying attuned to the wounded child inside and allowing her to express the pain she still carries, you will create a space of understanding that is even wider than it is now."

Then Spirit created an image in Pamela's mind, a metaphor for Debbie's healing.

"I see a tree that is already strong, but if it gets more water and sunshine, the roots will go deeper and the tree will become green and grow abundantly. The tree stands for your energy, Debbie. As I see it now, it radiates strength and perseverance, a deep inner knowledge, and the sense that you 'made it through.' But, the tree I see has no leaves, and the ground it stands in is a bit dry and a bit in the shadows. The tree would benefit from more water and being in a more open spot, where it can catch more sunlight.

"Water stands for emotions," Pamela explained. "You may allow yourself *to go with the flow of your emotions* a little more. Trust that these will bring you to a point of balance if you let them freely flow through you, without judgment or attachment."

This was a crucial insight. When we judge an emotion as bad, we create an energetic attachment to it. This attachment can strengthen the emotion and, if strong enough, fix the emotion in our experience. Thus, we create more of the very emotion we most want to dispel.

"The open spot and the sunshine," continued Pamela, "stand for allowing yourself to take up more space, coming out of the shadows, and owning your strength and radiance. It is about a sense of self-worth and taking yourself seriously, which have nothing to do with ego. You may allow yourself to more deeply sense your own greatness, your alignment with your soul and Spirit. By honoring your accomplishments and taking yourself seriously, your spiritual energy will become more rooted, more anchored to Earth, and therefore touch others even more deeply.

"I will now look at the karmic roots of the incest in your life. There has been a past life in which you knew your father. In that lifetime you were the manageress of a brothel. As a young girl you were forced to work as a prostitute. Your father in that lifetime—who is not your father in your current lifetime; I will come to your current father—was a bitter man. He and his wife lived in poverty and had several children. You look Spanish; it might have been in Latin America. He had ambitions but wasn't able to fulfill them because of his low social status. He was angry about that, and he took it out on your mother, who was a gentle woman but weak and unable to stand up to him. As a child you wished there would be more harmony in the family.

"When you were about sixteen years old, a man in the street abused you sexually. You were a virgin and did not know what was happening to you. When he was finished, he threw you a few coins, which you took home.

"I see you coming home, frightened and shocked, with dirt on your face and arms, throwing those coins on the table, and the eagerness with which your father received them. Your mother was happy, too. You did not tell them how you got the money. You noticed how bringing in the money brought happiness in the home. That's how you started to work as a prostitute. Your parents inquired as to how you got the money, and you made something up so as not to embarrass them. They did not ask further. They really didn't want to know because they valued the money so much.

"As you became a young woman, your sense of self-esteem suffered because of all this. Working as a prostitute on the street was a very tough life. At about twenty-one years of age, you sought the protection of a brothel. Life there was hard and unfair, but you did have the companionship of the other girls.

"You could not stand to see injustice done to these girls. Whenever you saw them being treated unfairly and even violently, a deep anger and indignation rose from within your belly, and you were not afraid to stand up for them and help them as best you could. You were less inclined to stand up for yourself than for others. Because of your fiery temperament in this respect, you made it to head of the brothel when you were older. By then you had grown a deep sense of distrust toward men and a fierce protectiveness toward 'my girls.'

"You were in your forties when your current father entered the stage. He was a man visiting the brothel, having an affair with one particular girl. He fell in love with that girl and wanted to marry her. He was decent, quite sensitive, but also frustrated because he wasn't as manly as one was expected to be by that society. He came to the brothel to prove he was a man. He was insecure and did not mean to harm or look down on the prostitutes.

"The girl loved him, too. She was a shy girl with low self-esteem. You thought this man would only use her and not keep his promises. The man's feelings were honorable, and the girl wanted to go away with him, but you refused to let her. You talked to her vehemently and persuaded her to stay in the brothel with you. She agreed; she was impressionable and unable to make decisions for herself. I sense she would have been happy with that man.

"He, your current father, was very upset by your interference, and his disappointment and indignation were great when he found out you had turned the girl against him. He never forgave you. You forbade him entrance to the brothel. The girl grew weary and sad after that, and got into a state of apathy. Seeing this, you did sometimes have the feeling you might have made a mistake, but you did not allow the man back in. Your heart had become closed toward men, and you felt it your mission to be the protector of the unfairly treated women. Your current father died in that lifetime with hatred toward you. This set a karmic wheel in motion.

"In this current lifetime, your father wanted to avenge himself on you and did so through the sexual abuse. An old part of him wanted to get even with you. That part of him could not see the innocent, vulnerable girl you were as his daughter; it saw only the powerful woman from the past lifetime that robbed him of the love of his life.

"The tragedy is that revenge never works. It only makes the karma—unresolved trauma—thicker and harder to release. I feel, however, that you have moved beyond the emotional trauma and are not bound anymore to that particular wheel of karma.

"The reason you did not remember the incest for a long time is that the contradiction between your image of him as a loving father and his actual, brutal behavior was so great that you could not wrap your mind around it, so you instinctively repressed the memory.

"With your grandfather I also sense a karmic relationship, but from a different lifetime. You were once his daughter. You were rebellious toward him. He was a traditional man, quite well off. I see him in a white suit with brown—Indian?—skin. You were an imaginative girl, wanting to explore the world, very independent. Your mother had an obedient attitude toward your father, but behind his back she did what she liked and made fun of him. You, however, did not like to be so secretive and subdued in your ways, and you openly opposed him. You had many arguments. He was very irritated by your independent and proud attitude as a woman. You managed to find your own way in life, independent of his support. As a grown woman, you had a sense of having triumphed over him.

"Because of your rebelliousness, your mother became much more assertive and divorced him. When he was old and sick, he was alone and expected you to take care of him. This was traditional in that society. You did so reluctantly, but you clearly radiated an air of contempt for the male conservatism he represented. Even in his frail, old state, you could not find it in your heart to forgive him and treat him with kindness. This set a karmic movement in motion.

"There was an opening for the two of you to make peace, to at least respect each other in a basic sense. He felt lonely and, despairing on his deathbed, longed for your presence to comfort him. You, however, kept your distance. This made him feel you were treating him cruelly, and it instilled in him a desire to hurt and humiliate you. I feel this to be the karmic background for the incest that took place in this lifetime.

"In both cases the men involved felt deeply humiliated *as men* and struck back by humiliating you as a woman.

"In the deepest part of you, at the level of your soul, you wanted to make peace with both men in this lifetime. Your soul consciously allowed the incest to happen, even if it caused deep emotional trauma. Your soul wanted to move forward and deal with this issue of hatred/distrust toward men. It wanted to move beyond these emotions and create a new openness to men at the level of the heart. In your heart chakra, I sense a remnant of the energetic shield you put there in past lives to protect yourself from pain and fear. Here again, allowing old emotions of anger, feeling betrayed, or sadness to surface will help to remove the armor and let your heart shine free and open once more.

"I will now let Jeshua speak."

Jeshua Discusses Incest

"Debbie," Jeshua said, "you are honored for your strength and perseverance, your faith and optimism, and your loving heart. We see the light of your soul shining on Earth and rejoice in it.

"I wish to say more about how to heal fully your emotional wounds. Always, healing one's own emotions is the key to creating more love and lightness in one's life and in those of others. There's still some unresolved anger inside you that needs to be addressed. Anger is an emotion that you often screen and only permit selectively into your awareness. Allow the full force of anger to enter your body. Do not fear it, for you are strong enough to hold the anger consciously and not be swept away by it. Holding the anger consciously will enable you to connect fully to your male energy again, allowing it to help you stand up for yourself and be very vigilant about your boundaries.

"The boundary issue is important. When you experience incest, by definition your sense of boundaries gets lost and confused. A child always wants to accommodate the parent's desires, and when the parent or grandparent violates your boundaries at a sexual level, a very basic sense of safety gets lost. Through this act the parent is basically telling you that it's good to give up all your boundaries and, really, to give up yourself completely. You believe this because you want to believe the parent; he is your anchor and safety net in life. Sexual violation is a very aggressive act of violence. If it is done to a child, the aggression is even more pervasive because the child considers the parent's behavior as right and trustworthy by definition. It absorbs the parent's lifestyle and statements uncritically up to a certain age.

"Incest always creates deep issues of trust. It may make you distrustful later in life toward sexual partners. But, it can also make you *too trustful*, thinking it's normal to neglect body signals that tell you your boundaries are being violated. Those who experience incest need to learn anew the language of their own emotions and body signals. They need to rely again on these signals, which tell them what they like and don't like in relations with others and in the area of intimacy in particular.

"I ask you to—on a daily basis—pay attention to body signals and emotions that are just at the threshold between consciousness and subconsciousness. This you can do by frequently tuning into your body and noting whether it is relaxed, whether you feel grounded and centered, aware of your needs in the Now moment. As you do so, your awareness of yourself will grow and reach below the threshold of what you normally register within your awareness. You will find new areas of yourself that want to be heard and expressed. There is an angry part of you that seeks expression, but as it surfaces, as it moves past the threshold and is openly received by you, the anger will transform into creative power. With this power you will be able to manifest yourself even more clearly in the outside world, reach out to more people, and inspire them with your kindness, clarity, and compassion."

"Jeshua," I asked, "why did Debbie plan before birth to experience incest?"

"She wanted to meet the two men involved in the incest, her father and grandfather, because she wanted to resolve old issues with them. These issues had to do with past lifetimes in which she ridiculed them, specifically their masculinity. Debbie's soul knew that both these men harbored an old grudge against her. She allowed them to express this hatred. Her soul's plan was to be able to cope with the abuse and *to forgive them in the end*. Her soul had the hope that she would be capable of it if she would call upon all her spiritual strength. Being able to heal herself and forgive the two men would allow her to move past her difficult relationship with the male energy and achieve an inner balance between the male and female energy."

I asked Jeshua to say more about why Debbie had planned the experience of incest with *two* individuals.

"She wanted to heal the family karma that was present in her biological family for several generations," Jeshua explained. "This karma had to do with a repressed female energy and a twisted and frustrated male energy that enacted a painful dance through several family members. By experiencing the incest and rising above it, she has offered her family the possibility of breaking free from an old chain of action and reaction. Energetically, she has offered them a pathway to healing that she herself has carved by her own inner struggle and liberation."

I now had an understanding of Debbie's intentions at the soul level; still, it was hard to accept that other souls would agree to a plan that would cause such suffering for Debbie. "Why did Debbie's father and grandfather agree to participate in such an experience?" I asked Jeshua.

"They were both unable to let go of their indignation and resentment. They felt belittled and humiliated by Debbie in the past lifetimes mentioned, and their souls allowed them to play out this dark aspect of themselves to eventually overcome it. Both their souls knew that Debbie's soul gave permission for the experience. There was sadness in both their souls as they planned the likelihood of this experience. Their souls' plan was to be confronted and awakened by the shame and guilt that would arise because of what they had done to a vulnerable, young girl.

"No one who commits incest," Jeshua continued, "can escape the sense of having deeply violated the sacredness of young and innocent life. No past life emotion of hatred or grudge can ever outweigh or take away the deep sense of shame and guilt that arises because of incest. The soul feels bereft of its inherent goodness, its liveliness and joy, and will experience deep self-hatred because of it. To betray a life so young and innocent is a grave shock to the offender's own soul. Debbie's father's and grandfather's souls knew that the deed of incest would turn their grudge toward and hatred of another person—Debbie in the past lives—into a deep shame and guilt about themselves. This shift in experience from victim to offender would allow them to go deep within and address their own feelings of unworthiness without blaming anyone outside them. This would free the way to their spiritual awakening, if they would choose so."

These words from Jeshua felt particularly important. I had long wondered how we as souls could move beyond learning through the victim-offender paradigm. Here was the answer: facing and exploring our own feelings of unworthiness rather than projecting them into the world from the vantage point of either offender or victim.

Clearly, though, the enactment of the plan described by Jeshua would have required the cooperation of Debbie's mother. "Jeshua, did Debbie's mother know before birth that incest would occur? Did she agree to allow it to occur? Why?"

"Yes, she did." he confirmed. "She knew beforehand that she would be torn inside over this issue. She had a sense of loyalty toward her husband and father, and at the same time she had to stand up for her daughter, who needed her protection. She chose to be confronted with this dilemma in this lifetime. She had to learn to trust her own instincts, her own sense of right and wrong, and this was difficult for her. As a result she was confronted with heavy emotions of powerlessness, fear, and shame. Her soul wanted her to deal with this. Through these emotions she would have to face her deepest fears, which would offer her the opportunity to find her own power and courage again.

"Debbie's mother's soul knew that Debbie's soul gave permission to experience incest. Before birth, her mother's soul felt deep respect and gratitude to Debbie for allowing her [the mother] and the other family members to play the roles they did. All souls involved recognized Debbie's greatness and courage during the planning stage. They all knew she had the potential to bring great healing and to be a teacher to them."

"Did Debbie plan not to remember the incest for many years?"

"Yes, she did. The timing was important and carefully planned by her soul. She planned to let the memories surface at a time in which she was able to deal with them in a way that was healing to her soul. She wanted to deal with the incest experience as an adult in order to have the best chance of overcoming the traumatic emotions in a balanced and peaceful way. This was a wise soul choice and a blessing for the personality."

"If we have memories that surface after a long time has passed," I asked, "how can we know if the memories are accurate?"

"It is very helpful if there is some way to objectively verify the memories, which will often mean that a family member is willing to speak about it. If it is not possible to find objective evidence in this way, then it is impossible to be completely sure, and this is often something that troubles the one who experienced incest. If verification is not possible, it is important to take the memories very seriously. They are there for a reason, and it is very probable that real events caused them."

"In our culture," I pointed out, "people sometimes doubt the accuracy of others' memories if those memories return years after the event in question. More specifically, if the person who experienced incest undergoes counseling, people sometimes wonder if the therapist created the memory simply by suggesting the possibility of incest."

"It is possible to create memories through a process of hypnotic suggestion," answered Jeshua, "but in the majority of cases the memory is real and the incest really took place. The temporary repression of the memory is a natural defense mechanism of the human psyche.

"When memories are artificially created, the person experiences them as real. They often indeed refer to real events, but events that do not belong to the person's life but rather to other people's lives. Sensitive people may pick up other people's memories and regard them as their own, just like sensitive people may pick up other people's moods and feelings and regard them as their own. There is, however, a way of distinguishing this. Other people's memories do not truly fit in with one's own life, meaning that you can feel at a core level that they are not your own. For people who are balanced and grounded, the distinction is not so difficult to make. It is, however, more difficult for people who are psychologically unbalanced, very open to outside influences, or very insecure and fearful.

"So, if there is genuine doubt about the veracity of the memory, one should start by checking for any objective evidence that can decide the matter or else look carefully at what method is chosen in the therapy and to what extent the client is capable of distinguishing between her own experience and other people's experiences. One should start, however, by taking very seriously what the client is experiencing and consider the memories to be true unless proven otherwise. In any case, if the memories that surface have a great emotional charge, they have great meaning for the client and therefore should be treated with care and respect."

"Jeshua," I inquired, "for what other reasons do souls plan incest?"

"The soul is not perfect and all-knowing," answered Jeshua. "It is in a process of learning and growing. There can be ignorant parts in the soul that need Earth experience to become enlightened. There can be darkness in the soul that attracts lifetimes as offender and perpetrator. The reason the light part of the soul, the knowing and wise part, allows this to happen is that the soul knows it is learning through experience, that it will go beyond duality only by having experienced it to the extreme. The soul knows it has to dance with darkness to become whole and truly wise. By becoming the darkness at times, it will truly sense the meaning of light and love. This will truly bring the soul Home. No one else, not even Spirit, can bring the soul Home. Only the soul itself can do it, by its own free choice.

"This is, generally speaking, why darkness has a justifiable place in the Universe, and why atrocities like incest are allowed to happen. More specifically, souls who plan to commit incest have had painful experiences in past lives with regard to their sexual identity. They may have been victims of sexual violence themselves. Often, men who commit incest have a deeply troubled relationship with the feminine energy, which shows in their relationship with adult females and also in their relationship with their own feelings and emotions. They often subconsciously think that women are all-powerful and that they are helpless against them; hence, the need to use power against a small girl and the inability to see the innocence and vulnerability of the child. To perform the act of incest, their female energy of empathy and compassion has to be shut down. The incestuous man is shut off from his own female energy and is incapable of having a healthy emotional relationship with grown females."

"What can we as a society do to help people who commit acts of incest?"

"It is a sign of maturity," Jeshua replied, "if a society is willing to help people who have committed acts of incest. By wanting to offer help to these people, even if their acts are unambiguously denounced, the society shows that it recognizes the humanness of the offender and the possibility for healing, even if one has strayed so far.

"To begin the healing process, the people involved [the offenders] first need to be willing to open up and share their emotions with another person. They will need to feel safe to express their emotions freely, and thus the one helping them will have to release judgment about them. You may disapprove of their behavior, but you have to be open to their *humanness*, the fact that they are at their core a human being like you, with the same emotions.

"When expressing their emotions, they may at first be unable to face up to their responsibility and may want to attribute the incest to external factors like their upbringing or other outside 'causes.' It is only when they start to take responsibility that healing can occur. One cannot force them to take responsibility. One can, however, listen to their stories and not judge any of their excuses but simply listen and wait. Through your lack of judgment, they may enter into a different space, a space of compassion that will eventually let them embrace their responsibility.

"If they do, they will be faced with their burden of shame and guilt. Now their female energy of empathy and compassion will open, and they will start to imagine and feel what the victim has gone through. They will be deeply disgusted with themselves. This is a delicate point, for if the disgust and self-loathing become too overwhelming, they will shut down again. If you are helping these people, you will need to lead them beyond the self-hatred by discovering with them why they were ever led to commit such an act of violence against a child.

"You can now explore their past with them and uncover the causes of their behavior while they are still taking responsibility for their acts. Slowly, they may start to get a deeper understanding of themselves. Self-forgiveness will be a long way off, but at some point they will be able to have some compassion with themselves. They may want to connect with the one who experienced the incest, and if she or he is willing to communicate, it can often make a huge difference. If they are able to express their deepest remorse to the other person, and if it is received by that person, it will speed their healing tremendously."

"Jeshua, the wound from experiencing incest is so deep that people may wonder how it can be completely healed," I said.

"Yes, it can be very difficult for people who have experienced incest to feel a basic sense of well-being and joy again," Jeshua acknowledged. "It is not so much that they long for a complete healing, but that they desire to have their basic sense of safety and liveliness restored. From there they can grow and heal more joyously, in a gentler way. To restore this basic sense of wellness, they need to face the deep sense of unworthiness incest always leaves behind. When your boundaries have been violated so fundamentally, in such a precious area as sexuality, you cannot get back your sense of safety and wellness unless you have a true spiritual breakthrough. You have to realize at some point that you are *not* the broken spirit of the child, that you are *not* the violated body or the betrayed trust, but that you are the grand and inviolate soul who has experienced all this and is capable of embracing the child and carrying it Home safely. To come to this realization, you have to open to the deepest emotions of fear, despair, and outrage that incest invokes. As soon as you do, you will see the light of your soul shining at the end of the road. Facing your darkness will summon the light within and will make you aware of your true nature, which is freedom, courage, and love."

"Jeshua, what else would be helpful to know in order to heal?"

"It is important to have great compassion for those who have experienced incest but not to *pity* them. Pitying them sends a signal that they cannot heal themselves, that they are beyond help or hope. This is the wrong signal. People who have experienced incest should be encouraged to communicate openly about their emotions, to release the shame and guilt they feel or even the loyalty they still have to their parents or family. There is much hope for those who have experienced incest if they are approached as capable human beings who have the power to heal themselves."

Debbie had told me she had only one question for Jeshua. "How can I best serve the planet?" she now asked.

"You serve the planet by *being yourself*," he replied. "You are yourself when you feel joy in expressing yourself. Whatever expression you choose, if it feels joyful and fulfilling to you, it will be inspiring to others as well. Compare it to a flower. What is a flower's mission? It is to bloom. This is not something it has to do; it is something it does because blooming belongs to its very nature. The flower fulfills its mission by being itself. In doing so it enriches the planet and it touches the hearts of humans who enjoy its beauty. It is your mission to bloom like a flower, to take care of yourself, to heal your wounded parts, to trust your visions and dreams, and to embrace life without reserve.

"To serve the planet, do not think of the planet but focus on yourself. Spirit is always communicating with you through your feelings. Whenever you feel peaceful and joyful, both quiet and inspired, you can be sure you are attuned to the spirit of Oneness that holds the world together. When you feel joyful in a grounded, peaceful way, you are serving that Oneness, which *is* Spirit, and serving yourself at the same time. There is no difference at that level.

"Put yourself first, and all else will follow. You have the ability to empower others. Think of the qualities you radiated in the past lives we investigated. You were a passionate fighter for justice, someone who stood up for repressed women. Although these qualities were not completely balanced in those lifetimes, at the core of them is a beautiful, radiant energy that is yours still. Now that you have come so far in embracing and integrating all your past lives and old inner wounds, you are invited to embrace again your true strength and serve as an example to others. This time, however, your power will be balanced, balanced by your acceptance of the male energy, your willingness to make peace and forgive, and your true knowledge of the Oneness of all life. This time your power is borne from an inner alchemy, a transformation of the lead of pain and trauma into the gold of the energy of All That Is."

Debbie's Session with Staci

Pamela and Jeshua had provided a moving and detailed explanation of Debbie's pre-birth decision to experience incest. For even more insight, Debbie and I turned to Staci and her spirit guide.

"Debbie," Staci opened, "you seek to find emotional balance within yourself in this lifetime. As with most souls who choose this, you've also chosen relationships that will turn you back to yourself. You created a life, especially with your parents, of some troubling relationships so that you would be redirected back to yourself because you wouldn't be able to find that balance, that place of absolute, unconditional love, with your parents.

"There are so many ways in which your experience with your father has served your growth. My spirit guide tells me that out of great love for him you agreed to play this role in his life. This can only mean that at a soul level you view yourself as very strong.

"I'm looking at your pre-birth planning session now. You're sitting cross-legged above, not quite touching, the floor. You are in your lightbody; I see whiteness and softness and light. In front of you is the pre-birth planning chart you are creating for this life. On the opposite side of the room is a spirit guide. My viewpoint is from where the spirit guide is. Let me listen.

Debbie:	I will cast myself with a personality conducive to the breakdown and repair of certain structures created through habit over [other] lives. My behavioral path taken in the past, if taken in this life, will lead to closed doors. In the personality structure I have created over the last six lives, I have built a stronger platform, and I feel strong enough now to overcome the many adversities I have planned for this life.
Spirit Guide:	Do you?
Debbie:	Yes. The restructuring and rebuilding I have planned at certain intervals in my life will guide me most assuredly on a steadier course toward compassion so that I may lead through better understanding of my own nature.
	I'm concerned for others, so may I complete this journey of learning to give blessings to all, not to see others in a demeaning way as less or lower than myself, but instead to see the thread of love that connects us all at the heart, and also to see the many foibles of human personality as structures that guide us upon our way and lead to growth, prosperity, and harmony of spirit within.

"Part of the structure you chose for this lifetime," Staci continued, "is to give yourself periods of alone time, more than what most other people have in their lives, so that you have the time to go within and figure out what you need: What is my truth? What is it that really fulfills and sustains me? My spirit guide tells me that thinking deeply about things is something you've been refining over several lives. You have come from a place that was much more impulsive in previous lives. In the last few lives, you've wanted to strengthen the ability to think deeply about things instead of reacting.

"Spirit tells me there's more I need to say. There are people who will turn on the TV or radio, or do self-sabotaging, self-destructive behaviors to avoid being alone. If they persist in doing this and not utilizing those alone times to do that work [on self], they will begin to manifest times of not enough money so that they are limited in their ability to distract themselves with things like going to a movie, dinner, or shopping. They're giving themselves opportunity to come face-to-face with themselves. If they still don't do the work, then the next step is manifesting some sort of illness. Usually that illness is of a kind that will take you out of the flow of life for anywhere from a few days to a few months to even lifelong.

"In my mind's eye," Staci described, "I see many lives where you were in a leadership position. In those lives you used your power unwisely and sometimes for the wrong purposes. My spirit guide says 'for self gain.' In that period between lives, when you review life, you became less and less satisfied with what you had done. You began talks with your main spirit guide. You came to understand that the less you needed to manipulate others the more you treated them with genuine respect, which is an expression of the unconditional love that connects us all. In this current life you desired to experience yourself as a leader. You wanted to inspire others.

"At a deeper layer underneath what I've told you is a desire at the soul level to experience compassionate service to others. You chose your family to give you an experience in which you could at some point understand their pathology from a compassionate point of view instead of anger, blame, and victimhood; so that you could be of compassionate service to others, which would in the process enable you to come to a place of emotional balance within yourself. It's interconnected and interrelated.

"Last, you wanted to work cooperatively with others. The first arena for this was your family. But, you also wanted to have an effect on humankind by doing something that would help others make their lives better. You chose to come back at a time in human evolution when the energies were most appropriate for it. You came back with a larger group who wanted to have a domino effect: one affects the other and the next and the next. This would cause a shift, a course correction in humankind's evolutionary path on this planet.

"I'm seeing once again a moment from your pre-birth planning session. I see both your mother and father wearing the cloak of the personality, what they will look like as adults. Your mother is standing behind you, arms bent, elbows pulled back, the palm of her hands facing out and flat toward you, like she is standing behind you, giving you a push. Your mother's purpose in this life was *to push* you forward to take a big evolutionary step.

"I shift my focus now to your father. What stands out to me is this genetic structure he built for himself that's mentally ill. I have the sense that he had issues of obsessive-compulsive disorder and something that either is, or is like, bipolar. My spirit guide is telling me it was more pronounced earlier in his life. I see and empathically feel that he set himself up for a life of problems— emotionally, mentally, physically.

"Let me tell you what I saw earlier today, a vision. I saw your father sitting across from you in your pre-birth planning session with your planning chart in between. His left arm was reaching out to you, and what would be his hand was energetically blending into your lightbody. I heard,

Debbie: You will not impact that which is the heart of me, that which is my true being. You will not damage me in a permanent way. I am strength and strong enough to withstand the experience of being manipulated and used by you. I will learn from it. It will not thwart my destiny. It will not change who I am or what I come to do. It will be another opportunity, just as it is another expression of my unconditional love and support of you. But after this, if you choose to create this entanglement

again, it will be without me. My time with you
and this journey will be done. I will move on to
the next step, and you will continue this journey
with someone else.

"He shakes his head up and down.

Father: Yes, I understand. I know.

"I have the feeling that he is full of guilt already, guilt I don't
think he has been able to express in this life; however, I'm being
told that when he leaves this life experience, he will come to a
place of greater understanding. He will understand his motivations for these actions in a way he has not before."

"Staci, what *is* his motivation?" I asked.

"He is learning at the soul level to build a more compassionate personality, but he is not as evolved as Debbie and so is still
learning from negative expression. Although he runs away from
his responsibility for this [incest] in this lifetime, as he has in
others, he learns all the more from it after the life is over. Debbie
understood this on the soul level and so volunteered.

"Let me see what else Spirit might show me. I am seeing an
energetic link between their [Debbie's and her father's] souls.
This is something I see a lot. We talk about the silver cord
that connects our spirit with our physical body. These cords of
connection are like that. I see one that extends from your solar
plexus, Debbie, to that of your father and mother. I also see these
same cords of connection between your third eye and your father
especially, and your mother secondarily. Both of them made the
decision together.

Father: I planned a child to be born here *[points to his
own pre-birth planning chart]* as a vehicle through
which I may experience a challenge to my self-
esteem and self-worth, a challenge that would
cause me to become more contemplative, to

think deeply in a very quiet, internalized way about what I have done. This is the point in my marriage with your mother where I have planned to withdraw, to be there but not be an active energy in the marriage relationship.

"I see a lot more detail suddenly filling in your pre-birth planning chart. A large part of your life then begins to take shape and form.

Debbie: This experience with you as my father will help me be a gentle guide to others, form a more compassionate nature, and acquire a more complete understanding of my own sensitivities and the compulsions of others. This, I feel quite certain, will help me complete this journey of self-mastery, so that I may break free of the grid which long ago we formed to connect our lives and paths in physical form, so that in my next sojourn I may rise above this and go on to a higher level of creation and Beingness.

"I'm seeing what you've got in mind for your next step," Staci told Debbie. "It's a couple of hundred years in the future. You come back at a time when the land on Earth has changed somewhat. I get the feeling of you living in the northern part of the North American continent. There's a lot of nature involved, a lot of peace, harmony, and alone time. I see you being a writer, writing about something that aids humanity's quest. I see you speaking before very large groups. Once again you put yourself in a position of leadership, but you are far above the personal issues of your current life. You're on to something else, another part of that journey."

Speaking with Staci and Her Spirit Guide

"Staci," I said, "Debbie's memories were repressed for many years. Could your spirit guide speak to people who are dealing with repressed memories either from incest or perhaps another life experience?"

"Do not be afraid of these memories," came the slow, measured reply. I knew immediately from her altered speech that Staci's consciousness had stepped aside and that her guide was now speaking directly through her. "They return at a time when your physicality is able to deal with the emotions carried in those memories. To let them out from the corners of your mind will lighten your burden, release years of pent-up energy, and propel you toward your karmic goals. Know that your journey in this particular life includes great personal development through one of the harshest experiences. Know, too, that you chose it. In planning your life, you felt there was no greater way to make this growth step. At times there are agreements with the other individuals with whom you have interacted. You are also serving a great purpose in their lives. As your focus turns around and you embrace yourself and all with unconditional love, you dissolve the energy blocks that have been holding you back from your potential, like heavy bricks weighing down upon you. Once these lift, you begin a journey of great growth at the end of which is wisdom. Many people choose this experience to direct them onto the path of service to others. It is through the most extreme experiences that humankind experiences its greatness. It is true for each of you."

"I'd like to say something," I replied, "that I think will occur to many who read these words, and that is, There's got to be a better way."

"When you are planning your lives from the soul level, you often forget how it feels to struggle with these sorts of emotional problems," said the guide. "It's like pregnancy and childbirth: you forget the pain and remember only the good you experienced in other lives in which you've gone through emotional extremes and extreme experiences."

"Then are we not in some sense making uninformed decisions?"

"When you have lived hundreds of lives in several dimensions, you see things from a different perspective. When you are in physical form in a denser vehicle than your lightbody, particularly so on Earth, you have forgotten what is real, what is your true Home, and what you really are. This is part and parcel of the Earth journey."

"Here's what troubles me," I persisted. I did not want to badger Staci's guide, but it was impossible not to pursue this line of questioning given the intensity of Debbie's suffering. "As I understand it, the planning is done largely by the soul, then the lifetime is lived by the personality. The personality sometimes suffers tremendously, and yet the soul that planned the life is not experiencing any of the suffering. From a human perspective, that seems unfair."

"It is not that the soul does not experience it," explained the guide. "The connection between the soul and the personality is always present until such time as the body is left behind and the personality construct, gently over a period of time that is determined by each individuated soul, dissipates. The harsher aspects of the personality soften; it dissipates and eventually melds into the soul body. The soul most definitely perceives the struggle of the personality. It feels it as an energy pulse through the silver cord. The feeling resonates in the soul but with a sense of knowingness the personality often does not have. The sense of knowingness contained within the soul is from the greater, higher perspective. The soul understands the reasons for the experience, and there is certainly compassion from the soul."

"It's possible to learn and grow without suffering," I pointed out. "Why are we not there now?"

"Many of you are!" he exclaimed. "Many of you live a life that by human terms is a breeze. These lives are often rewards to the self for other lives that may be considered harsher or more challenging. Oftentimes it is a reward to the self for a job well done. When you submerse yourselves in a pool, it is a different experience than floating on the top."

"But a lot of people may wonder, 'When do I get to float?'"

"When you decide. That truly is the answer. When you decide. That choice can be made during one's lifetime, but so many personalities are not able to rise above because they retain the baggage of guilt, blame, shame, and anger. Even for those personalities who feel they have forgiven, forgiveness is a process, and many times it will take ten, twenty, thirty, or forty years to accomplish fully. Only those who have been through that experience will truly understand this statement."

"People who have experienced incest," I said, "or many other types of life challenges must deal with negative emotions, just as you mentioned. How would you advise people to heal these emotions?"

"You already know the answer, and the answer is Love. These conditions, these experiences, will often set up a tremendous challenge, a challenge the soul desires in order to learn to love itself in all forms. As we've discussed in some of our work together, it's also a challenge chosen by the soul in order to come to a true experience of profound compassion. This sometimes enables the soul to make a change within a lifetime or just enables the soul truly to get on the path it wanted to walk.

"In Debbie's case she used the pain and insights not *just* for her own healing, but also to arouse compassion so that she would rise to her true calling. In many lives Debbie has demonstrated an affinity for and an enjoyment of helping others, even though in so many of her lives she has also been a great leader who uses and manipulates others. There are two sides to this aspect that Debbie is trying to bring into balance, first within herself and then in her dealings with all other individuals. In this choice of incest, she has aroused a compassionate nature within her that is so strong it cannot be extinguished. It was simply a choice for the most direct, quickest route to that goal. The soul is willing to undergo these extreme experiences in order to get there."

I asked Staci's guide to say more about why some souls plan the experience of incest.

"There are those souls who, in their desire for emotional independence, will create an experience so that the personality construct will be motivated to push away from its dependent connection on others," he answered. "Some souls make several sojourns to undertake this process and find they are unable to make that step toward emotional independence and wholeness. They will then choose a life experience similar to Debbie's in order to lead the personality to greater contemplation, isolation, or both so the personality will make that jump from one level of understanding, thinking, and behaving to the next. More self-awareness results from the process."

"What would you say to those who have committed acts of incest and are trying to forgive themselves?"

"You've said the right word: Forgiveness. Forgiveness. Forgive yourself. Seek to understand and forgive yourself. Seek to be kind toward yourself. Seek to understand the purpose this behavior has served in your life and the purpose it might have served in the lives of the persons you have abused. And while you do that, always come back to forgiveness. If you hold yourself in a place of blame and shame, which you may choose to do for as long as you wish, you will not be able to perceive the truth behind it all that will lift your soul from the dungeon you've placed around yourself."

"Is there anything else," I asked, "Spirit would like to say to someone who has experienced incest?"

"First and foremost, learn to love yourself unconditionally," suggested the guide. "Learn to love yourself in a way your parents or abusers could not. Allow that place of unconditional love for yourself to lead you to a compassionate viewpoint toward your abuser. Understand that it is a choice you made to propel yourself toward tremendous growth, growth that on the soul level you felt you could not achieve in any other way. Choose to lift yourself out of anger and blame. Choose to see from a higher perspective."

Debbie's Session with Barbara and Aaron

Because it is inherently so difficult to accept that an experience like incest would be planned before birth, Debbie and I sought a third source of wisdom in Aaron, an enlightened being. I began the session with the fundamental question: "Aaron, did Debbie plan before she was born to experience incest with her father and grandfather, and if so, why?"

"Remember first that you are a soul," Aaron said lovingly to Debbie. "You're not a human who has a soul; you're a soul who is presently incarnate in a human body. The soul is seeking to experience so as to learn and to grow. For you in this lifetime, Debbie, the predominant intention was to deepen in compassion.

"In past lifetimes there has been a habitual tendency for you to blame others and the self. When something is uncomfortable and anger comes up, one wants to push it aside. One mode of doing that is to find something to blame, some reason for attack. Let's take it out of the realm of incest and into a simple situation, say, driving your car. Perhaps you are pulling out of a parking lot, somebody backs into you, and anger flares up. The impulse is to find some place to put this anger rather than simply to sit and hold space for it. Anger, frustration, sadness; one wants to get away from those difficult emotions so one moves into the habit of blaming somebody.

"This has been a habitual pattern in many lifetimes. The intention in this lifetime was to move beyond that pattern, to learn to simply hold space for the pain, the fear, the anger that life had brought to you, release the habit of blaming, and open your heart to greater compassion."

Here I was reminded of Debbie's own words in the pre-birth planning session Staci had heard: "I will cast myself with a personality conducive to the breakdown and repair of certain structures created through habit over [other] lives." Evidently, one of the habits Debbie had desired to correct was the habit of blame.

Aaron then asked Debbie for her year of birth, explaining that he needed this information to delve more deeply into her Akashic Record.

"I want to clarify," Aaron continued. "Debbie, you—the child as a personality—did not create the incest. You were helpless. What happened is not your fault. It is important that you not misunderstand me by taking responsibility. It was your father who had the responsibility. He was acting out his karma.

"The question then is, Where do you go from here? This is about compassion: seeing that your father is the product of his karma, just as you were the product of your karma, just as all beings are the products of their karma, and yet to know that one can change this karma. One can release and balance unwholesome karma and come into a much more open-hearted place."

"Aaron," I inquired, "how likely was it that Debbie would experience incest?"

"In many birth situations incest is possible, but in some it would be very improbable," Aaron explained. "In this life situation it was much more likely. Because of the father's tendencies, it was likely he would be abusive to her. One must also regard the father's history. I will not look in the Akashic Records to learn about Debbie's father, which would be a violation of his privacy, but I suspect that he felt unworthy and afraid in past lives. This was why he expressed domination and power over others in both past lives and the current lifetime. Debbie, is your father still living?"

"Yes," Debbie replied.

"Do you speak with him?"

"I saw him two or three times in the last year. And I sent cards; otherwise, I communicate through my sister."

"I think the work you need to do with your father, Debbie, is more in your own heart than through verbally talking. You don't need his apology. I want you to open your own heart with compassion to his pain and to look within the present self [your personality] and ask, 'Are there any ways in which I do not acknowledge my own Divinity?' That is the healing.

"It's useful to watch those small situations where you receive pain from others through actual, active abuse or just through being ignored, and to ask yourself, 'How can I say no to this situation with love?' If someone has said something that feels cruel, simply say, 'I hear you're angry, but you may not speak to me in that way.' Watch the anger and fear that come up in yourself. As you learn how to do this in simple situations, then play back in your mind situations with your father. Have a dialogue with him in your heart. I know you have done that to some degree already, but it was with a fear that he could not hear you." This, I gathered, was information Aaron had gleaned from Debbie's Akashic Record. "I would ask you to do it with the full expectation of being heard, because you are a Divine Being. You have the power to be heard."

"Aaron," I asked, "for what other reasons do souls plan the potential for incest before they're born?"

"One might be if they were people who had been physically abusive to others in past lives, not choosing incest as punishment, but to learn from the firsthand experience how that feels. Also, there are rare but occasional situations where a very old soul with a strong past life connection to a younger and more violent soul will agree to be the recipient of violence from that person to help teach that person to be more responsible, to see the terrible results of the actions."

I asked Aaron if he could say more about Debbie's pre-birth plan with her father.

"Your intention at that pre-birth meeting," he said to Debbie, "was to try to help your father, which you have not really been able to do. That is not a fault, Debbie. For one to teach another, the other must be willing to learn. He was not ready. There are still ways in which you can help your father in this lifetime, but the most important starting place is that of which I have spoken: deepening your own compassion."

"Aaron," I said, "people who have experienced incest are trying to heal, forgive, let go of anger, and feel greater self-worth. What do you say to them?"

"What you have experienced has been extreme, and you may not feel ready to forgive. Forgiveness is one step in a much larger process. Begin simply by understanding that each human is expressing his or her own conditioning. Ask yourself, 'If I had been raised with that condition,' in other words, with that cultural and psychological condition, 'might I not have done harm to others also?' Let yourself *feel* the grief, the pain, of these people. Hold them in your heart with compassion.

"Then watch yourself in those moments when you are irritated or impatient and you speak sharp words to another. A far less hurtful action than incest, certainly, and yet sharp words can cause another pain. Can you also hold yourself with compassion? Without blaming yourself, see that your own conditioning led to the impatient response. Can you simply hold space for all of that pain? Open your heart as you heal yourself. In this way the heart opens more and more to the situation you were in [the incest], and your readiness to forgive increases, not conceptually but because you were practicing.

"When anger comes up, the part of you that knows anger is not angry. If when anger arises you say, 'Oh no, I won't be angry,' that's just more anger. But if anger arises and you say, 'Certain things have happened to me that brought up this anger' and you hold space for the anger, that which is holding the space is loving. This is the way you heal."

"And to people who have committed acts of incest?" I asked.

"I would say this, my brothers and sisters of the light: You are indeed that. It is only you who hold yourselves in darkness. Begin to watch the movements, the inner tides, of fear, of greed, of anger in the self, and find the place in you that is strong and does not need to react to such impulses. I would like to suggest that you practice in a very simple way. Take a mouthful of water. Watch the cool water in the mouth and the feeling of swallowing it. Then take another large mouthful of water, and hold it in the mouth. Feel the texture of the water. There may be a strong impulse to swallow that is unpleasant. Watch the tension that comes up. There may be a feeling of, I can't breathe. Just because there is an impulse does not mean you have to act out that impulse. Practice until you learn what I mean when I say, 'Hold space for it.'

"When there is a strong impulse, be it a sexual impulse, or an impulse to harsh speech, or any kind of negative impulse, learn how to hold space for it. During the time you are practicing this, reflect to yourself. Is there a commitment to change, to learn to live your life with more kindness? When you are able to hold space for that water in the mouth and the impulse to swallow, begin to watch how this works in small situations in your life. When something doesn't go your way, do you want to lash out? When there is something you want, do you grab and force your way? You can learn to control these impulses. As you do you will start to know yourself, not as one who does harm in the world but as one who is deeply capable of doing good. In this way you will begin to heal.

"When you are ready—and it may not happen in this lifetime, but if it does—try to find ways to make amends to those you have hurt. You may want to start small. If you were verbally rude to somebody, just say, 'I am sorry. I was tense. I should not have said that.' Then reflect on the ways in which you have been more deeply hurtful to others through the cycle of abuse. I cannot tell you what kind of apology is appropriate. It must go deeper than just words, and words may not even be appropriate. The person you have abused may no longer be alive, but that doesn't mean you can't heal. Remember that this is a process. Your whole incarnation is a process of healing and of finding your wholeness. *There is no point in which you are too deeply into negativity to reverse things.* Please trust that. You truly are brothers and sisters of light.

"Those who are abusive have usually been abused. Another step in your healing of these impulses and acts is to find compassion for those who have abused you.

"I simply want to remind Debbie," Aaron concluded, "that you are not responsible on this physical human level for the abuse you experienced as a child. No child is responsible for the actions an adult forces upon her. No child has invited those actions in any conscious way. The child is doing her best to survive. The adult is responsible. This is on the level of the personality; yet, you are also the soul, and this is part of the soul's journey. Begin now to ask yourself more fully, 'Where is the fullest healing to be found?' 'What ways can the heart more fully open and flower?

"My blessings and love to you."

Debbie's story is that of a woman who opened her heart to love—love for herself and, by extension, love for her life. In that opening of the heart was she reborn, her life imbued with new meaning and purpose. What does it mean to open one's heart to oneself? It means, as Jeshua told us, "to open up to the deepest emotions of fear, despair, and outrage." For Debbie it meant opening to shame and self-hatred as well. Unsure of her strength and afraid of what she might find, for years did she conceal aspects of herself from herself, burying them in the dark recesses of her mind.

Eminent psychologist Carl Jung said, "The gold is in the dark." He meant that our greatest power and deepest healing are found in the repressed, unloved parts of ourselves. When brought into the light of conscious awareness and accepted with love, these aspects of self *become* power, light, beauty, and grace. As Jeshua said of anger, "as it surfaces … and is openly received by you, the anger will transform into creative power." And so it is for all our hidden, rejected parts: that which we most loathe and cannot bear to face are the very traits that ultimately ennoble and uplift us, recreating us into beings of even greater majesty. This is the "restructuring and rebuilding" of which Debbie spoke before she was born, a complete reconfiguring into "higher levels of creation and Beingness."

The power of darkness to create light is so great that Debbie, her father, and her grandfather all designed lives to use it. Just as Debbie planned before birth to face emotions like fear and rage, so, too, did her father and grandfather hope to confront the deep feelings of unworthiness, shame, and guilt that would result from their actions. These three souls share the same underlying intent: to have the pain of darkness drive them within, where they would discover the unhealed parts of themselves, love those aspects of themselves into wholeness, and in so doing render a shining transformation.

I have said that this current lifetime is the one in which so very many incarnate souls have a pre-birth plan to heal the darkness, the discordance of all other lifetimes. Such is the total inner alchemy we as souls desire at this time on Earth. The process is similar to that by which a light bulb generates light: electrons flow from a negatively charged area to a positively charged one. Both negative and positive play important roles in a silent, invisible process that ultimately generates light.

When we are in body, life itself is an alchemical process that uses both negative and positive to create light. If we are receptive to our inner negativity, we facilitate our healing. It is for this reason that Jeshua spoke of receiving anger. Indeed, the courageous decision to receive anger or explore any aspect of our inner darkness literally creates an energetic vortex that attracts light. In this way the Universe always supports a courageous decision.

Receptivity is the key that unlocks our hearts and opens them unto themselves. This is the opening to love Debbie has experienced in this lifetime. It is the healing she created for herself and the healing that her father and grandfather desired for themselves before they were born. For you who judge your inner darkness, be assured: Your darkness carries within it the healing you have sought in every life you have ever lived, across time and space, through body after body. Like Debbie, her father, and grandfather, each of us has carried into form the discordance, the "not love," of all our past thoughts, words, and deeds for healing in this present lifetime.

Does judgment of our painful emotions prevent healing? Judgment of anything, including emotions like fear and rage, is a form of attachment, and what is attached is difficult to release. Too, judgment creates separation. We feel apart from that which we have judged; we separate ourselves from ourselves. Inner darkness is healed when embraced with love, but we cannot embrace what we have separated from. Such is the paradox of judgment: it tethers us to what we would release, yet distances us from what can only be healed by love's most intimate embrace.

Still, healing *will* come, whether in this lifetime or the next, because judgment of inner emotions always calls to us others who possess those same emotions. This is universal law. Like a magnet, judgment pulls to us more of what we judge. Many wonder why the same type of person—a type they judge and would prefer to avoid—repeatedly appears in their lives. The answer is that those individuals have judged some of their own emotions as bad and then banished them to a level below conscious awareness. There, like magnets, they draw others who have those same emotions.

Receptivity to painful emotions requires awareness, for we can be receptive only to that of which we are aware. For this reason Debbie planned before she was born to encounter triggers to awareness along her healing path. In her clients' faces she glimpsed her own reflection; they mirrored to her the inner darkness she needed, and her soul desired, to heal. For much of her life, Debbie was unready to look into the mirrors placed before her and so averted her gaze. We know before birth that we may choose when in body to exercise our free will in this way, and so we write into our life blueprints multiple paths to the same end. When in our nonphysical Home, we value the destination—the healing, the learning, the evolution—more than the route taken. When incarnate, we may lament the arduousness of the trail, but our souls have a higher perspective and so lovingly guide us to the desired end with no judgment of the detours we may choose to follow. Ultimately, all paths lead to healing.

As Jeshua said, Debbie's soul hoped before she was born that she would find her way to compassion and forgiveness. In truth, it is her compassion for her father and grandfather that permits her forgiveness of them. And her compassion for them sprang from the compassion she developed for herself, for her own inner darkness and painful emotions. When aware of those emotions, she chose to be receptive to them. When she received them without judgment and an open, loving heart, she was able to express them, howling like a wounded animal. Because expression *is* healing, Debbie was able to free herself of much of the inner pain she had carried throughout her life. When free, she could look upon the pain within her father and grandfather and know compassion for it.

If you have experienced incest, your mind may tell you that the one who committed the act is undeserving of compassion or forgiveness, or that compassion and forgiveness are simply not possible. Such thoughts are natural, understandable, and not to be judged. Compassion and forgiveness are not logical and may be difficult to reach through thought, even if one believes in pre-birth planning. *Feelings* of compassion and forgiveness for one who was abusive are reached *through the heart* in a way that is beyond intellectual understanding, though an awareness of pre-birth planning can be the fertile soil in which this understanding first takes root. Perhaps more important, genuine compassion and forgiveness for an abuser may coexist with thoughts that speak of their impossibility, much in the way that harmony throughout most of the body may coexist with dis-ease in one part of the body.

In developing feelings of compassion and forgiveness for an abuser, one must avoid arguing with thoughts that condemn the abuser. To argue with one's thoughts is to strengthen them. When such thoughts are accepted without resistance and are permitted to abide, their emotional charge is gradually diffused. At the same time, feelings of compassion and forgiveness may be cultivated through healing meditations. Such meditations literally send healing energies back into the past, thus healing the past and in turn both the present and future. The essential element of such meditations is that they access and open the heart. The opening of the human heart is a very real physical and emotional process, one that engenders the type of profound healing the logical mind can neither comprehend nor create. The experiences we plan before we are born are intended not to harden our hearts, but rather to open them in this way so that love flows freely through them.

Ultimately, only the strongest and most loving of souls plan incest. Out of great love for her father and grandfather, Debbie granted them the opportunity they needed to heal. With tremendous strength she agreed to descend into the depths of rage and despair, heal herself, and then offer healing to her family and the world. All those involved in Debbie's planning recognized her greatness and courage. That same greatness and courage reside in the hearts of all who have known incest. So that they might see that light within themselves, Debbie found that light within herself.

∞·∞

CHAPTER 9

Adoption

EVERY YEAR HUNDREDS OF THOUSANDS of children are adopted all over the world. During my study of pre-birth planning, I have learned that children who are born into and remain with their families choose their parents, and the parents choose them. Do adopted children and adoptive parents make similar, mutual choices? If so, why would a soul plan before birth to be adopted? Why would the parents plan on the soul level to adopt children?

And what of the emotional ramifications of adoption? Often, children who are adopted grow up questioning their self-worth, perhaps feeling they were not good enough for their birth parents to keep them. Anger toward the birth parents may accompany these doubts about self-worth. Do souls know before birth that these feelings may occur? Do souls actually want to experience such feelings? How would feelings of unworthiness or anger foster a soul's evolution?

To discover the answers, I spoke with Carole Billingham. Forty-three at the time of our conversation, Carole is married to her second husband, Barry, with whom she has a daughter, Ania.

Carole

A personal coach who specializes in empowering women, Carole was born to Pierre and Jan, who were then in their mid-twenties.

Jan was in graduate school studying to be a teacher; Pierre was in his first year of medical school. They were engaged to be married. When Jan told Pierre she was pregnant, "he freaked out and said he didn't want anything to do with having a family," Carole told me. "My mother went to a home for unwed mothers to go through the last part of her pregnancy and then deliver me."

Carole was adopted two months after birth by Dorothy and Richard, the supportive, loving parents who raised her. As a child she experienced attachment disorder—difficulty bonding with her adoptive parents. Yet as a young adult, "I thought I was healthy with my adoption," Carole said. "I believed that stuff everybody tells you about being the chosen child."

Carole's seeming peace in regard to being adopted was shattered at the age of twenty-five, when she went through a divorce. "It's very common for a woman, when she turns the same age as her birth mother was when she put her up for adoption, to go through some major life change," Carole explained. "My divorce catapulted me into wounds I didn't even know were there.

"The rage piece presented itself. Part of me was pissed beyond belief, and I didn't know what to do with that. As a woman I'd been taught that it's not okay to be angry. And it's certainly not okay to express anger. So, I turned the anger inward and punished myself."

Carole held that anger inside for nine years until a severe auto accident at the age of thirty-four motivated her to work with it.

"As I was being put in the ambulance, I prayed," Carole recalled. "I asked, 'What is this about?' The first thing [I heard from Spirit] was 'slow down.' The second thing was I needed to learn how to receive. And the third thing was that I had been praying for an opportunity to heal my rage, and this event was going to give me that opportunity." The accident resulted in a brain injury that to this day causes Carole to be unusually sensitive to sensory stimuli and to have difficulty maintaining focus.

As I listened to Carole, I thought of others who had shared stories of so-called accidents. A common theme had been living life at too fast a pace, often in an unconscious manner. These individuals had created the accidents to force themselves to slow down and be more reflective. Many souls anticipate before birth that they may live in an unconscious manner and so build the potential for an accident into their pre-birth plans.

Learning how to receive had been another common theme. Often, people were busy giving to others but did not permit others to give to them. The flow of love in the world is circular, and giving love to others constitutes only half the circle. The other half is receiving love. When we refuse to accept love from others, we block the flow of the love in the world just as effectively as if we never give love to others.

"I didn't realize at the time of the accident that I had a brain injury," Carole said. "One of the side effects is that it catapults you back into any past traumas that need healing. It took me right back to birth memories—memories of my birth father wanting to abort me, memories of confusion and shame and guilt and lots of adrenaline during my birth mother's pregnancy. I remembered her shutting me out and not talking to me. She later told me that in her seventh month it got to be so painful for her that she couldn't talk to me. I think that had a profound effect on how I felt my whole life, feeling shut out and like I don't belong anywhere."

The brain injury allowed Carole to recall even statements that were made in the delivery room when she was born. "I remembered the doctor saying, *'This woman is not to have any physical contact with this child, as it is being relinquished.'* I never did get to touch my birth mother. I also had memories of waking up in what I call a box, screaming bloody murder. *'Where's my mother?'* I remembered nurses with masks on, looking at me and not responding to my screaming."

"Carole," I suggested, "tell me more about why your mother felt she couldn't keep you."

"In 1963 abortion wasn't legal. My birth father made it clear to her that he didn't want anything to do with a baby. Then she found out he was cheating on her, so she broke up with him. In 1963 a woman who wasn't married didn't have an option. She had to give up her baby for adoption.

"My birth mother kept my birth a secret from everyone," Carole added. "To this day she still has shame. I've had to work really hard at not making that about me and recognizing it's not my fault."

I asked Carole to talk about the attachment disorder she experienced as a child.

"By the time I got adopted into my family—and I have very wonderful parents—I was like, 'You're my third mother! My first mom dumped me. My second mom only had me for eight weeks. Forget it. I don't want anything to do with you!'"

"Has this been a challenge for you in your adult life as well?"

"I think so," Carole said. "My first marriage was to a man who on the outside looked perfect but who treated me terribly. The way he treated me was a direct reflection of what I thought I deserved. I thought I was unlovable and unworthy, so I married a man who was good at literally telling me that. Finally, I realized that I deserved something more. I broke up with him, which for an adoptee is a very difficult thing to do. We've suffered such great loss that when we do get intimate with someone, whether we break up with that person or they break up with us, we are catapulted right back to that initial loss. It's horrific."

"Carole, do you believe you planned before birth to be adopted?"

"I do."

"What makes you believe that?"

"I believe it is truly impossible to be a victim," she answered. "But it's bigger than that. It's a *knowing* that I signed up for this. I tell my clients, 'If you look at the attributes you are most proud of as an adult, you'll find that most of them go back to your early difficult experiences as a child.' Also, I clearly remember wanting to die when I was in that box in the hospital. I remember saying 'I want to go back' and hearing some voice say, 'No, you've got important work to do.'"

Here, Carole was affirming something I hear often: When we plan certain challenges prior to birth, we also plan for those experiences to instill within us the very qualities we will need to heal. In addition, in ways that are beyond human understanding, our souls endow us prior to birth with certain innate traits that will be vital to our healing. The combination of the two sets of qualities makes healing possible.

"Carole," I inquired, "why do you feel you wanted before you were born to have the experience of being adopted?"

"I have a deep craving that's bigger than me, bigger than my humanness, to help others heal."

In her work as a personal coach, and more broadly through her vibration, Carole is a *lightworker*, one who plans before birth to bring light, sometimes in the form of healing, to the world. Carole's words had beautifully expressed the essence of a light-worker's pre-birth contract. In such a contract, the lightworker often chooses to have the very experience or the emotions she plans to help others heal. The healing of any energy is most powerfully accomplished from *within* that vibration. Such is the nature of true transformation.

"Carole, what qualities did adoption cultivate in you that allow you to do your work?"

"The adoption laid the foundation for the trauma and the feelings of isolation and confusion. The head injury brought me into my intuitive abilities, the memories. And also becoming a mother. Those three things have woven a tapestry for me."

"I'd like to hear the story of your reunion with your birth mother," I said. "How did you find her? What did you say to each other?"

When Carole was twenty-eight, and with her adoptive parents' blessing, she hired a private investigator to locate her birth mother, Jan. For a while she and Jan exchanged letters. Eventually, they agreed to meet at a restaurant.

"The big question burning inside me was, *Why? What did I do that was so bad to make you give me away?* Here's the woman who has hurt me more than any other person on the planet, and I'm opening myself up to being rejected all over again.

"As I got out of the cab, I saw Jan there. I remember thinking, Wow, that's her. We hugged, but nobody cried. I'm sure she was feeling as traumatized as I was.

"We had dinner for many hours. There are a couple of things I remember clearly. One was we had read all of the same books on spirituality. The other thing I remember was asking about my birth father and Jan being very hesitant to say anything. Finally, she said, 'I'm trying to protect you.' In that instant I thought, Oh my God, this is a woman I don't even know, who I lived inside of for nine months, and she really does care about me. She's trying to protect me. That's one of the most powerful memories I have."

"Carole, what would you like to say to adoptees who may be struggling to understand the spiritual meaning?"

"You're not alone. This feeling that you don't belong and that you're not lovable—it's a universal feeling we all have. We just have a different story around it. One of the healthiest things you can do is talk with people who can validate those feelings. Adoptees need to feel validated. It's okay to be angry, and it doesn't have to be at anyone or at society or at birth mothers. It's just anger. Love yourself enough to know that whatever you're feeling is normal.

"There are a lot of adoption support groups now. They bring together adoptees, birth parents, and adoptive parents—and boy is that healing! For everyone. To be in a room where you can be validated for feeling confused, angry, and lost. The adoption wasn't your fault. The feelings you're feeling are not your fault. If you can have an outlet to vent, that's the first step in healing."

Carole's Session with Staci

Carole had spoken poignantly of the challenges she had faced as an adoptee. To discover whether and why she had wanted prior to birth to have this experience, we worked with Staci. I knew Staci and her guide would provide insight and wisdom to all those who have been adopted, adopted a child, or given up a child for adoption, and more broadly to all who wonder why they chose their particular parents and children.

"Carole," Staci began, "I see a past life of yours in the early days of the United States. You lived on the frontier, the eastern edge of Oklahoma. You were a prairie wife. You had six children in that lifetime, five of whom survived. The one who did not survive lived a few short weeks and then caught a fever and died. You didn't realize that was as long as the baby wanted to stay. This baby was your mother in a previous lifetime and your birth mother in this lifetime.

"You two have had this dance in some of your lives where you're with each other only for a short time. I hear and sense that it's a gift you give each other, the gift of carrying the fetal body, the gift of giving life.

"I pick up immediately that this is something you planned and that it has helped you in your quest for emotional independence because you've always felt a certain disconnect with your adoptive family."

"Yes," Carole confirmed.

"It's this sense of being part of them but not *of* them," Staci continued. "It's subtle but fundamental. So, you've had to learn to be there for yourself, to be your own support. It also serves the purpose of having you go within yourself. In fact, it's part of your spiritual growth and evolvement karma this lifetime, because you've enriched the relationship with yourself and your inner being." In previous sessions Staci's spirit guide had defined "inner being" as the intelligent interface between the personality and the soul. "The most important karmic lessons you're working on in this lifetime are to create your own sense of self-worth and self-esteem. You did a profound job of setting the stage.

"There were two things your birth mother had to learn by going through the pain, grief, and even remorse of giving you up for adoption. One was not to be so impulsive, to not let her sexual desires control her to the extent they did when she conceived you. That was a lesson for your birth father as well. The other was to teach her more about being responsible to family. In fact, it was out of a sense of responsibility to you that she gave you up, but she always felt regret. I feel that she never forgave herself."

Spirit then took Staci directly to Carole's pre-birth planning session.

"What I'm seeing now is a conversation on the soul level between you and Barry," Staci said. "I see you both sitting just above the floor in front of this large square that has the diagram of your life on it. It looks like black and white squares, each square representing something in your life. The two of you have human bodies, but they are translucent. They don't have the same density we have when we embody on Earth. The soul is wearing the cloak of the personality it's going to take on in the coming life.

Carole: I don't know how I will survive. All I see is trouble and confusion.

Barry: I will wait until you are ready for me. I will help you.

"He seems very patient, kind, and gentle. He reaches out and touches you with his hands on both of your arms, as if to get you to focus on him instead of what you're going through inside. I am hearing that you had been brothers in a past life. There have been other past lives, too. You two are so close.

"I want to touch on your daughter for a moment. The agreement with your daughter was made on the soul level while you were asleep. It occurred over several nights. 'She will learn from your heartfelt experience' are the words I am told to tell you. One of your gifts to her is to support her self-esteem. You give love more than your birth mother was capable of giving to you."

Staci's description of the conversation between Carole and Barry surprised me. Generally, the feeling among souls in the pre-birth planning session is one of joyful collaboration, even when great challenges are being discussed.

"Staci," I asked, "why does Carole wonder how she will survive? That makes it sound as though she's reluctant about the plan she herself set up for her life."

"She was not reluctant. She was struggling to find her way through the emotionally challenging maze of her life. She saw herself at the age she would be when she met Barry and saw that issues within her would not be resolved completely. So, she was caught up in the emotions of that time in her life."

I then asked Staci if she could hear the pre-birth conversation between Carole and her birth mother, Jan. Immediately, Staci's inner vision took her to that part of the planning session.

"As this soul who is the one who becomes your birth mother approaches, I see you sitting down, Carole. I feel an emotional charge between you two. I hear her say, 'Here we go again.' At this point you are very emotional, but she seems serene. I see images of some of her past lives where there have been babies born to her that didn't live long. I see about five different babies like that, trailing behind her in thought bubbles. She reaches out and puts a hand on you to blend her energy with yours so that you intuitively hear her.

Jan:	You know I love you and always have, but what is meant to be is meant to be. I want to serve you and help you better yourself, but I must also serve me. I'll know when you are ready to come to me, but you know I won't be able to hold you. You know I will want to continue to be free. Is this your choice?
Carole:	Yes.

"You knew this was going to create emotional disruption, but you also knew this was something you needed to do."

Carole: I understand our special relationship, though I may not always while I inhabit my physical Earth body. But I do understand it now, and I thank you for the gift of life you will give me. I will take from you all that I need to live, and we will meet again when the time is right.

I know that I will never have your love as the love of a mother should be. I understand that you have your own challenges that prevent you from wholly loving me and including me in your life. It is in my awareness, though I may not be aware of it when the time comes. I give the gift of my life to you, to have me, if not to hold me. It seems so clear to me now, yet I know there will be times when I will feel desperate in my longing for you. I know, too, that this is only part of what I need to enrich myself.

Jan: I know how hard it is to leave a baby. I watched you grieve over me twice.

"So, there were two times, Carole, that you gave birth to this woman and lost her to illness.

Jan: The depth of that grieving knows no bounds. It is as deep as the soul, bottomless. I know that. The depth of my grieving over giving you up will be a double-edged sword to me. It will be with me my entire life, and yet as I am aware of it now, some part of me will always know I did the right thing. Will you forgive me?

"I see you reach out to her and look into her eyes.

Carole: Yes. I can forgive you now, and I will forgive you in time again. I know this will bring balance into both our lives. And this will balance a long-standing energy that has connected us for centuries. This will be the last time you or I will have to give each other up. In our next lives we will be together always, but not now.

Jan: There are some aspects of the personality I will be working on in my lifetime that will not be conducive to your growth and your sensitive nature. This is part of the reason why I must step aside and allow you to be with another family.

This is a gift of love to you, that I may bring you into the world and give you up, so that those who may not conceive you will have you, love you, nurture your growth, and foster your independence. This is my gift to you. I love you.

"There are tears. There's great love, but also sadness, because you know what's going to happen. You embrace for quite awhile. At that point I see her disappear. So, this probably happened while she was actually alive [incarnate], in her sleep, because otherwise she might stay and witness the rest of the planning.

"I want to describe the room a bit more. Normally, I see a room that is well lit, though I don't know what the source of lighting is. Usually there are a lot of souls in the room. In this room it's a little bit darker, and there isn't a big crowd, maybe half a dozen souls. A few souls come and go at the appropriate time when needed for the planning, but mostly it's you, a couple of spirit guides, and a few very close souls. The focus of light is smaller. The whole room doesn't need to be lit, just the area you occupy."

"Staci," I said, "please ask your guide if he can take you to a conversation Carole has, perhaps with her birth mother, perhaps with a spirit guide or another soul, in which she explains why she wants to be adopted."

Staci paused as she allowed impressions to come to her.

"I see you with a spirit guide," Staci told Carole. "This is toward the very beginning of this planning session, when you are talking about karmic themes you want to focus on in this lifetime. It's at the point of choosing parents for the learning experiences they can give you. Your spirit guide suggests your birth parents. You haven't thought of them before. Your birth mother seems to be a source of pain to you even on the soul level, and so, of course, this guide brought it up. I'm seeing a male spirit guide, an active, assertive force.

"The man who is your birth father is somebody you've not been in a life with since Roman times. He was of the ruling class and thought highly of himself. He had money, rode in a chariot, and wore a lot of gold."

"He's still that way," Carole quipped. Staci and I laughed.

"This ostentation, this self-aggrandizement didn't appeal to you, but your guide brought him up," Staci continued. "There were certain qualities—strength of self, focus, and purpose—you wanted to inherit. You didn't need the rest, so adoption was a way you could remove yourself from that. That appealed to you.

"You said to your guide that you did not want to be around the ego problems that both your birth mother and father would be dealing with in this lifetime. So, it was a good choice to be of them but not with them. You said to your guide that you felt if you were to remain in your mother's life and not be given up for adoption, you would still be cast aside in favor of another child that would come along later. You didn't want to experience that either. So, this seemed like a way to please everybody and accomplish your goal."

"Staci," I asked, "how do souls arrange for the adoptive parents to find the children they are going to adopt?"

"I'm hearing that there was an intermediary planned, some person or organization between Carole's family and the adoptive family," Staci answered. "I don't know what the circumstances were after you were given up for adoption."

"I was put into foster care for eight weeks," Carole said.

"The adoption agency is the intermediary, then. I'm hearing that the recognition was in the name of the agency. That was what guided the mother's choice. There was trust when she heard or saw the name of the agency."

Carole then asked Staci if she could pick up anything else about her adoptive father.

"I see you two talking about this on the soul level," Staci told her. "He's been a brother to you in a past life. He volunteered to be your adoptive father. He had known you before, not just between lives, but during a few lifetimes, and already loved you. I hear him say, 'I will be delighted to have you in my life.'

"Let me now turn my focus to what occurred in the pre-birth planning session with your adoptive mother [Dorothy]. She was about fourteen years old when you and she had this conversation on the soul level. This conversation takes place when her body's reproductive organs have gone into their puberty phase. She senses on a subconscious level that all is not right. I see her point to her uterus. She says, 'I know it's not right.' She's talking about her uterus being tipped and one of her ovaries not forming correctly, bringing about an imbalance that results in infertility. But she also talks about needing to have a child. And she does use that word *need*.

"Mmm hmm, that's my mom," Carole offered.

"I'm asking to be shown why she wants you. At this point she already knows that your mother will be giving you up for adoption. You two have been together in a past life. She enjoyed that very much and wants to be with you in this life again.

Dorothy: You would be doing me a great favor and service by coming to me.

Carole: At times [during this planning] I have felt very alone. Just knowing that I will not be with my birth mother through childhood makes me feel alone.

Yes, I would like that very much. I would like to be with a friend.

"Her excitement energizes you, which energizes her. It's wonderful to see. I see you embrace. You talk about wanting to remember this embrace, so that when she picks you up, you will remember what she feels like. There is this recognition you'll feel physically. It will calm you as a baby; you'll feel it's right when you're in her arms.

Dorothy: Having you as my child from the time you are a baby will fulfill me in a way nothing else possibly could.

"It excites you, Carole, to be given the opportunity to affect somebody's life in such a deep and positive way. You're overjoyed by it. You wholeheartedly agree to this.

Dorothy: I want to help you find your voice so you can express yourself. I want to nurture that.

I don't always feel wonderful about myself. I apologize for anything I may say or do that may hurt you. That is never my intention, but I know I have this weakness.

Please know that I want to strengthen and support you in as many ways as I possibly can. If nothing else, all your life I will care for you, love you, and hold you as if you were my own.

"In my mind I see her thinking about bottle feeding you, how that will be her first gesture of nurturing. I sense how much she would be fulfilled by having you in her life. You've been silent through this because you're in agreement with everything. You love how it feels.

Carole: I am grateful for your desire to love and support me, and for your generosity.

"You hug and smile at each other. Then she goes back to sleep [returns to her sleeping physical body on Earth]."

"My adoptive mother loves me very much," Carole told us. "The agreement that I would fulfill her—that has absolutely been our relationship."

"Staci, is there any place in the planning session where Carole plans to have attachment disorder?" I inquired. "That's something she feels she may have had as a result of the early experiences."

"I'm told she speaks about it with her spirit guide.

Carole: Will I ever be able to trust anyone in this lifetime?

Spirit Guide: You will have a tendency to live in your head and not be aware of all that is spoken by those around, specifically mother and father. This is part of your growth process. One must experience the absence of something in order to find it in oneself. You trust in your being [Self] right now and in the choices you are making for the life that will come. That is the same trust you will learn to employ in those who will comfort and care for you.

Carole: I know I will have trouble trusting that those I am handed over to will love and support me. I will always be afraid of too much or too little love and support.

Spirit Guide: No, you won't always be afraid. It only feels like you will.

Even upon finding your birth mother, the question of trust will not be answered, and the resolution of trust will not be established. The trust issue is really self-trust: trusting yourself to be in the right place at the right time and to always take care of yourself in any situation. This will give you great strength in the long run. Though at times you may feel you are not up to the task, you will learn to give in. The trust issue will make you keep yourself separate from others. Though it is what you will know early in your life, it is a pattern you will one day learn to discard.

"As the spirit guide says this to you, Carole, you understand it in a nonverbal, emotional sense. You see the path of evolvement a soul takes through this process, and you accept this as one of your challenges."

"I can say sitting here, at this point in my life, that I've healed thanks to some wonderful opportunities," Carole said. "The birth of my daughter brought a whole new knowingness of what my birth mother went through. I also had a head injury nine years ago. I knew it was about learning to trust my inner guidance. I can safely say that I absolutely trust myself.

"Staci," Carole continued, "when you talked about my agreement with Jan and that she would have cast me aside for another child, that really resonated. She had two more girls right after me, and the youngest one had triplets. I have noticed a marked difference in our relationship since the birth of all these grandbabies."

"If you had remained in that family, you would have felt that from the time you were a small child," Staci replied.

"Yes," Carole said. "Another thing: What you shared in my conversation pre-birth with Jan when she asked, 'Will you forgive me?' I was in tears, because that's a piece that I'm still working on. I can forgive her from an intellectual level, but my soul certainly wants for me to be able to truly, wholly forgive her."

Carole's Session with Pamela and Jeshua

Carole's last comment in her session with Staci had been a candid acknowledgment of her need for more healing in regard to forgiveness. As Carole wisely pointed out, forgiveness can begin and some forgiveness can occur on the level of the mind, yet true forgiveness must be *felt* in the heart. It is true for deep healing in general. We may heal some guilt by understanding that we are not responsible for another's actions, some shame by knowing we did our best, some feelings of unworthiness by learning that we are divinity incarnate. Yet even more profound healing occurs when we *feel* our innocence, *feel* our beauty, *feel* our infinite worth.

To learn more about how we may heal in such deep ways, Carole and I sought the wisdom of Pamela and Jeshua. Although Pamela typically begins a session by giving her impressions, this session began with Jeshua sharing his insights into adoption.

"Dear friends," he said, "it is I, Jeshua, connecting to you in this moment. I feel your energies, and I ask you to feel me present in your hearts, not a teacher from outside, but a presence deep within you, a presence with whom you are One. I am the teacher from the heart. I speak to you from your feeling side.

"I hope to tell you a bit about adoption and the questions you have around it. I love when you ask questions about this because it helps me to clarify and to elucidate the human reality on Earth, and in that way create an opening to more love and understanding of yourselves. You are working on this process by asking me for advice. Know that you are also contributing to the healing process that was set in motion. You are not doing this just for you, but for humanity, to change some of the general views on adoption and to set free the minds and spirits of those who have been burdened by grief, guilt, and fear.

"I first want to say that there is no blame or guilt regarding the parent who has to separate or who chooses to separate from the child. There seems to be a relationship of offender and victim in this interplay. The parent feels deep guilt when it separates from the child, especially the mother, who feels an almost physical sense of being ripped apart. Even when the mother on a conscious level rejects the child, still there is deep grief and a sense of guilt within her. Most mothers feel this consciously, even when life situations are such that it is better for the child and themselves to give the child up for adoption.

"Let us take a step back to before the child is born in physical reality. Before that, the child spends time in the motherly womb. In this stage the infant is closely united with the mother, so deeply that it hardly knows its boundaries. The mother's energies are absorbed deeply by the infant as it first gets acquainted with Earthly reality in that lifetime. The mother's energy has a huge impact on the child's mind and emotions even when it is inside the womb. Because the child is deeply merged with the mother, it will take on her feelings as its own. It will think it is feeling sad or depressed like the mother when it is actually happy and joyful. There is not yet a distinction between child and mother.

"When the child is born, this connection, which is in many respects a psychic connection, a connection from the heart, is still there. So, although the umbilical cord is cut, psychically there is still a form of union. They are still almost one organism. Whenever a child is permanently taken away from the mother at birth, the child experiences turmoil and chaos. This leaves a huge trauma in the child's mind, but what it feels, what it is actually experiencing, is for the most part the mother's emotions, her tremendous guilt, her grief, her deep sense of having to care for the baby and of failing in this respect. One might say that guilt is the most powerful emotion of the mother who has to let go of a baby, and the baby in this very open and vulnerable state swallows this guilt as its own. It thinks it is guilty. It thinks it is at fault. It senses tremendous fear and abandonment, and thinks it did this to the mother. The burden placed on this child is immense. The child cannot yet experience itself as a victim, so it experiences itself as responsible.

"Because of the openness a child has when it enters the Earth realm, the first imprints in life are very influential. Whenever there is separation between mother and child, especially in the first three months, this will have a huge impact on the child's development. Even when growing up in happy circumstances and cared for by loving parents, still there is this sense of abandonment, confusion, guilt, and having to achieve much in order to be worthy of love and acknowledgment. This is a very painful energy, a wound in the child's spirit.

"A child may also be parted at a later stage from the parent. In this case, even if there were problems in the family, there has been a bonding between mother and child in the first year so the circumstances are a bit different. Still, the separation causes a deep injury in the child's awareness. When a child is adopted at a later stage, the pain caused in parents and child is essentially the same.

"If the child is older when it happens, the hurt is more conscious, and this may seem worse from the human perspective. It may seem less cruel when the child is separated directly at birth from the parents, but this is not so. When the child is not able to experience consciously what happens, then it is kept alive in the subconscious. It will play out at a later age in a sense of not being good enough, having to achieve more, a deep insecurity. The fact that a child is very young when it is separated from the parents doesn't take away from the trauma that occurs.

"The adoptive parents tune in to the child's emotions and help it as much as possible to understand that it is not responsible for what happened. Children are especially sensitive to feeling guilt. When they feel the parent is lacking in love, happiness, or joy, they naturally think of themselves as the cause. So, it is very important to explain to the child, whenever it is capable of understanding, that it is not guilty for anything that happened on the part of the birthing parents. To release the child from guilt is probably the most important gift one can give to it for the rest of its life.

"Also, when a child is in the care of adoptive parents, it is important from early on not to hide the fact that it is adopted, to ask the child to speak up, express emotions, and ask questions about the situation. Whether or not a child expresses questions and emotions, it is not right in any way to ignore that the child is adopted because sooner or later the underlying emotions will show themselves in certain character traits in or behavior by the child."

The Birth Parents

"Jeshua," I asked, "how does giving up a child affect the birth parents?"

"It leaves deep traces within their hearts and minds," Jeshua replied. "Giving up one's own child leaves one of the most painful scars on the human soul, because when a child is born to you, you are entrusted with its soul. The soul, though grand, has chosen to incarnate in a vulnerable, little body. It needs your care and unconditional love as a parent to grow up in this world, to feel safe, to feel welcome.

"All parents know they are endowed with a sacred task when they receive a child from Heaven, even though they may not believe in God or anything religious. Even if they have much trouble themselves, even if the mother is not ready to receive a child, and even if she consciously doesn't want to have a child, there is a deep sense of responsibility within any parent's spirit. To violate that sacred responsibility causes deep, deep suffering in each biological parent's soul.

"I ask you, Carole, to feel for a moment what it is like to receive a child from Heaven, the pure innocence of such a being, and then not to be able to make space for it in your life, to have to say no to it, to have to separate from it. There is deep injury in the soul because of that, and there has been deep injury in your birth parents' souls because of this. I am not asking you to forgive them; I am asking you to see from a distance how this would affect a soul when it feels it has failed the child at such a deep level. Giving up a child for adoption instills a deep sense of guilt and failure in the parents. It will take all their strength and inner wisdom to forgive themselves. No one can do it for them, not even the child that sprang from the womb.

"This is a difficult task. One might say it is even more difficult for the parents to forgive themselves than for the child, because the parents consider themselves to be the offenders. The parents have to learn to see themselves as innocent children, to embrace their own inner child. That inner child is often filled with fear and insecurity and suffering from self-judgment. These parents must come to terms with their own inner child, who represents their deepest emotions. When they do, the process may bring them a peace in their hearts, something that could not have happened if they had not gone through this process of taking on the burden of guilt."

Here, Jeshua was calling attention to one of the major reasons for planning any life challenge: the conversion of darkness, pain, or negativity into light. The darkness may have a past-life origin, for example, guilt left unhealed in past lives and carried forward energetically into the current lifetime for healing, or the pain may have originated in the current lifetime. Regardless of its origin or nature, the healing of that pain infuses light into the soul, magnifying its brilliance. As the negativity is transformed by self-love, the soul's radiance intensifies, and it ascends to new heights.

"There is meaning in all that happens on Earth," Jeshua continued. "There is no such thing as coincidence. A child does not coincidently come into a mother's womb. Often, a child enters when a situation needs to be cleared. For instance, a mother may have certain psychological problems for a long while, or both parents may have certain problems and may have become stuck. The situation seems to have no solution.

"When a child enters, the problems may get solved, or the child's coming may give rise to a crisis in the parents' lives. This makes their emotions more intense and therefore, in a sense, by making things worse the possible solution comes nearer, for crisis sets in motion a new dynamic. The soul of the child—and I am speaking here of children who are put up for adoption—knows that it will bring certain energies to a climax, that it will enable the parents to make more conscious choices."

As I took in Jeshua's words, I was reminded that parents sometimes plan before birth to lose an unborn child in a miscarriage in order to force themselves to face the unhealed parts of themselves and their relationship. Similarly, parents and child may agree prior to incarnation that a child will return to Spirit at a young age, the pain of its death intended to propel the parents into a new awareness and way of life. (In both instances the souls of these children are often highly evolved, and they are working in loving service to the parents.) To give up a child for adoption, even though the decision is made consciously by the incarnate personality, is to lose the child in a similarly painful way. That pain may well be the catalyst for profound healing and change.

"Often," Jeshua said, "a child's entrance will either make the parents more loving and warm or bring conflicts to the surface, conflicts that were only half conscious before the child entered. The child tends to bring certain problems into sharp focus. Often, after a child is born the mother's awareness of who she is and what she wants in life becomes much clearer. She may separate from her partner because she discovers the relationship doesn't truly fulfill her needs. This, in fact, was the child's purpose—not to separate its parents but to empower the woman. Whereas it may seem tragic to separate when a child is still very young, on the inner level it may be important for all involved because it may accelerate their spiritual progress. So, a child, though beautiful and innocent, doesn't necessarily create peace and happiness by its presence. It may confront the parents with deep issues within themselves, and this may turn the lives of the parents upside down. This is part of the child's intention for entering the lives of its parents."

Pre-Birth Planning and Adoption

"We have now spoken about children at a very young age, and before, when they were inside the mother's womb. I will now go farther back and speak of pre-birthing planning and how souls choose their life plans, especially in regard to adoption.

"When a child is adopted, in almost all cases it knows so beforehand. It is an experience the soul wants to go through for several reasons. One reason is that some souls have inflicted pain on others, pain they want to balance in this lifetime. The soul has a deep longing for balance, and it wants to experience both sides of any issue. But, that is not in the way of punishment, and it is not that a soul is directed to do so. Whenever a soul has hurt people, it carries a deep sense of guilt within. It wants, therefore, to relive this experience and to rise above it. By doing so it will have balanced the karma.

"There are other reasons for incarnating as a child who will be adopted. Sometimes the soul embodying the child is very conscious and has a longing to reunite with its adoptive parents, and the adoptive parents themselves cannot have children. That may be for a number of reasons, but from the standpoint of the child to be adopted, it wants deeply to unite with the adoptive parents because it knows these souls. So, it has to enter through the channel of the birthing parents. The more conscious souls are willing to take this upon themselves because they know the birth parents will learn from this process. The more conscious a soul is, the more it is able not to take upon itself the guilt and grief of the birth parents. The child, when a conscious soul, may already have a sense of not fitting into the birth family. So, there is a readiness in this child's heart, and therefore the process of being adopted is easier. There is a sense of being at home with the adoptive parents. This child will suffer, but the healing will be easier because there will be a more evident connection between the child and the adoptive family. They will be very sensitive to its needs and desires.

"I have now named two possible reasons for souls to have the experience of being adopted. In the first case, the soul carries burdens that make it more unconscious, less aware of its own divinity, one might say. Still, it is very courageous to choose such a difficult process. When the soul is more conscious, the path is easier. In a sense I am now describing two ends of a spectrum. In between there may be, for instance, souls who are conscious in that they realize they have deep issues regarding their self-worth. Whenever a child is separated from its parents at an early age, it raises issues of self-worth. A soul in the middle of the spectrum may want to solve issues of self-worth that it is already carrying from earlier lifetimes, and so it may take on the emotions caused by adoption. This child may be subconsciously aware that it is there to become more free and independent of outside judgments. This middle point in the spectrum is where most adopted children are. They have to go through heavy internal struggles to create a sense of self-worth and independence. But if they do so, they will experience tremendous healing on the soul level."

Once again I was reminded of the significant role feelings or beliefs of unworthiness play in pre-birth planning. Time and again souls who in previous lives questioned their inherent worth planned life experiences that would bring that issue front and center where it simply could not be ignored. The specific form in which the issue presented varied considerably from soul to soul, but underlying these different challenges was a sense of unworthiness the soul desired to heal.

"Much healing can also take place in the adoptive parents," Jeshua told us. "Many adoptive parents have a life theme of letting go of expectations. They had a desire to have a child and had to let go of that expectation. There is an issue of releasing control, of opening to things life wants to give them in other ways. Often, the child will bring surprises into their lives. Adoptive parents need to let go of certain pictures they have of the happy child or the child they always wanted. They are challenged to be truly open to the soul of the child. This is the gift the child brings to them. Even when the child has psychological problems, those problems are actually a gift because it helps them embrace the child unconditionally."

Adoptive Children's Healing

"I will now address the question of how adoptive children should deal with the emotions caused by adoption," Jeshua continued. "Almost all adoptive children will experience rage at the biological parents. The children will want to know why they were put up for adoption and how the parents justified the decision. It is important to accept the anger. Whenever you are helping these children, offer acceptance so they are allowed to feel the anger thoroughly. They should be encouraged to cry, yell, or write angry letters to the parents, not sending them but as a means of self-expression. Before they can get to peace and forgiveness, they first must give anger its rights, its truth. It has to be felt within the body to be truly released. At this stage it is about expressing the inner child, which is the seat of the emotions.

"Bodywork may be helpful—to feel the energy of the anger as a flow within by stamping your feet on the floor or beating a pillow. It is important not to be afraid of the anger, to trust the body's wisdom. Emotions speak through the body and show themselves in an inner tension that wants to be released. The anger is truthful, and there is no use ignoring it. When ignored, it grows. When repressed, it seeks other ways of expression that are far more destructive than crying out in anger. So, if you feel pure anger inside because of your past, that is a good thing. Welcome it. Far better to feel it than to have it express itself in destructive behavior like addictions or obsessive thinking. Those are perverted forms of expression. The first step in therapeutic healing is to address the anger in pure form as the energy-in-motion that it is. Do not be afraid of the power of your anger.

"If you let anger speak through your body, at some point it will be released and you will find deep grief behind it, a sense of wanting to cry a river for the betrayal and abandonment you felt very early in life. When you get into the state of grief, cry, let the tears come, and do not hold back.

"You will find suddenly that you are also grieving for your parents, that you are sensing their grief, their tremendous guilt and pain. There you get into the union between you and your birth parents, the unity that was once there and that caused you to absorb their feelings. You will first cry about yourself and the child who experienced the abandonment. That child lies deeply buried inside you, only semiconscious. But when you go into this grieving, you will find you are grieving because of your parents and what they have lost.

"At a conscious level you experienced anger at your parents, but when you go through this process, you will find you are not angry with them. You will find that you feel for them. The compassion can go so deep that you even feel responsible for their pain, feeling guilty in a sense. This is what you felt like as a child: *'I got them into trouble.'* That's the basic feeling of the child. So, the next step is to investigate this area in which you are in fact grieving for your parents, in their stead because you absorbed their emotions.

"When you do this, you begin to address the guilt that may be buried deep within you: *'I am not good enough. They must have had a reason for letting me go. I failed.'* All those kinds of deeply hidden thoughts are there and need to be addressed. And when you address them with consciousness, they will go. You will release them. Whenever you have gone through the process of experiencing their grief, your grief, and the guilt you have absorbed, then you will have entered an entirely new space of consciousness. You will already be healed to a great extent. Having released the anger, and having gone through the grief and self-judgment in the light of compassion and understanding, it is there that most healing takes place.

"When you see yourself as the little child at whatever age it happened, you will see the child's mind saying, *'I must have done something wrong to deserve this. I am not worthy of their love.'* When you see this clearly from your conscious mind, then you can reach out to that inner child and tell it, *'Of course it is not your fault. You are not guilty at all. You even chose this experience to come to terms with your own feelings of unworthiness. You chose this experience as a soul to help your birth parents come to terms with their own issues. You are such a beautiful being, so whole and lovable unto yourself.'* And when you can see this, when you can reach out to that child you once were, you reach through time, back into your past, and you heal that child. Through your own awareness, you can be the parent you so longed for. You can imagine picking up the child you once were and erasing all the guilt and self-judgment by embracing it with the mother energy. The mother energy is a universal, cosmic energy of complete acceptance and safety. When you get to this deepest level of self-healing, you are doing the work you planned to do as a soul when you started this lifetime. You are healing the most hurt part of yourself, and you therefore spread light in this world, both to yourself and to others.

"When you are a child who is adopted, you will find that even when you get to this level, which takes a lot of inner work, it will still take a long time to heal. The self-judgment, the notion of being unworthy, goes deep and needs a repeating of this process to finally erase the negativity in your soul. Again and again you have to remind yourself that your light, your divine core, is unscathed and whole throughout the experience. So you see, whenever you restore [in your own perceptions] the beauty of this inner core, then you will radiate this divinity to other people. You will spread an energy so beautiful and pure that you will make a difference in the world you could not have made if you did not go through this deep process of being wounded and then healing yourself. There is spiritual meaning in the process of taking this injury upon you and releasing it," Jeshua said.

Birth Parents' Healing

"I will now say more," he continued, "about how parents who have put their child up for adoption can come to terms with their feelings. In many ways the process for them is the other way around. They start with the feelings of guilt, and this can be a suffocating burden for them. If you cannot get beyond guilt, you cannot truly heal yourself. Often these parents feel they have to keep the guilt alive to punish themselves for wrongdoing. True healing, however, comes from going beyond the guilt and connecting to the emotions that were present when they made the decision to give up the child. They have to connect to the despair and also to the anger that was probably there at the people around them and at their situation in life. This is a human instinct: to place the burden on others when the experience is too heavy. Humans project outward and accuse the world around them. They feel angry about life.

"This anger should now be expressed fully, without judgment. When the anger is experienced fully, in the way I have described, a layer of grief is exposed: grief for not being able to hold the child in one's arms, grief for not having been able to watch it grow up. This grieving and mourning will come to the forefront. When the grief is fully experienced, then healing will take place and parents will embrace spiritually their own inner child and say, *'I did the best I could. It is okay not to get everything right all the time.'*

"The parents may then sense there is spiritual meaning in the experience. After they go through these stages, they may come to terms with their own vulnerability and forgive themselves while taking full responsibility for the choices they made."

Pamela's Reading for Carole

Jeshua had spoken lovingly and poignantly of the challenges inherent in being adopted, giving a child up for adoption, and adopting a child. Now that we had his wisdom on which to build, we were ready to look in a more personal way at Carole's experience. Pamela began by giving her impressions.

"Carole, when I look at your auric field—the energy surrounding your body—I feel a genuine kindness in you, an openness to others that is beautiful. You seem to be appreciative of the good things people give to you. Also, you seem to be modest about yourself; you do not fully value your own gifts and power. I see a dark purple energy inside your head and moving through the rest of your body. This dark field brings critical judgment about yourself, and that is quite opposite to the soft and gentle kindness you express toward others. I see inside your heart chakra—an energy center inside your chest—a soft and warm pink energy you have been developing in the course of your lifetime."

Pamela then described a past life in which Carole was with her birth parents, Pierre and Jan. In that lifetime Jan was her daughter and Pierre her father. A widower, Pierre lived with Carole, her husband, and Jan for many years. In his loneliness he demanded much attention from Carole. He was also highly critical of her. Eventually, Carole and her husband asked him to leave their home. Years later, as he lay on his deathbed, he told Carole that the years he had lived with her were "the most beautiful years of my life." He added, "You had a kind of love and purity that made me envy you. I wanted that, too, and therefore in my behavior I was not fair."

Pamela explained that by entrusting herself to Pierre as a vulnerable baby in their current lifetime, Carole had contributed greatly to his soul growth. To my surprise, Pamela then relayed a message directly from Pierre's soul to Carole: "You have confronted me with my deepest darkness, and you have done so in a most gentle and loving way by being a vulnerable, small child entering my life. You have been a precious angel to me."

In that same past life, Carole's relationship with Jan [her daughter] was often strained, with Carole frequently disapproving of Jan's behavior. When Jan eventually took up with a man of whom Carole disapproved, Carole refused to help financially, and great hardship followed for Jan. Jan died before Carole in that lifetime, their relationship unhealed. "By being born through her [in your current lifetime]," Pamela told Carole, "you wanted to tell her, *'I value you. I do not look down on you. And I truly love you.*'" In this way Carole brought healing to Jan's soul, and she healed their relationship from the past life.

Pamela's consciousness now stepped aside, and Jeshua returned to speak with us.

"Carole," Jeshua said, "please accept me as your brother. I am close to you, never above you, but next to your heart. You are beautiful as you are, but your heart has been closed to some extent to your beauty, your integrity, your kindness. You have withheld appreciation for yourself.

"When you were born into this lifetime, you had a certain plan, some goals you wished to accomplish: to surrender self-judgment; to place no authority above you; to trust your own heart completely; and to see beauty in every expression, even if it does not match outside standards, standards that are not your own. You wanted to feel the beauty of life itself unfolding through you.

"In a previous lifetime, the one before this one, you were a nurse working in a warlike situation. You were a young woman at that time, and you had great sense of duty and responsibility for your patients, giving all of yourself to help them, almost at the cost of yourself. You also had a tendency to obey higher authority figures, to believe they knew best.

"In particular, there was a doctor who had certain views on how to deal with patients. You did not have his medical knowledge, but from your day-to-day contact with your patients you had hands-on, practical knowledge about their illnesses and the emotional pain they went through. So, it occurred at some point that you disagreed with this doctor but you were afraid to stand up for yourself and to go against his authority. This put you in a difficult situation. On the one hand, you knew the intuitions of your heart. When you looked into the eyes of your patients, you knew very well what you had to do. But, there was this harsh voice from the doctor, ordering you to follow a certain method that did not comply with your heart's desire.

"The doctor urged you to be 'more professional' as he called it, to have more distance from the patients, but you felt called to sit with them, to be with them when they were dying. You were like an angel, very compassionate and kind. This energy is still with you, but in that lifetime you were taught that this was not fitting. In the end the doctor threatened to send you away or to fire you, so you complied with his wishes, repressing your feminine, feeling side. This was a huge conflict psychologically. After you died in that lifetime, you realized you were working from the heart as a nurse and that that was a good thing. You were sorry for not having been disobedient toward that doctor and for not having chosen your own path.

"In general there is a male energy clinging to you, speaking with an authoritarian voice that has become an inner voice for you. It tells you to achieve, to be ambitious, to do everything you can. There is nothing wrong with being ambitious if the ambition flows from true inspiration in your heart, if you feel joyful and inspired to follow that ambition. But, in your own history there has been a repression of your joy and inspiration because of the inner voice telling you that you are never good enough, that you have to obey and be a good girl.

"When you started this lifetime, you as a soul wanted to develop the giving from the heart, the being from the heart. There was deep insecurity about whether you would be valued if you did so. You wanted to shine your soul's qualities out to the world, but you knew you would have to solve your insecurity about this. The brain injury you experienced was indeed part of your pre-birth planning. It was something that was very likely to happen to help you become more aware of yourself and accept unconditionally your compassion and kindness.

"If you get upset about your limitations [from the brain injury], please remember that you are in essence an angel bringing your light to Earth, which needs it much. You extend your light through your kindness, your understanding, your compassion. See yourself as the nurse you once were, sitting at the side of people in pain, making them feel cherished and loved in their final moments. It is in these qualities that your true power lies. If you feel angry or frustrated because your brain doesn't work the way you would like, remember there is purpose behind this. The limitations free the way, so to speak, to concentrate on other qualities, the ones of the heart.

"Know there is deeper meaning. You will see it yourself. You will see the beautiful things that happened because of the injury and the limitations you have experienced. You will see that it has opened another dimension in your life. After you depart from this lifetime, you will see that it has been a blessing. You surely will.

"I will now address your adoption," said Jeshua. "You wonder if this was part of your life plan and what the purpose behind it is.

"The higher purpose of your adoption has been to develop a self-esteem that would not rely on anything outside you. When you are born on Earth as child, your parents are the first authorities you meet, the first persons to whom you cling unconditionally and on whom you are completely dependent. When there is a separation from your parents as a child, you feel rejected and even guilty. It is important for you to find that place inside in which you still feel you have failed your parents, that you did something wrong.

"This was exactly the experience you were looking for as a soul. You wanted to have the experience of seemingly being rejected and pushed aside. You wanted to rise above it in this lifetime, to feel truly validated and appreciated for who you are, and to base this evaluation solely on you and not on anyone outside you. You wanted see your own beauty and power, even if this was not mirrored back to you by your environment. This is a repetition of what occurred between the nurse and the doctor when you were rejected by an authority, and it was magnified in the beginning of this lifetime when your parents gave you up for adoption.

"Your parents were torn at an inner level. It is not that they consciously rejected you, but that is the way a child experiences it, even if the child is not consciously aware of it. There is inside you a deep insecurity because of being adopted, a feeling of being completely abandoned and alone. You chose this experience to learn from it that you are never truly alone. There are always healing powers surrounding you who will catch you when you fall.

"You are still recovering from your early childhood experiences. You have done very well. You have made beautiful progress on your inner path in this lifetime. You have given love to and received love from others, and what better way to show that you have survived your inner wounds. Be proud of this. That is your goal in this lifetime—to develop self-love, true self-esteem, not relying on anything outside you. That is your true mission.

"I wish to say, do not have the attitude of 'I have to make the best of it.' In that way you undervalue your own true power. Instead, expect a new chapter in your life to begin. Know that because of the qualities of your heart, and not so much because of the qualities of the mind, you will reach out to others in the world in a way that will make a difference.

"I take you back to the previous lifetime in which you were a nurse attending to people who had disabilities. It never crossed your mind that they were anything less than whole. On the contrary, whenever you looked into the eyes of severely injured persons, you could see their beauty and innocence, their souls shining in the midst of physical but not spiritual limitation. That you could sense the soul's radiance was your gift, your power. You can now extend this gift to yourself and deeply sense your divinity.

"Your husband, Barry, and your daughter, Ania—one of the reasons you are together is to experience what it is like to have a loving family. Both you and Barry have a need of this, to experience the safety and love, the intimacy of forming a family together. In both of you there are fears of not being good enough, of failing, of not achieving enough. Ania is helping both of you with this fear. She has a sense of spontaneity, of doing what her heart tells her to do, something that is liberating for both of you. You can be inspired by her vitality and love of life.

"You and Barry knew you were going to meet in this lifetime. Indeed, you know each other from previous lifetimes as well. In one, Barry was your son and you were his mother. In view of the situation in your life with regard to adoption, this has a deeper meaning. Before you started this lifetime, you and Barry planned to help each other with your insecurities and to inspire each other. In both of you the issue of self-trust is important, and your relationship will flourish most when you truly accept yourself and enjoy the gifts you have to share with the world. It is helpful to Barry if you can truly appreciate yourself; it will inspire him to do so as well. Receive his love, and that will help both of you, too.

"Ania has come into your life to encourage you to trust yourself and be spontaneous. Do not reflect too much on yourself and think about things that need change or feel painful; just feel joyful and embrace life. These are qualities she wants to remind you of. She wanted to be your daughter in this lifetime because of the innate kindness that radiates from your soul.

"She has been quite powerful in previous lifetimes, and she is coming to terms with the issue of how to balance her own power. She needs the emotional safety you provide. Experiencing that safety, that steadiness, will enable Ania to express her power and vitality in a balanced way. Opposite to both you and Barry, who are sometimes afraid of outside authorities and the judgments of the outside world, she is much more one who stands up against authorities and goes her own way. This creates a balance between the two of you and her. You are working, in a sense, on opposite issues.

"You can help Ania reach her life goals by being steady and unconditional in your love but at the same time firm about what you like and don't like, need and don't need. Being clear about your feelings helps her relate to you. If you speak to her from your heart, she can relate to your feelings. If you speak from the mind, she has a tendency not to listen. She wants to hear your innermost feelings.

"You want to be here in peace and service to each other."

Discussing Adoption with Jeshua

It was now time for questions. "Jeshua," I asked, "what role does adoption play in advancing the consciousness of humanity?"

"Being adopted raises deep questions about one's identity," he replied. "The questions you tend to ask when you are adopted are, 'Who am I? How does my bloodline affect my character? How much of my identity is determined by my biological makeup? How much is determined by other factors, by my social environment, by my adoptive parents? Is there also a layer of identity that is independent of all of these factors?' This layer is your soul, the eternal you.

"So, sooner or later being adopted stimulates you to look beyond the human factors that determine your identity and to find your divinity within. Therefore, separation from your birth family may open up a spiritual awareness of your soul consciousness. It may help to create an understanding among humans, which is much needed in this age, especially when children are adopted from another country, when they look different, or when they come from a different race or culture. In that way adoption can give rise to unity consciousness, a universal recognition of one another's humanness across cultures.

"Adoption enhances spiritual growth, although it often happens in a very painful way. Suffering is not needed to create spiritual growth. There are other ways of becoming aware of who you truly are, but you have become used to suffering on Earth. But, we are now on the verge of a collective change, and there will be different ways of learning for mankind."

"Jeshua, what percentage of adoptions are planned before birth? What percentage of souls plan at least one lifetime in which they will be adopted?"

"Roughly eighty percent of adoptions are planned before incarnation, but to speak of percentages and numbers is difficult because there is not a finite number of souls or lifetimes. There are an infinite number of souls and they go through an infinite number of lifetimes, not only on Earth but also on other planets and systems as well.

"Although souls have life plans, nothing is fully determined beforehand. It is always about likelihoods and potentials. Some potentials have a very high probability, and therefore one might say they have been predetermined. But, there is always a margin of freedom, because the personality always has free will and can always choose a different path. When that happens, when you choose a less likely path, a new life plan will come into play. So, there are always alternatives at hand.

"Souls are at different stages of evolution. At some point ninety percent will choose to experience being adopted, but how it will fit into their life plans is dependant upon how evolved they are at a soul level and how much unity there is between the soul and the identity at the Earth level. The more unity there is, the more they are open to their souls, the more adoption can lead to an awakening of their divinity. But, if a soul is not that evolved, adoption can lead to a difficult karmic cycle of lifetimes, repeating the issue of being abandoned and feeling lost."

I asked Jeshua how souls decide whether to be adopted as infants or later as children.

"When you are planning your life," he answered, "you are assisted by your guides, who help you go through different scenarios that may come into play in the lifetime. You, as the soul who is ready to incarnate, are often less aware than the guides surrounding you. You are aware of certain life lessons you want to experience. You are drawn to those lessons and to the emotions that accompany them. The guides will show you different possibilities. You will intuitively feel which scenario, which life plan, will suit you best. Sometimes you may shrink from the life plan that seems too challenging, but your guides will explain the meaning behind it. You have free will, but most souls have to trust their guides, and sometimes they have to be pushed a bit to take on the challenges they need to fulfill their missions.

"When you are a soul whose life plan it is to be adopted, very often whether you are adopted as a baby or later on is not a factor that stands on its own. The choice for a certain age is one factor, but other factors are the kind of family you will be in and the prior karmic relationships with the adoptive parents. There are many factors, and age is often not the determining factor that makes you choose a specific life plan. The decision you make will often be guided by an intuitive sense. It is almost like each of the possibilities has a different radiance or color, and you intuitively choose the one that appeals to you the most

"You will, for instance, be able to feel some of the emotions you will feel as a child, and you will be able to compare these emotions with other possibilities, with what you would feel in other families in which you might be adopted in different circumstances. You will make your choice based on these different emotions. At one point you will have an overwhelming sense of, *This is the right choice.*

"This scenario shown to you by your guides, the one that will eventually be your choice, will radiate an energy of joy. But, at the same time it will also radiate an energy of challenge. You will feel a bit fearful but also excited. If it is the right mixture of joy, excitement, and tension, then this precise mixture will make a soul aware that this is what it is drawn to. You will have a deep sense of meaningfulness with the life plan. Souls choose according to their intuition, their feelings."

"Jeshua, how do the adoptive children and adoptive parents know they will be able to find each other?"

"This is something that cannot be comprehended by the analytical mind. If a life plan is put into motion, certain events will take place that will make it highly likely you will meet the adoptive parents you are destined to be with. You use the word *synchronicity* for these kinds of events. You often recognize when these events take place. You experience a clarity of mind, a sense of meaningfulness, a sense of things having to be that way. It is your Higher Self influencing certain possibilities in your life.

"In general, the adoptive parents will often feel drawn to a particular child. This child may have certain character traits or a certain look that fits the adoptive parents' desire. There may be something specific in this child that touches them and makes them reach out in their hearts, an emotional thing they cannot explain. But, the fact is they already know this child at a soul level, and they want to join with it. Often adoptive parents will have a sense of the child belonging to them even when they only just met. This shows that there is a life plan at play, a decision from before incarnation.

"In the case of Carole's adoptive parents, they wanted to meet Carole again in this life; they knew her from other lifetimes. They had a desire from the soul level not just to have a child in their lives, but to meet Carole specifically. They had a bond of friendship from the past; in particular, Carole's adoptive mother had been a good friend of hers in another lifetime in which they were the same age. They were very loyal to each other. From a soul level, Carole's adoptive mother wanted to help, in this lifetime, to provide her with love and safety. But, from a higher perspective the relationship is of a mutual nature. Carole's adoptive mother also wanted to learn from Carole, from the things she went through emotionally, from her wisdom and kindness. Through taking care of Carole as a child and helping her grow up, both the adoptive father and mother have enriched themselves. It was arranged before birth that they would meet in this way. They love each other, all three of them, at a soul level, and they wanted to enhance one another's growth. They have given one another love and understanding."

∾

We who are One can never be separate from one another, but we can create the illusion of separation in the physical realm. In our nonphysical Home, where no such illusion exists, we know that we are cells in the heart of one Divine Being, united by Love in one cosmic pulse. On Earth, seemingly confined by the apparent limitations of a human body, we perceive ourselves as distinct from one another. Only the most powerful of beings can create such illusion. Only the most courageous challenge themselves to live in it.

To be adopted is to repeat and intensify the original decision to separate from the One. Child and mother are naturally one, and family recreates, though dimly, our feeling-knowing of the unity that is our natural state of consciousness. The experience of separation from both Home *and* mother or family may bring great light to the soul, but it is not for the faint of heart. Carole's pre-birth decision to experience both is the bold act of the spiritual warrior.

One of the higher purposes of Carole's adoption was for her to develop a self-esteem that is independent of anything external to her. Carole's pre-birth intent to derive esteem from a sense of Self, from *knowing* that she is a majestic, vast, limitless soul, is but one expression of a common and broader type of pre-birth plan: the desire to be self-referencing. Across millennia and in dozens, even hundreds, of incarnations, we as souls seek to discover and then lead lives based on our own inner wisdom, our own heart's desires, our own strength, our own knowings, longings, and passions. In the Oneness of Home we retain our individuality, but when we isolate that individuality on the physical plane, its contours become more pronounced, its facets deeper and more striking. The diamond that glistens in a long necklace may be brilliant, but its light is immersed in that of the other jewels. When removed from the necklace and standing on its own, its unique radiance shines more brightly for all to see.

This is the value, the power of the feelings of separation and abandonment created by adoption. As Jeshua put it, Carole sought to place no authority above her own, to trust her own heart completely, and to set aside outside standards for beauty, choosing instead to see beauty in every expression. When Carole returns to her eternal Home, the pain of abandonment no more than a wispy memory, she will know experientially her own brilliance. And with that knowing at her core, she will not hesitate in future lives to heed the call of her inner wisdom or follow the promptings of her heart. As souls, our deepest desires are to serve and to love. We serve most wisely and love most selflessly when aware of, and able to draw upon, our own strength and wisdom.

When we plan before birth to experience great challenges like being adopted or giving a child up for adoption, we also plan the means by which we may heal from those experiences. The soul's intent is not to become lost in trauma, but rather to rise above it. The basis for much healing is *expression*. It is for this reason Jeshua spoke of expressing the inner child, perhaps beating a pillow or stomping one's feet on the floor to release anger, for example. The inner child is more than mere metaphor for internalized pain; it is a real being who simply exists in a dimension beyond the perception of the five senses. In holding and loving that inner child, we send the energy of love into the past, thus healing the past and, in turn, both the present and the future. What we call imagination is real, and what we imagine actually occurs, though on a different plane of existence. Loving the inner child is an act of literally reaching into the past and changing it.

Imagination derives its healing power from intent, and intent may heal the present just as potently as it heals the past. The emotions experienced by Carole and her birth parents—anger, guilt, grief, resentment, blame—are energetically present within the physical body and aura, much like dark clouds in an otherwise clear sky. The intention to heal is the gentle breeze that begins to clear the clouds away. (Prayers for healing, which are always answered, strengthen the breeze.) As those heavy emotions clear, more light literally enters the human aura. When Carole tells Jan in the pre-birth planning session, "I will forgive you," that statement of intent creates a healing energy Carole carries into body for expression later in life. For you who were adopted and feel you lack the internal resources to heal from the experience, rest assured: You set a similar intent in your pre-birth planning and so placed a similar healing energy within your body. That energy is activated now by your conscious awareness of it. Your intent to heal, first formed before you were born and remembered now as you read these words, initiates the healing you seek.

Ultimately, Carole's story illustrates how nothing is as it seems on the physical plane. The child who is given up for adoption may appear to be a victim in a harsh, unwelcoming world, but he or she is really the powerful soul who courageously chose and embraced the experience. The birth parents may seem to be selfish or irresponsible, yet in truth they are engaged in an act of profound service: the giving of physical life to a soul who seeks to reunite with the future adoptive parents and can come to them in no other way. This act of service requires tremendous strength and selflessness, as Jan demonstrated when she spoke of the guilt she knew she would carry for her entire lifetime. The adoptive parents may also appear to be victims of an indifferent Universe, one that coldly denied their longing to give birth to a child. Yet they, too, planned their lives, and the seemingly uncaring Universe lovingly granted their wish in the only way possible.

Each soul plays its part in this intricately choreographed dance, a dance expressed in lives of beauty and grace.

CHAPTER 10

⚭

Poverty

WHEN IN SPIRIT, WE CREATE instantaneously
with thought. If we desire a beautiful home, we
manifest that home simply by envisioning it. Any
furnishings we may want—a plush rug, soft bed, a soul-stirring
painting—come effortlessly into being. We may place our home
next to a quiet brook or along a roaring oceanfront, in a majestic
forest or tranquil, flowered glade. We are limitless in our ability
to create. This abundance is our birthright as Divine Beings.

Why, then, do so many struggle on the physical plane with
financial challenges or outright poverty? Certainly much hardship is created by our belief in and thoughts of lack as well as
our difficulty remembering ourselves as the powerful creators we
truly are. Yet, how do we explain the millions of people who
are born into deprivation? Since we as souls choose the time,
location, and circumstances of our birth, why would anyone
knowingly incarnate into poverty?

Rolando Lopez grew up impoverished in Nicaragua. Now a
sixty-three-year-old widower without children, Rolando lives in
South Carolina in much greater comfort than he had known in
his youth. Why had he planned such destitution for his formative years? Rolando could have chosen to be born to a wealthy or
middle-class family in Nicaragua. He also could have incarnated
in a wealthier country or on a planet where the inhabitants never

experience lack. How had Rolando hoped to evolve through this decision?

Rolando

"My full name is Edgar Rolando Lopez Gutierrez," Rolando began. He spoke softly and radiated gentleness. "I was born on a coffee farm in Nicaragua, Central America, in the northern city of Jinotega. I have been a scientist most of my life. I became a Ph.D. person at the University of Massachusetts in 1997. My Ph.D. is in entomology, specializing in biological control of insect pests. I was hooked into that since my early ages when I grew up on a farm and my father was a farmer.

"One day my father took me to visit a friend. His friend had a small piece of land planted with beans in front of his shack. That was all he had for his family—beans. When my father asked how the beans were growing, he said, 'Fine so far, but I have infestation of white flies, and I don't have money to get an insecticide. That means I'm going to lose my beans that represent the food for my family.' At that moment he started crying."

And as he told the story, Rolando, too, began to cry.

"I will never forget that," Rolando said, choking back his tears. "I decided that very moment that there should be a way of helping poor people. I was at that time seven years old."

I asked Rolando to tell me more.

"My mother and father had eleven children. I was the eighth. I was born on that beautiful farm. The lesson I learned very early in my life from my father was that you can do whatever you want if you make the effort to achieve it. That expression— *'You can do whatever you want'*—stayed with me all my life.

"I was eight when my family lost the farm. One year during the coffee harvest there was bad weather. There was a week of rain, constant rain, and so the coffee ripened in a hurry. In two or three days all the coffee was ripe. We didn't have enough hands to harvest this coffee. So, the coffee dropped to the ground and spoiled." In order to repay business loans, Rolando's father was eventually forced to auction the farm.

"We were left with nothing," Rolando said sadly. "So, my mother came up with the idea to make potato chips." He pronounced it *cheeps*. "It was a very small home business that had all my sisters and my parents peeling and frying potatoes by hand all day long and then making the small packages that me and my brother sold at the baseball and basketball games in town. We also sold potato chips at the local movie theater in the evening, because people hang out around the entrance. That was our salvation. The potato chips were a big hit.

"In the beginning I felt humiliated and didn't want to go, but I never showed that because it was needed for the family."

"Rolando, how many years did you sell potato chips?"

"I sell potato from eight, nine, and ten years [of age]."

"How were you able to sell potato chips and go to school at the same time?"

"We run after school to get home and get the chips," explained Rolando. "I remembered my father told me in the very early years of my childhood that I needed to keep working hard for what I wanted. I wanted to be first in my class, but I didn't have much time to study. I got back home and had dinner, and everyone was so tired they went to bed right away. I had to stay studying alone. Many, many days I remember my mother waking up and coming to me and saying, 'You need to go to bed.' And I said, 'I haven't finished my homework.' I stuck with my father's comment that you need to put effort to get what you want. I was getting my first of the class recognition and at the same time I was selling potato chips."

I asked Rolando to describe the process of selling the chips. What did he say to people? What did people say to him?

"I didn't have to say much except *'Papas! Papas!,'* meaning potatoes. The people knew what they were going to get for a peso, which was like fifteen cents. Sometimes they were happy, and sometimes they were insulting because they wanted me to let them get the potato chips and then pay later. But my mother told me to never do that.

"Once, I remember losing the money. I felt so badly because I had to come home with my empty bag and my empty hands." Rolando started to cry again. His voice was pained. "I put my bag with my money somewhere, and I started playing, and probably some of the kids stole the money. By the time I realized, it was too late. I felt really, really badly. My mother saw me coming back crying. She said, 'You need to be careful and responsible, because otherwise the whole family will be affected.' Those experiences still are with me now."

As a child Rolando had one pair of shoes, two shirts, and two pairs of pants to wear. Wet clothing was hung in the courtyard, so Rolando wore one outfit while the other was drying.

"Rolando, what was your home like?" I asked.

"Three rooms and a half. There was the father and mother room, the room for all of my sisters, and a room for me and my brother. It had a big yard. My father planted fruit trees—oranges, lemons, pomegranates, mangos. We sold the fruits. The house was falling apart. It was made of mud mixed with grass. We had a latrine and a bathroom outdoors. The bathroom was falling apart because the wood, with the humidity, was getting rotten. It was open [without a ceiling], and the water came from the tube. If it was a rainy day, we were lucky because we didn't have to struggle who got in the bath first."

"Rolando, what did you do for Christmas? Were you able to give gifts?"

"The first year after my father lost the farm, my parents didn't have anything to give us," he explained. "One of my younger sisters went to the store, talked to the manager, and told him to give her apples. There were no apples growing in Nicaragua, but for Christmastime the richest store imported them. She got apples and put them under the pillow for me and my brother. When I came to the United States and tasted a good apple, I realized that those apples were dry. But at the time, I didn't think about it. It was great to have an apple! It was Christmas, and we were enjoying Christmastime as any other kid."

"What did you do for medical care?"

"I don't remember going to the doctor anytime," Rolando said. "My mother had the idea of talking to the pharmacist. 'I have this kid with diarrhea; what would you give me?' In my country even now there is no need of prescription to get whatever medicine you want, if they have it."

Rolando told me about his education, the journey that brought him to the United States, and his eventual marriage to Linda, the love of his life and a fellow naturalist. They shared a passion for the land, the forests, and the Earth, and they worked to heal the planet. Linda died of ovarian cancer, but before her death she received an inheritance from her family. This financial security now allows Rolando to serve the world through another form of healing, Quantum Touch, something he studied years ago.

"I've been learning more and concentrating more on how I can help people with pain, and many times troubled people," he said. I sensed his great compassion, a compassion born of his own suffering. "That doesn't allow me to accumulate money, but I don't need that money. I can live with whatever I have.

"In these years I've been alone," he continued, "I've been thinking that the point of my existence here is to help other people, not to be richer. For example, it would be great to have an ice skating rink for the kids to enjoy a sport that has not been available here. I can allow the people that can pay to pay, and the people that cannot pay—the poor kids, the African Americans, the Mexicans, the immigrants that are struggling, the kids wishing they could have a sport the parents cannot afford—can come in, too.

"When I was little, one of the things I wanted to do but never did because my family was not of that status, was play tennis. Growing up under those conditions made me realize how important is kids' sports. I want the kids, especially the poor kids, to enjoy an ice skating rink; otherwise, they only see it on TV. They dream of being able to skate but don't have the chance. If I had the money, I would use it for a rink."

"Rolando," I said, "as I understand it, before we're born we're shown the various parents we may choose. You may have been shown your parents in Nicaragua and other possible parents in other parts of the world. Why do you think you chose your parents?"

"Because they both insisted it's not what you get in life, it's what you share in life that's important," he replied. "Time and again, whenever a person needed help, they were there to help them. It didn't matter how poor they were. It didn't matter how much suffering there was. They suffered together with them."

"Your heart is very open, Rolando."

"Exactly."

"I wonder if the poverty has helped you to open your heart like that."

"It was the poverty itself," he said. "It was having the opportunity to do something for anyone and restore the smile on their faces and share whatever I could to make people happier, no matter what."

"When you look back now on the experience of poverty, how do you feel about it?"

"I don't feel sad. I only feel very, very strongly when I read about the suffering of poor people. That experience I went through made me understand how much the suffering of the poor people is. I am grateful because that kept me from really being attached to money."

Corbie Channels Rolando's Soul

I was moved by the poignant way in which Rolando had spoken of and cried about poverty. His emotions were strong and still raw, yet he had been comfortable sharing them. It was clear to me that poverty had left an indelible mark on his soul. He *felt* it viscerally. Rather than allow his childhood experiences to leave him angry or bitter, he had opened his heart and had grown in compassion and empathy.

Because the limitations of poverty stand in such stark contrast to the unlimitedness of the soul, I was eager to speak with Rolando's higher self about his experiences in this lifetime. How had Rolando's soul expanded as a result of the hardships he had endured? Had the pre-birth intent been to grow in compassion and empathy? What had been his soul's other intentions? And what would Rolando's soul say to the many people who face poverty or financial challenge to help them see its deeper spiritual meaning? What sort of healing perspective would his soul offer?

After the session Corbie told me, "Rolando's soul is a warrior. He is strong. If I had to paint a face on the soul, it would be jut-jawed and hawk-nosed, crow's feet by the eyes, squinting into the distance to see what else is coming up."

"Mother/Father God," Corbie prayed as we began our time together, "surround us with Your unconditional white light of love, protection, wisdom, compassion, service, and truth. Let only truth be spoken, let only truth be heard. Let me be a clear channel to bring Rolando and Rob the information they seek today, and let me be always head, hands, and heart completely in Your service. In the name of the Christ this is asked. In the name of Christ this is done. Amen."

We paused for a moment as Corbie's consciousness stepped aside and another took its place.

"You seek the soul of Rolando Lopez. I have come." The timbre of Corbie's voice was suddenly more deep and resonant. I sensed an energy of strength and authority.

"Thank you for joining us. Did you plan for Rolando to experience poverty as he was growing up, and if so, why?" I asked, opening with the central question. As I spoke, I imagined a young Rolando selling potato chips in front of a movie theater in a small town in Nicaragua.

"There is a great arc of learning," answered Rolando's soul, "of which poverty is only a small part." There was a solemnness to the tone that told me the responses we were about to receive were carefully considered. "Many, many lifetimes I have sought to examine poverty. To understand the depth and breadth of something, one must have an opposite canvas on which to paint. My soul family is very brave. They have come with me often on this journey through the jungle of human desire and need, and I am grateful for them. Yes, it was planned. It was agreed upon. The more that is learned about how one in form [body] creates lack, creates efficiency, uses greed—all these things will help balance many, many souls when the information is returned [to the soul group].

"When a soul has learned its curriculum, then the learning can be brought back and is useful for all souls. I may never meet in the flesh one who has spent many lifetimes in France, China, or on the planet Neptune, but what they learn is freely shared with me and may make the experiment and learning I choose more efficient and profound."

I understood and appreciated the soul's need to learn through opposites, but this general statement did not explain why Rolando and his family had to suffer to such an extent. I decided to be more pointed in my questioning.

"Respectfully, the poverty Rolando experienced as a child brought great pain to both him and his family. This can seem cruel to humans because we suffer, but our souls do not." I trusted Rolando's soul would know that my intent was to understand, not to judge or be critical of the life plan.

"You are separating yourself [from the soul]," came the reply. "A child may say, 'I did not like that needle [inoculation] you gave me. You made me suffer. You are cruel.' The child does not understand viruses, inoculations, or the immune system. That is language the child would dismiss as so much nonsense. Poverty may look like that, but the truly advanced soul does not suffer in poverty. The difficulty Rolando and his family suffered was part of the learning. It makes the learning less objective and more subjective. One can read about global warming and say, 'That is terrible. We should do something'; but if you stand in the midst of an empty lake and see people dying of thirst, plants not growing, and animals scarce, then it will hit home."

"What did you hope Rolando would gain from the experience of poverty?"

"That compassion would grow. Also, that he would understand, intuit, and take to the cell level the idea that there is always enough. A fish in the ocean never wonders if there will be enough algae to eat. An eagle does not look from the top of its mountain, count the number of rabbits, and divide by the number of other birds. The greater the contrast the bigger the impact and the stronger the fire grows for change."

"When you created Rolando," I wondered, "did you give him any particular traits or qualities that would equip him for the experience of poverty?"

"A good brain," said Rolando's soul. "His memory is sharp. He can recall sounds, words, and senses and use them as part of the fuel for his fire. Emotionally, he feels more deeply than many. The most important thing he was given was a double dose of compassion: the compassion a male would normally have and also as much compassion as a mother for her brood. There is a greatness, a largeness that I place within those incarnations where a leap forward is hoped for."

"But you said you had hoped the experience of poverty would cause his compassion to grow."

"A child prodigy still needs to do his scales and exercises. A child prodigy, if never put in front of a piano, may never know he can play. Rolando has an ability to sense his compassion, stretch his compassion, own his compassion, and realize it is one of his most superb tools."

"After Rolando's incarnation is over, how does the enhanced compassion serve you as the soul?"

"Compassion is like a wellspring. The deeper the compassion runs from lifetime to lifetime, the closer it is to the surface and the more the personality is willing to use it for itself." Here, I understood the soul to mean that Rolando had cultivated deep compassion in other lifetimes and that this compassion was available for him to draw upon in his current life. Like Rolando, each of us has cultivated certain skills and qualities in other lifetimes, and these are always available for us to tap into.

"Too often humanity will have compassion for everyone around them yet treat themselves the way they would not treat a dog," continued Rolando's soul. "Also, compassion very often comes with guilt. If compassion can take over where guilt resides, that is a great step forward."

"From your perspective as a soul," I inquired, "why don't people treat themselves with compassion?"

"They are too focused outward. They judge themselves against everything—the fashions of the times, other people's opinions. They do not look in the mirror. If they did, if they were able to reach inside and touch, however briefly, the soul inside the shell, they would be filled with such compassion, gratitude, and awe that they *would* value themselves more. They would be aware of the profound gift they are. When the connection with Spirit is muddied, the pure water of Unconditional Love, which you so much want to help us spread throughout the world, is blocked. Therefore, in this time when there is too much to pay attention to—money, possessions, fear—these things block one. Poverty was a way to make sure this was not the case in Rolando's early life. A child today who has everything, all kinds of electronic and social stimulation, has no need either to look inside and connect with compassion or to see the child who sits next to him in class and say, 'I am you.' In older civilizations and simpler times, compassion came closer to the surface."

"But if souls want their incarnate personalities to look within and feel and know their worth, and if there are so many distractions in the current era that make that difficult, why not choose another place or time? You could have the experience of poverty in many other times and locations."

"What we can learn in this very fraught time is different from what we can learn, for example, in the eighteenth century, pre- what you call the Industrial Revolution. But, some things are universal and timeless: compassion, sustenance, peace, self-worth, and connection with God. Your current era is just an advanced class."

"Let's talk," I suggested, "about the specific circumstances of Rolando's incarnation and his poverty. Why did you choose Rolando's particular parents and this specific era?"

"The middle of the twentieth century was a time of great change," explained Rolando's soul. "The razor's edge of before and after the creation of the atomic bomb—what it did to the vibration in and through which you live—is not fully understood even now. The family has been with me many times. Part of what is deemed difficult on Earth is separation." Here, Rolando's higher self was referring to one of the primary illusions of life on the physical plane: the fact that we *appear* to be separate from one another and from God or Source, though in truth we are One. "When you are separated from nothing, there is no concern about not having enough. You know you are connected with All and can have all you need. Therefore, being put in a place where poverty was in high relief with a family who felt it keenly served a great purpose. Certainly, it was more to Rolando's advantage than coming into a place where poverty was seen as genteel and all feel it at one time or another. Poverty had to have a sharp tooth and pierce deep for him to make it his heart's work this time."

"If you wanted Rolando to develop greater compassion through the experience of poverty, why choose that life plan as opposed to, say, relative wealth in the United States punctuated by periods of loss or great financial setback?"

"Because that has been done. Remember, there is not only one life. If you look at the numbers of lives in which I have sought to understand poverty, sufficiency, selfishness, selflessness, and wanting and not wanting, there have been periods of enormous wealth. Just as periods of wealth are useful, so are periods of poverty. Poverty is not a punishment. It is a tool. It was decided that tasting the depth of it would bring emotional and spiritual wealth. It would also bring the condition of the world into sharper relief. That was felt worthy of exploration."

"As I'm sure you're aware," I said, "there was a particularly difficult three-year period in Rolando's childhood in which the family supported itself by making potato chips that Rolando sold on the street after school. He then came home late every night and had to stay up until the early hours of the morning studying. He was exhausted and drained. Was this experience planned, and if so, why?"

"It was," declared the soul. "This was a way at a very early age to—your phrase is 'push the envelope.' Rolando had a choice. He could have not done the homework and lived forever in poverty. Or, he could have sold the chips and stolen the money, yet he did not. This was a way for him to develop those spiritual muscles of resilience and faith while relentlessly going after what he wanted, and what he wanted was an education and a way out of poverty. Much of Rolando's strength and knowledge that there is always a way was created during that three-year period. He did well."

The reference to faith was important. Often, we are not able to understand why suffering occurs. Its causes are nebulous, its sources obscure. In these most difficult of circumstances, when *why* cannot be grasped, the soul's intent is generally for the personality to learn faith. To grow in faith that all is well, that we live in a loving and benevolent Universe, is one of our primary objectives in coming to the physical plane.

"Rolando is now better off financially in his current life in the United States. If so much is to be learned from the experience of poverty, why not continue it for an entire lifetime?"

"Once you have completed four years in college, why not stay there?" the soul answered. "Because you have gained enough knowledge at that point to go out and use it in the world. In the United States, Rolando has the stability to take what he has learned and the compassion that has been born within him and do more for the world. It is certainly easier to ease poverty in a country that has less of it than in a country that has a great deal.

If you are in the desert, you cannot look to others and say, 'I need to build a well. Lend me some of your water so that I do not thirst while I do it.' You make your plans and gather your materials where there is enough to drink. You bring enough with you that you will not die of thirst as you dig the well in the desert that will then save others."

"Now that Rolando is in that position, and now that he has developed so much compassion, what would you like him to do?"

"The first thing I would hope for him is to use that compassion for himself and look upon his time as a child in poverty as a brilliant lesson, one well learned. Then, find that which touches him most deeply. If it is a hungry child, feed it. If it is a mother left alone from a war, help her. If it is to manage one of your microbanks, making small loans to people who, like he, are resilient and wish to pull themselves out of poverty, it is a task well done. Those who have always been wealthy and who have never starved can get distracted. For every person whose eye is laser-bent on helping those who hurt, there are those who do it because it is fashionable. When something else interesting comes along, they perhaps remove themselves from the actual experience of the poverty and the joy of assisting in the change. One can donate to a food bank or one can hand a bowl of hot soup, a cup of coffee, and a roll to a rheumy-eyed man who has been on the street in the cold for two weeks. You feed him soup, he feeds you gratitude. Both are fed. Both are nourished."

"Even in a relatively wealthy country like the United States, there are many people in poverty," I pointed out. "Just yesterday I heard some statistics in the news: 50 million Americans live with what is called food insecurity, 37 million receive food stamps, and 17 million live in extreme poverty. If some of those people pick up this book and read your words, they may say, 'I understand that this experience benefits my soul, but I'm suffering and I need some practical, real-world help.'"

"No one is condemned to poverty," answered Rolando's soul. "You are not forced into it forever. Always look to the next sunrise. Realize that you are not poor in worth, heart, or mind. If your mind is clear and your heart strong, there will be ways for the poverty to lift. But at the same time, self-judgment, anger at the poverty, or resentment at those who have more keep you where you are. That is part of the problem. People see poverty as an affliction. The words 'It's not fair' and 'What did I do to deserve this?' ring out too often. It is not a matter of deserving. It is a matter of bravery and what you have chosen. Too many times people spend countless hours creatively explaining to themselves why things cannot change. Take that time and find one step forward. It may take years, as it did for Rolando, or it may take weeks, but you can move from the position where you are. But, *you must believe that there is more for you. You must believe that there is enough in the world.* You cannot say, 'If I get this and he does not, at least I've got mine.' That is thinking there is only so much to go around. That is also cutting off your compassion for others and often for yourself. If you believe you must fight to get what you need, it closes the doors of compassion in your own heart. Anger and fighting do not necessarily strengthen you. Pursue what you want with love and hope."

"Let's talk," I requested, "about an experience that's more common than poverty: the experience of just getting by. Millions of people live paycheck to paycheck and feel that life is nothing more than endless toil."

"You are what you think. If there is just enough to keep a roof over the head and simple food on the table, then feel gratitude for what is given. Even if you work at a minimum wage job, feel gratitude for the money you receive, gratitude that there is a place for you, however small or simple. When one believes one *is* what one has, that is when it is difficult. In India there are sadhus [ascetics] with nothing but a begging bowl, and for them it is enough. Are they poor? They think not. If in a simpler time there was just enough to get by, gratitude was more likely because you were not surrounded by a society that said you should have an easy life and everything you want. There need be no lack if one goes straight to the heart, appreciates everything one is, and in each moment says, 'I am doing the best I can, and when I am not, I will change.'"

"We've talked about some of the reasons you wanted Rolando to experience poverty. For what other reasons do souls plan either poverty or financial setback or struggle?"

"For Rolando it was primarily compassion. For some it is inventiveness. With struggle they stretch their minds and creative faculties. Others wish not to be distracted by the responsibilities that come with having much. They may want such a one-pointed focus in life that money cannot hold any importance for them. Also, it is a good way to eliminate fear. When you experience something you fear, you learn what you can do in those circumstances, and often the fear resolves."

"People who are on Earth at this time live in a period of great change," I noted. "It's said that as the vibration of the planet rises, old financial structures that are built on greed will collapse and make way for a new Earth."

"That is correct."

"People who hear that may feel afraid and fearful."

"Such people have put their worth on the outside, on that which they cannot control," said the soul. "Fear occurs when you look at the future and, because you cannot precisely predict or control it, feel that you will be out of control. But, you are never out of control. You always choose what you think and how you respond. The collapse of the financial system may indeed be what is required to bring people back to an awareness of what is valuable, where instead of constant competition there is cooperation. Therefore, see whatever comes as an opportunity to get to the heart of your life. Realize that the bigger you build your fear, the more violent the collapsing structures will seem to you. When a child is afraid of something because it does not understand what that something is, an adult who understands change may stand strong, guard the child, and say, 'It's all right. We are still here.' Why do people look at a house burning to the ground with everything in it but their families, and some mourn and wail and say, 'It's not fair. God must hate me,' while others say, 'I have my family. Those are only things.' It is all perception. How you perceive your life and your ability to move in and make a difference in the world will inform your existence, whether you are rich or poor, sick or well, wise or unwise."

"On the new Earth, will there still be poverty?"

"If people choose it. But, if people reach into that well of compassion in their hearts, then everyone will have enough. Yet, it will take great change in the mind of man to understand *enough*."

"What is the soul's concept of *enough*?"

"Peace. *Enough* changes in terms of quantification. If one is at peace, one has enough. For one man three hours of sleep is enough. For another it is nine. It is not quantification; it is what brings him enough sleep to function well and be at peace."

"What else would you like to say about poverty?"

"Please understand that poverty is not a condemnation. Poverty is a perception, and it is a perception held both by rich and poor. People fear that if all have the same amount, no one will be inspired to do anything. 'If I do not get more because of my work, why should I bother?' You bother for self. You bother because it brings to you a feeling of accomplishment and creativity. Poverty is simply a tool. When humankind as a whole realizes that enough truly is enough, poverty will no longer be necessary."

"I have no further questions. Thank you for speaking with me today," I concluded.

"I am pleased to assist," said Rolando's soul.

Rolando's Session with Pamela and Jeshua

Corbie's channeling helped me to see the soul-level perspective on poverty and how it instills deeper compassion in the human heart. Clearly, Rolando's soul had sought over many lifetimes both to grow in and to express compassion on Earth.

Yet, I had also sensed in Rolando a need for healing. Some of his tears had flowed from empathy as he talked about the poor, but other tears, I felt, were caused by unresolved inner pain. I hoped that Pamela and Jeshua would offer both a greater understanding of why souls plan the experience of poverty and how they may heal from the suffering it may cause.

"I see a past life," Pamela told us, "in which you, Rolando, were a man living in Greece. You were wealthy and wanted to stand up for the poor. In that lifetime you grew up in poor circumstances in a family with six kids. You had a warm and loving heart, and it was very important to you that there was harmony in the family. You would rather have an empty stomach and peace than a full stomach through conflict and competition. As a boy you always wanted everyone to share what little they had, and you were teaching this to your younger brothers and sisters. You had a great ideal of equal and honest sharing, for you felt, even as a little boy, that this would strengthen both the family and the community, and then it would be much easier to overcome the problems of poverty.

"When you were a young man, you rose above the poverty and got a good position in society. You were talented and intelligent, but most important, you never felt that you were less worthy than others simply because you had a poor background. You were convinced of the integrity of your ideals. This helped you rise above not just the physical poverty but also the poverty consciousness that had become a part of the minds of the people you grew up with. Poverty consciousness means that subconsciously you believe you are worth less as a human because you are poor. You feel powerless and like a victim. Poverty consciousness can deplete a basic sense of dignity.

"Because you did not have those negative beliefs about yourself, you rose above the poverty as a tradesman. When you were older, you pleaded with the authorities to change certain

laws to create a more favorable and fair arrangement for poor
people. They refused; they looked down on the poor and saw
them as a lesser kind of people. This upset you deeply and
stirred an anger inside you that went to the core of your being.
You decided then to act on your own to help poor people with
your own means; however, you remained frustrated because
you could not help everybody, and also you bumped up against
their poverty consciousness. Some people became dependent
on you, begging for more help every time, and they were indig-
nant when you sometimes had to refuse. This truly upset you.
You became aware that helping people out of poverty is not
just about giving them things on the material level but also
about helping them to create a deep sense of self-esteem and
empowerment.

"This awareness was awakening inside you in that lifetime, but
you felt torn inside by all the suffering you perceived, the unwill-
ingness of the authorities to help, and your inability to solve
the problems. When you died in that lifetime, you carried an
emotional wound inside because of this. You felt deeply involved
with the poor people, whom you regarded as your brothers and
sisters. But, because you had to some extent become an outsider,
you also felt lonely, and you often thought you had failed your
soul's mission of achieving justice for the poor. This was very
painful to you.

"In your current lifetime," Pamela continued, "you still want
to fulfill this mission, but now your soul has grown in awareness and wisdom. Your soul wants to fulfill this mission now
by *being a teacher by example*. To help people rise above poverty,
they first and foremost need to believe they can. They need to
have faith and trust in themselves. You are one who displays that
faith and trust, for you have let go of poverty, not just physically
but also psychologically and spiritually. By doing this you are a
living example of how one can transcend poverty and poverty
consciousness. By being who you are, through your vibration you
are creating an energetic trail that other people can follow. You

are radiating to others the energy of the solution. This energy is something you have added to collective consciousness, and it is available to all.[8]

"At a human level, you may think you are not doing enough for the poor and that you have to help them in a more concrete, palpable way. But, you are being a teacher by example, and even if you would not speak at all to people about the issue of poverty, you are still radiating the energy of the solution.

"Apart from the lifetime just mentioned, there has been a lifetime in which you yourself were a ruler, part of the oppressing powers in society. You were raised in a disciplinary way, with much emphasis on the male energy and a suppression of the female qualities of feeling and empathy. I feel an association here with the Roman Empire in the time before Christ. As a boy you had to relinquish your sensitive, caring side and focus on the male qualities of leadership, competition, and ambition. As you came of age, you became the successor to a powerful ruler and felt you had to emulate him to be accepted.

"There was much fear inside you of falling short of expectations, and therefore you did things that went against your sense of justice. You were unfair to people who had hardly any rights and who could not defend themselves. Your unfairness was born from fear; you dared not step out of line for fear of being eliminated yourself. You were always afraid of conspiracies against you. You died in anguish, with a deep sense of guilt and doom, feeling you had lost your integrity. After this lifetime you felt a longing in your soul to make right what you had done. You wanted to help the poor and to redeem your soul."

---

8 For more information on the notions of an energetic trail and the energy of the solution, see "Letting go of your birth family" and "Three pitfalls on the way to becoming a healer," both channelings by Jeshua published on www.jeshua.net.

Speaking with Jeshua

With the information and insight Pamela had provided, I now had an even better sense of the intent behind Rolando's life plan. I was astounded by how accurately Pamela had described what I perceived as the essential nature of Rolando's character. The man—indeed, the soul—she had described was exactly the person with whom I had spoken. It was now time to learn more about Rolando and the experience of poverty from Jeshua.

"Jeshua," I inquired, "did Rolando plan to experience poverty, and if so, why?"

"Yes, he did," Jeshua confirmed. "He has been exploring the issue of poverty and wealth for several lifetimes. His soul wants to understand the spiritual essence behind poverty and how he can teach people to release poverty from their lives."

"Did Rolando have any beliefs that he is not worthy of wealth, for example, or that wealth is bad that led to his choice to experience poverty?" My question was based on my understanding that our beliefs influence our pre-birth choices.

"Rolando did not have such negative beliefs about himself in relation to wealth," Jeshua replied. "With respect to the issue of poverty, he came in as a teacher. His soul also has a second positive reason for choosing poverty. He wanted to experience the strong sense of connectedness and love that sometimes arises in extreme situations of poverty. The bond with his sisters, the love he received from them, was a positive motivation for choosing poverty in this lifetime. Love was also something he gave to others in past lives and that was now returned to him."

"Why did Rolando choose to be born in Nicaragua?"

"He wanted to be part of that particular birth family. He had a strong bond with several of his family members on the soul level." Evidently, Rolando's parents and perhaps some of his siblings as well had already decided to be born there, and Rolando had wanted to be with them. This is a common reason for choosing to be born in a particular location and at a particular point in linear time. Others whom we love dearly have already selected that place and time and we simply wish to join them.

"Did Rolando plan before birth to move from Nicaragua to the United States, and if so, why did he want to experience both the poverty of his home country and the relative wealth of the United States?"

"Yes, he did. He wanted to experience both countries because his spirit is quite an adventurous one. Also, the spirit of the United States, the sense of freedom and of 'making it on your own' resonate with Rolando's inner development. And by being in the United States, he is, with his particular background, radiating an energy to others that is healing to and helpful for them."

"Why did Rolando choose to experience poverty at this time in human history?" I asked Jeshua.

"First, he wanted to join his birth family. Second, he wanted to have the opportunity to move from Nicaragua to the United States to experience the freedom and mobility in that move. This would have been more difficult to realize in older times. This time allows for more individual freedom and self-expression than many ages in the past. Third, Rolando wanted to be born in this era of spiritual transformation. He wanted to be a part of it and to help and encourage others."

"Why is the experience of poverty important to Rolando's soul?"

"Rolando's soul wanted to free itself from attachment to—in the sense of basing one's identity on—either wealth or poverty," Jeshua explained. "By freeing himself of this, he enabled himself to connect to people's souls, whatever their social background. This ability to look behind appearances, this awareness of the divine core of each living being, is part of Christ Consciousness. Rolando wants to embrace Christ Consciousness in this lifetime. Christ Consciousness can be realized or achieved in various ways. This is one of them."

I asked Jeshua to speak about other reasons why a soul might plan before birth to experience poverty.

"Many souls choose life on Earth because it is such a valuable experience, even if it is lived in poor circumstances. So, many souls choose a life in poverty, not because they want the poverty but because they value life on Earth so much. This is hard for humans to understand. You watch the lives of people who live in poverty and ask, 'How could this be meaningful?' Still, each life is sacred and precious and holds a promise for the soul, a promise that often remains hidden to the eye of an outsider." By *outsider* I understood Jeshua to mean someone who was not living that experience.

"Life on Earth is so precious," he continued, "because it offers such an intense experience of all the emotions humans are capable of. Even a short lifetime lived in poverty offers the soul a range of experience and a level of understanding that would be hard to achieve in many centuries on the other side of the veil.

"There are also particular reasons why a soul wants to experience poverty on Earth. First, the soul may want to develop certain qualities that poverty invites them to develop, such as courage, perseverance, or the ability to appreciate the simple things in life. For women, poverty may inspire them to become more self-empowered and independent. If a woman is successful in this, she is an example to others, not only by showing them the way out of poverty but also by radiating a more positive self-image for women.

"Second, the soul may want to help others and so comes in as a teacher for humanity. Often, such souls are born in poverty to experience the challenge from within. This will make them powerful teachers for others." Here, Jeshua was describing the pre-birth blueprint of a lightworker, one who places himself within a particular vibration in order to transform it.

"Third, the soul may have karmic reasons for being born in poverty. For example, the soul may have developed a poverty consciousness in a previous lifetime, thinking it is doomed to experience oppression and hardship or believing it is not worthy of wealth and abundance. On the other hand, there are souls who have exploited others in previous lives, taking wealth away from them and using it for themselves. These souls may feel the need to experience the other side of the coin, to feel what it is like to be exploited and humiliated so they will understand the preciousness and value of each human life."

Jeshua's choice of the words "feel the need" echoed my understanding of karma. We are not punished for previous bad behavior, nor are we judged. Instead, we ourselves often choose to experience that which we created for others. From the level of the soul, we view this as a step along the evolutionary spiral.

Variations on a Theme

"Jeshua," I wondered, "why do some souls choose to experience poverty in so-called undeveloped countries while others choose to experience it in wealthy countries?"

"People who experience poverty in wealthy countries often have to deal with the social stigma it creates for them. This is a much more important issue for them than for people who experience poverty in an environment that is poor on the whole. Souls who choose to experience poverty in a wealthy country as their challenge often want to learn to deal with the pain and rejection that arises out of being social outcasts. They want to grow an inner sense of dignity, independent of the environment. They want to learn that their true self, who they really are as soul, is independent of social status. If they are successful, this challenge will help them find true self-esteem and, often, their natural gift, their soul's passion and joy, what they naturally feel like doing even if they are not supported by material abundance or help from society. This discovery brings them in touch with their soul. From there, a life path will unfold that often brings deep fulfilment and abundance."

I asked Jeshua why some souls choose to experience poverty not from birth but rather as the result of a financial reversal.

"Souls who plan to experience poverty after great financial reversal," he explained, "often plan this challenge because they want to deal with their dependence on money and social status.

If you have been wealthy and powerful and then experience the loss of it, you either become desperate or go deep within and find a sense of self-worth that has nothing to do with money, power, or social status."

As I took in Jeshua's words, I was struck once again by the way in which we as soul learn through opposites. People who experience poverty in a wealthy country may cultivate—and indeed are *motivated* to develop—true self-esteem when those around them do not hold them in esteem. Similarly, souls who experience major financial reversals may discover their true power and worth when they lose outward status and influence. Both experiences, typically viewed as terrible hardships from the perspective of the personality, are extraordinary opportunities for self-discovery when seen from the vantage point of the soul. Truly, little in our world is as it seems.

"Jeshua, do all or most souls who incarnate on Earth want to experience poverty or financial reversal?"

"I would not say that the experience of poverty is something most souls seek out for purposes of learning and growing. Most souls who live in poverty now did not desire the experience of poverty; rather, they wanted that lifetime for other reasons and accepted the poverty as a by-product. The soul may want to meet certain friends, relatives, or foes in a lifetime, and these people live in the impoverished area in which the soul chooses to incarnate.

"Poverty is a relative notion," Jeshua added, echoing the perspective expressed through Corbie by Rolando's soul. "If you live in the western world, you are considered poor if you cannot afford a television or a phone. In other countries these are considered extravagances. It is your own consciousness that determines whether you experience abundance or lack in your life. Experiencing abundance is about feeling truly fulfilled and grateful for what life offers you. It is as much an inner state of mind as an objective level of material wealth."

Poverty and the Experience of Incarnation

"Are there souls, Jeshua, who never have physical incarnations, and if so, how do they learn the lessons offered by poverty or any other challenges we face here?"

"As soon as there is an individualized consciousness, which a soul is, there is the experience of I versus the other, me as opposed to the world. This experience of separation is truly the hallmark of incarnation. Incarnation means that you as a limitless soul take on a particular form and from there start to experience life and reality. This form may be more or less material, more or less dense and physical depending on which dimension you live in, but there is a form that limits you and lends a focus to your perception. That is what incarnation is about.

"When you are in form—incarnated—you will experience lack at some point. The individual consciousness will sense a yearning for wholeness, a desire for completion that will motivate it to grow and search and experience. This is the beginning of the notion of poverty. The notion of poverty sets in when one experiences lack. It may be lack of material goods on your Earth, but it can also be lack of love, lack of safety, lack of emotional well-being.

"I would like to define poverty in a broad way," he clarified, "meaning 'the experience of lack.' People who suffer from poverty hardly ever suffer from lack of physical means alone. They also feel unrecognized, undervalued, abandoned, and ignored. The wound poverty inflicts is much deeper than lack of physical means. It is the wound of the soul I wish to address.

"To answer your question, poverty in the broad sense of experiencing lack is present everywhere in the Universe, in very different places. In general, experiences on Earth are more intense than in less physical, less dense realms. Souls who live in those realms learn more gradually. Some souls do not feel inclined to have the Earth experience. Souls who incarnate on Earth are the passionate and bold ones, very adventurous.

"In a deeper sense, however, all souls are connected and share one another's experiences. There is a universal mind that all souls are tapped into. All that you experience on Earth is available to souls who do not incarnate on Earth. They will not experience it like you, but they will be able to distill the essence of your experience and gain understanding from it. Likewise, you can tap into the experience of less physical beings, for instance angelical beings, and get a sense of support and love from them. They are often more deeply aware of the interconnectedness of life and can give you a sense of peace and harmony. So, although all souls have their own individual paths, together they form a tapestry of interacting energies, which support one another and help them grow as a whole."

Jeshua's Lifetime on Earth

"In your lifetime as Jeshua, how did you feel about the poverty you saw or experienced yourself? What was your response to that poverty? Would you share with us a story of how you responded to someone's poverty?"

"I was appalled by it," Jeshua stated. "I noticed how the political system not only unjustly divided the means available among people but also looked down on and humiliated certain groups. There was indignation inside me about these circumstances. I had to learn not to lose myself in anger about this issue but to remain centered and calm in the midst of it.

"My teaching was aimed at making people aware of their inner light, which is there whether you are poor or rich, sick or healthy, male or female. I was to guide them to that inner realm of freedom and abundance that cannot be touched by outer circumstances. If I talked to poor people, I discovered I could often reach into their hearts quite easily, for they had little to lose and were quite open to my message. The rich and wealthy were more identified with their social status and worldly power and therefore less inclined to open to the inner realm. There were exceptions, of course.

"My main purpose when speaking to the poor was to remind them of their inner worth, their inherent equality to others, for they were often treated with disdain and cruelty. This has great impact on the human mind.

"I once attended a wedding" he continued, "in which a young woman of simple background married a wealthy young man, quite uncommon in those days. The young woman felt embarrassed by all the richness, silently thinking how much her family would benefit from even a small part of the money paid for the wedding festivities. She felt torn inside and had trouble enjoying it. Meanwhile, people were gossiping about her, saying she had married the man for his money and had abandoned her family. She was portrayed as a mean and manipulative woman and was heartbroken because of that.

"During the wedding she shared her burden with me. I understood very well and told her that she was richer than most people present because she had a kind and pure heart and never wanted to marry the man because of his money. I implored her to hold on to her self-worth and pride and keep her inner light alive. I told her that by remaining pure and simple of heart, she would become a teacher for the rich as well as for the poor, showing them a way of the heart that goes beyond wealth and poverty.

"Indeed, she became such a teacher, not so much teaching through lectures but by spreading a vibration of purity. In fact, her husband was so open to her energy that he rose above his own upbringing and was willing to share his wealth with people who lived in poor conditions.

"What I did was to make her aware of her own light, which is there independent of upbringing or social background. This is what I tried to do with all people I met. It is the awareness of the divine spark of light you are that will liberate you from all the labels society puts on you. One of my goals on Earth was to break through social hierarchies and make people aware of the incomparable worth of every human being. I was a democrat in that way, although politics was not my main focus. My aim was to open the human heart to the spiritual notion behind democracy: that each individual being is a Divine Soul, that all of us are directly connected to Source or Spirit, and that we can understand and forgive one another if we connect from the place of oneness that binds us: the human heart."

Poverty and Spiritual Responsibility

"Jeshua, are the wealthy morally or spiritually obligated to share their wealth with the poor? Are we our brother's keeper?"

"I do not like to speak of moral or spiritual obligations, for the very notion of obligation suggests there is no spontaneity or natural inclination behind the action. I am interested in what connects us on the inner level. In the deepest sense, all souls are connected through a giant web of life. In the end, separation is an illusion. As you grow spiritually, as your heart opens and there is freedom in your mind, you will naturally understand other humans more easily. You will look at them with compassion and withhold judgment. You will try to help them as much as you can, not out of obligation but because you feel an inner connection. It is like a family connection. You feel they are part of your family, and therefore you want to reach out to them.

"I would say, though, that you are your own keeper first and foremost. Each soul walks its own path and has all the means available inside to evolve and become who it truly is. Helping others means primarily that you radiate the peace and compassion that naturally accompany you when you have healed yourself, found your own inner path, and are walking it joyously. Paradoxically, if you want to be your brother's keeper, go within, find the universal field of oneness of which you are a part, and feel the joy of surrendering to it. If you do so, you will weave threads of light into the web of life, spontaneously and naturally helping others simply by being who you are.

"The most valuable thing one can give to people struggling with poverty," Jeshua added, "is the notion that they are powerful creators able to change their lives on their own. Make them aware of their true power, the power that resides within, for that will create miracles and attract to them changes and opportunities that will enrich their lives."

"Jeshua," I said, "in the United States there is some sentiment against the government doing too much for people. Some say this would be socialism and that it would create a 'nanny state.'"

"Spiritually, there is worth in both outlooks, socialism and capitalism," Jeshua responded. "The liberal standpoint, which stresses individual freedom, actually goes back to the energy of the pioneers who first set foot on the North American continent. They were a rather sturdy folk, independent and strong, averse to authority. The urge to free oneself from external authority is a valuable thing and marks the beginning of taking full responsibility for oneself; however, it can also lead to a certain harshness and lack of compassion for others. The socialist movement, on the other hand, goes back to the notion that each individual has certain rights. This also is valuable, because it recognizes the inherent worthiness of each individual human being. It can, however, lead to suffocating rules that impede individual creativity and freedom.

"Both traditions have a true spiritual insight at their core. The question is not so much which one is right; the real question is how humanity can lift its consciousness in such a way that individual freedom and caring for others are seen to be complementary rather than opposite. An individual who has truly accepted freedom and responsibility will want to contribute to society out of joy and because it makes life meaningful. In a society based on the values of the heart, people will share freely of their gifts and talents, and they will receive what they need through the natural gifts and talents of others. There will be more freedom but also more sharing and connecting. Both go together in a heart-based society. There will be less need for a large government to control or regulate people's behavior because the morality that is now embodied by the government will then be a living reality in each person's heart."

Our Future

"In 100, 300, 500 years, what will Earth be like in regard to the distribution of wealth, and how will attitudes have changed toward wealth and poverty?" I asked.

"This depends on the choices humanity will make," stated Jeshua. "There is such a thing as human collective consciousness, which has a certain vibration. The energy of this vibration attracts a particular future. At this moment there is much confusion on Earth. There is a financial and an ecological crisis that affects the whole of humanity. Humanity is called upon by these crises to act as one, to cooperate on a global level, and to recognize what really matters in life. This crisis is really about getting back to the basics of life on Earth. It is about recognizing the value of life, whether human, animal, or plant. The very planet on which you live has become endangered by the way the human species has interacted with Her.

"There is now a growing awareness among people that things need to change. In the richest countries there is a conscious or subconscious longing in many people to go back to basics, to live life in a simpler but more fulfilling way, not relying so much on material wealth or status but more on truthful connections to others and doing what you really love doing in your life.

"How will it all evolve? It is not certain because it depends on the individual choices of billions of people. What is certain is that all individuals can make a contribution and change consciousness on Earth by becoming aware of their divine core and their interconnectedness with all other living beings. Such individuals can set the example for a new way of living and being. There is a great need for such examples now. If you feel drawn to break free from society's demands, to connect to your innermost longings and visions, I ask you who are reading this to have faith in your own powers. You are a Divine Being and can make a difference on Earth. Believe in yourself, and you will find your unique path, contributing to the transformation of consciousness in your own way."

I asked Jeshua if people would eventually master the Law of Attraction to such an extent that there would be no poverty.

"This is entirely possible," he assured me. "There is much fear on Earth now. Fear blocks faith in one's creative powers. Fear tells you that things won't work out, that you are powerless. To break free from fear, people need to go within. The only remedy for fear is to connect to the part of you that is not dependent on anything outside you: your divine core, your soul. The soul knows it is able to create reality from its deepest visions and desires. The soul is completely aware of the Law of Attraction.

"How does one connect to the soul? Listen to your feelings and emotions. Your feelings tell you what you truly desire. Thoughts may tell you it's not possible, but these are just thoughts. The flow of your feelings, your true passion, is much stronger than that. If you truly allow yourself to feel what you feel, and use thought to support that flow rather than block it, you will know you are a powerful being, able to attract outer circumstances that reflect your inner needs.

"When you are in connection with your own divinity, your soul, you will not attract poverty anymore in the sense of an experience of lack. You will experience abundance. Whether this means you own many material things or just have enough to get by comfortably is of lesser importance. It is the experience that counts. Some people do not have the need for great material abundance. In fact, most people who live life from their souls do not care so much anymore about material wealth. They are not poor. They will surround themselves with a living environment that satisfies their physical and emotional needs and also their sense of beauty. But, they will simply not be focused on money or material things because the expression of their souls' passion gives them much more satisfaction than any material thing can offer."

Healing

"What else would you like to say to those experiencing poverty or financial difficulties and are wondering, 'Why? What does it all mean?'"

"Do not despair," Jeshua advised. "Even if the situation seems bleak and hopeless, know that there is always a possibility for change. There is always hope. Find two things in your life that you are thankful for. It can be material things you own, the presence of a loved one, or the body you dwell in. Feel grateful for those things, and you will place yourself in a flow of receiving, a flow of abundance. By looking at what you have, you are replacing a sense of lack with a sense of abundance, and your energy will change.

"Changing your energy, your feelings, is the most important thing you can do. Trying to solve the situation only through your mind will not work. The situation you are in requires surrender first, acceptance of what is right now. When you are in a state of acceptance, you can feel emotions of grief and sadness rise to the surface. Let them be. Embrace them. Then, when you have recognized these emotions, there will be stillness in your heart, a sense of peace in the midst of trouble. You will have connected to your soul. From this connection miracles are born. You may not know the meaning behind the poverty you experience, and you may not have practical solutions right away, but you will have become empowered in the deepest way possible, and change will come."

"What if we have beliefs about wealth that led us before birth to plan the experience of poverty? How can we heal those beliefs? What if the beliefs are subconscious?"

"A soul may choose to experience poverty for a variety of reasons," Jeshua reminded me. "There may be positive reasons: A lack of material wealth may enable the soul to deal with certain issues without distraction; the soul may want to let go of its attachment to power and wealth built up in other lifetimes. If that's the case, the belief is quite positive, something like 'I choose poverty because I want to go back to the basics of life and find out what really matters.' In such cases the human personality may feel dissatisfied with the poor living conditions, but the soul is aware of a deeper reason.

"If a soul chooses poverty because it reflects an inner belief in unworthiness, the soul's plan is always to heal this belief. Very often, opportunities present themselves in the lifetime of such a soul that offer a way out of poverty. For instance, the human personality will frequently be challenged to have faith in self and find inner strength. If it does, it will find that beautiful opportunities come along to rise above the poverty and build a meaningful life. Whereas in the case mentioned above souls will experience a lack of such opportunities, here opportunities will miraculously present themselves when the soul has built true self-worth.

"Beliefs about not deserving abundance are almost always subconscious," he pointed out. "That's why they are so hard to let go of. It is part of your culture to give people a sense of unworthiness. Children are taught to behave, to repress and distrust their emotions, to trust their minds more than their feelings. There are religious and moral traditions in your society that make it hard to believe in your own innocence as a human being, to trust the flow of your natural feelings and the kindness of the Universe you live in. To heal these beliefs in unworthiness, it is necessary to realize that you are unconditionally loved by Spirit or God. You are innocent and beautiful and are meant to live a joyful and abundant life. It may be difficult to believe this, but I am here to testify to your innocence and beauty. It's the very reason for speaking to you in this way. I am not here to judge you or to tell you what to do. I am here to love you, and I am asking you to accept this love."

"Jeshua, how else can people heal beliefs, both conscious and subconscious, that led them to create suffering for themselves, whether planned before birth or not?"

"First," said Jeshua, "these beliefs have to be recognized as such. Many times beliefs that cause suffering are taken for granted. As mentioned, beliefs in the unworthiness of the human being are widespread on Earth. Some of them are even considered to be moral standards or religious tenets. To heal the negativity you have absorbed from these beliefs, you need to become aware that they are *beliefs* and that they are not set in stone. That is often the most important step, because when you recognize they are mere beliefs, you have opened up a new space of awareness and the possibility for change.

"For this change really to take effect, you have to release the false beliefs not just from the mind but from your emotions and feelings as well. This may take more time. It requires the releasing of emotional habits that have been with you for a long time. This can be done if you have patience with yourself and if you are willing to address your emotions honestly time and again, as though you are dealing with children who need a new upbringing. They need to be raised anew with a sense of trust and compassion that you, as their parent, need to bring from the level of your soul.

"Emotional healing *is* possible, and as more people are committed to this, the more easily culture will change and people will grow toward a more respectful way of treating themselves and others."

Who we are—our vibration—is far more important than anything our bodies will ever do, and Rolando is a living example of a teacher who powerfully affects the world in this way. Though he speaks of poverty and thus teaches through words, his most profound contribution is the energetic trail he has blazed, and that is one of *compassion*. As souls we desire before we are born both to cultivate greater compassion and to express and thus know ourselves as compassion on the physical plane. These twin intentions form the touchstone of many pre-birth blueprints and are a driving motivation behind the planning of a wide range of life challenges, including poverty.

The first seeds of Rolando's extraordinary compassion were planted in early childhood, when he witnessed a grown man crying over the loss of beans, the sale of which would have fed the man's family. Only one year later, Rolando looked on helplessly as his own family lost the coffee harvest and with it the family farm. That seeming tragedy was followed by three years of selling homemade potato chips on the street and toiling late into the night with schoolwork. All this transpired within Rolando's first ten years of life.

Emotionally powerful experiences, particularly when they occur in the tender and impressionable years of our youth or when they cannot be sidestepped by free-will decisions, are reliable indicators of the soul's intent. Rolando's soul knew that the young boy who cried *"Papas! Papas!"* in front of the movie theater would evolve into the loving, open-hearted man who now seeks to bring play and laughter into the lives of neighborhood children. His soul knew, too, that the child who never saw a doctor would grow into the adult who offers healing touch to those in pain. Poverty was the midwife who birthed Rolando's intense desires to alleviate lack and suffering and to foster joy. In the nonphysical realm from which we come, scarcity and suffering are nonexistent, joy ever-present. Such was Rolando's plan: to immerse himself in a reality that is precisely the opposite of what he knows to be true, then wend his way through that illusion in order to recreate the beauty of Home on Earth. It is Rolando's deep compassion that now drives him to do so, a compassion so strong, so enduring that it could only have been forged in the fires of his own childhood pain.

When we as souls plan life challenges like poverty or financial hardship, we also plan the means by which we may use them to fulfill our pre-birth intentions. Rolando sought before birth to be a teacher, one who would empower others to know they can transform their lives. He therefore needed to know he could transform his own and so wisely chose a father who taught him, *"You can do whatever you want."* Our beliefs are all-powerful, and the Universe responds with circumstances and events that confirm them. Rolando therefore teaches not only that poverty can be transformed but also that it is transformed specifically through the power of belief. The experience of mastering the physical plane through belief instills within the soul a more profound knowing of its own power. A deep awareness of that power can and often does emerge from circumstances in which one feels powerless. Truly, poverty and the feelings of powerlessness it engendered were the means by which Rolando realized that he can do anything. Had more comfortable circumstances been chosen, his awareness of his power would not have been as great.

Belief plays a primary role in the creation of wealth or poverty not only while we are in body but also *before* we incarnate. Unlike Rolando, many who plan prior to birth to experience poverty or financial hardship do so because they believe they are either unworthy of having or incapable of creating abundance. These false beliefs, which are discordant to the soul, are learned in other lives and then carried into the current lifetime for the purpose of healing them. In the pre-birth planning process, one who holds such beliefs is energetically drawn in accord with the Law of Attraction to parents and other life circumstances that mirror the false beliefs. A classic learning-through-opposites plan is then created as one chooses disempowered parents, a lack of basic material comforts, or financial strain or loss. Experiences are selected that will speak of one's unworthiness and powerlessness in the hope that such lies will be utterly excoriated. And lies they are, for every soul is of inherent infinite worth and unlimited power. If you have suffered or suffer still from poverty, your soul's wish for you is not that you reject the harsh circumstances you see outside yourself but rather the false beliefs that may reside *inside* you. The act of seeking power or worth in anything external to self creates the very sense of powerlessness and unworthiness one seeks to heal. Your soul would have you know this, and you *will* come to know this, if not in this lifetime, then another.

Resistance sends energy to and thus strengthens that which we hope to release. To resist poverty or financial strain is therefore to create more of it. Human consciousness has now evolved to a point at which many realize this truth. What is less well understood is that resistance to *any* aspect of life blocks the flow of *every* form of goodness into our experience. Energetically, saying no to financial hardship is the equivalent of hanging a large No! shingle on the front door of one's home. The Universe does not recognize that No! is intended specifically for poverty; rather, it hears No! in regard to all the many blessings it seeks to deliver. Not only is material abundance blocked but also love, joy, peace, health, and even wisdom and spiritual clarity. Our souls ask of us, then, that we respond to lack by appreciating even the smallest pleasures and joys in our lives, much as Rolando savored an apple at Christmas, or better yet with gratitude, as Jeshua suggested. Vibrationally, appreciation and gratitude create a large Yes! sign on our front doors, one that grants our angels and guides permission to shower us with Love and blessings of all kinds.

We come, then, to the question of how best to respond to others who face material hardship. This question was posed to the great American psychic Edgar Cayce late in his career, after he had already read for thousands of people. In a private session, two wealthy sisters from New York City told Cayce that they were desperate to help their brother. "Our brother lives under a bridge," the sisters informed Cayce. "He drinks too much. He has squandered his share of the family fortune. For years we have done everything we can think of to help him turn his life around, all to no avail. What can we do?" they cried. "Our brother is beyond hope."

Cayce went into trance and accessed the Akashic Record. He then informed the two women that their brother was the single most highly evolved soul about whom he had ever obtained information. Out of his great love for you, Cayce explained to the sisters, your brother agreed before you were born to play this role so that you might develop greater compassion. Astonished, the sisters returned home with a newfound and deep respect, admiration, and gratitude for their brother, the courageous soul who so lovingly, so bravely enacted his very difficult role in service to them.

Poverty, then, is a master teacher that calls forth the blossoming of profound compassion in the hearts of those like Rolando who experience it firsthand as well as those who bear witness to it.

If you find yourself walking down the street one day only to see a homeless man sitting in a cardboard box, consider the possibility that this person was part of *your* pre-birth plan. He may well have agreed to be there in that moment so you could choose to put aside judgment, remember this man's infinite worth, and in so doing remember your own. That seemingly powerless individual may be the highly evolved soul, the spiritual brother who sits there in service to you so you may feel and thus know yourself as compassion, the compassion you came here to be.

CHAPTER 11

~

Suicide

TO LOSE A LOVED ONE is always painful, but when that loss comes as the result of suicide, the pain sears to the very core of one's being in a uniquely excruciating way. Nothing is ever again the same. Often, the people left behind are wracked by guilt and self-blame, and they may feel anger toward those who ended their lives. (I will not use the phrase "committed suicide" because it may be taken to imply an act of wrongdoing. No such judgment is rendered here or by Spirit.) Grief is deep, stark, and seemingly never ending. The heart is plagued by countless unanswered questions.

As you will see in the story that follows, we as souls do not plan suicide as a certainty; rather, we plan various life challenges, well aware of the possibility—and in some instances probability— that we may respond to these experiences by ending our own lives. The souls who plan to be with us know that suicide is an option in their pre-birth blueprint, and they willingly accept this risk in order to join us in an incarnation.

Worldwide, more than one million people die by suicide every year, and an estimated ten to twenty million people make non-fatal attempts. To offer understanding and healing to the many whose lives have been touched by suicide or suicide attempts, I spoke with Carolyn Zahnow. Fifty-two years old when we spoke,

Carolyn had lost her only child, Cameron, to suicide when he was eighteen. She has since founded a suicide support group and wrote *Save the Teens: Preventing suicide, depression, and addiction.*

What, I wondered, had happened to Cameron after he ended his physical life? What happens to others who choose the same path? How does Spirit view suicide? What can we as a society do to bring more love and healing to those who are suicidal? And how can those who have lost a loved one to suicide heal their deep wounds?

Carolyn and Cameron

"In every picture he was happy."

That's how Cameron looks in the many photos she took of him in his youth. Since his death four years ago, Carolyn has kept one particular picture in their family room. Taken at a beach in North Carolina, the state in which Cameron was born and spent much of his childhood, it shows a two-year-old Cameron wearing "this little tropical print shirt and shorts, and he has this beaming smile. It reminds me of the happy days," Carolyn said sadly.

Carolyn and her husband, Jim, separated three months after Cameron was born. Then thirty years old, Carolyn raised Cameron on her own until he was six and starting first grade, at which time he went to live with his father.

"I went back to college so I could make enough money to raise him without having to depend on someone else," she said. "How did I give up my son for so many years?"

Carolyn recalls that as a child Cameron showed a deep love for animals, raising turtles and chickens. As a 4-H project, he raised a baby lamb, which he affectionately named Lambie. When a grown Lambie was sold at auction, Cameron asked the buyer, "You aren't going to kill her, are you?"

"No, we won't kill her," the man replied gently.

"Okay," said Cameron, assured that Lambie would be properly cared for.

Carolyn married her current husband, Dan, when she was forty. They moved from North Carolina to Flower Mound, Texas, where Cameron came to live with them when he was eleven.

"Cameron fought living in Texas for about a year," Carolyn told me. "But after he made friends, he did fine. He was by nature very outgoing, easy to get along with for lots of people."

Carolyn has fond memories of driving Cameron to school every day when he was in seventh and eighth grade. Often they had to stop at a traffic light next to a pasture in which long-horned cows grazed. "When the cows were close enough, we'd sing to them," Carolyn reminisced. "A silly song, something like 'Moo moo moo' to the tune of 'Jingle Bells.' I'd drop Cameron off at school with a smile on his face."

As a teenager Cameron continued to show a love of animals, becoming active in an animal rescue group. He developed interests in sketching and photography and displayed real talent for both. And he was popular with girls. "They all thought he was a hunk. He was very sweet, very giving." When he was fifteen, Cameron asked his first girlfriend to give him two bunnies for Christmas.

Cameron was also known and loved for his quirkiness. "He took Latin for two years," Carolyn said. "You have to be smart to take Latin. He would confide in his Latin teacher so they became very close. You know the old saying 'Take an apple to your teacher'? Well, Cameron, being different, took a fresh pineapple to her." Carolyn was laughing now. "She told me she ate it. After he died, she said, 'You know, I still remember that: Here comes Cameron with a pineapple!'"

Cameron's life changed forever during his freshman year of high school when his father died of cancer, Cameron at the bedside as his father passed. "When we got back home after the funeral, the depression showed up. He was seeing friends, but he wasn't talking about it with anybody. He just clammed up.

"He was taking photography that year. One of his assignments was to take pictures of eggs at various places. When he finished, he said, 'Mom, can I break the eggs?' I let him break them on the side of a building. He was hurting so bad that he just wanted to break something."

To encourage Cameron to open up and talk about his pain, Carolyn shared many stories of his father. "Oh God, I tried! He wouldn't say anything. He was missing his dad a lot, holding it all in."

In the months following his father's death, Cameron's grades fell and he started to smoke and to use alcohol and other drugs. Carolyn took him to an outpatient rehabilitation program in which participants were encouraged to draw to express their feelings. "They told us, 'Watch your kid's drawings. If they're black and white, that's the sign of depression, because there's no color in their life.' Well, Cameron was creating black and white drawings."

"Carolyn, what was he drawing?" I asked.

"Vicious-looking cartoons, like a bunny holding a cigarette. I learned in rehab that his drug of choice was methamphetamine. His last year, when he was doing meth heavily, he was drawing this scary monster mouth. There weren't even eyes. It was this morbid mouth with drool dripping off the fangs. He drew that over and over. I think it meant that Cameron felt like the drug was eating him."

Cameron's struggles with grades and drugs continued throughout high school, but a combination of rehab, antidepressant medication, and psychiatric counseling made it possible for him to earn his degree. "He *did* graduate," Carolyn said proudly. "That was a high point in my life. He even graduated with honors because of his art. He was talented.

"He graduated on May 28. The next day he turned eighteen. We went to one of our favorite restaurants for his birthday. He was very glum. He didn't eat. There are pictures of all of us, and we all look happy, except Cameron. This was his eighteenth birthday, and he'd graduated. Why wasn't he happy?"

A few days later, Cameron was to begin a summer job at a camera store. Excited and hopeful that the job might raise his spirits, Carolyn purchased new clothes for him. "He said, 'Thank you, Mom,' and gave me a little, sideways hug. That was my last hug from Cameron."

Cameron worked one day at the camera store. Very early the following morning, at an hour when Cameron should have been at home and asleep in his bed, Carolyn was eating breakfast in her kitchen. Suddenly, "Cameron appeared at the back door. It was glass; I could see out. He had this black shirt on. It was still dark outside. When I saw him, it scared me. He looked like a ghost! It was like seeing something before it happened."

"You gotta work today, right?" Carolyn asked him, concerned.

"Yeah, I got time," Cameron answered. "I'm going to bed now."

"He seemed perfectly fine. He was a little wet, because it had been raining. This was August the 11th. It was very hot; it's Texas. I thought, 'I'm going back to bed to sleep for a couple more hours.' It was still so early, and it felt so good with the ceiling fan on.

"Cameron's phone started ringing at 7:00. Ringing and ringing. I ignored it the first time. The second time I got up and went upstairs. I saw that the attic stairs were pulled down. I thought, 'Why are those stairs down? That's bizarre.' Then I moved in a little further, and I saw Cameron's feet hanging there. *'Oh, no!'* I thought. I looked up and saw that Cameron had hung himself. I went up the attic stairs and pulled up on him, thinking that maybe he'd just done it and I could save him. I was screaming, *'Oh, please, Cameron, no! I'll do anything you want! Please don't leave me!'*

"Pulling on him was useless, so I got a pair of scissors and cut the rope. It was that sisal rope; I couldn't look at that kind of rope for years afterward. I cut it, and he fell into the hallway. I called 9-1-1, then gave him mouth-to-mouth as the operator advised. For the longest time after that I could taste Cameron. And I could smell him, too, because he had peed in his pants.

"Then emergency medical services arrived. They put a syringe in his heart to get it going. As they were working on him, I said, 'Guys, he's already gone.'"

Later at the hospital, Carolyn was asked if she wanted to see Cameron one last time.

"I went up to him and grabbed his hair. I told him, 'You weren't just my son, you were my friend. I love you.'"

Carolyn began to cry. We sat in silence for a few moments.

"Something else I remember about that day. Cameron's eyes weren't totally closed. They were open just enough so I could see his brown eyes. I looked at those eyes for the longest time. Gosh, I remember those eyes."

I asked Carolyn what it was like for her in the days and weeks that followed.

"For the first few days, I hugged myself so hard that I left bruises on my arms," she replied. "And when I washed my hair, I scrubbed really hard so it would hurt. I just wanted to feel something because I was in shock.

"I couldn't go to sleep without reliving the whole thing. All the thoughts that went through my head! What if I'd taken Cameron away the year before he got addicted to meth? What if I'd moved back to North Carolina to the beach? What if I'd not let Cameron live with his dad? What if I'd done this? What if I'd done that?"

For the next year, Carolyn held two jobs in an attempt to stay as busy as possible. At the same time, she planned her and Dan's move back to North Carolina. Finally, the day arrived when it was time to clean Cameron's room so they could put their home on the market.

"I did what I had to do," she remembered. "I didn't stay long. Cameron's shoes were on the floor where he had left them. His bed was the same. Everything was the same. Then I saw these pieces of paper folded up beside his computer. It was like a suicide poem."

"What did it say?"

"That he hadn't thought of suicide as a way out until recently. That he had a noose ready in the trunk of his car. He was very smart, but he spelled noose like the river here in North Carolina, N-e-u-s-e. He knew how to spell *noose*. I think that was his way of saying he was going Home."

"Carolyn," I suggested, "let's talk about your healing process. What was that like?"

"The first year I was in shock. I was crying a lot, but the crying tapered off over time. At first it was hourly. The second year I started coming out of the mist a little bit. I started learning how to handle the anniversaries, Mothers' Days, other holidays. They are totally changed.

"I speak as the mom of an only child. People who have lots of kids and who lose one say they have to go on with life because they've got other kids to take care of. But I didn't. I had a husband, me, and a dog. Just taking care of myself was hard. I had to fight off the doctor giving me antidepressants. My thought was, 'I'm grieving. If I don't feel it now, I will have to feel it later.'

"The people left behind often, and I did, consider taking their own lives," she continued. "I vividly remember one day when I was driving to work a few months after Cameron's death. I thought, Some people drive right off the road and into a tree. I had to fight that urge. I was hurting bad. Very bad. I stopped and thought, What am I going to live for? Simple things, like daffodils in March. And helping others. I now facilitate a suicide support group. When Cameron ended his life, he ended the Carolyn that once resided inside me. I'm a new Carolyn now, one who is determined to save teens and others from depression."

"Carolyn, how is day-to-day life for you now?"

"Much better, but yes, I think of my son every day. I think of what he would be doing if he were alive. I don't feel like a good mother anymore. I lost my son. I couldn't keep him alive. I'm getting better, though. I'm getting better.

"I don't forget him on birthdays. He loved strawberries, so I always make a cake or something from strawberries. This year I didn't feel like baking, so I had a strawberry daiquiri in his memory. If he were alive, he would have had one with me, because he'd be old enough.

"You never go back to the way you were," she added. "It's different. Totally different."

"Carolyn, is there anything else you'd like to say?"

"Cameron kept a journal that last week. Don't know why. Maybe he thought that was going to be his last week. On the cover he wrote, 'beautiful disasters.' Those two words say a whole lot. He was beautiful, and what happened was a disaster. That is him in a nutshell.

"We all miss his sweet smile, his jokes, the way he listened … but his friendship is what I miss the most. His friendship.

"God speed, Cameron. God speed."

Carolyn's Session with Pamela and Jeshua

In my conversation with Carolyn, I had felt both her great love for Cameron and the tremendous pain she bears. Pamela had told me prior to the session that she knew she could reach Cameron. This will be the first time since his death that Carolyn can speak consciously with him. I knew she longed to talk with him, to find out if he is well, and to ask at last the many questions that still lingered. I hoped the conversations with Cameron and Jeshua would bring a renewed and deeper healing to Carolyn and to all who have lost a loved one to suicide.

"Why did you take your life?" Carolyn immediately asked Cameron. She had wondered for four years. Silently, alone, she had asked that question countless times each day. She asked now not as an accusation, but in a true and sincere search for understanding.

"First of all," Cameron began, "I am deeply sorry for the pain and grief I caused you and the ones I left behind. It was never my intention to hurt you. I did not see a way out at the time of my suicide. I was desperate. I wanted a quick fix. I wanted to be done with the depression once and for all. It had crossed my mind to commit suicide before that time, but it was still an act of desperation. I wish to offer you and my next of kin my sincere apologies for the pain I caused you."

For a moment I was surprised by Cameron's diction and maturity; he sounded more like an adult than a teen. I then reminded myself that he was no longer behind the veil of forgetfulness through which we pass when we incarnate. We were speaking with the real Cameron, fully conscious and unburdened by depression.

"I love and care for you deeply," Cameron told Carolyn. "My action was my decision, and you were in no way to blame for it. There is always hope, you know. This I have learned on the other side of the veil. There is hope for everyone. You can get out of the darkest spot if you accept help and are willing to reach out to others. I know this, because they have helped me a lot here.

"When I came here, I was bewildered and confused. I had not counted on an afterlife at the moment I took my life. But, there were guides present, beckoning me. I was very lucky to *see* them. I reached out to them, and they told me what had happened. 'You're on the other side now,' they told me, and I was struck with grief. They actually showed me my dead body to convince me that I was really dead. I wasn't aware of this, as I was in a state of panic when I killed myself.

"After I crossed over, they took me to a place of learning and recovery. The first period of time was very difficult. I wanted to go back to Earth, to you, my family and friends. I could not accept that it was so final. I was full of regret and bewilderment, and it was hard to find peace of mind. I often traveled back to you and my friends, wanting desperately to talk to them, to let them know I was around. Some listened; others I couldn't get through to. Some I reached in the dream state.

"I certainly got in touch with you. We had some deep conversations with each other during the dream state. You were full of sadness and questions. My guides had to stand by me during those talks, because I was so full of grief and sadness myself. I just wanted to come back to you and try again. It took a long time before I accepted that I had done it, that I had really left my life behind and that I had to start over again. In my talks with you, I tried to tell you that I truly appreciated who you are as my mother and that you didn't fail me. No one failed me. I want this message to help other people struggling with suicidal thoughts, and I thank you, Rob, and the channel sincerely for offering this opportunity to me."

Cameron's words moved me. I felt saddened that he had suffered not only while in body but also upon his transition back into Spirit. Yet, I was heartened that his guides had been there to greet him and that he had been able to see them despite his initial, overwhelming confusion.

"Will you return as another person during my present lifetime?" Carolyn inquired. "Will I know you?" I felt her profound yearning.

"It is not time yet for me to plan another lifetime," said Cameron. "I am still in the recovery zone, but I have progressed a lot, I am proud to say, since my crossing over. I am even helping others, Mom! This gives me great satisfaction. I am helping teens who have crossed over due to suicide. I help them understand their situation and assist them in their mourning process. Even if you take your own life, there is a mourning process to go through on this side as well as for the ones left behind on the other side. You have to let go of your loved ones and also come to terms with the guilt that arises in you when you see the sadness of the ones left behind. This is really very tough. I am so glad to have come so far that I can help people with this on this side.

"But, I am in no place yet to plan my next lifetime. I do not yet feel the urge to do so. Life is meaningful to me here right now. As long as it stays meaningful, I know this is my place. They will let me know when I might have to go back to Earth."

Present all along, Jeshua now spoke to Carolyn's question.

"There is no plan yet for Cameron to incarnate. Much depends on his development. Different strands of possibilities and probabilities will at a certain point come together and create the opening for a new lifetime. It is best not to speculate about that now. Rest assured, however, that you [Carolyn] and Cameron are deeply connected to each other. You will meet again, whether on Earth or in the life in between incarnations. You are actually connected *now* also, although it is hard for you as a human to truly believe this because you cannot feel, see, or touch your son. He is there. He was frequently around you after he died, but the connection is much clearer now because of his greater awareness. He has evolved. You can be proud of him! He has come to terms with what he has done. He has taken responsibility for it."

"Are you regretful about taking your life?" Carolyn asked Cameron.

"Yes, very," he replied. "After I came here, I could see into the probabilities of the lifetime I left behind, the scenarios that would have been possible if I had chosen life. This was very difficult to watch. But, the guides that accompany you here are very skilled at pointing out that it's okay to make mistakes, that it's no use blaming yourself forever, and that there will be new opportunities available even if you take your own life. God is always merciful. I am thankful for their help. I now am slowly getting over the regret and guilt.

"I tried to get through to tell you that I loved you, that I was sorry, that it was a mistake and that I wanted to get back to you. I felt frustrated that I could not talk to you in the normal way. I was confused at that time. But, I also wanted to let you know I was still alive."

"Will you continue to visit me, at least in my dreams?"

"Yes, I will," Cameron affirmed. "I now do so much more consciously, with the help of my guides. I am more aware now of when it is the right time to reach you. I am calmer now. You are still coming to terms with my death, and that is what we are working on in our dream-state meetings. *I want more than anything else to help you heal from this trauma.* We are making progress. You also have guides who accompany you in our meetings. They are very gentle and caring.

"You have to get to a place of full acceptance of my death, Mom. I know this is very hard, but it is the only way to really move on with your life and make the best of it. There is nothing more I wish for you than to reach a state of peace about my death. I wish you'd see that I made this decision on my own, even if I was desperate and lonely at that time. I am entirely responsible for this action, *and I want it to be that way.* I would not like to be portrayed as victim. It is okay for you to *miss me,* but it's time to stop the 'what ifs' and 'couldn't we have done things differently.' Let that go. We are past that point now. I am past that point now. I wish to cooperate with you on a new level. We can make a difference in the world by helping other teens and perhaps prevent them from taking their lives."

"Are you okay with me sharing your story, your poetry, your artwork to illustrate the depth of your depression?" Carolyn inquired. She was intensely motivated to see that Cameron's death was not in vain.

"Yes, you can," he agreed. "I'd like to share everything with the world in order for them to understand what happened to me. I can be an example for others. Sometimes it's hard for grown-ups to understand what's going on in the minds of young people. Young people are much more sensitive to mood swings, fears, and insecurities due to the changes they are going through in puberty. They are becoming a man or a woman, and the transition from being a child to a grown person with a sexual identity can be hard. There are a lot of doubts accompanying this transition.

"It's important for teens to talk about their insecurities, their fears," he continued. "They hardly do that, because they're so busy building their identity for the outside world. They're much more occupied with the impression they make on others than with what's inside. They seek to alleviate their fears and insecurities by creating a personality they think is desirable. They look at the images available in society about how to be a good, attractive man or woman. These images are often not aligned with what the soul wants, and therefore a gap arises between what a person actually feels inside and what is presented on the outside. This gap can cause a problem for teens who are very sensitive. It's hard to be untrue to your own nature for a long time. That's when psychological difficulties arise, such as fear and depression."

"Cameron," asked Carolyn, "what can I tell teens to help them out of depression?"

"First of all, it's important to recognize the signs of depression. When teens are unusually withdrawn and seem shut off from you, pay attention. It's normal for teens to stand up against their parents, to disagree and fight with them. If, however, there is a substantial lack of communication, it's important to find out what's going on in their lives. Perhaps speak with their friends or teachers in a careful way. They're not just 'minding their own business' if they don't communicate with you anymore. If they don't communicate emotionally with other people, there is something wrong. Perhaps you are not the one they are intimate with, but there should always be someone. This is important.

"Next, it's very important to let teens know they can talk about their feelings of insecurity or fear. It's important they get the message that it's *they* who really matter, not the things they accomplish in the world. They need to open up about their deepest emotions. That will set them free. The people helping them need to be prepared for the depth of their emotions, to have no judgment about it, and to invite them to express even their darkest thoughts. Nothing is scarier than a thought or emotion held inside for a long time. If it's out in the open, the solution is at hand.

"Inviting teens to speak with each other under the supervision of a skilled and compassionate therapist is a good thing," Cameron concluded. "One could create circles of open and genuine communication in which groups of teens share their thoughts and feelings about certain issues in their lives. It's important they connect to each other."

Jeshua Speaks

"Suicide is not wrong," Jeshua stated. "Spiritually, suicide is simply a possibility, a choice one can make among others. It is not necessarily the worst choice one could make. Let me explain.

"Sometimes a person can get so stuck in a certain mood, a state of mind, that it is very hard to get out of it without taking drastic measures. Life is all about change. If you get stuck in one state of mind for a very long time it becomes unbearable, and life itself will force you to do something, even if it means you take your life.

"Cameron, for example, landed in a deep depression and tried several ways of getting out. He did his utmost to come to terms with very difficult emotions. He had a fierce temper, combined with a very sensitive and kind-hearted side. It was hard to balance the two. There were angry parts inside him that he dared not face. The energy got stuck there, and in the end it became impossible for him to stay in touch with the natural flow of his feelings. He became shut off from himself. He felt as though he were dead while alive. This is a very painful state of being. He committed suicide as an act of desperation but ultimately also as an act of hope—a hope for change, *any* change.

"Now," Jeshua continued, "would he have healed if he had not killed himself? It is not certain. We do know that right after he killed himself, he regained his feelings. He awoke in the shock and horror of realizing that he had cut himself off from the ones he loved. While physically alive he could not feel his love for them anymore. When dead he realized the full extent of his love, and from the soul's perspective this was a great breakthrough. The suicide forced change upon Cameron, and in his case it worked out well. It was a turning point for his soul.

"It does not work that way for everyone. People respond differently after having taken their lives. It is not the case that suicide is in any way a thing I recommend. Of course not. I only wish to state that from a spiritual perspective there are no acts that are absolutely wrong or sinful. The deepest act of self-betrayal can lead someone into a state of inner clarity that may help forever. The darkest point may become the starting point for a new direction toward light. You see, spiritual evolution does not proceed in a linear fashion. It uses the polarities of light and dark to create dynamics and change.

"In saying this I wish to take away the traditional judgment about suicide, that it is the gravest sin. God or Spirit does not feel this way. God has the greatest compassion for people who take their lives in despair. There is always help available for them on the other side. They are never abandoned.

"With regard to your question about teens and depression, Carolyn, I wish to add to what Cameron has said—that it should not be your primary focus to prevent teens from committing suicide. The primary aim of your work should be to invite teenagers to share their burdens, to open their hearts and tell you of their deepest fears. Even if a teen later kills himself, if you have reached out to his heart and touched him, he will take that with him forever. Your help reaches across death. It is when you are open to all possibilities that you are most able to hear them truly and reach out in compassion. Of course, this will diminish the risk of suicide. Do not, however, measure your success by that criterion."

As I took in Jeshua's words, my feelings about suicide shifted. I had never considered it to be a sin, but it was helpful to hear Jeshua say that suicide can actually be the beginning of a movement toward growth and light. Each of us is a sacred being who lives forever, and any moment, even that moment we consider darkest, can serve as the catalyst that propels the soul to new and greater heights along the spiral of evolution.

"Cameron," Carolyn asked, "is there anything you want me to tell Dan? Your friends in Texas?"

"I love them all," Cameron said. "I am sorry that I did what I did, that I didn't see any other way out at the time. I thank them for their companionship, and I still visit them every now and then. You have no idea how strong the bonds are between souls once they have connected from the heart."

Carolyn then asked if he visits his father often and how his father is doing.

"I don't visit my father often, only once in awhile. He is very busy preparing himself for another incarnation on Earth. He is in the process of making a life plan with the help of his guides. He wants me to let you know that he is with us and will stay with us, even after he has crossed over to that new lifetime. Part of him remains here in the afterlife and is always available to us.

"When I meet him, he appears as I remember him. He has learned a lot here. He is at peace now with his early departure from life. He still visits you often. My contact with him after I died has not been extensive. I have primarily been in contact with guides who are very specialized in suicide. I want you to know that he is fine and that he will be there for you when you cross over. He loves you, admires you for the work you have done on yourself, and wants you to take good care of yourself."

Having asked Cameron her most pressing questions, Carolyn now turned her attention to Jeshua.

"Jeshua, how can I best help depressed individuals?" she inquired.

"Help them understand themselves better," Jeshua counseled. "They need to know what is happening to them. You cannot tell this to them by handing them a book or a list of characteristics and tools. They need to find out themselves by being given the opportunity to tell their story to someone who listens with no judgment and with complete compassion. When they are able to open up and tell their story, then you can help them find meaning in it, and you can show them that they are not crazy but often are very sensitive, kind-hearted people. You can help them by reflecting a point of sanity in their confused world. By *sanity* I mean the energy of trust and compassion, encouragement and inspiration. Make them aware of their strength, the qualities they have already shown, their accomplishments. Often these people have very low self-esteem and need to be made aware of their beauty and incredible strength.

"The form in which you help depressed individuals will evolve over time," he added. "Whenever you wonder, 'Do I have to do this?' ask instead, 'Do I *feel* like doing this? Does this give me a sense of joy and inspiration?' Spirit communicates to you through your feelings of joy."

Carolyn's questions had addressed much of what I had sought to understand, particularly in regard to Cameron, but I still had questions about suicide in general.

"Jeshua, is suicide ever planned by a soul before birth, and if so, why would someone agree to be close to a soul who was planning to commit suicide?"

"Suicide is never planned before birth," Jeshua stated, "although there may be a likelihood of it happening due to problems the incarnating soul is going to meet on the way. The life plan of a soul has some fixed points but also a range of possibilities depending upon the choices the soul makes [when in body]. Suicide is never a fixed point, but it can be a probability, in some cases a high probability.

"Some souls choose to be close to someone who has the potential for serious psychological imbalances. They may choose to do so to gain more understanding of the human psyche, to become more empathic, or to learn to keep their distance when necessary to create boundaries around themselves and not be swept away by the other person's pain."

"Jeshua, what happens to people after they take their lives? Cameron has shared his experience with us, but what other sorts of experiences are possible?"

"It depends on the state of mind in which they arrive. There is always help available. There are guides present to explain the situation to the deceased and to help them cross over to a place of recovery. Some souls, however, do not hear or see the guides; they are too caught up in themselves and their worrisome thoughts. They may roam around for some time until they find their way to the light. The places of recovery help souls come to terms with what they did, look at the reasons behind the suicide, and find ways of addressing the hurt and emotions beneath."

"How quickly do they reincarnate?"

"That is entirely up to the individual. Some incarnate quickly; others take some time to reflect."

"Do they have to continue with the same lessons?"

"Yes. They will meet the same lessons in different circumstances."

"What else did Cameron experience after his suicide?"

"He reached out for help quite soon after he passed over. He noted the friendly face of a male guide nearby and asked him,

'What is happening with me?' He was in a state of shock and surprise. Because he was so open, the guide was able to get through to him and tell him that everything was all right and that he was on the other side now. The guide offered to help him, and Cameron said yes. He followed the guide and was taken to a place where he could rest and gradually come to terms with what had happened."

"Where is Cameron now, and what is he doing?" I asked.

"Cameron lives in a house in the astral realms," Jeshua informed us. "It is a white house, and there are paintings hanging on the walls that he himself made. The paintings are alive, like a canvas of moving energies. They are very colorful and somewhat abstract. He is still seeking to come to terms with the issues that depressed him during his life. He works on himself by painting and talking to his guides. Also, he assists others who have just crossed over due to suicide. Cameron is evolving. After some time he will leave this realm and go to a lighter place. From there he will travel to other places in the astral world in order to learn and understand more about human life."

"Jeshua, after Cameron took his life, what kinds of adjustments did Carolyn's soul make in her pre-birth plan? Since Cameron was no longer here to play the role he agreed to play in her life, did her soul make arrangements to bring in other people or create other learning experiences that will teach the same lessons Cameron would have taught her? If so, what were they?"

"Yes, Carolyn's soul made adjustments after Cameron died. She went into a very intense growth process psychologically. The intense emotions activated or attracted different possible lifelines [timelines]. A life plan is a web of probabilities, as mentioned, and one might say that due to Cameron's suicide certain threads in the web suddenly started to glow and become activated. Whereas they at first were only dim possibilities, they now became much more real.

"It is not so much that Cameron will be replaced by another person teaching her the same lessons, although she will meet people who have problems similar to Cameron's. Rather, it is more the case that her lessons have gained in intensity. On the one hand, her homework has become heavier. On the other hand, it carries a greater promise of inner growth. Carolyn wanted to learn lessons in this lifetime about staying true to herself, not giving away too much of herself in taking care of others, and not being too action oriented but rather letting go and letting life take care of things. She would have learned these lessons if Cameron had stayed, but she is now learning them in a faster and more intense way. Due to her inner growth and courage, she will now attract situations and opportunities that will fulfill her deeply. The road may seem steeper, but it will lead her to beautiful vistas she might not have visited otherwise. There is a benevolent flow in life that brings the circumstances that help one grow.

"Life plans can be reviewed several times during a lifetime," Jeshua added. "New plans are made, but these new plans already existed as possible alternative realities. I know this is puzzling from a human perspective. God's mind is infinite, and there is no limit to the possibilities, even in one lifetime.

"Also, people exist in alternative realities [parallel dimensions]. In these alternative realities, different 'yous' are playing out different aspects of life. It is mind-boggling for a human, and one does not really need to understand this. The important thing to remember is that there is always room for choice; no lifeline is fixed once and for all. You can always choose a positive course of action under any circumstances. If you lose someone through suicide, your life plan will be changed to accommodate the choices you subsequently make. Life will always offer you possibilities for healing, and you will attract the alternative reality that offers you the best circumstances to do so."

I asked Jeshua how people who have lost loved ones to suicide can heal the guilt and self-blame that are usually felt.

"Guilt and self-blame are human reactions to suicide," he responded. "In the beginning they can be all-consuming. You keep thinking about how you could have made a difference, or you get angry about other people having failed to make a difference. This is okay. This is how the human mind responds to such a situation. Don't resist these thoughts. Don't fight them. Their hold on you will diminish when you open to other people's perspectives on what happened. Often they will tell you things about the loved ones you did not know. You slowly understand that they had lives of their own, that they are souls unto themselves, and that they steer their own course in life, even if you try your utmost to help them change or recover.

"You gradually realize that you did the best you could and that you could not have prevented the suicide. There comes a point in the decision-making process of people contemplating suicide when it is between them and themselves. It is their choice. Respect this. Guilt and self-blame ultimately express an overestimation of one's power. It was not in your power to prevent the suicide. No one has such power. To accept and respect one's own humanness can help to release guilt and self-blame."

Jeshua's reference to preventing suicide made me think of a powerful story in author Irene Kendig's book, *Conversations with Jerry and Other People I Thought Were Dead.* Irene presents a discussion she had through a medium with her friend Bill, who had taken his own life. She tells Bill about her two friends Dan and Denise, a brother and sister. Dan took his life on an evening when Denise had planned to meet him for dinner but canceled. After Dan's death, Denise felt guilty for canceling, believing she might otherwise have saved her brother's life. Bill responds by telling Irene,

> Even if she had dinner with him, Dan still would have had to be willing to create an opening in order for her to have made a difference. If he'd been willing to create an opening, someone—in this case, Denise—would have stepped in. And even if she hadn't, someone else would have. Something as simple as a smile or kind word from someone would have made the difference. Everything is orchestrated. If Dan had needed someone's assistance to guide him in a new direction,

someone would have been there. There is always a response to our needs. Had he been open to such a change ... the universe would have responded to the opening.

I shared this story with Jeshua. "This story seems to suggest that every suicide that could have been prevented *was* prevented. Is that true? If it is, this awareness would do wonders to relieve the guilt people feel at not preventing a suicide."

"If there is an opening," Jeshua answered, "the Universe will mirror this positive attitude and will respond, for example, through kind, helpful acts from others. In opening up, the suicidal person aligns with his soul and chooses for light and positivity. This is an act of free will; such acts are not pre-determined. Throughout your lives you repeatedly face the choice to open up or close down, and it is not pre-determined or pre-planned that you will choose to open up or not in specific circumstances. Although some situations are fixed and pre-planned, your way of responding is not. If that were so, there would be no sense in incarnation as a learning process."

"But are you saying that every suicide that could have been prevented was prevented?"

"All suicides preventable *by outside forces* were indeed prevented," Jeshua declared.

This statement stopped me. Here was one of the most important and powerful pieces of information I had come across in the years I had been exploring pre-birth planning. If only this were widely known! Millions of people would then be spared the heartbreaking agony of wondering whether they could have intervened to prevent a suicide.

"Acknowledging the fact that one sometimes cannot help someone, even a loved one, involves a sense of humility," Jeshua continued. "This can be a liberating sense of humility. It can set you free from the notion that you could have prevented the suicide. It can help you, also, to forgive the person who wasn't able to open up. In forgiving, you recognize the person's responsibility while being compassionate and understanding at the same time.

It releases guilt, because in forgiving you also recognize that you were not responsible."

"Jeshua," I asked, "how can we heal the anger that is often felt toward the loved one? And how can we deal with the overwhelming feeling of missing the person?"

"What does healing really mean?" Jeshua queried. "Healing does not mean that one will return to how one was before the incident took place. Healing is about change. To heal truly means to accept the things that happened, even if they still hurt you. With acceptance there will be peace as you allow the emotions of grief and anger and the passing thoughts of guilt and self-blame to be there without being attached to them.

"Healing from losing someone to suicide *is* possible. Again, you will not experience life as you once did. After you have gone through the mourning process and the guilt and self-blame have started to lose their grip on you, you will become more thoughtful, quiet, and reflective and also capable of truly savoring moments of joy and laughter. You will even start to reminisce about your loved one with a smile on your face. Perhaps the smile will be accompanied by tears at first, but there will be a moment in the future when you can be thankful for having had the loved one in your life. There will be a moment in which you wish the person well from the bottom of your heart and focus on your own life again, doing things you enjoy and that fulfill you. That is when true healing has occurred.

"Anger is one of the emotions one comes across in the mourning process, alongside grief and the sense of missing. With anger it's important to allow yourself to feel and express it in a safe way. Beating on a pillow, for instance. If you do so, you will find that beneath the anger is pain, deep pain. When you get in touch with that pain, you will start to cry. That is a good sign. Crying is releasing. It is healing.

"Missing your loved one is an honest emotion that just needs to be felt. Do not resist it. Cry a river of tears. It will cleanse you. The missing will remain, but it will change in quality over time. It will lose its sharpest edge."

"Jeshua, please speak to those who are contemplating suicide."

"It is a choice one can make. In an enlightened society, people with suicide plans would be permitted to talk with a counselor who would consider this option with them. By allowing it to come into the open, and by not immediately rejecting it, the therapist could create a sense of liberation in them, which might help them, paradoxically, to release the suicidal thoughts and consider other options.

"When something is forbidden, it has a particular attraction. If suicide is completely taboo, then those who suffer from depression will be drawn to it, and they will feel even more depressed because of that attraction. If those who are drawn to suicide are asked openly about how and why they would wish to end their lives, there is a release of the pressure.

"To someone considering taking your own life, I say that you need not be ashamed of this thought. You are simply seeking a way out of your despair. I say to you that nothing you can ever do will take God's love from you. There is always help available to you, whether on this side or the other. God or Spirit does not condemn suicide and instead favors a humane, compassionate approach to anyone considering this option. If you will allow suicide to be one possible pathway to take, you will see, again, paradoxically, that the number of suicides decreases."

Carolyn's Session with Barbara and Aaron

In talking with Carolyn after the session, I sensed that it had been deeply healing for her to at last speak with Cameron, to know that he was well, and to hear him say that he loved her. I felt, too, that his acceptance of responsibility for the suicide would bring even further healing to her over time as she released more of her self-blame. Jeshua had shared with us much healing wisdom, including the non-judgmental view that suicide is not a sin but rather a choice. Carolyn and I were now ready to talk with Aaron, who I knew would provide a different yet still enlightened perspective.

"Carolyn," Aaron began, "my deepest sympathy. I understand what a painful experience this is." There was great warmth, tenderness, and compassion in his tone. "The strongest teaching here, Carolyn, is that no one ever leaves, and nothing is ever lost. So, although you cannot still embrace the loved one and talk to him in the physical form, you can learn to transcend the illusion of physical form and know that the loved one is never far away. How could you lose anyone? This is a primary lesson. It helps to draw the one left behind a bit further out of the illusion of separate self. It invites that one to transcend separation and know the unity of All That Is.

"On occasion, the one who is left behind has in a past life abruptly left the one who died by suicide. So, the one who remains behind may have caused enormous pain to the one who is leaving. It is never punishment but rather the recognition [on the soul level] that 'This is what my beloved experienced when I did this.' This helps people learn to be more present for others. It's not necessarily about suicide; it may be about desertion, abandonment. All these lessons are being learned."

"Aaron," I asked, "why do souls care about learning how to transcend the illusion of physical form while in body?"

"You are lost behind the veil," he responded, speaking not just to Carolyn and me but to all who would read his words. "But, at some level you always remember that you are a soul and that you are here for a reason. It may not be in the conscious mind, but it's still there. This is especially true for the older soul, who is aware both of the pain and loss on one level and that this life is about spiritual growth and learning, and that whatever comes is there to enhance understanding, kindness, and love if one will but permit it. Thus, one can steep in anger and feelings of abandonment or betrayal, or one can find compassion for the loved one who is gone, whether it's through suicide, abandonment, or mortal illness. As your heart opens in compassion and you no longer blame the loved one or take the leaving personally as an affront to you, then you are learning. You are learning to let go, and you are learning compassion."

"Aaron, what happens to those after taking their lives?" I inquired. "How quickly do they reincarnate?"

"What happens will differ depending on the spiritual level of the individual, the level of awareness, the openness to guidance. In the worst case, they move into that transition hardly aware that they've moved into a transition, filled with whatever pain and anger drove them to the transition. And they will reincarnate very quickly. This is no different from a person who dies in an accident, for example, a sudden trauma or in a war, a military skirmish. It may be very hard for the soul to be aware that it is no longer in a body, and it quickly grasps at the first reasonably appropriate body available.

"At the other end of the spectrum is the soul who has thought deeply about its reasons for leaving the body. Whether that is through suicide or through war, it has pondered the very real possibility that it will die. It is willing to stay open to its guidance and to wait quite awhile before it moves very consciously and lovingly into a new incarnation.

"Carolyn, you would want to know if this is the case with your son: *What did he experience after the suicide?* A brief period of sadness more than anything else. Fear, trauma, disbelief. But also, because he had a strong spiritual sense, he was able to hear and connect with his guides, to be reassured by them."

"Aaron," I said, "some people believe that suicide is a sin and that those who commit suicide will be punished."

"Suicide is merely a form of transition," Aaron replied. "The most common reaction after one has moved through the transition is sadness that one lost this hard-earned opportunity to be in physical body and learn. This is true even if the physical incarnation seemed impossible and unbearable. From the perspective of the other side, one sees opportunities one did not see while one was feeling thus so trapped.

"But it is not a sin; it is simply a loss. Cameron did experience it as a loss. He began to look at his situation and why he had chosen thusly. He is presently in a space where he is counseling others who have made a sudden planned or unplanned transition by accident, by their own hand, or through violence. He is one of a group of guides, still third density [third dimensional] and knowing he will need eventually to incarnate, but he is able to use his experience to help others move through that initial trauma of finding themselves out of a body, to comfort them, to help them to be merciful to themselves. And this is part of his learning.

"Let me come back, then, to the question of what happens to people after they take their lives," continued Aaron. "The same thing really that happens to all people who move through this transition known as *death*. They suddenly experience themselves separated from the physical plane and the physical body. At first there may not be acceptance—they may become what we call an 'earthbound spirit'—but more usually they are helped past that phase.

"Whatever anger, fear, pain, or confusion drove them in their lives will still be there, but they are able to see the whole life experience from a bigger perspective. There is always loving support. If they are very caught in anger and negativity, they will experience a place of darkness. They are not being punished and held in a place of darkness; rather, they hold themselves there, and the darkness is that of their own fear, anger, and confusion, their own negativity. Always there are loving guides, but they may not be able to perceive them. Carolyn, your son was blessed in that he was able to perceive these guides.

"Eventually, all beings, no matter how they die, will open to their guidance. We look here at beings who were deeply negative and did great harm to others, such as a person who killed a roomful of schoolchildren and then killed himself. Somebody like that may be deeply immersed in negativity and finds himself in a place of deep despair and darkness, but he is still loved and supported. Such a person may have so much negativity that he cannot tolerate the light for a long time, but eventually he will open to it.

"On the other hand, a person who has a more tender heart may feel he does not deserve the light, but slowly he will open to it. Then this traveler will be given the opportunity to look at the past life to see what unwholesome choices were made and why, to see what he was seeking to learn and what was or was not learned. There will be an opportunity to balance some of the karma, as your son is doing now, Carolyn, as a guide to others."

I asked Aaron if he had ever ended his life in previous incarnations.

Reasons for Suicide

"Of course, in so many thousands of past lives, yes, there were times when I did that," he answered. "In one situation I was losing both body and brain function. The body was in great pain, and the brain could no longer think clearly. I wanted to die consciously. So, at one point when the brain was a bit clearer and there were painkiller pills available to me—please don't think of your present-day morphine; this was thousands of years ago and herbal medication was used to control pain in those days—I took a great overdose, consciously choosing to leave the incarnation.

"Immediately upon awakening on the other side, I was aware of the choice I had made and grateful that I had been able to make that choice, because my extreme pain and frequent confusion were very distressful to my loved ones. It was more restful for everyone that I go at that point. The [nonphysical] body I woke up into was whole, and the mind was clear.

"What seems to bring impairment after the suicide is holding on to negativity, which can happen all the way through the transition. Such souls are always surrounded by loving energy until they are finally capable of seeing the light and allowing themselves into the light, however long that takes. And then they are supported further along their journey."

Aaron's past-life decision was a concrete example of what Jeshua had told us: that to end one's life in a conscious manner can under some circumstances be a reasonable choice. Aaron had spared both himself and his loved ones further suffering. After returning to the nonphysical, he was not judged or punished either by himself or by others. On the contrary, he was grateful he had been lucid long enough to make that choice.

"Aaron," I asked, "do those who end their lives have to pick up with the same lessons in another lifetime?"

"Yes, but perhaps not in the next lifetime. If the issue was too difficult, they might move in a different direction for some period of time before they return to the lesson, but eventually they would need to pick it up again.

"Your son, Carolyn, has chosen to look at what he was learning and failing to learn. I cannot tell you whether he will come back in an incarnation in which he plans to face those particular lessons again or whether he will give a break to it, but now on the astral plane he is working with it."

To offer as much healing as possible to those left behind, I then asked Aaron another question I had asked Jeshua: "Aaron, how can people heal the guilt and self-blame they feel after loved ones take their lives?"

"Remember that it is about them, not you. Of course, sometimes the ones left behind will have been part of what happened, for instance, a child who was abused and takes its own life. In that case, one [the parent] must look deeply at one's participation, acknowledge one's responsibility, ask forgiveness for it, and bring forth some kind of balance for that responsibility.

"Since beings interact, there is always some participation. But, for the most part, the ones who take their lives are souls on their own track, learning their own lessons. There's little the loved one could have done, whether it's a child's parent or a person's partner who dies. The one left behind needs to know, 'The other person made this choice, not me.'

"In most cases," added Aaron, "the practice is about compassion: to see how deeply this one was suffering, and that this one, no matter how hard he or she tried, could not successfully learn the lessons that he or she came to learn in the incarnation.

"When we look at what is sometimes called mercy killing—for example, someone with cancer who has been treated through surgery, chemotherapy or radiation, and the cancer has spread throughout the body; the person is in terrible pain; the person asks to leave—it's heart-wrenching. You love this person. You might not pull the trigger, but you might leave certain kinds of pills within reach. There's such deep compassion, not wanting the loved one to suffer and recognizing that the loved one has tried everything and has no further recourse.

"It feels a bit different when it's an emotional issue. Sometimes the pain is so strong that the person simply needs to leave and start over.

"There is one more type of situation that comes to mind," Aaron continued. "There is a friend of Barbara's whose seemingly healthy nineteen-year-old son abruptly ended his life through suicide. He had not seemed suicidal. He was not using drugs. He seemed to be not happy or unhappy but dealing with and making something of his life.

"At some level this young man knew that his body was developing malignancies that were not yet visible and that he was going to experience what would probably be a completely untreatable form of brain cancer. He did not know this consciously, but after meeting with this young man after his death, I could tell that at some level he understood his body was moving in that direction and he simply needed to leave.

"Let me give a different example. A man of age sixty whom Barbara and I knew, who seemed perfectly healthy, with a loving wife, children and grandchildren, and work he enjoyed, developed a sudden stroke and died within minutes. There was no prior sign of illness; in fact, medical tests had shown that he was healthy. But, the autopsy showed the beginnings of cancer in his body, tumors that had not been known to be there. At some level he was aware of that and rather than face a prolonged illness, he simply chose to leave. Now, he did not jump off a building or shoot himself; he simply had a stroke. But, of course, he participated in that stroke."

Aaron's reply made clear to me that death and suicide are complex topics about which much is still not understood. I thought of the nineteen-year-old man who had taken his life. He had known subconsciously that incurable brain cancer was developing and did not wish to have that experience. Yet, following his suicide, his parents had undoubtedly blamed themselves. What if they knew then, or later learned, exactly why he had taken his life? How powerfully would this knowledge have brought healing and self-forgiveness to them? I hoped that Aaron's words would prompt those who have lost loved ones to suicide to realize that little in our world is as it seems and that much is happening beneath the surface. This awareness alone could engender deep healing.

"Aaron," I wondered, "how can a person heal the anger that is sometimes felt toward the loved one who dies by suicide?"

"Look deeply at the suffering of the loved one and at one's own suffering, offering kindness to the one who has departed and to oneself. We do not wish our loved ones or ourselves to suffer. When one can acknowledge the anger without feeling guilt for that anger, then one sees that the anger is really based on a feeling of abandonment. It's very important *not* to say, 'I shouldn't be angry,' but rather to say, 'Anger is present; or sadness, grief, fear, and confusion are present; or feelings of abandonment, betrayal, and loss are present.' And then to work with lovingkindness, wishing oneself well. 'May I be happy. May I have peace.' And wishing the loved one well. 'May you be happy. May you have peace.' Very gradually, the feelings of anger begin to give way to genuine compassion and the deep love one has felt for the other.

"That which is aware of anger is not angry. It is the deep, centered aspect of the Self that is capable of seeing with an open heart. So, anger arises. Instead of taking it personally and feeling guilt or needing to act it out, one simply holds oneself. 'Breathing in, I am aware of the anger. Breathing out, I smile to the anger,' smiling to the self, holding the self mercifully, and then turning one's attention to the one that has departed. It's a gradual process." Here, Aaron was speaking of meditative and breathing practices that allow one to dis-identify from anger or other negative emotions.

One comes to realize that one is not anger but rather that anger is something that passes through one. Such spaciousness and dis-identification from the emotion bring peace.

Aaron then shared two other past lives in which he took his own life.

"I told you about one life in which there was sickness," Aaron said. "There is another lifetime in which I was one of a number in battle. A country had invaded, and we were completely out-numbered. I knew the cruelty of these barbarians, who would torture their enemy. So, when it was clear there was no way I could continue to fight, I took my own life.

"In that lifetime I died with hatred of the enemy." Here, I understood that Aaron was using the term *enemy* to refer to his viewpoint during that incarnation, not his viewpoint now. As an enlightened being, Aaron sees no one as an enemy. He now knows experientially that all are his brothers and sisters. "That hatred held me in a dark place for some period of time. When I speak of time, please remember there is no sense of time when you leave the human plane. I'm speaking figuratively in your terms. There was an unknown period of darkness. Within that darkness I became aware of light. There was a feeling that I did not want or deserve to be in that light, so I maintained myself in darkness. Somehow the light continued to comfort me, even though I rejected it, until eventually I was able to let it in.

"Now, this soldier that I was had seen his wife, children, and loved ones brutally slain. So, there was much hatred of what this enemy had done. I recognized finally that I was being given the opportunity to balance old karma and to offer forgiveness, that in forgiving my enemy I was also forgiving past aspects [incarna-tions] of myself [my soul], who had been brutal and who had harmed others.

"To forgive does not mean to condone. I was not condoning my enemy's behavior, but simply seeing that his behavior was the outgrowth of his condition and conditioning. In the same circumstance, I had done the same in past lifetimes. It's not so easy to condemn oneself, so gradually the heart opened. It was an awakening, because I finally saw how hatred only engenders more hatred and that only love can heal.

"Further on in that transition," Aaron remembered, "when I was open to the light, my guides brought me to a very dark place where the ones who had killed my people had gathered. They were suffering badly. They held themselves in darkness. They were terrified of everything. They were consumed by hatred and fear. I was given the opportunity to be for them what others had been for me—a surrounding energy of light—and to hold that light for as long as was useful until some of them began to be able to tolerate and then yearn for light. In this way one learns.

"There is also one very long ago, very ancient lifetime in which the being I was consumed by the darkness of greed, lust, and desire. What he most wanted was taken from him. He was a well-to-do landowner, a man of some power. He had several wives and families. Then an enemy came in and killed his sons, took his wife and daughters as hostage, and made him a captive, a slave. In despair and anger he killed himself. I would call that an emotional suicide. That being also lived in darkness for quite awhile until he finally understood this same principle: I have a choice to live in light or darkness, to live in hatred or compassion. And thus he grew and healed."

Aaron had now eloquently described three past lives in which he had ended his life and how he began to heal on the other side. I asked if there had been previous incarnations in which he had lost a loved one to suicide, and if so, how he healed emotionally while still in body.

"I had a son, a beloved son," Aaron recounted, affection in his voice. "Because of the state of the world as he grew up, he did not have the deep training I had and that I had wished for him. He did not know how to balance his emotions and not take them so personally.

"He saw loved ones around him being persecuted and put to death for religious principles. He despaired both because he felt betrayed—he felt some of these loved ones had the power to save themselves and did not do so—and because he did not have the power to save them. He despaired at the cruelty in the world.

"He did not literally kill himself with his own hand, but he acted in ways he knew would lead to his capture and being put to death when he could easily have stayed quiet in the background or gone away. We certainly could call that a kind of suicide.

"I grieved because I recognized I had been so busy with the state of the world that I had neglected my son, his education, his support. I felt that I could have prevented his death. I was angry at him, myself, and others who had been put to death before him and who had seemed not to enact the power they had to save themselves.

"Two things helped me most. One was a very wise and beloved friend, who helped me to see … let me put it this way. If my son had repeatedly gotten on a wagon on a hill, and each time I stopped him, lifted him from the wagon, and said, 'No, you will crash. You will go over the cliff,' and he insisted on getting back on the wagon, then eventually I would have to acknowledge, 'This is his path.' All I could do would be literally to imprison him, to tie him. He was determined to do what he did. This is who he was. My wise friend helped me to understand that this is his karma. 'The best thing you can do for him is simply to love him and let him go. You brought him into this incarnation with the hope that he could learn lessons he was not yet ready to learn. He had hoped to learn those lessons. Perhaps he will learn them on the astral plane after the incarnation. Let him go with love.' That helped.

"The other thing that helped was simply to remember him as a boy, to remember all that was beautiful about him, and to keep that alive in me, not in a cruel or deceitful way but rather to recognize, 'He is gone. This human is gone, but the love he gave to me and others is not gone. I can cherish that love, cherish the human being he was and all the good things about him.' That was a great help."

I was touched by Aaron's words. Though he had lost his cherished son to suicide in that past life, he had kept the love alive in his heart. From the astral realm, his son would have strongly felt his undying love, just as Cameron could still sense Carolyn's immense love for him.

Adjustments

"Aaron, after Cameron took his life, what kind of adjustments did Carolyn make at the soul level in regard to her birth plan?"

"She is still making them," Aaron informed us. "On one level there is no duality. Carolyn and Cameron are part of the same Divine Oversoul, part of the Unity and Love of the Divine. But in another sense, Cameron never belonged to Carolyn. He simply came into the Earth through the route of his mother. He was nurtured but never owned by his mother. A big part of the lesson for Carolyn is that of loving without grasping, knowing you literally cannot hold on to anything and that that is not a reason to love less but to cherish more deeply. It's a very painful lesson. Nothing can be held onto. Everything changes.

"Do you love the beauty of the rose any less because you know tomorrow it will be wilted? Do you hold yourself back from it? Let me say this very specifically: Cameron did not take his life in order to teach Carolyn this lesson. Many things in her life could have taught her this lesson. But, since her son did take his life, it gives Carolyn an opportunity to go deeply into this lesson."

"Aaron, since Cameron planned before birth to be with Carolyn for a much longer time, does her soul now bring new people into her life to teach her whatever he was going to teach?"

"Rob, there are always new teachers in every moment. It would depend whether the lessons were learned. Carolyn does not suddenly go out and invite in new teachers because she no longer has her son. She observes that her life is filled with teachers, and they come in their own time. It's very important for Carolyn to stay open to new teachers. One of the challenges of anger and despair is that it closes one's energy field, contracts one. One armors the heart and is not willing to open the heart to new teachers and teachings. It's very important that Carolyn observe that possibility and work very gently and lovingly with herself to stay as open as she can, and she is doing that."

Thus far Carolyn had listened quietly to the conversation between Aaron and me, but she now asked her first question. "Aaron, is Cameron aware of me and what I'm doing?"

"Yes, your son is quite aware of you and what you are doing," Aaron assured her, "but he is working hard not to create personal stories based on that. Let me say this carefully, Carolyn. You and your son have known each other in numerous lifetimes. There is a strong connection. Love does not dissolve, but the personal relationships of mother-child, siblings, friends—these personal kinds of relationships dissolve. He is no longer your son in that way, but simply one who is connected to you by these bonds of love. He sees what you are doing and holds it in love."

"Will Cameron reincarnate in my lifetime?" Carolyn asked.

"That is unknown at this time," Aaron told her.

We paused for a moment. We had now discussed how both those who have ended their lives and those who have lost loved ones to suicide may heal. But what about healing for those who feel suicidal?

"Aaron," I said, "please speak to those who are thinking of taking their lives."

"I would ask them to consider the enormous gift of human incarnation, painful though it may be at times," he responded. "I would ask them to consider that a year or five years down the road they might see things in a different way and may have learned something of enormous value if they're willing to stay. I would remind them that it is not a sin but there is a loss, a loss of the opportunity to learn. They've worked so hard to come into this incarnation and prepare the way for the learning they sought. I would ask them to ask themselves, 'Is there any other option besides taking my life?'

"Finally, I would ask, 'Is your choice to take your life one of fear or one of love?' If it comes from a place of fear, anger, feeling

betrayed or hopeless, or feeling enormous body pain and needing to escape it, please remember that when you move through
the transition, any strong negative emotion comes with you. If,
however, you are choosing to leave the body from a place of love,
for example if you are desperately ill and in enormous pain, you
see the drain it's creating on those around you, you know you
cannot live much longer and are able to say, 'I am ready to leave
now. I don't need to go through this anymore,' then you can take
that step literally with an open heart."

Sensing that we were coming to a close, I asked Aaron if there
was anything else he would like to say.

"With a suicide," Aaron replied, "there is more likely to be
anger, confusion, blame, guilt. It's hard to lose a loved one to
cancer or a car accident and one always wonders, 'Could I have
done something differently?', and yet the act of suicide seems like
such a violent one against the self that it is much more likely to
bring up anger. For the one who remains, then, it's so important
to be merciful to the self. You can never stop anger by saying, 'No
more anger.' That's just more anger. 'I won't be angry' is a very
angry statement.

"How does one acknowledge the presence of anger with kindness and compassion for the self and hold the self in that field
of compassion? The strength of the compassion and mercy itself
will create a field of gentleness and love. As you learn compassion
for yourself, you learn it for the one who has departed.

"It's very important not to be afraid of the emotions that arise
and also not to get caught up in the stories. 'What did I do wrong?'
is a story. 'How could I have prevented it?' is a story. 'Why did he
do it?' is a story. Rather, simply know the direct experience of loss,
grief, anger, and confusion, and hold it with mercy."

"I truly miss my son," Carolyn suddenly interjected. "Is there
something I can do?"

"The best thing you can do, Carolyn, is literally to talk to him.
Be assured he can hear you. Tell him you miss him. Tell him you
love him. Tell him what was most special to you about him, what

qualities brought you the most joy. As you hold him in love in that way, it helps him to hold himself in love and supports his progress.

"As you speak to your son in this way and hold him in this circle of love, you must also continue to acknowledge the sense of loss and sadness. Carolyn, please look at the difference between sadness and grief. Sadness is a very natural arising upon loss. It's based on the open heart and on the love that was there, and missing it.

"Grief is based more on fear. 'Is he okay? Will I be okay? What will I do without him?' There's a contracted energy to grief, a tension. Look at that tension whenever it comes. When you are feeling grief, know it as grief and see if you can find the sadness that's openhearted and uncontracted underneath. It's okay to be sad. It won't last forever.

"At this point you have passed through a lot. As you reflect upon the loss of your son's companionship in your life, the loss of his literal hug and smile, find that of him that is still with you, that which can never be lost, and enjoy it.

"Watch when grief with contracted energy and fear and grasping come, and simply note, 'This is grief. This is fear.' Is the mind creating some kind of story then, trying to get away from anger or some other kind of pain? Do you understand the distinction I'm making?"

"I understand," Carolyn said. "I have more sadness than grief now. It's still hard, though. Thank you for your words."

"Carolyn, please be assured that your son is well, doing his work, and aware of you. He loves you and holds you in the circle of love. He is doing exactly what he needs to do to balance his life and his death, to help others to progress, and to make himself ready for the next steps he will take. He is well, and he is happy. Be assured of that."

∼

"All suicides preventable *by outside forces* were indeed prevented."

This one awareness, this single knowing, is the healing balm to those who extended a hand to a desperate loved one, only to feel that person's fingers slip through their grasp. As Jeshua told us, when we take responsibility for another's suicide, we overestimate our power. For you who lost a loved one to suicide, be certain: There was nothing more you could have done. Within that humble recognition is your self-forgiveness found.

And as Aaron made clear, "no one ever leaves, and nothing is ever lost." There is, in fact, no place apart from us where those we love so dearly could be. The higher dimensions overlap and interpenetrate ours, and though our five senses tell us otherwise, we are forever one with those for whom we care, connected through the unseverable bonds of the heart. The love we gave to them is with them always, just as the love we received from them is forever within us. This is more than mere comforting sentiment; it is, indeed, spiritual truth. Like indelible oil painted on the canvas of the soul, the love we give and receive—for giving *is* receiving—becomes part of us literally for all eternity. It is for this reason that Jeshua told Carolyn, "Even if a teen later kills himself, if you have reached out to his heart and touched him, he will take that with him forever. Your help reaches across death." Love is expressed by bodies, but it does not perish with them. When created and shared, it can never be lost.

Society does not yet recognize that there is sanctity in suicidal thoughts. The one who contemplates suicide is a Holy Being standing at a crossroad. From that crossroad, regardless of the decision made, one being will die and another will be born. If suicide is not chosen, then the one who wanted to die in fact died, and a new person, equally holy and now laying claim to physical life, is born. If suicide is chosen, then the one who wanted to die in fact died, and a new being, equally holy and now laying claim to *nonphysical* life, is born. For the soul a divine rebirth occurs at the crossroad and there is no judgment of either form the rebirth may take. Whether physical or nonphysical, the new life is known by the soul to be sacred. If the rebirth is into the nonphysical realm, the soul does not view the suicide as bad, sinful, or an affront to God. In complete nonjudgment and with utter compassion and unconditional love, the soul simply says, "The lessons are unfinished. Let's try again."

Indeed, from the perspective of the soul, suicide may permit spiritual evolution that had stalled in the physical realm to begin anew. As Jeshua said, "Sometimes a person can get so stuck in a certain mood, a state of mind, that it is very hard to get out of it without taking drastic measures. … It becomes unbearable, and life itself will force you to do something, even if it means you take your life." As Aaron echoed, "Sometimes the pain is so strong that the person simply needs to leave and start over." When removed from the density of the Earth plane, those who have ended their lives are often more receptive to guidance and healing. Cameron opened to his guidance in ways he could not while in body, and in so doing created a new life in which he is healing and helping others to heal. Though the soul does not desire suicide, the soul also understands that suicide does not end life. Because life *is* everlasting, and because growth on Earth is potentially so rapid, our souls are willing to accommodate the potential for suicide in our pre-birth plans. Before birth we hope we will embrace our evolution with joy and excitement, but when we cannot do so in the physical, we will most surely do so in our eternal Home.

How do we embrace life after a loved one died by suicide? We begin by choosing to believe that healing can occur. A fundamental spiritual tenet is that our beliefs create our reality. To choose to believe that healing is impossible is to seal one's consciousness in an energetic darkness that prevents healing light from entering. As Jeshua and Aaron said, pre-birth plans are modified after trauma occurs, and a loving Universe brings to us the people, events, and circumstances needed for healing. Yet, nothing can come into our experience unless our vibration so permits, and belief is among the most potent of vibrations. "Healing from losing someone to suicide *is* possible," Jeshua stated. The refusal to accept those words closes the door to the benevolent flow of the Universe, but an openness to the *possibility* of healing marshals healing forces. Angels, spirit guides, and even the loved one who ended their lives are thus summoned and permitted by us to our side, where they literally envelope us with love. That love supports us in ways beyond the understanding of the human mind. Life then proceeds to rearrange itself, bringing us opportunities for healing that will affirm the belief that healing is possible.

Healing also occurs as we stay in relationship with the loved one who appears to be gone, and communication is the foundation of all relationship. Words, whether thought, spoken, or written, are the energy that ripples across the dimensions. As Aaron told Carolyn, "The best thing you can do is literally to talk to him. Be assured he can hear you." The thoughts of loved ones call them to us, and they feel our love more acutely, more clearly, than when in body. As eager as we are to continue in relationship, deceased loved ones may communicate with us in our dreams, through electrical phenomena like phones ringing or lights flashing, or perhaps by creating the familiar scent of cologne or perfume they used. As they reach out and touch us in these ways, grief is healed. And as grief is healed, the loved one's ongoing presence becomes easier to feel. Perhaps most healing, though, is the simple knowing that we can still make a difference in their lives. "As you hold him in love," Aaron explained to Carolyn, "it helps him to hold himself in love and supports his progress." Like all love, Carolyn's love for Cameron is limitless and unbound, transcending the illusions of time and space.

Healing comes not only from staying in relationship with the loved one who died but also from the relationship we have with our own thoughts and feelings. We can engage with and perhaps even fight the emotions of guilt, self-blame, and anger, or we can choose not to resist them, instead simply allowing them to be, touching them with gentleness, mercy, and love. As Jeshua observed, there will be peace "as you allow the emotions to be there without being attached to them." A recurring message of this book is that acceptance *is* transmutation. To resist thoughts or emotions is to strengthen them; repression pushes their energy into the cells of the body where it awaits expression at a future time. By contrast, acceptance slowly dissolves pain. The wounded heart is something one *has*, not something one is. It becomes a vessel that holds pain as pain gives birth to greater awareness.

Too, repression is a powerful form of communication with the Universe. When the one in pain says, "No, I will not feel this way," the Universe hears only no, thus blocking the flow of understanding, love, spiritual clarity, and abundance in all forms. By contrast, saying yes to pain is the energetic equivalent of saying yes to the Universe; it permits all of life's blessings to flow freely to us. In time this flow of Love washes away guilt, self-blame, and anger. Profound compassion then takes root, and an abiding appreciation for the beauty and sanctity of life is birthed.

One might ask: What does it mean to know the sanctity of life? Aaron said to Carolyn that it means to love without grasping, to know that we cannot hold on to anyone and that this is not reason to love less, but rather to cherish more. Cameron now cherishes his physical life in a way he once could not and so works on the other side to counsel teens who, like he, did not see the essential, inherent beauty of their lives. Like Cameron, Carolyn, too, now cherishes life in a new way and so works on this side to counsel teens who do not see the essential, inherent beauty of their lives. Here, mother and son who lost each other step forward hand-in-hand, extracting deep meaning from stark pain. Carolyn's love for her son flows to and through him to the teens he counsels; Cameron's love for his mother flows to and through her to the teens for whom she cares. In this circle of life, Carolyn and Cameron teach others to cherish themselves in the way that they, as mother and son, now and forever cherish each other.

CHAPTER 12

∞ ∞

*R*ape

ONE YEAR AFTER THE PUBLICATION of *Your Soul's Plan,* I gave a talk at the Unity of Birmingham church in Birmingham, Alabama. During my visit I was hosted by two members of the church, Beverly and her partner, Tom. Meeting Beverly was like reuniting with a long-lost friend; throughout my visit I was struck by her warmth, kindness, and openness.

Late one night as we talked alone in her kitchen, Beverly confided that she had been raped many years earlier. Because my work focuses on the planning of life challenges, it is not unusual for people to share deeply personal matters with me. What *was* unusual was one of the details Beverly related.

She told me that after the rape had occurred, the rapist fell asleep next to her in the bed. Seizing the opportunity to escape, Beverly slid quietly off the bed and made her way toward the bedroom door. As she walked past the side of the bed on which the rapist lay, she did something that at the time was utterly incomprehensible to her.

"I leaned over and kissed his cheek."

That statement stopped me—not only because Beverly kissed the man who had raped her but also because the kiss immediately struck me as something that could be explained by a pre-birth relationship. I sensed there was indeed such a connection between Beverly and the rapist and that she might have known before birth of the potential for the rape. The idea stunned me, even though I already knew that some extremely dark roles are agreed upon before we come into body. Nevertheless, I wondered if healing could be found within this perspective. Two years later, when it came time to invite people to share their stories in this book, I reminded myself of my own pre-birth plan to speak my truth courageously. I took a deep breath and, unsure of what I would find, asked Beverly to talk with me again.

In the conversations that followed, I discovered that Beverly had traveled an arduous yet very healing path. Traumatized for years by the rape, she told me she had turned to alcohol, experienced two divorces, and for a very long time been unable to have "a healthy relationship with [her] sexuality." Yet, now at the age of fifty, she enjoyed an emotionally and physically intimate relationship with her partner, and she had completely forgiven the man who had raped her. Some time after our talks, she became a volunteer counselor at a rape crisis center.

What, I wondered, had Beverly done to heal and to reach a place of forgiveness? Was her healing journey now complete? And if not, what else could she do to heal her wounds?

As you read Beverly's story, bear in mind that not all rapes are planned; some are the results of freewill decisions made by people after they are born. (Such is the case with most experiences.) Of those that are planned, there is great variability in the likelihood that the rape will occur. If you have experienced rape, your intuition is your best guide in deciding whether the rape was part of your pre-birth plan. Your intuition—which is your soul communicating with you—will lead you to the perspective that is true, and therefore most healing, for you.

Beverly

Beverly expected the summer of 1978 to be a fun, carefree time in her life. Twenty years old and home from college, she thought she would spend the hot Texas summer visiting with her parents and enjoying the company of old high school friends.

One night Beverly and two of those friends, Gary and Amy, drove into Houston for a night on the town. In 1978 disco was all the rage; Beverly and her friends chose a pulsing, two-story nightclub with a particularly big dance floor. It would be great, Beverly said to herself, to cut loose with Gary and Amy.

At one point during the evening, the three were sitting at one of the backgammon tables in the disco. A man who appeared to be in his late forties and who was wearing a suit approached and introduced himself as Steve, the manager of the club. He said that he hadn't seen them there before and asked a few friendly questions to get to know them. "Glad you're here. Hope you come back," Steve said at the end of their chat.

"Later, I got up to go the bar," Beverly recalled. "Steve saw me, walked up to the bartender, and said, 'That's on me.' I said, 'Thank you, but no.' So, I paid for the drink. I thought it was a little unusual. After a bit Steve came by again to visit some more. I got up, went over to the bartender, and said 'Is this guy for real?' The bartender said, 'Oh yes, he runs the place.' I sat back down and felt comfortable at that point." Beverly would later discover that the bartender was lying for Steve.

As the evening went on, Gary and Amy moved to another part of the club and Beverly found herself in a backgammon game with John, a man who had introduced himself as Steve's friend. Then Steve reappeared.

"Gary invited me out to his place," Steve lied to Beverly. "I told him you would ride with me and John."

"No, I want to ride with them."

"Well, they left."

Puzzled as to why her friends would leave without her, Beverly walked to the parking lot to look for their car, Steve following her. When she was unable to find the car, she told Steve she was going back inside to look for Gary and Amy. "No, you're not," Steve ordered. "Stay here."

"I became very nervous and was in a bit of shock," Beverly remembered. "So, I stood there. I wonder now why I didn't just run and scream."

Then John drove up. Steve opened the car door, pushed Beverly inside, and sat to her right, trapping her in the middle of the front seat. "Gary and Amy must have left," he said to John. "We'll just go."

"I didn't know Houston well," Beverly told me, "but I did know that to get to the side of town that Gary lived on you had to follow the signs to Dallas. Well, the car started to go in the direction away from Dallas." When Beverly objected to the direction in which they were headed, Steve told her they were going to pick up something at his house.

"I remember staring at the emblem on the hood of their Cadillac," Beverly said, more emotion now in her voice. "There's that emblem … I went into shock or dissociation, because I lost track of time. I came to when all of a sudden the car parked in a driveway." When Beverly made no effort to get out of the car, Steve took her arm and forcefully led her into the house, through the kitchen, and into a bedroom.

"Look," Beverly pleaded with him, "no one knows I'm here. If you let me go, I'll call a taxi. I won't tell anyone. There won't be any problems. *Just please, please let me go!*"

"No."

"If you harm me, my family will see that you're punished."

"That doesn't scare me. You're never gonna see your family again."

Beverly began to sob. Steve told her to undress. And Beverly refused.

"Then he took my clothes off," Beverly said, her voice trembling. "When he climbed on top of me, just like in the car I lost … I didn't remember anything until I was lying there looking up at the ceiling. I realized he was lying next to me. I didn't know how much time had passed. I thought, This could be my only chance. How many people are here? Can I get out? I slowly scooched myself off the bed, trying not to move it at all. I put on my pants and shirt and held my shoes in my hand. As I walked by his side of the bed, I leaned over and kissed his cheek. When I left the house, I was very careful to close the door quietly."

"Beverly," I jumped in, "what prompted you to kiss him?"

"I don't know. It shocked me! I had a hard time telling anybody that. How could anyone accept that? How do you explain that?"

Her heart pounding, Beverly ran down the street. Afraid that John or Steve might follow, she stayed close to the homes and away from the streetlights that would make her visible. She knocked on the door of the first home with a light on. "I've been raped!" she cried to the startled man who came to—but did not open—the door. "You'll have to go somewhere else for help," he told her.

Beverly ran to the next house with a light on, and here she was taken in. She called her parents and told them what had happened.

"A strange thing," Beverly recalled. "My sister was home with my parents when the rape happened. Earlier that night she awoke very upset and crying, having had a vivid dream of herself being raped. My mother got up to comfort her. Not long after my mother returned to bed, her phone rang. It was me calling to say I had just been raped."

Beverly's parents called the police, who took her back to the crime scene. There, she identified Steve, who was still asleep, and John. Both were arrested. Beverly was taken to the emergency room at the hospital, where she received an injection of penicillin. "I've been allergic to penicillin ever since," she said. "When you've had trauma, your body will react adversely to anything associated with it.

"Then I went to my parents' home. I curled up in a ball on my bed, my hands up over my head, all curled up, scared. I remember my mom asking how I was doing. 'He's stolen me,' I said. 'There's nothing left of me. Beverly is gone.'"

The next day Beverly's parents called Amy's parents to tell them about the rape. "I learned later that Amy's parents looked down on me for the rape and said that probably I had brought it on. That felt horrible. How could someone think that? It amazed me."

At the trial, Steve claimed that Beverly had been his girlfriend and had willingly come to his home. To Beverly's astonishment the neighbor who had sent her away, a friend of Steve's, corroborated aspects of Steve's story. The defense attorney asked Beverly how much alcohol she had consumed that night and why she had walked into the parking lot with Steve, implying that the two of them had been in a relationship. Nevertheless, Steve was convicted and sentenced to twenty years. He was paroled after five years and died sixteen years after his parole.

Healing

I asked Beverly how she felt in the time following the rape.

"I felt completely dirty," she exclaimed. "I could not imagine ever, ever wanting to have sex again. I'd been completely violated. I felt like I was damaged goods. I could not see ever getting beyond that."

"How did you work through that?"

"It took a number of years. I used alcohol to numb my feelings. I convinced myself that I was okay, but I was self-medicating to make pain go away. I was in my thirties before I went to a therapist. It took from my mid-thirties until my early forties before I started to really heal. I went into Alcoholics Anonymous and got sober. That's when I finally starting making some headway.

"I was in a marriage I wasn't happy in," she continued. "Our sex life had problems. I didn't know if I would ever be able to be a good partner to anyone. I felt sorry for my husband because I couldn't show up in a relationship the way he deserved and needed.

"When I finally got into AA, I started to open up and express myself. I had stuffed everything. I thought that if I tried to work on the rape and my emotions, I was giving power to the rapist and saying that he was still having an affect on my life. I didn't want to do that, but I was destroying myself by not expressing the pain and anger."

"Beverly, what did you do to release the pain and anger?"

"I started to see therapists. I went to a ten-day Healing Your Life workshop, where I did a lot of journaling. We recreated some events to let anger out. We used punching bags. I did heavy breathing.[9] I took a course that used rituals to release issues. I had a picture of him. I wrote a letter to him the last night of our class. I read the letter and then burned it along with his picture."

I asked Beverly what she had said in the letter.

"I told him he had cheated me and taken something precious, and that is having control over my own body." Beverly began to cry. "You just—you don't feel that you have control over anything. If I can't say when someone's going to touch or be intimate with me, then what do I have control over? I also said in the letter how I was going to let go of it. As much as I didn't want to acknowledge that this was having an affect on me, I wanted to get rid of it as if it were.

"I remember saying to someone, 'How do I know when I'm going to be healed? When will this stop?' It seemed like it wouldn't be possible."

A major breakthrough came when Beverly told her life story to her home group at an AA meeting. "It was the hardest thing I'd ever done. I cried, I shook, but I got it all out. After I did, it was amazing how much better I felt! I realized that speaking and writing about it, just letting it out—how much of a difference that made. After that, if I ever felt like crying I would let myself without having to figure out what it was connected to. I realized that I will know what I need to know if and when the time is right. I need not press for answers."

"Beverly, you mentioned problems with intimacy," I said. "How were you able to heal that?"

"I remember thinking, I don't care if I ever have sex again for

---

9 Breathwork can give one access to suppressed emotions. When brought to the light of conscious awareness, the painful emotions may be embraced with love and thus healed.

the rest of my life," she replied. "It wasn't until after I had been in AA and quit drinking that my body starting having sexual energies. I would actually wake up from sleep having an orgasm. There was all this sexuality that I had repressed all those years. It wasn't my decision anymore; my body was telling me, yes. With tantra and a sexual healer, I worked through the issues. I was concerned about being intimate and sober at the same time; I didn't know how I would show up. It was scary. It took a while to get to a place where it wasn't all about me, where I knew that sexuality can be a healthy, spiritual coming together.

"One of the things I'm most proud of," she added, "is that I don't carry hatred for that man."

"How *do* you feel about him?"

"I pray for him. And I don't hide anymore from my story. I just live a healthy, engaged, honest life."

"Beverly, what would you like to say to someone who is healing from a rape?"

"Just don't give up," she said passionately. "You can get to a better, whole, healthy place. I am more in control of my life, in closer relationship with myself, and more whole than I ever was before the rape. I chose this path on some level, and it got me where I am. I'm grateful for feeling so connected with myself and Spirit."

Pamela's Impressions of Beverly

After talking with Beverly, I was still left with only one possible indication of a pre-birth plan between her and the rapist: the kiss. Unsure what to make of it, and struggling intensely with the idea that any soul would knowingly and willingly agree to participate in any way in a rape, I was eager to pose questions to Pamela and Jeshua. Had Beverly and Steve in fact known each other before they incarnated? Had either or both of them been aware of the potential for the rape to occur, and if so, why had they created such a plan?

Prior to the session, Beverly told Pamela that she prays for Steve's soul, and she asked Pamela how any karmic connection remaining between them might be healed.

"I will start by connecting to your aura, Beverly, and describing what I see and feel," Pamela began. Again, I reminded myself that Pamela was using the word *feel* in reference to her gift of clairsentience, her ability to enter Beverly's energy field and sense firsthand, experientially, what is there. "As I look at the energy surrounding you, I feel openness in your heart, an openness to learn and to understand life and what you have gone through. I feel a connection inside you, with Spirit, with God, meaning that you are open to a higher guidance in your life. I also view that you have gone through a lot of heavy emotions. Your aura feels fragile, vulnerable. It feels open in a very positive way to receive guidance, but also open in the sense of unprotected, open to an insecurity inside you, whether you feel things right, whether you are doing well.

"I feel that you should be more proud of yourself, all the things you have accomplished and gone through, not losing your faith in the process. I feel you may have more self-trust. At the same time, I can feel that it has been very difficult for you to have that reliance on yourself because of things that happened to you in the past, not just the rape but also things in your childhood.

"When I go to the energy of your childhood, I feel there has been a kind of aggression toward you. I strongly feel that it is your soul purpose this lifetime to handle aggression, to put boundaries around yourself and not let the aggression take all of you or enter deeply into your soul and body. This lifetime is about standing up for yourself. It is about self-esteem and not being drawn into other people's energies, people who do not feel right to you.

"In your first and second chakras, the energy centers at the base of your spine and in your belly, there are still unresolved emotions, especially anger. I feel there is a tendency within your personality to be very nice and sweet in adapting yourself to others, but in those lower two energy centers there is anger about your needs being denied and violated. If possible, it is desirable to go back to the experience of being raped and enter the body at that time. I understand this is a difficult thing to do, but the hurt that was inflicted on you, both physical and emotional, was perceived by your body and still needs to be addressed at all levels for you to become completely free of it."

Though Beverly had come far in her healing, Pamela's statement did not surprise me. When we cannot or do not express emotion—and certainly Beverly had not been able to express anger as the rape occurred—that energy is literally pushed into the cells of the body. There it sits, potentially causing illness and always awaiting release. That Beverly had dissociated during the rape did not matter; her subconscious mind as well as the elemental consciousness of her body were well aware of the assault. Beverly later released some of her anger—the portion in her conscious awareness, in her healing work—but apparently there was more.

Pamela continued. "More generally, this lifetime is about consciously using anger and feeling the healing power of it. Anger, if addressed openly and accepted, can make you more aware of your true boundaries and help you become more centered and grounded. If you go back to the experience of the rape and imagine that you are not outside your body but inside it, you can find out what you really felt in that moment. You can experience the humiliation, the despair, the powerlessness, and also the hatred and the anger against this man who violently crossed your boundaries. It's important to feel these emotions. It may seem too destructive to go back to the experience and relive all this negativity, but by doing so you are releasing it from your energy, from your body, and you will feel liberated because of that."

The process Pamela described is profound in its ability to bring healing. It is important that the reliving of the rape must be done gradually and under the skill of a trained counselor; otherwise, there is a risk of being retraumatized. Loving support from family and friends assists the process immeasurably.

"During the rape," Pamela told Beverly, "you couldn't deal with these emotions. In fact, the emotions you had were so strong that they reached your sister. She experienced some of the anguish you were not able to feel. Your emotions were 'in the air,' energetically floating around, not owned by you. Your sister, who was connected to you at an emotional level, tuned into this. She helped you to ground and integrate the emotions, not literally in your body, but she took away some of that burden by physically experiencing it in her body. You are not indebted to her; this is something she wanted to do for you, though perhaps not consciously. Your response at that time, the dissociation, was all right. It's important to accept what happened and to look at yourself with compassion.

"Go back in your mind to the experience of the rape. Imagine that as you are undergoing this act, you are there as an angel standing by your side. You can now, as the angel that you are, see yourself as a child screaming or crying. Ask the child, 'What are you feeling?' By entering a dialogue with your inner child at that time—the inner child represents the pure, spontaneous emotions—you can help her come to terms with the experience and integrate all the emotions that were part of it."

Again I was hearing about the importance of emotional release. We release emotions by expressing them, and to express them we must feel them. Healing requires feeling.

"I can see," Pamela told Beverly, "that at the emotional level, the level of the inner child, what happened in that moment of the rape is that you actually had very ambivalent feelings toward the rapist. The human part of you was overwhelmed by the experience and had much fear, but there was also a part of you that somehow felt connected to this man. This was inexplicable at that time. This is, in fact, a part of you that goes back to a past lifetime in which you knew the rapist. This accounts for the fact that you gave him a kiss before you left.

"I will now go to this past life energy that I sense between the two of you. I feel and I see that at one time you were the mother of this man. He was separated from you at an early age, about eight or nine, and was terribly upset because of this. He never forgave you.

"I will review this past life from the start to clarify why this happened. I see you in this past life as a baby. You are held by a mother who is very friendly and who loves you. She is a bit of a dreamer. She likes to fantasize and is not fully present, but she is kind and loving. Your father is a religious man with strict morals, very conscientious.

"At some point your mother dies. You are still young, about four. The relationship with your father is not warm; emotionally, you experience abandonment and are lonely without your mother. You are angry; you feel that everything is taken away from you when your mother dies. But, you also sense your father's grief, and you feel sorry about that. You almost feel it's your fault. Psychologically, you tend to feel guilty for other people's grief, even if it's not your fault at all.

"You try to help him alleviate his grief about your mother and even try to fulfill the role of your mother for him. His reaction is mixed. On the one hand, your father is a moralistic man who doesn't know how to deal with emotions. Your energy is so warm, loving, and compassionate that he doesn't know what to do with it. He seems unable to receive it. On the other hand, he is drawn to you in a way that is not pure. There is a sexual attraction toward you. He seeks comfort in your presence, almost like you are the woman he lost. This is very confusing for you. At some point he touches you in an inappropriate way and asks you to lie in bed with him. He's holding you and seeking comfort, but it's not just as a father. He is very mixed up about sexuality in general. He looks down on it but cannot fully repress it. It's difficult for you to feel your boundaries or get angry with him. You feel guilty, like 'Shouldn't I give him more?' It's twisted in your mind.

"When you are a grown woman of about eighteen," Pamela continued, "he tells you to marry a man. You do not love this man, but you consent because you dare not stand up to your father. You still think he is wise, that he knows things. You had been fully dependent on him as a child, so you trust him.

"You do not feel at ease with the man you marry. This man is a friend of your father. He is quite possessive and jealous. You are afraid of him. Then you get pregnant and carry his baby. This baby is the soul of Steve, and when he is born and you are holding him in your arms, you feel truly joyful.

"It is one of the most beautiful moments in your life. You are in awe! The baby in your arms is splendid, and you feel that for the first time you have someone for yourself, someone to love, someone with whom things will not be so difficult. You look forward to caring for him and being his mother. But, things turn out differently. Your husband gets very jealous of his own son for taking all your attention. He notices that you are happy in a very authentic way with this boy, and he gets angry because of that. He even becomes physically violent, hitting you, and very distrustful.

"The boy, who I will call Steve, hates his father. He cannot get along with him at all. He feels protective toward you. He also feels dependent on you, because you are the only ray of light in his life. He wants to be with you all the time. He is possessive in the way of a child.

"When Steve is nine or perhaps ten, your husband forces you to separate from your son. Steve is sent away to school to be educated in a very strict, disciplinary way. Your husband tells you this is good for the boy, because 'you have an unhealthy relationship with him. You are too close.' He is still jealous and suspicious, quite sick psychologically. But, you again feel unable to stand up to him, because you are afraid he will hit you or harm your son. You decide to respect his decision, but it's excruciating. You do not want to part from your son, and he doesn't want to part from you.

"You take Steve away to that school. It doesn't look very hospitable. You do not tell him clearly that you are about to leave him, that he will be separated from you permanently. You are afraid to tell him, because he has a temper, too. He has this possessive side that becomes very angry if you do not meet his demands. When you are separated by the people who are leading that school, it breaks your heart. Steve actually has to be separated from you with force. He is screaming at you, very angry that you are letting him go, that you have not been able to go against the will of your husband.

"You feel like you betrayed him. You feel guilty, and you are torn inside between your loyalty to your husband and your loyalty to your child. In that very moment of separation, Steve feels so betrayed and abandoned that a deep anger arises within him toward you. The anger he felt at that time sets in motion a karmic energy, a need on his part to take revenge on you, but also to come close to you again.

"After you left him, there were mixed feelings inside him of both love and hatred toward you. These emotions were never resolved in that lifetime. For your part, you felt guilty for the rest of your life. You felt much self-hatred."

Here we had it: Unresolved emotions between two souls, particularly a lack of forgiveness, create karmic ties that must be resolved, if not in one lifetime, then another. It is said that forgiveness is the untying of the ties that bind. Those ties had not been undone in Beverly's past life with Steve and had therefore been carried forward into the current lifetime for healing.

"The lesson to be learned from this experience," Pamela explained, "is that you need to stand up for yourself and your feminine energy." Here, Pamela was referring not to the rape, a situation in which Beverly had been powerless, but rather to life in general. "The rape has brought you to the center of your mission this lifetime: to learn to cope with the emotions you have; to truly honor and stand up for yourself, being both loving and very firm in protecting yourself; to know the balance between giving and receiving.

"At this point the most important step you can take toward healing yourself even more is to address the unresolved anger still inside you because of the rape, but also because of other events in your life in which you had to deal with male aggression in other forms. Become aware of the anger. That is sometimes difficult.

It may be helpful to let the body express anger, for instance, by hitting a pillow very hard or stamping your feet on the floor. In that way the body can help to awaken the anger.

"Anger can be a healing force. It's not a bad thing. It is when we repress our anger and feel unworthy because of it that we get twisted and depressed inside. But, anger in its original form just states, 'No, I don't want this.' That's a very genuine response. I feel you have gotten used to repressing this response.

"It is so important to go back to the original feeling and let it just be. Then it's like a huge wave in the ocean: after it reaches its highest point, it flows onto the beach and becomes quiet and peaceful. Emotions have their own dynamics. If you let them free, they will bring peace and liberation. They have a natural tendency to balance themselves.

"You told me that you pray for Steve's soul and that whatever karmic connection you had be healed in this lifetime. You asked whether this has happened, and if not, what you can do toward that end.

"First and foremost, it's about resolving your own karma. Karma is not really shared by people. They can work out their own karma in a relationship with each other, but you have your karma, and he has his. You are each responsible for your own. Steve had a great sense of guilt and of even being damned because of what he did to you. Now that he has crossed over, he has come to understand that you were responsible for what happened to you, like he was responsible for what he did and what happened to him." Here, I understood Pamela to be referring to the level of the soul, not the level of the personality. "This knowledge has relieved him from his darkest self-hatred. He is getting help on the other side. He is learning and growing. But, I want to state clearly that whether or not he is learning from the past is his business. Whether he does or does not resolve his karma will not affect you.

"What will affect you," Pamela advised, "is how you deal with your own issue: forgiving yourself for having attracted this event into your life. It's empowering and very courageous to see that at some level you are responsible for the things you attract into your life. It's a major spiritual breakthrough to let go of the notion that you are solely a powerless victim and know instead that you have power over your life, not only to attract things into your life but also to rise above them and to heal yourself.

"You have this awareness. It is very important now to look at yourself with compassion and to allow the part of you that still is traumatized by the rape to fully express itself. Self-expression brings balance. In allowing yourself to feel the repressed emotions, you are saying to your inner child, 'I love you so much. You are so worthy of being loved that I allow you to fully express yourself, for then you can come to a point of again feeling the joy and love you truly are.' The joy of living, the creativity, the love and innocence of the inner child—these can be set free. The original nature of the child can be unveiled if you allow the negative emotions to simply be there and express themselves.

"If you pray for the rapist's soul, look deeply within yourself to see whether there is some guilt. Someone who is raped can feel guilty in that you have also done something to the rapist. You may think, 'Now he is going to hell because of me.' This is not right; you do not have to pray for his soul for that reason. But, if you come to that point of feeling deep compassion for yourself and releasing all the emotions that go with the rape, then you may come to a stage at which you say, 'I forgive him. I can see how this would arise from his past, how who he was led to this action.' By forgiving the rapist in that way, you are truly releasing yourself. That's a beautiful thing to do.

"Forgiving happens naturally when you are fully in love with and forgiving of yourself and able to embrace every part of you that has been hurt and traumatized. At that point the forgiveness will be there, simply as something you realize: 'I have forgiven him.'

"You do not have to pray for his soul out of guilt. Pray for yourself that you may be healed in this lifetime. That will set him free, for when his soul feels that you are free of the pain caused by the rape, that will ease his suffering. It is first and foremost by helping and healing yourself that you also help him to grow and to evolve.

"With regard to the past-life karma I described, this has been *balanced* now. You are even, if you want to speak in those terms. But, to truly *release* karma is both to see what responsibility you yourself had for this event and then to work out your own hurt emotions." I took Pamela's use of the word *responsibility* as a reference to energy. In other words, what sort of energy had been present within Beverly, below the level of her conscious awareness, that had made it possible for the rape to come into her experience? "That's what resolving karma is really about," added Pamela. "You are doing this, Beverly. If you pursue this path of self-healing, becoming stronger and having more self-esteem and a sense of self-worth, then there will be no need whatsoever for you to meet Steve again under such painful circumstances. You will not attract each other anymore."

Speaking with Jeshua

Pamela's clairsentience (which allowed her to feel Beverly's both conscious and subconscious emotions as well as her emotions in a past life) and clairvoyance (which allowed her to see Beverly's past life) had permitted a clear explanation of the connection between Beverly and Steve. To expand our understanding, Beverly and I asked Jeshua to address the question of why a soul would plan before birth to experience such a painful challenge. Beverly allowed me to pose the majority of the questions on behalf of both of us.

"We wish to tell you that we honor the path you have chosen," Jeshua told Beverly. "You have been courageous and willing to face up to your own darkness at pivotal points in your life. Your soul is awakening and is deeply thankful to you, Beverly, the aspect of itself that has experienced darkness and difficulties in her life and is learning how to rise above them and embrace her true, lovely Self. We recommend to you that you take time every day to honor yourself, to give yourself a blessing by doing something kind and nurturing for yourself. It's important to recognize every day how far you've come and how beautiful and worthy you are right now."

"Jeshua," I said, "please tell us about the past-life connection between Beverly and the rapist."

"Beverly was the rapist's mother in a past life," Jeshua replied, verifying what Pamela had seen. "As his mother she inflicted pain on him by separating from him at an early age. He felt deeply hurt, offended, and enraged. At some level she agreed that he was right, that she had abandoned him and deserved to be punished. These emotions of unworthiness on her part and anger on his part were not resolved during that lifetime. In this current lifetime they met again, the son now appearing as a violent man raping Beverly. He still wanted her recognition, her love, but could ask for it only in an aggressive way."

"Why did Beverly kiss the rapist goodbye before she left the room?"

"There were mother feelings in her soul when she did this. The past life dynamic was playing out during the rape. At some level she felt sorry for what she did to him in that past life. The kiss was a gesture of forgiveness toward him that came from the soul level. On the level of the Earth personality, she would still have to deal with the powerful emotions of fear, anger, and sadness the rape caused."

"What about the people who judge Beverly for kissing him?"

"It is wise to look beyond outer appearances and be open to the possibility that the relationship between victim and offender is very complex psychologically. Also, Beverly did not want to kiss the rapist, as in a conscious decision. It just happened. She was in a dream state at that moment and was reliving soul memories that caused her to reach out. Judging this kind of thing is a way of reducing the complexity and making the victim feel shameful and guilty, whereas it is precisely the unexpected and so-called forbidden emotions that can throw another light on the situation and enable one to understand the feelings of the victim on a deeper level."

"Did Beverly plan this experience before she was born," I asked, "and if so, why?"

"The soul of Beverly knew it was necessary to come to terms with the issue of self-denial, which played a major role in several lifetimes. In a previous lifetime [the one Pamela described], Beverly had a problem standing up against male aggression and protecting her boundaries as a woman. Beverly chose to plan the potential of rape into her life path because she wanted to come to terms with this issue. By being raped she was forced to deal with very deep emotions of feeling unworthy, powerless, and unable to stand up for herself. This would give her soul the opportunity to rise above these emotions and old negative beliefs about herself. Also, her soul felt indebted to the rapist personally because she had left him as her son in that same previous life."

"Why did the rapist plan this?"

"The soul of the rapist still experienced anger, hurt, and indignation with regard to Beverly for having abandoned him in a previous life. The more ignorant part of his soul followed the urge to avenge himself. The higher part of his soul allowed the lower part to have his way because it knew that through this course of action, potentially the soul could finally realize that one cannot get anyone else's love through violence. Love has to be offered freely or else it is simply obedience and fear. The rapist's soul had to learn this, and he has partly learned this, although he still has to face a lot of inner fear and turmoil.

"Life plans often play out over several lifetimes," Jeshua continued. "A soul can work on a certain issue for many lives, each lifetime making some progress. Planning a life challenge that forcefully brings the particular issue to the fore enables the soul to make new and better choices.

"Both an evolved and a less evolved soul may plan rape into their lifetimes. They may recognize it as something that resonates with certain deeply ingrained beliefs about their own unworthiness.

Deep down, every soul wants to face its inner darkness in order to rise above it. Like attracts like. The soul is drawn to bring into the light what is dark by attracting outer circumstances that reflect the inner darkness.

"Generally, more evolved souls will have a better chance of facing the spiritual challenge inherent in rape. It will be easier for them to face their emotions and rise above them because there's a stronger connection to Spirit. In Earth life these people may seem incredibly resilient and positive, and they are an inspiring example to others. The less evolved soul may more easily remain stuck in the trauma and heavy emotions caused by rape and need more time, even other lifetimes, to grow and to evolve. But, in both cases the soul chooses this experience because it can grow only by attracting in the outer world what it wants to change on the inside."

"I do not believe in evil," I told Jeshua. "Instead, I believe that some people are in enormous pain and that in their pain they do things we call evil."

"You are right," said Jeshua. "There is no pure or absolute evil. Evil arises from pain *not recognized*. It is not the pain itself that gives rise to evil; rather, it is the denying and repression of the pain that eventually creates a desire to inflict pain on others. If pain is consciously addressed, accepted, and allowed to be felt at all levels, it will dissipate and even make one a more loving and wise person. If, however, pain is repressed, the personality believes that part of it is bad and not welcome. The initial pure emotions of fear, grief, or anger become perverted. By being judged and repressed, they turn into negative beliefs such as 'I am a coward' (for being fearful), 'I am incapable of overcoming grief,' 'I am far too sensible and not able to cope with life,' or 'I should be nice and obedient because anger is wrong.'

"Whenever the initial emotions are repressed and turned into judgments of unworthiness on the part of the carriers of those emotions, the people involved become tense, depressed, and even violent. They are in constant struggle with themselves. When the struggle becomes unbearable, the aggression turned against one-self may be turned outward toward others. Then it becomes evil, as you call it, but there always is much aggression toward oneself first. Underlying the aggression is unaddressed pain. Addressing this pain is the key to dealing with evil at the most basic level."

"Jeshua," I wondered, "what was the likelihood prior to Beverly's birth that this rape would occur?"

"Very likely, say 80 percent. The percentage is not absolute. It was 80 percent given the state of Beverly's soul at the start of this lifetime and the way humans generally develop during Earth lives. Humans do not generally wake up easily. Often they need a crisis to change on the inner level. There is great fear on Earth pervading the minds of humans and making them resistant to change. Humans tend to cling to old ways of avoiding pain, even if those ways themselves are painful.

"Beverly had a pattern of self-denial in her psyche, a ten-dency to give too much to others, neglecting her own needs and ultimately the sanctity of her own Self. This painful pattern of self-denial eventually resulted in attracting the rape into her life. On some level she allowed it to happen. On this level a negative belief about her own unworthiness allowed the rapist to enter her physical reality.

"Now, what happens as a result of this ultimate act of violence is that Beverly stands at a crossroad: She can either lose herself in the experience of victimhood and pain, or she can decide to stand up and see this pain as the result of a negative pattern inside her that now, because of the rape, stands out clearly, ready to be addressed and released by her conscious decision. The event of the rape is a spiritual catalyst, inviting her to address the issue of unworthiness.

"At a deep level she knew this [at the time of the rape]. Souls know that such events bring them to a pivotal crossroad. They know they have attracted these events into their lives. They know these events offer them possibilities for deep, inner change. To choose not to see oneself as a victim but to embrace the challenge and grow because of it is the soul's greatest victory. Whenever you see humans choosing this path, you see their greatness, their divinity, clearly shining through."

"Jeshua, was there anything Beverly could have done to avoid the rape? More generally, if someone has planned a painful experience, can that person find a way after birth to learn the lessons in a less painful manner?"

"There is always a possibility of awakening in life earlier than expected," Jeshua answered, "thereby canceling certain events that were likely to happen. Theoretically, Beverly could have awakened earlier, thereby making the rape unnecessary. I say this to make people understand that they are always free to change their lives. I am not saying this as a judgment of Beverly's choices. Practically speaking, given the way she started this life carrying the memories of past lives as she did, avoiding the rape was hardly a possibility.

"There is no judgment on our side about whether the soul does or does not participate in a self-created challenge. We respect and celebrate both when the soul manages to avoid the challenge through self-discovery and when the soul goes through it and learns through suffering. Both take great courage and a clear and determined spirit.

"The aim of becoming more conscious is to become aware of one's divinity and creative power and therefore to grow through joy instead of through suffering. The nature of the soul is joyful; pain is not necessary. When you are trapped in dualism, you can use suffering to wake up, but that doesn't mean the suffering is intrinsically necessary.

"If you seek to enlighten yourself by reflecting on your life, psyche, and relationships with others, if you face your own emotional pain and dare to look your dark parts straight in the eye, that will certainly have an impact on the kinds of circumstances and events you attract into your life," he continued. "In this way you may avoid getting sick, being fired, or having an accident. You have a conscious grip on your life, even if you do not know what events you are sidestepping with your conscious intention to grow. There are certain wake-up calls planned into your life, but a fair number of them are there as possibilities only. If you do not need them anymore, they will vanish from the timeline you are on. Life plans are flexible. They may change because of your inner growth."

"Jeshua," I pointed out, "some people may feel offended, angry, or even appalled by this discussion because they may feel it denigrates the one who was raped or absolves the rapist of responsibility for his actions."

"Yes, it is quite a stretch to say that people are at some level responsible for the crimes committed against them. One should always be very careful in stating this. My advice would be for the victim herself to find out whether or not this perspective is healing for her. No one should ever tell a raped woman that she herself is at some level responsible for the rape, especially since raped women are already liable to feel guilty and ashamed. These women should feel free to express in a safe way all their anger and rage against the offender. At some point, however, they themselves may feel the urge to claim their responsibility, initially not so much for the event itself but for the way they deal with it. They realize that it is empowering to take back their responsibility. If they feel open to a spiritual perspective, they may even embrace the notion that the rape was an event that, from the soul level, they drew into their lives. It is only when this perspective is liberating to them that it has true spiritual value.

"On a practical and legal level," Jeshua added, "the rapist should be held entirely responsible for his acts. The legal system should reflect the spiritual truth: that all women are to be respected in their sexual identity, and that violence is wrong. The legal system should not reflect the dark and ignorant parts inside either the offender or the victim; rather, it should be a beacon of light reflecting to them the counterparts of these blind or dark spots. By holding the rapist accountable, the legal system radiates a positive statement about how people should treat each other in an enlightened society."

"Jeshua, if a rape is planned before birth, does that mean the rapist accrues no karma?"

"The rape always occurs from a part of the rapist's soul that is blind to the truth, a part that is in fear and ignorance. This act will create karma whether it is planned or not."

"If a rape is not planned before birth, what happens to the rapist in his life review after his death?"

"This depends on how the rapist has evolved after the rape. Has he taken responsibility? Has he opened up to what the person he raped went through? Has he faced his own darkest emotions?"

"Are you saying that if the rapist is truly sorry for what he did, there is less karma to be balanced in another lifetime?"

"Yes," Jeshua confirmed. "Taking responsibility for one's own darkness always connects one to Spirit more strongly. Then room for healing and forgiveness arises. Even so, the rapist may still attract a lifetime in which he will be the victim of sexual violence. The soul may feel the need to go through the emotions of the one who was raped to be able to truly let go of its own mistakes.

"If, however, the soul of the rapist has taken responsibility and has become more evolved after the rape and in the afterlife, it will more easily rise above the trauma of rape in the life to come than if it had not taken responsibility and felt genuine remorse. So, the karma may create the same consequences—life challenges on the physical level—but they will be lived through more easily, with more grace."

"Jeshua, the act of rape is such a terrible violation of a human being. Many people may find it hard to believe that a loving God would allow such a thing to happen."

"Spirit allows the soul to experience life without limitation. To exclude certain experiences, even if they are acts of darkness, would go against the nature of Spirit, which is boundless creativity. Spirit does not, however, stand outside creation. Spirit is present in the one raped, suffering along with her. Spirit is not an outsider. You *are* Spirit having a human experience."

"Why did Beverly's soul not plan to learn in some less painful way?" I inquired, thinking of Jeshua's earlier statement that suffering isn't necessary.

"It felt unable to learn through another, more joyful way. Often the soul needs to see its own negative beliefs mirrored in outer events to finally realize they are false. Sometimes, by taking things to their extremes you finally realize that you are part of Spirit, unconditionally loved as such and therefore able to grow through joy rather than through suffering."

More about Healing

"The emotional pain from a rape is so deep and long lasting," I said. "How can one heal truly and completely from such an experience?"

"To be raped is one of the deepest injuries one can experience as a human," Jeshua observed. "On Earth this has happened to women on such a grand scale that one can speak of a collective female wound, which is in great need of healing in this day and age. Today humanity is on the verge of experiencing an awakening. Humanity is breaking free from a past that has been full of violence and massive suffering. Within the current transformation of consciousness, the healing of the female wound is of great importance. The female energy is needed to create the new awakening, for it is in connecting to the powers of intuition, feeling, and empathy that humanity will find balance again.

"How can this wound, the collective trauma of having been raped, humiliated, and looked down on, be healed by the women of today? How does one deal with the deep emotional injury of having been raped? The first thing that is necessary in dealing with any trauma is to relive the emotions involved in it consciously and with compassion. One cannot leave behind the trauma of being raped without facing the emotions it has caused within you. Almost always these emotions have been repressed by the woman involved because they were too overwhelming to face in the moment the rape happened.

"Many women experience that they go out of their bodies during rape and are only half-present, and they shut down in the lower chakras or energy centers of their bodies. The energy inside their genitals and bellies *freezes*, so to speak. This happens almost automatically as an attempt not to feel the pain. The result is that women lose touch with their emotions after a rape. It is often hard to feel the anger, pain, and sadness that are inside them because of the rape.

"At some point many women even start to accuse themselves of having caused the rape [at the level of the personality]. They feel guilty or ashamed. They have negative judgments about themselves. This is the result of not truly allowing the original emotions of fear, anger, and sadness. When these are repressed, they turn into negative self-judgments, and this may turn into depression, addiction, or self-destructive behavior of another kind.

"The key," said Jeshua, "is to go back to the experience and allow the pure emotions of fear, anger, and loneliness that were there during the rape to fully enter one's consciousness. Feel them without judgment. It may be helpful to have someone there to help you through this, someone who is comfortable letting you express your emotions freely and openly but in a peaceful way, not harming yourself or others. In this way you will integrate parts of you that have become shut down and repressed because of the rape. The anger, grief, and sadness have healing power when you let them flow through you freely. They will allow you to become empowered and create a level of self-love you did not know before.

"After you relive and integrate these emotions, and this may take years, it is possible to feel free again, free within your body and at ease with your emotions. The memory of the rape will still be there, but it will be surrounded with compassion toward yourself instead of self-loathing. It is possible to heal from the emotional scars that rape causes, and when you do, you become a shining beacon of light to others who have experienced it.

"If someone has risen above the trauma of rape, she will have built a strong sense of self-worth and dignity as a woman. And she will not only heal herself but also help other women heal, because she is touching and changing collective consciousness by her inner light.

"At this time much depends upon the healing of the female wound, for it is only through the rebirth and empowerment of the feminine energy that humanity will be able to move forward to a more loving and respectful way of living, with one another and with planet Earth herself."

"Jeshua," I said, "you spoke of the healing power of experiencing the emotions repressed at the time of the rape. If these emotions are largely or even completely subconscious, how would she know she needs to do such healing?"

"One knows because one does not feel complete and whole," Jeshua answered. "There is a lack of joy and creativity in the personality when important emotions have been repressed, even if it was a long time ago. There is a sense of not being fully present in one's own life, of not being able to feel and express emotions in a deep and sincere way.

"Also, in a person with repressed emotions there is always fear of the emotions, and therefore there is the need to distract oneself continually, possibly through activities and relationships, but also through addictions or other kinds of self-destructive behavior. One can recognize the need for healing when the person is always restless, finds it difficult to relax, or is being destructive toward the self in a seemingly irrational way."

"Jeshua, though we as a society tend to focus on women in regard to rape, men are raped, too."

"Rape of men involves the same pain and emotional trauma. The way of healing is generally the same for them. In addition, however, men have to deal with the disbelief and ridicule of society because they are often not taken seriously. To heal,

I would encourage these men to speak with women who have experienced rape. Finding the common thread, the shared pain, will help them find peace with the female energy again. They need that peace to fully enter their emotions, which are part of their feminine, feeling side."

Beverly Questions Jeshua

"Everything you mentioned about my struggles and what I need to work on in this lifetime—difficulty handling aggression, setting healthy boundaries—are things I clearly recognize," Beverly told Jeshua. "What is the best approach for me in dealing with these issues?"

"Use your male energy, the part of you that is grounded, self-aware, and centered," he advised. "Your problems with boundaries originate from a lack of trust in your own male energy. You have felt resistance toward the male energy for many lifetimes because you have associated it with aggression and oppression. You retreated into the female energy, but it is not possible to live in a balanced way without using the male energy. The male energy is about maintaining a healthy separation between 'I' and 'others.' Practice saying no whenever you feel like it. Dare to trust your impulses. Allow yourself to be angry if you feel this emotion inside. Greet the anger as a friend, a messenger. If you make friends with anger and trust the message within that anger, setting boundaries will become much easier. You repress anger because you fear its power; however, you can let in your power. It will save you, not destroy you. Embracing the dark emotions makes one whole and radiant. The power that surfaces in this conscious embrace is not bad power but truly the magnificence of your natural Being."

"Some of my closest relationships have been with men—my father, brother, and nephews," observed Beverly. "So, relationships with males have been positive and powerful as well as negative and violent."

"You have attracted both positive and negative models of male energy in your life," Jeshua noted. "The positive experiences are the result of your soul's desire to make peace with the male energy, outside and inside. In a very ancient past of yours, you misused your female energy in the sense of exerting power over men. In these lifetimes you were offender rather than victim. At some point you did not want this anymore. You gave up your power and went to the opposite—being powerless and abused for several lifetimes. As a soul you were trying to find balance between a domineering, manipulative female energy and a too-soft, submissive femininity. The answer lies in embracing a balanced male energy. This will also make the female energy balanced. The fact that you attracted both negative and positive relationships with men shows that you have both resolved old karma and received the fruits of that, and that you still have to work out remaining issues."

Parallel Dimensions

Our discussion of healing now complete, I asked Jeshua about an important related topic: parallel dimensions. "Jeshua," I wondered, "did Beverly's decision in the past life to send her son away to school create a parallel dimension in which there is a Beverly who kept the son at home?"

"Yes, it did. In that alternative timeline, she separated from the husband. This was a challenging but very liberating parallel life."

"Can you explain in general what parallel dimensions are, how and why they are created, and how they serve the soul?"

"Imagine the Beverly-personality to be like a tree," Jeshua replied. "The trunk represents the basic character traits of the personality, the parameters it has to work with. The trunk is rooted into the soul. The branches represent different life paths for the personality. The splitting into different branches, different life paths, occurs when the personality is at a crossroad, an important moment of choice. When the personality is torn inside about which path to choose, the soul enables it to pursue both paths, to experience what the different paths are like and to learn from them.

"This splitting of the soul energy does not happen when you make little choices in everyday life; it concerns major choices that deeply affect all of your life. The parallel reality takes place in a different dimension, just as real and physical as this one. Yet, all these parallel realities are part of the same personality, connected to the same trunk."

"Is there a dimension in which Beverly was not raped?"

"Yes, there is a branch on the tree that represents a timeline in which Beverly was not raped. At the time of her birth, this branch was only a twig, so to speak. It had not so much life power in it, but it was there. Now, although this path was not chosen by the Beverly you know, she can activate the energy of that twig—the other Beverly—by healing her emotions around the rape. When she comes to the point where she recognizes that she does not or did not necessarily need the experience of rape to grow, she changes the energy flow through the tree. She will give energy to and receive energy from the other Beverly who did not choose rape. She will even *become* her in a sense, and therefore that tiny twig will now turn into a sturdy branch.

"In this way one can interact with parallel realities through inner work and growth. When Beverly heals from this lifetime's trauma of rape, she will affect all other timelines in a positive way, and her chosen life path (with the rape) will become more of a twig, containing less life energy. It will fade out eventually, not meaning that the physical event will be uncreated, but rather that its energetic weight will diminish because Beverly will have removed the trauma around it. In this process Beverly herself will not fade out, but she will merge more deeply with her soul, the roots of the tree."

"Jeshua," I wondered, "how many 'Beverlys' are there? And how do our other selves in parallel dimensions affect us?"

"At this time there are about four parallel personalities that are relevant to Beverly here and now. The number is not fixed.

Reverting to our tree metaphor, parallel realities are connected to one another through the trunk. They are constantly interacting. Through the interaction new realities are born, and others fade away in a constant process of growth and learning.

"This is difficult to imagine from your point of view, because you have a concept of time in which past, present, and future proceed in a straight line. The concept of parallel realities can be understood only if one embraces a different concept of time in which past, present, and future realities exist simultaneously in one great Now, like a vibrating web of energies, always flowing and interacting. The personality has the power to endow a certain thread in the web with life energy and to remove it from others. This is the personality's freedom.

"Do you create parallel timelines out of nothing when you come to an important crossroad, or is the timeline already there waiting to be activated? In a sense both are true. The tree, a potential of many different life paths, is already there. But, which timelines are actually activated, which branches will be endowed with life energy depends on the free choice of the personality.

"Your other selves in parallel dimensions interact with you in several ways," Jeshua explained. "First, through dreams, including daydreaming. You may connect to a parallel self without knowing it consciously, experiencing some of its dilemmas, even helping it to solve them or being inspired by its talents and accomplishments. Second, the death of a parallel personality may give one a sense of liberation or of mourning, or an increase of life energy. Third, the rise of a parallel personality to a higher level of consciousness can help you heal and grow. It is also the other way around: you help a parallel self through your efforts to face your inner darkness and increase self-love. Fourth, it is possible to connect consciously to a parallel self through hypnosis or relevant relaxation techniques and send them support, or receive advice and support from them."

Beverly's Session with Barbara and Aaron

Pamela and Jeshua had explained in great detail Beverly's pre-birth connection to the rapist, why the rape had been part of her life blueprint, and how she could continue to heal her emotional wounds. To learn more about both Beverly's plan and healing from trauma, Beverly and I spoke with Aaron.

"Good day. My love and blessings to you. I am here at your service," Aaron greeted us warmly. It was joyful to be in his presence again. I began by asking Aaron to speak to Beverly's intentions before coming into body. We paused for a moment as he accessed Beverly's Akashic Record.

"Part of this situation is the pre-birth intention to learn how to find compassion for one who was abusive," Aaron informed us. "Are you able to find, if not forgiveness, at least compassion for the rapist? Can there be compassion, understanding that the rapist is also a victim of circumstance?

"Beverly, you in no way invited the rape, but you in some sense co-created it simply by bringing yourself into a time and place where it could happen. This was the playing out of the karma. People will ask, 'Why was I in this place rather than that place, at this time rather than that time? Why me?' There is always some kind of agreement to be there.

"The rapist was working out his own very unwholesome karma. At some level there was an agreement that you would experience this kind of trauma to give you the catalyst to develop compassion and also to begin to understand that the rapist in this lifetime and many who do terrible deeds are also the products of their environment, culture, and karma. They are responsible, but one must still have compassion rather than hatred for them.

"Having been raped," Aaron continued, "it's easy to fall into the role of victim and act in subtle, subconscious ways that continue to invite various kinds of abusive behavior in one's life. In other words, this is a life-altering and personality-altering experience.

The important question for the person who has been raped is, 'Where do I go from here?'—going not only into the healing of the sense of violation, but also into growing in compassion and watching to be sure that one lives one's life in a way that says no compassionately to abuse to oneself and to others."

"I may begin working with rape victims in a volunteer program," Beverly said. "This may be a way of helping other people where I failed to help in past lives."

"Beverly, this is accurate, and I am glad you see this. There are always two parts to karma—resolution and balance. The resolution of karma comes with understanding, with compassion, with forgiveness. But, the karma must still be balanced. That volunteer work is a way of balancing the karma through reaching out to others. It will be a very wholesome act for you.

"I would add here, Beverly, that as we speak and I look in the Akashic Records, I note that you are an old soul. Now, here we have a distinction. An old soul's reasons for experiencing will be quite different from those of a new soul. A younger soul may be stimulated by violence, much in the way people watch violent movies or stop to see accidents by the roadside. The older soul, seeing an accident by the roadside, will usually drive on, saying a prayer for those who were injured in the accident. This is not bad; this is simply a matter of maturity. But, for an old soul, a major part of pre-birth intentions is to finish with some of the karma of the past, to be of service to others, to learn deeper love and compassion, and to release judgment of others and self. The experience of rape is one part of accomplishing the purification of karma.

"Given that you are an old soul, a major part of your learning here is not just compassion but taking that compassion into everyday life in the ways you planned pre-birth. The question for the old soul is always, 'What blocks the most loving action in the world, and how can I release that blockage?'"

"Aaron," I said, "let's talk about healing. Please speak to those in the process of healing from rape."

"I would remind these sisters and brothers: Don't let anyone, including your own inner voice, tell you, 'I *should* forgive.'" Aaron's comment reminded me that words like *should, need to,* and *have to* are admonishments of the ego. The soul, by contrast, motivates the personality through feelings of love and joy. "Rather, be present in as loving a way as possible with the pain you feel and without self-judgment for that pain. Then, reflect on the fact that throughout the world many beings experience the pain of abuse from others and that the abusers also experience terrible pain to have been driven to abuse. It is with this kind of reflection that compassion grows, and without compassion there cannot be that final step of forgiveness. Forgiveness is a process, not an event, and one moves into it gently and gradually."

"Aaron, just as women are raped, men are raped, too," I said. "Do you have words specifically for men who have had this experience?"

"Rob, as you know I have been in both male and female bodies, and like all humans I have sometimes experienced rape or sexual abuse. I have experienced it both as male and female. There is a subtle difference in the experience for a man, because there is a sense of humiliation. The woman will feel deeply violated, as will the man, but for the man that sense of being helpless at the power of the other man can create great feelings of shame. It's very important that a man who has experienced rape or any sexual abuse look at these feelings of shame, not with the idea 'I should not be ashamed,' but simply be present with shame until one sees the anger that is within the shame. Then hold space for all of that."

I asked Aaron to explain what "holding space" means and how one does so.

"When there is a strong emotion like fear or anger," Aaron replied, "it's very uncomfortable. One usually wants to get away from those emotions. Sometimes fear masks anger; sometimes anger masks fear. One will be more at the surface, more intense. If there is a lot of anger, one wants to lash out and find somebody to blame. Deep down one would be using this anger as a smoke screen, wanting to avoid the experience of fear and the helplessness that comes with fear. There is an almost existential experience of helplessness. No matter what one does in a lifetime, one cannot keep oneself safe. You're going to die. There will be pain; there will be suffering. This is the human experience. I am not stating that as a negative. It's simply a fact that people suffer enormously. Because they don't want to accept that fact, they keep seeking some way out.

"To hold space means simply to be there with a direct experience of pain, humiliation, fear, anger, confusion, whatever may be there, and to watch the stories that come up. For example, with anger comes the story of 'Who's to blame? How do we fix it?' When you see a story like that come up, you can notice how consciousness is giving rise to this story as a way of escaping the pain of the direct experience. What is the direct experience of anger without any stories? What is the direct experience of pain without any stories? Then these emotions begin to break up. We can't really say what anger is or what shame is. At a certain point, we have to stop thinking about it intellectually and just be there with a broken heart with sadness. When one is spacious with it in this way, creating a bigger container for the emotion, then one is no longer controlled by the emotion. One sees that the emotion exists under certain conditions but that it will pass away. Then there is not so much fear of experiencing that emotion. This is what I mean by 'hold space.'"

"Aaron," Beverly said, "I came to a place where I was not denying that there was pain I needed to feel in order to get to a healthier place. I knew I had to go through some processes in order to move beyond it, to have it no longer affect me in such a negative way."

"Sister, you are very wise," came his loving reply. "Yes, one needs to allow oneself to be intimate with one's pain. Then it ceases to be your pain, and it literally becomes the pain of all beings. So many humans all over the world have been raped and abused in various ways; one can no longer separate oneself. One stops asking 'Why me?' and instead begins to ask, 'Where does healing begin for our whole world?' It's a very different question, and it comes only through that willingness to stop denying pain and to allow oneself to be touched by it."

"Aaron, many people wonder how a loving God can allow things like rape to happen," I said.

"Rob, God gives us free will. If we have free will, then we create our own circumstances. God doesn't allow or prevent. God doesn't create rape; humans create rape. God does not create the response to rape, but God is there to support a compassionate response to any human violation. God *is* that compassionate response! That which I call God, which is the core of loving energy in the Universe, is always there to support us when we choose love. As more and more people choose to live their lives in loving ways and to respond to abusive acts in the world with a strong compassion that says no but without judgment and hatred, we move in the direction that will allow a much more peaceful world in which we co-create with that loving element we might call God."

"If a person commits rape," I inquired, "what kind of experience will he have when he returns to the nonphysical?"

"It depends, Rob, on whether there has been true remorse for the act or whether there is ongoing justification of it. For one who has experienced deep regret and then has done everything one could do to make amends, to create balance, and to help prevent such acts not only in oneself but also from others in the future, it's likely after the incarnation that the person will be asked to be responsible for what he has done. He will need to move into a new lifetime that gives him the opportunity fully to resolve and balance that karma, but he will still be greeted by loving guides. He will experience love.

"For the one who is not at all remorseful, who is filled with anger, and who blames others, that one will also be greeted with love but will be unable to accept that love. After the transition nobody judges you, but if you are not able to open your heart to the experience of love on Earth, how can you open it to the experience of love on a heavenly level? Such a being will find himself in a very dark place, a place where he perpetuates the story, 'It's not my fault. Now look what happened to me,' until finally he becomes clear that 'I am the one who is creating this prison of darkness for myself, and I have a choice.'

"I like the term *compassionate regret,*" Aaron continued. "Compassionate regret lets us see ourselves with compassion, see the unwholesome things we have done and take responsibility, then seek the path to resolution and balance but without an unhealthy sense of deep guilt, shame, and self-judgment.

"If you have experienced rape or any other abuse, my heart goes out to you. You certainly have suffered. Now, make the wholesome choice to put that suffering to use for the good of all beings. Grow the heart into greater and greater compassion until you understand how to enact that compassion in the world, healing yourself and the world. Cease to separate yourself. Let your own pain transform you, not getting involved in self-pity but just opening to the direct experience of the pain that the loving heart can transmute."

"I stopped running from it," Beverly told Aaron. "I used to deny that it had a big impact on me. As you say, just feel it, be released from it, and get to the other side."

"Sister, I am very glad you have been able to do this," Aaron said. "You certainly are healing. Pain is odd in the way it works. We think that we have finally made peace with it, then suddenly something comes up that shakes us, and briefly we feel lost in it again. If that happens, just hold space, loving yourself and all who suffer such pain. This may not happen, but if it does, tend it with love."

"I appreciate all that you have shared with us today," Beverly replied.

"Sister, I appreciate you, too. I wish you well. Rob, thank you again for this opportunity to be of service."

"Thank you for speaking with us today," I said.

Staci's Supplemental Reading for Beverly

To gain even further insight into why a rape had been planned, Beverly and I spoke with Staci and her spirit guide. Prior to the session I had requested that they access that portion of Beverly's Akashic Record that would specifically address her relationship with Steve.

"Upon reflection in that time in-between lives," Staci said to Beverly, "and upon discussing with your spirit guide and members of your soul group, you came to know that your [less-than-honorable] behaviors [in other lifetimes] occurred because you were looking for answers outside yourself rather than internally, where everything you wanted could have been found. You wanted to be forced to turn back to yourself. When you have been raped, that makes you work harder on emotional well-being. From the soul-level perspective, that's exactly what you wanted in this life."

"This makes total sense," Beverly agreed.

"The next lesson is that your parents held back giving you some nurturing that would have been essential for the development of your self-esteem. That was part of their soul-level agreement with you. You wanted to learn to nurture yourself in this lifetime so you would form your own sense of self-worth from yourself. In so doing you would come to know your own truth. What's true for you is not necessarily true for others; nonetheless, it's important and relevant, and it has merit and value. When you recognize that, you achieve a level of honesty with yourself that becomes self-confidence and enables you to be more richly and fully expressive of who you really are instead of holding back. When somebody rapes you, you want to pull a shell over yourself, go inside that shell, and never come out. But, that's where you do your nurturing. Until the rape there hadn't been enough nurturing in your life. Not of you and not for you. And not by yourself for yourself.

"I would think that it would be very difficult for you to see the rapist in any sort of compassionate way," Staci added, "and yet that's exactly your challenge here: to understand him from a different perspective and allow compassion to express itself in your viewpoint toward him.

"Why else did you choose this? Because you recognized on the soul level that all comes from your connection to All That Is/ God. When I look out my window at the clouds and flowers and grasses and trees, there is an energetic connection I see between myself and all of that. It's through yourself that your connection with All That Is is made. When a soul chooses this path, it will create ample time and opportunity to meditate, to learn, to read a book, to spend time with self, enriching the relationship with self and eventually asking, 'What am I doing? Why is it I am not feeling fulfilled?' Then you figure out what you can do and how you can change yourself in order for your life to be fulfilling. Was one of your reactions at the time to withdraw?"

"Yes," Beverly confirmed. "I particularly withdrew from the situation. I wanted to not think about it, not talk about it. I didn't learn for years that by not feeling the feelings and looking at it and touching it and talking about it, it was affecting me hugely."

"You were repressing," Staci observed, "so you did not use that in the most fast track way possible. You know what, though? When we look at our lives from a soul-level perspective, time is irrelevant. I am telling you this because I don't want you to feel down on yourself for not using that period of time in your life to the best. It's all experience. It's all something you learn from, and so long as you learn, that's what matters. That's what you wanted.

"I am now being told that this soul, Steve, has a habit of developing personality structures [in his various lifetimes] that gets him into his head too much, thinking about things over and over to the point where he constructs rich fantasies that enable him to feel all right about what he is doing. He had cultivated a belief over a few lives that he did not have to work as hard as others to get by."

Staci paused. When she resumed speaking, her speech had slowed, indicating to me that her guide was now speaking directly through her.

"The feeling that it was okay for him to take something that was not his developed concurrent with these lives," Staci's guide told us. "Steve also had developed a feeling of unworthiness for love. This was an accumulation of many lives of experience chasing after love and nurturing. That and the attitude that everything belongs to him combined to justify within consciousness the taking of Beverly."

"Could these beliefs not have been healed through the classes and instruction we receive when we are in Spirit?" I asked the guide.

"Steve was not able to bring that into his consciousness [when in body]," he explained. "Although he achieved an understanding in the time between lives, he was not able to incorporate it into his consciousness enough to sufficiently strengthen that aspect of his personality.

"Steve has had lives where he wanted to be of humble service, but all too often he gets to the midway point in those lives and makes personality-based decisions that are impulsive and that affect the course of his life. The soul had been seeking some way to find an abrupt ending to that behavioral pathway. This individual we know as Beverly provided Steve with a uniquely extreme yet loving and compassionate service so that in his own life review he would be humbled and vow never to go down that pathway again. Indeed, this is what the individuated soul has done."

"How did Beverly and Steve know they would find each other?"

"There had been guidance from spirit guide entities to get them in the same area at the same time. If you would ask each one, they would tell you there was a sense that night of needing to be there."

"If the rape had never taken place, what effect would that have had on Beverly?"

"Beverly would have continued to deal with feelings of inequality and lack of self-sufficiency far longer than she did as a result of the rape."

"And what would be the effect if Beverly were still harboring intense anger toward Steve?"

"If Beverly had not come to a place of releasement within herself," said the guide, "it would have bound her to Steve for another life, and in this sense it would have been to work out the imbalance within her. Beverly gave her consent to closure of this dynamic that only came to a head, but did not begin, with the rape. She had to be motivated enough to want to let him go. Had she not, Steve would have felt the very real strings still attaching to him. The fibers would have connected these two individuated souls, and they would have chosen another life within which they could connect with each other again."

"From his place in the nonphysical realm, can Steve feel that Beverly has released this?" I wondered.

"Most certainly."

"What would Spirit like to say," I inquired, "to someone who has been raped and is wrestling with any of the emotions that come up naturally with rape?"

"We would say that being raped gives you a valuable opportunity to learn to love yourself. Since loving yourself is the foundation of all things and all growth in this Earth cycle, we would ask that anyone who has experienced the trauma of rape look at it as a place upon which to stand and then from which to step out and journey toward wholeness. It is an accelerated journey toward unconditional love and wholeness.

"We caution you, Rob, that there will be those who become incensed at the notion that rape could serve such a noble and worthwhile purpose. We say, step back and look from a higher and broader perspective. When you are encased in anger, you cannot grow. Look upon the experience as a new way to practice forgiveness. Quite often that means forgiveness of self, not just of the other person. We would ask such individuals to allow the process of life to unfold for them and reserve judgment until such time as they come to a greater awareness and understanding of All That Is and how all matters serve us all. There is also an effect created by experiencing or reading about rape in that it gives the individuated soul the unique opportunity to define for itself what is right, fair, and just, what is and is not tolerable. Upon the resolutions made there can be growth. Thus, the individual elevates itself and continues its journey toward enlightenment."

◡

Rape is a searing, primal violation of one's being. Rage, guilt, self-blame, shame, despair, and feelings of powerlessness and victimization are among the natural responses to such an assault. They are not to be repressed in a pained haste to arrive at an understanding of one's pre-birth plan. If you have been raped and are filled with rage, then feel the rage with the totality of all you are. If you feel guilty or blame yourself, do not allow your mind to dismiss or denigrate these feelings; instead, immerse yourself wholly in them. If you feel yourself to be a powerless victim, let go of the handrails of spiritual philosophy and allow yourself to free-fall into the abyss of that pain. Your feelings, whatever they are, are wise and true and noble and pure and right. They are to be honored. They are to be revered. They are to be felt, and felt again, and felt again, for they bring with them the dawn of healing.

If the time never comes that you can consider that a rape may have been in your life plan, then this concept is not part of your highest and best path. Leave the idea of pre-birth planning by the trailside and stride boldly forward without it.

Yet, if you have allowed yourself to feel all there was to feel, and if you continue to allow yourself to feel all that arises, then, when the inner chaos calms a bit and the dark clouds of pain part ever so slightly, *feel* your way into Beverly's story. Remember: Your soul has guided you to these pages, and your soul communicates with you through feeling. The logical mind knows only what it has been taught, thinks only what it has been conditioned to think. Ask yourself: How do the words in this chapter *feel* to me?

Do I *feel* there may be something here? If the answer is no, honor that. If the answer is yes, then even though the mind may scream in rebellion, honor that as well.

And if the answer is yes, and if you feel that your life plan is similar to Beverly's, then beyond your anger with the one who attacked you, you may also come to feel anger toward your soul for creating your life plan, toward yourself for agreeing to the plan, and perhaps toward God or the Universe for allowing such plans to be made. Do not judge, suppress, or try to talk yourself out of such anger. As Jeshua told Beverly, anger carries within it great healing power when accepted and allowed to flow freely. That acceptance *is* the healing; that allowance *is* the transmutation.

Granting anger, grief, sadness, and all other painful emotions their rightful place is a magnificent act of compassion toward self. It is for this reason that Aaron advises *not* to say, "I *should* forgive," but rather to be present in a loving, nonjudgmental way with pain. Then does compassion grow, and compassion is the fertile ground in which forgiveness takes root. As Pamela said, forgiveness happens naturally when we embrace every part of ourselves that has been hurt. For years Beverly ran from these parts of herself, fearing that to acknowledge them was to give power to the rapist. Only when she became receptive to them did her healing journey begin.

What, then, does it mean to heal from the trauma of rape? As Jeshua told us, by being raped Beverly was "forced to deal with very deep emotions of feeling unworthy, powerless, and unable to stand up for herself." Acquired in past lives, including the lifetime in which she believed she had betrayed her son, these feelings were deeply held within Beverly's consciousness. Bravely, she chose to carry them into body for the purpose of healing them, an act of great service to her soul. It is here that we come to a most fundamental and powerful of truths: *There is no unexpressed consciousness.* If we feel ourselves to be unworthy, we will magnetize to ourselves experiences that reflect this feeling so we may heal it. If we believe ourselves to be powerless, we will vibrationally attract circumstances that mirror this belief so we may heal it. To accept that we are the creators of all we experience is the ultimate step in self-responsibility. The Earth plane is a school in which the outer mirrors the inner, not for the purpose of suffering but so we may learn to take responsibility for all our creations in this and other lives, and so the inner may be healed. And one very potent way to heal is to bring the feelings and beliefs within us into the light of our conscious awareness.

At this time in the evolution of human consciousness, life plans similar to Beverly's are enacted all across the globe. On a massive scale, we as a race have brought into body feelings and beliefs of unworthiness and powerlessness so that we may become aware of them, feel them to their utter depths, and then embrace and thus transform them with love. Rape is but one of the more extreme expressions of these aspects of our consciousness. The pre-birth planning of myriad challenges, most of them less severe than rape, is often based upon the soul-level need to recognize and heal such feelings and beliefs while in body. In this lifetime—this one, current lifetime—rests the potential to heal all that is in need of healing from all lives past and present. For anyone seeking to participate in the planetary shift in consciousness, the time has long since passed to focus externally on only one linear life.

"Embracing the dark emotions makes one whole and radiant," Jeshua said. Within this embrace lay remembrance of our Holiness. In truth each of us is a vast, limitless being, infinitely worthy, gloriously powerful. Your soul asks you to come into this remembrance in this lifetime, not merely through intellectual understanding but through a *feeling-knowing* of your magnificence. Severe life challenges are designed to crack open the casing of false beliefs in which we have for millennia cloaked our Divine Essence.

Consider this: You who read these words are forerunners in bringing to a close the learning-through-suffering paradigm. Though rapid evolution may result from suffering, it is not necessary for growth. The human race is now ready to ascend into a world in which learning comes through love and joy. To help bring about this quantum shift, one must immerse oneself fully within the old vibration and transform it *from within*. Highly evolved nonphysical beings can provide us with love and guidance, but our leap from one paradigm to another is entirely dependent upon the frequencies of those of us who are in body.

Like Beverly, you chose before you were born to leave a realm of great peace, joy, and light in order to help our world make this monumental leap. To facilitate the shift in consciousness by planning to experience and then heal from a rape is an act of extraordinary service and great love. These are plans of boldness, plans few souls would dare undertake. From across the Universe, only the most courageous have accepted this challenge.

And when the healing is complete and all the inner darkness has been embraced, there comes a level of self-love we never knew before. As Beverly heals herself, she helps all who have been raped to heal, touching their consciousness through her inner light. As you grow to love yourself, you pave an energetic pathway that makes it easier for all others to love themselves.

In your remembrance of your own magnificence, the human race is reborn.

Yours is a life of sheer heroism.

CHAPTER 13

⬙⬙⬙

Mental Illness

A T SOME POINT IN THEIR lives, one out of every three people worldwide will meet the criteria for a mental illness. (I find the phrase "mental illness" to be misleading in that it does not reflect the innate perfection of every person; nevertheless, I use it here because it is widely recognized and understood. And I use it with only the utmost respect; anyone who faces such a challenge is indeed a courageous soul.) In the United States this figure is 46 percent. These figures may well be low because of inadequate diagnosis or low rates of self-reporting.

We live in a time in which ever-increasing numbers of people are coming into both a more loving, heart-centered way of life and the awareness that we are all One. Yet, at the same time we as a society judge mental illness and its attendant suffering as bad. That judgment often creates fear. If we apply the label of mental illness to others, we may fear them to some degree even if we do not acknowledge it to ourselves. If others apply the label to us, they may fear us. And if we apply the label to ourselves, we may fear our own inner darkness. Given the prevalence of mental illness, the fear engendered by this label constitutes a global barrier to our expression of love and our return to Oneness consciousness.

An understanding of the soul-level purposes of mental illness reduces this fear and makes a more loving world and greater unity possible. In my search for such an understanding, I spoke with Mikæla Christi. Born in Geneva, Switzerland, in the early 1950s, Mikæla attended the University of Geneva, then earned a master's degree in English and education at the University of Illinois. She has worked as a writer and editor for a variety of international institutions, including the International Committee of the Red Cross, as well as for several publications and non-governmental organizations that work with the United Nations in the area of human rights.

I felt drawn to Mikæla's story because she had experienced several forms of mental illness (psychosis, bipolar disorder, anxiety, obsessive-compulsive disorder, and bulimia), is herself a channel who can bring forth her own information about her pre-birth plan,[10] and most important, has courageously and brilliantly healed herself and come to a place of great joy in life.

Why do we plan before we are born to experience mental illness? How is our evolution served by such an experience? When in body and faced with mental illness, how do we create healing? I looked to Mikæla for answers.

Mikæla

"I chose a truly wonderful family—stable, loving, safe, secure—and a prosperous, optimistic time to be born in," Mikæla told me. "I had the best possible conditions to heal a lot of mental, emotional, and even physical issues. I feel that I chose those conditions so that there would be no disturbing influences from healing."

Mikæla's words echoed my understanding: We select the circumstances into which we are born. People often ask how they may determine the purpose of their lives. If you seek such an awareness, look closely at the family, country, historical

---

10 Mikæla's other channelings are available online at http://www. reconnections.net/meta_arc_index.htm.

period, and other circumstances of your birth. Therein lay important clues.

"Mental and emotional imbalance is experienced as illness as long as it is not seen as a choice at the level of soul," Mikǽla continued. "I see that now, but for thirty years I thought there was something wrong with me and I tried to fix it. So, I took on the beliefs of others."

"Mikǽla, how did your family respond to the mental illness?" I asked.

"I didn't talk about it to my dad that much. He was one of the most stable, well-adjusted people I ever knew, but he also never showed any openness to it. My mother, on the other hand, is an unbelievably loving, empathetic, and compassionate person, a real listener. She always put a positive spin on everything so that I wouldn't turn it into something horrible. That was useful for me, because it was, in fact, very difficult.

"Over the years my symptoms were many and variable, and they did not add up to a clear diagnosis despite all our digging. Lord knows we couldn't find a root cause, not in this lifetime."

For Mikǽla the experience of mental illness began at age four with nightmares that would continue to terrorize her until she was forty-five.

"The images were sometimes huge worms, spiders, sharks, monsters," she recalled. "Sometimes they were not nearly so clear; it was more like something was rushing at me and I was about to die.

"There were phases where I woke up and it was clear that it had been a nightmare. There were other phases, however, where I woke up in my room, but everything I was seeing in the nightmare was still there! I'd scramble across the bed, clawing the sheets, and fall onto the floor. I knew I was awake, but this massive, phosphorescent green worm was still buzzing at me. My terror was so strong!

"I remember one nightmare where I was in bed with my husband. When I woke up, something was moving up the wall.

Then this thing *became* the wall, and the entire wall was then moving. It was creepy, crawly, insect-like, and huge, and it was coming at me and *becoming* me. I screamed and went over to my husband. He was amazing. He woke up, looked at me, and said 'Oh, another nightmare.'

"It's the most awful thing you can possibly imagine," Mikǽla added, "particularly if it takes a form like a spider. It's beyond belief. I felt totally powerless. That's what really got to me. That's what pushed me into the arms of therapists. Then I actually heard the words *psychotic break*. They gave me pills to calm me down. The therapists didn't help so I stopped working with them."

During Mikǽla's childhood the horrific images originated only during her sleep, but in adolescence they started to appear spontaneously in the middle of the day, though never when Mikǽla was outside her house.

"Those images rarely took a well-defined form," she described. "It was more of a rushing, swirling, out-of-control, chaotic thing coming at me. It was very hard not to panic."

It was also in adolescence that Mikǽla began to experience bipolar disorder—episodes of euphoria followed by periods of depression.

"I loved euphoria," she said. "It gave me a complete escape from reality and responsibilities. I felt on top of the world, like nothing could harm me, like I could step off the roof and fly. I ended up doing stupid things. I spent my credit card way beyond the limit. I danced all night and went to fancy restaurants and bars. I'm lucky I didn't have a major accident.

"Depression was the opposite lens. It made the entire world totally gray. I had no pleasure in anything." Mikǽla was medicated for depression intermittently for fifteen years. One therapist gave her lithium, but she found that it took away the highs much more than the lows. "There was one episode where I got medical leave and just stayed in bed. I had suicidal thoughts. My mind was in a haze, and everything seemed totally hopeless."

"Mikǽla, as a child, how were you able to go to school and have friends with all this going on?"

"I didn't have friends," she said sadly. "I came home directly from school. I found it very difficult to associate with other kids. I didn't feel like a kid. Once I got a medical release so that I wouldn't have to go on a school trip. I just couldn't go to a place where I'd sleep with a bunch of other kids, because if I woke up from a nightmare, what would happen?"

"What did your parents think was going on?"

"Nobody made it wrong. It was just something very strange that they didn't understand."

Despite the ordeals she endured in childhood and adolescence, Mikæla made it to college. There she met the man she would eventually marry.

"It was almost an unspoken agreement between us," she explained. "I could be exactly who I was and do whatever I wanted without having to worry." I wondered if Mikæla had perhaps chosen her husband for the same reason she might have chosen her parents—to create the safety and security in which healing would be possible.

Mikæla and her husband enjoyed a happy marriage for ten years but eventually parted when he decided he wanted to have children.

"I was more invested in my inner life and trying to find out what the hell was going on with my therapists and medications," she recounted. "Me taking care of small people was impossible. I could barely keep myself together."

"Mikæla, what other forms of mental illness did you experience?"

"When I was depressed, I had obsessive thoughts and became compulsive. For example, I couldn't leave the house without going back and making sure that everything was turned off. When I locked the door, I had to lock it twice. It was so powerful. I couldn't not do it! And then sometimes I felt invaded by obsessive thoughts and stories."

"What were some of them?"

"In one it was Italy in the Renaissance. [In my current life] I was walking down the street, but inside my mind I was underneath a table and in danger. I had enemies all around me. I was carrying poison. Both of these things were happening at once. Later I realized this was a flash from another lifetime, but at the time it was just something invading me."

Mikǽla began taking Prozac, which allowed her to hold a job but which also caused her to be emotionally "flat lined."

"I wasn't feeling fear anymore," she said of her time on the drug. "I wasn't feeling at all. I was just noting these obsessive things going around and around in my mind.

"I also had an eating disorder since age eighteen. I've had eating disorders in the plural, mostly bulimia. I binged and purged for years.

"It felt like there was something deep down inside of me that was trying to get out," she said of all these experiences. "Gradually I was impulsed from within—impelled—to search for some other way of dealing with all this. Once I was open to it, synchronicities just dropped into my lap, one after the other."

Healing

"Mikǽla," I asked, "which forms of healing eventually worked for you?"

"Focusing,"[11] she answered, referring to the name of a specific healing modality. "It was invented by a therapist, Eugene Gendlin, who was dissatisfied with psychotherapy. He discovered that just talking about things, going in circles mentally, doesn't help most people. You have to connect with the emotions. He found that if you look for where you feel emotion inside the body, you quite easily find that place. Then you focus on that place. It wakes up something. It brings forth imagery, knowing, emotion, or a situation or event. It exists inside those cells, and you reconnect with it. The goal is to feel whatever is there for

---

11 For more information please visit www.focusing.org or www. focusingtherapy.org.

you to feel. When the emotion starts coming through, your body moves and twists."

In one of her first focusing sessions, Mikǽla saw an image of an enormous, fortress-like battleship in her mind. Then, abruptly, she developed a headache emanating from the center of her head. She understood intuitively that she was in the center of the battleship and that the battleship—her head—was protecting her in some way. As she focused on the pain, her body arched backward. And as her body arched, the pain subsided.

"Once I described it [to the focusing therapist] and felt it, it was healed," Mikǽla observed. "That was a key experience. Once I had done a few of those sessions, it felt like that was a way to heal."

Our bodies are wise, and when we involve them in our healing, miracles happen. The physicality of Mikǽla's experience had been an important aspect of her healing. Emotion is energy in motion and as such needs to flow freely. When it cannot, when it is repressed or suppressed, it crystallizes in our cells and chakras. By focusing on her frozen emotions, Mikǽla had loosened them. As her body twisted, the crystals of emotion broke up and began to move. The intention and attention of her mind, coupled with the wisdom of her body, had constituted a brilliant healing partnership.

After working with focusing for several years, Mikǽla delved into Biodynamics, a related type of healing system created by French therapist Gerda Boyesen.[12]

"In Biodynamics the healer works electromagnetically," Mikǽla told me. "It's a reiki modality. You lie down and close your eyes. The healer starts to feel almost at the same time as you where in your body the symptom is. She places her hands on or above

12 For more information please visit http://en.wikipedia.org/wiki/Gerda_Boyesen, http://www.appb.org, http://www.ecole-et-therapie.com/therapies-psychocorporelles-suisse.php, or the website of Gerda's daughter, Ebba, at www.ebbaboyesen.fr.

that place. You both focus on it. Then you start to get a feeling, image, or sense being someplace else."

"Can you give me an example from one of your sessions?"

"I actually became somebody else," she said. "I was still aware of being in the room, but at the very same time I was in a torture chamber. They were trying to get me to say something, and I wasn't going to say it. The feeling in my body was connected with that.

"As I focused into it, and as I *allowed* it to be—in the beginning I couldn't always do that; sometimes I popped right out of it—very powerful emotion started coming up. Then my body started to stretch and pull. I breathed more deeply. I was letting the emotions flow through me instead of through that person [in the torture chamber] who couldn't let them flow. That made the difference. That's what the healing is. The fact is, it works. Whether it was actually another lifetime or a symbolic story I projected doesn't matter."

Mikǽla continues to work with Biodynamics, though less frequently. She has also used past lives therapy (in which she did guided visualizations that took her to the extensive violent trauma in those lives), meditation, and visualizations of her own creation. In each she reconnected to moments in other lifetimes in which she had not allowed or accepted intense emotions. Usually those lifetimes came to her in brief flashes. Over a period of years she felt, and thus released, countless frozen emotions.

Then one day she suddenly, unexpectedly, started channeling.

"I was with two friends," said Mikǽla. "We were sitting around the living room. One asked a question, and I spontaneously started trance channeling. They told me afterward that I was speaking in a voice that was not my own and that I had answered the question. I was somewhere else. I didn't even remember what I had said.

"Channeling was the culmination of the journey for me in that I had been seeking a new understanding. It changed everything. It was a remembering of who I really am and of things, both individual and collective, that go beyond me. I understood some-how that things were back in balance for me and that imbalance is fascinating for our souls. We're drawn to imbalance because consciousness always finds a way to rebalance, and it's a wonderful challenge to do that.

"I began to see that I am not only my human body and mind," she added, "but also all these other lifetimes, a soul, the one creating all of this. I opened myself up to understandings I wouldn't have had when I was identified completely as one human in one lifetime, including why I as a soul chose mental illness and how I as a soul might feel quite differently from the way I feel as a human."

Pre-Birth Planning

"Mikǽla," I said, "what do you feel your pre-birth plan is? Were all the forms of mental illness planned before birth?"

"I think all the potentials were selected before birth," she replied. "There might have been others that didn't manifest.

"The openness to chaos within order was chosen because Switzerland is a very ordered place. Having chaos erupt in the middle of order is something I sought because I didn't want to shatter into a million pieces. Also, I—we all—chose this era because it has the potential for such rapid, far-reaching evolution about beliefs and judgment regarding 'normal.' When I was born in the 1950s, I was on the rigid end of normal; people knew what normal was. Luckily, I had parents, mother in particular, who didn't make me into somebody abnormal."

Mikǽla's insights reminded me of Pat, the man in *Your Soul's Plan* who planned to experience decades of alcoholism and a feeling of disconnection from God followed by a spiritual awakening and feelings of deep connection with God. As souls we learn through opposites, and that learning is profound when the opposites occur within one lifetime. Like Pat, Mikǽlaa had planned to experience two ends of a spectrum. By choosing to be born in Switzerland in the 1950s, she had elected to experience narrow, well- defined beliefs and judgments about normalcy. Yet, by choosing to be born into an era of rapid growth in conscious- ness, she put herself in a position to heal those false beliefs and judgments. Hers was a classic learning-through-opposites life blueprint.

"Mikæla, why do you feel the potentials for the various forms of mental illness were built into your pre-birth plan?"

"The whole plan was chosen for healing unfinished business from many other lifetimes and for remembering. My soul was healing stuck, blocked emotion because stuck, blocked emotion keeps repeating, attracting the same patterns over and over again. You cannot go anywhere."

"The emotions that got stuck in other incarnations of your soul in other lifetimes—are you saying that the various forms of mental illness you experienced were intended to create those same emotions in you so that you could feel and release them?"

"Yes."

"And by healing those emotions, you are also healing those other incarnations of your soul?"

"There is an overall process going on here from the point of view of the Higher Self," she explained. "All of this happens at once. My soul went deeply into studying violence and what kind of human motivation creates that violence. Is it possible to understand that? Is it possible to see violence as a soul choice in those lifetimes? In most of those lifetimes there was no con- sciousness of that type. It's in this era that we have the ability to remember ourselves as the Higher Self and connect with that in a *felt* understanding—it may not be verbal—that allows it all to be.

"If I embody no more struggle or resistance," Mikæla contin- ued, "and if I allow, then this wonderful ease and grace comes and I can be with all those things and understand the perfection of all creation. Then the story is healed. It's not blocked anymore, and there are no more refused aspects.

"By *allow* I mean that there's nothing I judge as wrong, bad, or broken. Feeling it as a choice I made gives it meaning and purpose, but also lets it be. That opens up a transition. We're the ones doing that for the Higher Self.

"And I can tell you what that transition is like. It's fairly recent for me. Gradually, over the past year, it's like a new birth. I have no more need for rebalancing or searching. There are no goals, no objectives. That was a tough one, because that's such a fun game! I truly remembered and integrated that I am this Higher Self, the one creating everything in my life and all those other lives. They all flow together in this dance of light and color and sound. It's amazing!"

I asked Mikæla what specifically she is able to do now that she was not able to do before she healed.

"I can be within the challenges of life. I can create freedom, joy, exhilaration, and all the feelings I seek simply by choosing to make that my way of experiencing life no matter what is happening at the time.

"I have the same challenges as anyone else. My mother is seriously ill and will probably die soon. In my office I have the same insanity as the next guy. But, now I can create any feeling out of absolute nothingness. I don't need to change anything in the outside world; I simply evoke the feeling. I align myself. There is a way of going to the still center of your being—where you go when you meditate—in the midst of daily life. It takes half a second."

"How do you do it?"

"I focus my attention in the high heart, a place above the physical heart. In Biodynamics that's where I felt the still center, which feels like calm water. From there you can create absolutely anything. So, I can be in the hospital with my mother, and she's in pain, and that's making me feel horrible and helpless, and at the very same time I can create joy. I am not bound by any one feeling. I can have several at the same time. The process I've gone through allows me to do that."

"Mikæla," I said, "some people, after they come into an understanding that we plan our lives before birth, become angry with themselves, their soul, or God for allowing suffering to occur."

"If you say 'My soul planned this, and I am angry,' you're act-ing as if those are two different things," she answered. "You, the human expression, have a certain independence, but the soul is not separate from you. You are that soul, and you are you, at the same time. I understand that there can be frustration or anger. I had this, too, at one point. It's like, 'How the hell could I have chosen this?' But, this whole process led me to know that there is always a purpose.

"I know someone who says, 'I could never have chosen to be abused by my dad.' Well, that's responding emotionally. If you're in the middle of the emotion, it's very difficult at the same time to step back from it. Years ago, when I was in the midst of some-thing, I was not able to step back from it the way I can now.

"It's a process, and there are stages to that process. All you need do is be open to the possibility that as a soul it's still you and that you had extremely good reasons for choosing something.

"It's the remembering who we are that's the most important part of it. That opens up everything else. That's how it was with me. It's remembering who we are that gets us past a horrible situ-ation and feeling like a victim to it. That's not how it is, and that's not who we are."

"Mikæla, what can you say to those who are experiencing mental illness and struggling to see its deeper purpose?"

"Getting lost in it is not ever something that any part of you wishes to maintain," Mikæla answered. "Some form of getting better is out there and is being drawn to you. Your soul is looking for the thing that will help you balance. That kind of base trust allows you to take a faster road. You yourself have—every single one of us has—a naturally evolving process going on within us. Trust that."

"Do you feel grateful for all the challenges you've gone through?" I asked.

"I wouldn't trade them for anything else. To get to where I am now, it was worth it."

Mikǽla's Channeling

Mikǽla had offered much keen insight into the purposes of the mental illness. Next, I wanted to ask questions of and hear the perspective offered by Spirit. How much of Mikǽla's mental illness had been planned before birth? What additional insight could we gain into the reasons this very difficult plan had been forged? What words of wisdom would Spirit offer to those suffering from mental illness and those who love and care for them?

Prior to asking Mikǽla to share her story, I read some of her channelings. I saw great wisdom in them and felt certain that equally helpful and healing words would come through in the session we would do together. My hope was that Mikǽla would channel her Higher Self. I was, therefore, quite startled when a very different consciousness, one I could not have anticipated, expressed through her.

Before the channeling started, Mikǽla entered a deep meditation, her consciousness stepping aside so that another could make use of her body.

"Please tell me your name if you use one," I asked as the session began. "Also, please tell me where you are." I knew that many nonphysical beings recognize one another other not by name but rather by energy signature—their color and sound—yet I felt that a name would still be helpful. I knew, too, that space is an illusion, but I wanted to see how the channeled consciousness would respond to a question about location.

"The group energy speaking here today is gathered in relation to the questions you have," came the reply. (As sometimes happens Mikǽla's speech had slowed, though her voice still sounded like her own.) "We understand there is a certain sense in which you would like our channel to channel her soul; however, in our view the human speaking these words *is* her soul. This has always been the case, although like nearly all humans, she forgot for most of this lifetime. Now she has remembered, so it makes no sense to speak of her channeling her soul, as that is what she is doing all the time.

"We are your future selves," they continued. I was stunned and excited by this revelation. Apparently, the questions I planned to ask had energetically summoned a collective of the future selves of some, perhaps many, of those now in body on Earth. This was, therefore, a rare opportunity to receive wisdom from humanity's more evolved future. "But, those selves contain billions of potentials and experiences from which to choose. You have questions and so does each of your readers. For that purpose one name cannot be given. Naming defines. It leads you to believe that you know, because you have named and placed outside yourself that which is also within. If you or your readers wish to use a name, feel within and allow a name to emerge. Your name for us will not be the same as the name that emerges from someone else, for each human is utterly individual and therefore so is the guiding or responding energy each one calls forth.

"As for our placement … you are in space-time in a paradigm in which space is extended and time enfolded. In other words, you occupy space but do not access time. We are in its counterpart. We are where space has enfolded and time extended; therefore, we have access to all the potentials of time but could manifest within space only if we crossed over to where you are."

Here on Earth we are in a place in which space appears to have been extended to three dimensions. Because time is linear to us, it is enfolded into the one point of time we experience in each moment. The term for this type of perceptual experience is *space-time*. By contrast, the channeled consciousness was experiencing multiple timelines—billions of them, evidently—from the one point in the space they occupied. The term for this converse type of perceptual experience is *time-space*.

"I'd like to talk," I said, "about Mikæla's pre-birth plan in regard to what we refer to as 'mental illness.'"

"You will forgive us if we first speak about a definition," replied our future selves. "For us a pre-birth plan correlates with a resonant moment when a soul group aligns a preliminary configuration of selected potentials for entry into a lifetime. There are far more of these potentials than could ever manifest in physicality; indeed, many are alternatives to ensure the evolution of the soul's purpose. The human lifetime is a process of choice, change, and evolution.

"Now, there were indeed—there always are—many potential, useful outcomes; however, if you are speaking about the elements in the lifetime that are linked to mental imbalance, the ultimate purpose was to expand the experience and understanding of all that she is by reconnecting within one human lifetime to a large network of lifetimes past, present, and future in relation to where the channel is now. This process clarifies and confirms the ways in which human lifetimes are connected and interactively evolving across space and time.

"For her, for the human, it means re-membering the whole self. Re-membering: it would be good if you were to print that with a hyphen. *Re-membering,* which is a putting back together of all that she is while within a human lifetime, was the most important purpose. It was inherently served by many of the mental symptoms. The purpose is of so much importance because it is leading both our channel and many other humans at this time to what you call ascension, which, in turn, leads to mastery, mastery of the creative process itself: the mastery to create worlds, other Earths, new Earths, and thus take life beyond what it has been."

In short, Mikǽla's understanding was correct. Her purpose in this lifetime, which she had so beautifully fulfilled, had been to re-member herself as soul.

"Could you say more," I asked, "about re-membering?"

"There are many ways in which this is being accomplished," said our future selves, "some of which were not predictable. It is not the same for different groups, especially for different humans; therefore, we can only speak about what it is for us.

"For us, within humanity there are themes and series of interconnected lifetimes. From our point of view outside space but within the corridors of time, the interconnected lifetimes are all evolving and expanding together at once. This concept is very difficult for a human. All the lifetimes have turning points that are linked across space and time. At those points it is possible for a human to remember in the classic sense of the word—to have flashes, visions, experiences, a form of 'sensed sight' or feeling. [The human then knows that] there are different lifetimes all occurring at the same time. This opens the possibility of knowing that you are much more than this one human, this one body-mind. You are also your soul, and your soul is part of a soul group, and that soul group is part of a soul family, and that soul family is part of the soul community. In the end the human is able to conceive of himself or herself in a completely different way.

"We apologize for the lack of clarity. It is quite difficult to speak of these things in human language."

"I understand," I told them. "I feel that humanity is at a point in its evolution when many people see themselves as flawed, limited, and lacking in power and worth. To me, re-membering means recalling that we are infinitely powerful and of infinite worth."

"Indeed, that is the truth," they replied. "There is nothing that is flawed or to be fixed. There never is. It simply seems that way because of mental judgments that have to do with the human collective. Individuals constantly find themselves faced with value systems, with beliefs and judgments that do not correspond to theirs. They therefore think of themselves as bad or wrong. Part of the process of re-membering is to understand one's full responsibility for the creation of one's own life and to stop making such self-judgments."

Our future selves had spoken of interconnecting lifetimes. I understood them to be referring to the other expressions, both physical (for example, human) and nonphysical, of our souls. These are sometimes called parallel lives. From the human perspective in linear time, some of these parallel lives are in our past, some in our future, and some in our present. Most of us perceive only our own lifetime, the one we are currently living, but our souls perceive all the lifetimes at once.

I asked our future selves if a metaphor I use to understand this difference in perception between the soul and the personality is correct: If a CD has seven songs on it, and each song represents one lifetime, then we as humans generally listen to or perceive only one song—our own. Our souls, however, are listening to all seven songs *at the same time.*

"Yes," they answered, "except that 144 different, interactive, 3D video games might be a better way of putting it because the games would all be running interactively with one another. You have access to them all. The complexity of that process is what humans are learning about and seeking to master."

"So," I asked, "throughout Mikǽla's lifetime, how many other lives did her soul have going on and how many are there now?"

"From birth until now, there have been thousands. At any one time, the least is a number under 20 and the most is a number in the vicinity of 144, which is why we used that number."

"How are those parallel lives created? When Mikǽla came to a major decision point in her life and chose A, did it spin off a parallel dimension with a parallel Earth where there was a parallel Mikǽla who chose B?"

"We would not say 'spin off,'" they clarified. "We would say that those potentials pre-existed, and she chose one of them. Potentials that were not chosen exist in nonphysicality."

The reference to potentials already existing is a reference to timelines, the flow charts medium Staci Wells sees in pre-birth planning sessions. Each line in the chart is a pre-existing potential, a path we may choose. For example, if we learn to give and receive love, we choose a relatively high-vibration path or timeline and experience a life filled with love. If, on the other hand, we close our hearts and refuse to give or receive love, we choose a relatively low-vibration path or timeline and experience a life lacking in love. Both potentials (and many more) already existed. We simply chose one.

To my surprise, our future selves had said that potentials not chosen exist in realms that are nonphysical. "Can you explain what nonphysicality is?" I asked.

"The average human today would probably talk about imagination and dreams and how they are not real. For us that is not the case. For us these are realities."

Here, our future selves were confirming an idea that had been shared with me in my personal channeling sessions: Imagination is real. That is, what we imagine is actually happening. That is how powerful our minds are. Initially, what we imagine happens on a nonphysical dimension. If we then imagine the same thing repeatedly, and particularly if we infuse strong emotion into the image, we may draw it into our physical experience. As the great psychic Edgar Cayce said, "Mind is the builder."

I asked if there were other physical and nonphysical Mikælas in existence.

"It would not be correct to say that there are other physical Mikælas," they stated. "There is no other physical one. There are many nonphysical ones, however."

"Mikæla is the only physical lifetime of her soul?"

"No. She is the only one who can truly be called Mikæla, because she is the one with that unique signature pattern. The uniqueness of the DNA of each individual is complete; therefore, whether in the fifteenth or twenty-seventh century, it [the personality incarnated by Mikæla's soul] is not Mikæla. It is another who is interactively creating that lifetime with Mikæla and who resembles her in many ways but not all."

As I listened I thought of the vision Mikæla had of herself hiding under a table during the time of the Renaissance. According to our future selves, that person was not literally Mikæla but rather another incarnation of Mikæla's soul that has much in common with her. Mikæla herself is a unique being who exists only in this current lifetime.

"If you were able to project into a nonphysical, parallel lifetime," our future selves continued, "you would have the impression that you had a nonphysical variant of Mikǽla that looked and seemed exactly the same. But, the physical one is the one that is resolving many of the most important issues and is answering many of the most important questions. It is through the physical one that that happens."

Here we had a crucial piece of information. Most of us have moments in which we feel small or unimportant, in which we wonder about the true value of our lives and whether what we are doing is of real and enduring importance. Our future selves just spoke directly to all who have ever felt that way: You matter. You are vitally important. It is through *you*, the physical self, that your soul—and by extension, the entire Universe—evolves.

I asked if one of Mikǽla's pre-birth desires had been to heal the mental illnesses she would experience and in so doing heal her soul's other lifetimes.

"Indeed, the purpose was to heal, but to heal from our point of view means to make whole again, to see as one that which had previously been seen as separate. Healing results in a serenity of being that permits perfect allowing. Allowing is a form of pre-mastery. One will never arrive at mastery of the creative process without allowing whatever happens during the creative process; therefore, allowing a low- frequency emotion is as important as allowing a high-frequency emotion.

"One of the reasons why bipolar tendency was selected was precisely in order to ride a wave where there would be very high and very low emotion. The goal was not to 'even out,' which, unfortunately, seems to be the goal for those humans who use medications. The goal was to arrive at a point where Mikǽla could be joyful and excited about even a very low-frequency emotion. The purpose was for her to ride up and down and then disengage from it so that she is fine with whatever is going on. This leads, as we have seen within her lifetime, to her no longer going up and down in this way."

"I think people who experience bipolar disorder will probably say, 'How can I possibly be joyful about that kind of suffering?'"

"Let us take the healing process in percentage terms over time. In Mikǽla's case, it was only when she completed approximately 85 percent of the process that she was capable of allowing herself to go down and also allowing herself to go up but without pushing the up. Before, when she pushed the up, she went higher, but then when she went down, she went even lower.

"For more than half the process, it is almost impossible not to add anything to it. For example, there is not only depression, but also despair about and fear of the depression. Reactions are added to it, and so it becomes more cemented into place because of that focus upon it. The healing process eventually leads to less focus being placed upon it. Everyone reading this will eventually be able to be within something without being completely focused on and identified with it. Re-membering and becoming whole again enables a slight distancing from and neutralization of the human experience so that you can feel depressed and at the same time lift your focus away from it.

"In the beginning you find something outside yourself to focus on. That is what humans do. That makes them feel a bit better. But, gradually, you learn to place that focus within yourself. That last step, which indeed happened in Mikǽla's case, happens only in the last 5 to 10 percent of the entire process. That final 5 to 10 percent is the part that gives you back your freedom. It is only in that final 5 to 10 percent that you have understood and have seen enough that you no longer need to create the situation itself in order to get there."

"Can you discuss the other forms of mental illness Mikǽla experienced in this lifetime and the purposes served by them?"

"The greatest and most important was perhaps the hardest to accept and to make sense of: the nightmares that persisted into daytime consciousness. Although psychotherapists would indeed view them as a form of no longer seeing consensus reality, each one was actually an opening onto another reality. Gradually, Mikǽla developed a willingness to allow them to be. That ability, those openings, allowed all the other lifetimes, both physical and nonphysical, to get through to her so that she finally became what some people call clairaudient, clairsentient, and claircognizant. That process opened Mikǽla to the rest of her being. The configuration of parents, era, and even therapists was carefully navigated to avoid a premature diagnosis that would have led to medications being taken to suppress the nightmares, for it was of extreme importance that the process be allowed to come to its term."

"Why is it necessary or desirable," I asked, "for there to be so much suffering on the part of the incarnate personality to benefit the soul?"

"The soul is not separate from the human; it only appears that way. The soul is actually fully present within the human at all times. Where do your deepest desires and greatest motivations come from, if not from the soul? You believe that you choose by a mental and emotional process, but that is not what actually happens. The soul guides through the use of feelings. It is how you feel when you consider one alternative or another. The soul level of you creates those feelings in order to direct you.

"But, it is not that the human is suffering and the soul is directing it. One of the purposes that work such as yours serves is to evolve understanding to the point when you know that suffering is, in fact, most often resistance. If in your pre-birth planning you choose potentials for experiences that are sufficiently outside the norm of the time, it will be that much more difficult for you to conform to society. Mental illness is a case in point. It is defined by others in a way that makes you resist and therefore suffer. You will attempt to flee from it and therefore suffer. You will find it unacceptable and therefore suffer. In a future time it may be possible for children to be brought up differently and for a far greater diversity of experience to be allowed and seen as simply diverse forms of experience. This was the case for Mikǽla with her mother. If her father had been home more, he would have imposed his highly adapted-to-society point of view. This would not have been useful.

"We are sensing at this time the potential reactions of your readers. We understand that a person who is deep within suffering can take only one step at a time. There are healing methods gradually evolving now within your society. We have been talking about the end of the process. Those who are suffering the most may not be able even to consider that right now, because in many cases they are not ready to take responsibility for their choices all the way down to every last experience or to see that it is simply impossible to meet all the expectations and demands they are placing upon themselves."

"You mentioned healing methods," I said. "If we are evolving through the experience of mental illness, then should we also try to alleviate it?"

"There is no 'trying to alleviate,'" stated our future selves. "There is a naturally evolving process. The point is not to stay within the mental illness; the point is to evolve through it. It is very, very difficult for any being who has not incarnated as a human to understand why a human would refuse certain experiences. From a nonphysical point of view, allowing is always the better choice. Allow these experiences and then return again always to the stillness at your center."

I then asked our future selves to discuss the other challenges Mikǽla had faced.

"The eating disorder developed for two reasons," they said. "The first was that she attempted to conform to a certain body type that is valued by the society but that was never intended to be hers, and therefore she began what you call dieting. In addition, she was seeking—quite literally in physicality and also in symbolic form—sweetness. From an early age she was in a family in which sweetness was highly valued. Given her nonconforming purposes at soul level, the eating disorder was a seeking of compensation for that. It gradually disappeared of and by itself after she took an extremely long look at it. This is why some healing modalities can be useful *at certain times*. Had Mikǽla attempted at age twenty or thirty to use a basic form of behavioral therapy to look at her eating disorder, she would have been incapable of using it for that purpose; however, by age forty she was able to use that modality, and the eating disorder went away.

"A lifetime in which re-membering the whole self is chosen requires what you would consider to be an inward turning. For us, inside and outside are the same; they are simply different manifestations of the same reality. For you the human, however, there is an outer world and an inner world. Turning inward is not seen as optimal in your society, and therefore in many cases it is medicalized. It is considered to be illness.

"Even what your great writer and therapist Carl Jung called 'introversion' is merely a different choice. It is the choice of placing the felt energy source inside the person as opposed to outside; therefore, the person requires, and the soul has created, a situation in which it will be drawn toward the inner world in order to be energized again. Without that it will no longer have any energy, because it is important for the purposes of the whole being that the person turns inward."

"From your perspective," I asked, "what are the most effective healing modalities in our world now for mental illness?"

"From our point of view, the standard care is useful only in the early stages or when things are so far out of control that people are incapable of distancing themselves from the imbalance. We do not have anything against solutions that simply calm matters down, because that is required to start looking at something differently. We do not believe, however, that medications are anything but a temporary help. Ultimately, they will not lead you to seeing things differently, which is what is needed.

"There are many of what our channel calls 'bridge modalities,'" our future selves continued. "She spoke of one called focusing. It was a temporary measure that allowed the physical body to be included. Many of the things that are not resolved at mental and emotional levels will eventually be physicalized, but even before they physicalize they are present within and therefore can be accessed through the cells. The book called *The Healing Power of Illness* talks about the symbolic value of physical illness.

"If you open to a different way of seeing, one will present itself to you. That is always the case, because your desire is calling it forth. A greater opening allows you to consider certain modalities that are now considered nonstandard. It is not our purpose to recommend. Indeed, it would not be a good idea to do so, because different people will come to different things. It is that sense of excitement or enthusiasm, the feeling of resonance with something, that will lead you to a modality.

"Mikæla eventually came to a moment when she wished to see if she could arrive at an independent and autonomous way of creating well-being. People may eventually find their connection to their own inner guidance. You are forever evolving, and when you resolve something you move on to the next thing and the next level. Mikæla now works with a healing meditation that is extremely good for her. It is a product of Esther and Jerry Hicks, who channel our good friends. We know this energy well; you call it Abraham. For Mikæla it helps maintain the level she has reached."

"I want to come back to the idea of resistance," I said. "People who are suffering from mental illness may say, 'Not resisting mental illness may be helpful, but how do I not resist something that causes me to suffer?'"

"No longer place mental illness as the focal point of your reality. Instead, turn your attention to what's working in your life. It's like what most humans do with the idea of their own death. They don't particularly like the idea, but they forget about it and focus instead on life."

"For what other reasons," I asked our future selves, "is mental illness planned before birth?"

"There are as many reasons as soul groups, and there are many, many, many soul groups. A lot of what's being dealt with in physicality are the things that are most difficult to understand and therefore seek evolution the most. They've been around the longest. It's precisely because they have been around the longest that they are physicalized. Anything that can be allowed and let go of very easily never becomes physicalized. Many have to do with the fact that you are so unbelievably different from one another. That is how all the Universe evolves: by creating a cauldron of diversity. Diverse points of view evolve all of humanity and therefore the entire Universe."

"We've talked a lot about how mental illness for Mikæla was of service to the other expressions of her soul, helping them to heal. For readers who aren't interested in past, present, and future parallel lives and who just want to be happy, what else can you say about mental illness?"

"Again," answered our future selves, "it is from our point of view very difficult to understand mental illness as a choice if one remains only within the perspective of one lifetime; however, each human believes that there is a way forward, a path. Trust that it is there and that you can find it. The divinity within you is showing you the way forward. Trust your own inner feelings. The right way for you is utterly individual, because each one of you is utterly individual, special, and deeply appreciated by all that you are. Focus on that, and keep bringing your focus back to that again and again and again. Within what you might think of as the chaos of your life, pieces of it are working. Focus on those. See yourself as someone unbelievably special who has your own way of doing it, and you will find the next step."

"Many readers will have loved ones who have some form of mental illness, and their concern is how they can best help."

"Truly, the best thing you can do is to be absolutely sure that you maintain and nourish your own process, because the best gift you can give to them is to be within your own well-being. Then listen to them and be open to whatever guidance comes through you. Be still and in nonjudgment as much as possible. Do not think you know what they need. There is no way anyone can know what anybody else needs. Allow their own process to bring what is best for them. Ask yourself, 'How can I bring their focus to what's working in their lives? How can I do for them what I have done for myself?' See them as people who are skilled, strong, and capable. Trust that they are capable of moving themselves farther along their path. Help them to see their own strengths and abilities. Help them to see that they have choices."

"Is there anything else you would like to say on the topic of mental illness?"

"The word *illness* is useful only in the preliminary phases," replied our future selves. "It is far better to see things in terms of what's useful at a particular moment. So, if one is at the early stages, when defining and treating something as an illness is useful, then by all means. But, there will come a time, and there always comes a time, and there has to come a time, when it becomes important to see it no longer as illness. At some point it becomes okay. Then you are able to say 'I chose it, but why? What can I understand from this? What did it allow me to do, or what did it allow into my life? What focus did it create?' Because very often that's what it is doing: creating a different focus.

"You created it in order to evolve it. When you can see it that way, then you can take responsibility for it. And when you take responsibility for it, you know that it's not you, the human, who created it, but rather another level of yourself.

"That's when you re-member."

Mikǽla's Session with Pamela and Jeshua

For me Mikǽla's channeling was eye opening and expansive. Never had I expected to speak with a collective of our future selves. Mikǽla had provided a rare and immensely valuable glimpse into the perspective we hold in the future. I felt a renewed and deeper sense of just how important and healing a physical lifetime is for the soul. In how many other lives, both physical and non-physical, was my own soul expressing, I wondered. If I were ever to doubt my own importance, I would need only remind myself that I am bringing healing across many lifetimes and dimensions to my soul. In the same way, all persons who are in body now may heal themselves and in so doing offer deep healing to their souls.

I now turned to Pamela and Jeshua for their perspectives. What insights would they share regarding our soul's reasons for planning mental illness? From their viewpoint what was the meaning of the specific forms of mental illness Mikæla had experienced? How had Jeshua helped those with mental illness to heal when he was in body, and how might we apply that wisdom today?

Our session started with Mikæla providing Pamela a general overview of her life. I knew that as Mikæla spoke Pamela was tuning in to her and receiving psychic impressions.

"I see certain images, and I feel your energy," Pamela began. "The first thing I see is the color pink in your energy field and especially at the beginning of your lifetime. You were very open, sensitive, and vulnerable as a child. The boundary between you and all your identities in past lives was very thin, and those old, traumatic energies were still part of your soul. It seems that you did not fully enter your body at birth and then become fully grounded; therefore, those energies from past lives easily entered your consciousness.

"I also sense a power inside you. I perceive the colors blue and purple, which show that you have inner strength and have been capable of handling all this. In the process of trying to make sense of all these difficult energies, you have understood deeply who you are. Do you recognize this?"

"Yes, absolutely," Mikæla replied.

"I can also feel the bipolar illness," Pamela continued. "I feel the depressions have been very deep and dark. The images I see now are related to the depression: images of being persecuted or violently rejected." Interestingly, in their conversation at the beginning of the session, Mikæla had not shared with Pamela any specific information about her past lives. "I feel that when you entered this lifetime, Mikæla, there was fear but also a deep knowing of, 'I want to do it.' You came back to Earth to deal with the pain and trauma that had been caused here in this dimension. It was a courageous step."

"This was *the* lifetime," Mikǽla confirmed. "This was *the* opportunity, however challenging it was going to be."

"Pamela," I interrupted, "Can you see one or two of Mikǽla's lifetimes and tell us how they relate to her current lifetime?"

"I see several lifetimes, but I am focusing on the one that comes to the front," Pamela said. "I see that you are male in this past life, Mikǽla. At one point you have to flee. You are alone out in nature, and you are hunted.

"I will now try to see what happened by going back to when you were a small child in that lifetime. It's a warm country. The people live in tents; the ground is dry and dusty. I see that you have an awareness that is a different from the other people. You are somehow connected to the sun, and you feel there is so much more to life than people ordinarily see as they go about their daily business. I see your mother. She, too, has this feeling for the mystical, and the two of you talk about it in secret.

"I now see you as a young man of about nineteen. You feel that you have to go away from home, which seems limited to you. You begin traveling, and you find a group of people with whom you feel very much connected at the heart. That's the first time in your life that you feel spiritually connected to others. They are different; they have a vision.

"At some point you decide to go among these people and bring to them the energy and messages of Jesus, but you meet with a lot of resistance. I see you sitting on a horse. You are taken off it, dragged away, and imprisoned. Sitting in a cold prison cell, you feel completely isolated and desolate. It's suffocating being in this dark cell and feeling the hostility of the people. You feel that you're going insane. In the end you are killed. A big part of you doesn't understand this violence, and when you die there is trauma in your soul about this.

"In your current lifetime you have experienced part of the fear, desolation, and despair that this man felt. When you connected to these very difficult moods and darkness, you entered that lifetime as well as others. They want to be healed. If I connect with that past lifetime in particular, I feel that this man has partly healed because of what you have done in your current lifetime. Also, he wants to connect to you. He represents your male energy. He wants to let you know that even now you can still become more grounded and more firm in expressing who you are and setting your boundaries, which was so difficult in that past life. So, this clearly is an interaction."

This struck me as a particularly important point. In Mikǽla's channeling, our future selves had also said there is an interaction among the various lifetimes of the soul, but they had not provided a specific example. I asked Pamela if she could explain in more detail just how Mikǽla's healing had brought healing to this man in the past life.

"One of his greatest wounds," Pamela explained, "was that he didn't feel welcome on Earth with his particular kind of inspiration. He felt it wasn't safe to be truly himself. Mikǽla has in this lifetime come into touch with her soul. She has gone from the outer layers into her spiritual essence, and she has created safety for herself on an inner level. Anything she does to trust life, to feel more grounded, has a direct effect on him and other lifetimes, which are still there, still alive."

Mikǽla then told us that years ago she had seen flashes of a similar, related past life. In that lifetime she had been interrogated, tortured, and burned by members of a church for attempting to bring spiritual knowledge to people. "At the moment of death," Mikǽla said, "there was a complete incomprehension of how it's possible for human beings to treat other human beings this way. That's why when I was birthed into this current lifetime I was late, because I wasn't sure I wanted to come. That's also why I have been afraid of people in this lifetime, even though there was nothing bad happening in the outside world. The fear was coming from the inside."

"Pamela," I said, "Mikǽla has talked with me about how her mother and husband were very nonjudgmental. Is that why she planned before birth to have her particular mother and husband—because they would give her the safety the man in the past life never had?"

"I see an image of you, Mikæla, before you were born," Pamela responded. "I see you saying, 'I need help.' This is related to your mother but also more generally to the environment you were born into. It was necessary for you to meet with those gentle energies on Earth; otherwise, you would have wanted to die and leave Earth. You wanted a soft landing, and it was given to you. Also, you and your husband knew each other from past lives."

"Yes," Mikæla affirmed, "there was familiarity and a feeling of trust right from the first moment. Both my father and husband are 100 percent trustworthy. I think that was very important for me."

In my exploration of pre-birth planning, I had discovered that as souls we learn through opposites. In regard to her family, however, Mikæla had chosen to forego the learning-through-opposites plan. Why, I wondered, do some souls like Mikæla choose to incarnate in safe, supportive environments while others choose families that are less than loving? I put this question to Jeshua.

"A soul always chooses the right circumstances, the best context for the central goals of a lifetime to be achieved," Jeshua said as he spoke through Pamela. "When a soul plans to deal with deep, inner issues, it is sometimes necessary that the outer circumstances are quiet and peaceful. This enables the soul to deal with other realities and dimensions that could not be entered if there were turmoil in the childhood."

Then Jeshua spoke directly to Mikæla.

"You are very brave, and I love you." I could feel his love streaming to her. "This fire in your heart that you sensed in the old past life and in many past lifetimes is the inspiration to recognize the oneness of all living creatures. You are able now to live from your heart. Trust even more, and dare to be who you are."

That Mikæla is now able to live from her heart is surely one of the greatest things to emerge from her suffering, I thought. Life challenges break open our hearts, not for the purpose of harming us or making us suffer but so the love we are on a soul level may flow more easily and powerfully through our hearts.

"*I know who you are*," Jeshua added, making a statement that would take on much greater meaning when we later talked about how in his lifetime he had helped those with mental illness to heal. "You have much to give to others who are on the same journey, a way of listening to people and understanding them. Truly see your own beauty. That's what self-worth is: truly seeing your innocence, integrity, and courage, and embracing all your dark and light parts. This makes you even more grounded and present on Earth."

"Jeshua," I said, "please discuss Mikǽla's pre-birth plan of mental illness in this lifetime."

"Mikǽla wanted to make peace with old pain in her soul, inner voices that were screaming out and not understanding. On a deep level she said yes to the things that happened, the highs and lows, the visions and the crossing of the dimensions. It helped her to discover her true strengths. And now, by living through this she has gained a very deep understanding of human life and emotions and how far the soul can travel from the light. That is very powerful."

"Just what is mental illness?" I asked him.

"In general, in cases of mental illness the person has too much to deal with," Jeshua explained. "The body and spirit need to be grounded and present in the now moment. From that basis one can integrate several emotions, feelings, and thoughts. In mental illness this basic groundedness is fragmented and the soul has no earthly anchor. It is drifting. There is no calm, inner space in the midst of hallucination or depression. The soul feels lost.

"What helps most in approaching people with mental illness is to stay in touch somehow with their essence, to feel the light of the soul within, even if they act very strangely or cannot be communicated with. It is a certain ability to keep in touch with the presence of the soul. This can sometimes help a person to be present again in the body and available for communication.

"If there is, for instance, hallucination or psychosis, the person is in a sense out of body and dwells in other dimensions. The person cannot integrate what he or she is seeing there; therefore, the link to the body and Earth is very important in order for all the visions and information to become meaningful. There *is* meaning in what a mentally ill person experiences, but it is difficult for the person, and also the people around, to grasp it."

Jeshua's answer reminded me of Eckhart Tolle's description of the counseling work he has done. Generally, his approach was simply to be present with the person. By identifying himself as soul, timeless and formless, Tolle is more readily able to see others as soul. And as he sees them as soul, they regain a feeling or sense *of themselves* as soul.

"Jeshua, how do we help people feel the light of the soul within?"

"That's the true gift of healers. They somehow feel the essence of the other person, and often they cannot do more than that. To be present in such a way—connecting to the soul, still seeing the light in the other person's eyes—has to do with having true faith in the power of the other person to heal herself. It also has to do with having patience and allowing the other person to go through the experience because sometimes you cannot stop it.

"This goes against what regular medicine would prescribe. It is a spiritual approach to mental illness. It's important to understand what the person is going through from within and not just try to fix it from the outside. It's important to establish contact with the soul and also pay attention to the body, for the body is the anchor to which the soul needs to be connected. So, sometimes physical issues like having enough sleep or enough to eat are important to address, but the true healing comes from the soul."

I asked Jeshua how he had healed people who experienced mental illness when he was incarnate.

"People suffering from this type of illness are always very sensitive," he observed. "It is not just a disorder; it is also a gift. So, when I met these people, I stayed with them in a space of silence, which was also a space of understanding. I let them be who they were. I didn't try to fix them. It was as though I were connected to each soul, and I knew each soul was capable of self-healing. It was more a transmission of energy than certain words or healing methods. I reached out to their essence. Sometimes they would look into my eyes and recognize it, too. They would suddenly feel, 'This is the truth of who I am. I am a being of light.' Some people suddenly awakened to this insight. Others needed more time because no one, not even I, can force healing upon someone else. The soul has to choose for itself. But, there is nothing more powerful than recognizing the core of someone, the beauty, innocence, and light inside. This is what healing is truly about."

"Jeshua, it's my understanding that there really is no such thing as mental illness," I said, "that what we call mental illness is only lack of love."

"That is exactly right," Jeshua agreed. "The label 'mental illness' is misleading. Essentially, it is about losing touch with your own essence, which *is* love, joy, peace, and creativity. It sometimes takes a long while for people to realize this truth, because throughout the history of humanity there has been so much judgment—and therefore so much self-judgment—in the religious traditions, which has affected people very deeply. Spiritual traditions were meant to bring people Home to their Inner Divinity; instead, they told people they were sinful or bad and there was a God outside and above them who acted as an authority, judging them. These ideas and images have influenced people and made it difficult to be in touch in a very simple way with their True Essence, with love, indeed."

"I don't like the term 'mental illness' either. What would be a better term?"

"There is no clear distinction between normal and insane," he pointed out. "The words *mental illness disorder* suggest that one is not normal, when in reality it is all very gradual. I would formulate it in the terms you used: a lack of love, a lack of being in touch with your soul. Also, be aware that those who have so-called mental illness are often very evolved souls who are able to feel much. It is precisely because they are able to feel so much that they can get caught up in extreme mental states. That is another reason why it can't simply be labeled a disorder."

I asked Jeshua for other reasons Mikǽla planned to experience mental illness.

"There was a personal reason why she planned it, but there is always more to it. By going through this type of illness and then finding her balance, she also has done something in a broader sense for her soul family. Her soul family consists of souls who have had similar trauma and pain from past lifetimes or during this lifetime. Mikǽla has created an energy trail that other people can follow, because when she has healed it becomes an existing energy pattern. So, she is helping other souls from her soul family, even if she doesn't know them. Apart from that, she has also, by bringing this energy into her birth family, challenged or invited the people around her to have a deeper understanding of emotions, psychology, and human life. She has affected their consciousness."

To bring as much healing and specific understanding as possible to people, I asked Jeshua about the forms of mental illness Mikǽla had experienced. I started with the nightmares.

"Jeshua, when Mikǽla awoke, her nightmares continued as visions in front of her. What was happening, and what was the underlying spiritual purpose?"

"Real energies from other dimensions and other lifetimes entered her reality. Her aura was open to receive this type of information. This was meant to happen because it would invite her onto the inner road where she would explore and in the end understand these images. When these images come to people in the waking state, their consciousness is not completely focused on their material surroundings. It is in a kind of trance state. Psychologically, the emotional weight of these energies is so intense that the energies 'bleed through' from other lifetimes in order to be resolved in the current lifetime. They become more strongly present than the direct physical environment."

"What about Mikǽla's bipolar disorder?"

"In both the depressive and manic states, one is not fully grounded," Jeshua told us. "In Mikǽla's case, the depression was sometimes too much for her, and so another part of her simply went into an altogether different state of consciousness in which she felt completely free and in a sense out of body. She was still in her body, but her mind was free of the limitations of the material realm. In general, the human mind and spirit are capable of experiencing extreme things. One can explain these things partly by studying the brain and chemical processes, but there is also a spiritual meaning. For Mikǽla the very high, light energies were essential for remembering who she really is. It was a way of seeking balance."

"I would also like to ask about the obsessive compulsive disorder. For example, Mikǽla had to relock her door again and again. Jeshua, what can you tell us about OCD?"

"The mind tries to find ways—behaviors, rituals—to control fear and other emotions. This is where the mind gets stuck. It cannot do it, which is very painful. It is in running away from fear that you can develop compulsive behavior. In essence, the solution to this type of disorder is to face the fear directly, and you may sometimes need the help of other people. In saying yes to the fear and welcoming it, you make more sense of it, and then it can eventually go away."

"Mikǽla also heard voices."

"She is extremely sensitive, and by *sensitive* I mean also clairvoyant and clairaudient. So, there was no barrier. It was on purpose that she was born with this type of nervous system and brain; it enables her to travel within in a deep and wide manner.

"Voices can come from past lifetimes," Jeshua added, "but they can also come from people who are deceased and in the astral realms. The solution is to enter your body completely. Then, usually, your energy field closes around you. This is a natural protection that you have. The problem with people who have anxiety or difficult memories from past lifetimes is that there is a resistance to incarnating and truly merging with the body, the reason why this type of mental disorder can be very difficult."

"Jeshua, what caused Mikǽla's bulimia and how did it serve her soul?"

"Mikǽla had a lifetime in which she experienced hunger and deprivation, and this caused an ambiguous relationship with food. In general, taking food is a symbol for saying yes to life. Mikǽla desired to live and to experience life, but she also resented and wanted to withdraw from life. The bulimia brought to the surface her inner doubt about whether she wanted to be here among people on Earth.

"Bulimia and anorexia—eating disorders in general—are never only about eating. They are about deeper issues of how you take care of yourself. Are you able to trust other people enough to receive from them? Or, do you need food to be 'nourished,' fed in a broader sense than just physically? Can you embrace life? Can you be yourself? These issues are at play in an eating disorder. These disorders are a way of controlling fear, and they can be very persistent."

I then posed some questions to Pamela.

"Pamela, when Mikǽla was planning her life and approached her future mother, father, and husband, what did she tell them in regard to mental illness, and how did they respond?"

"She felt very responsible," Pamela replied as she used her gifts of clairvoyance and clairsentience to access Mikǽla's pre-birth planning. "Mikǽla asked them if it was okay and they all said yes. They wanted to help her; that was part of their mission. It was not just that she was going to cause problems for them; she also had something special to give. They realized that her inner wisdom—her light—would mean a lot to them. Also, there were past life connections with all of them. They wanted to honor her for being different. Mikǽla is someone who always wants to know the essence of things, what's behind the ordinary. They explicitly wanted to honor that because in other lifetimes they did not honor it. They wanted to balance that and learn from it at the same time."

"What specifically did they learn?"

"Mikǽla's father connected with his own fears, fears that at first he didn't realize he had. It forced him to look inside and also to know when to accept and let go. He feels [on the soul level] in awe of Mikǽla's light and grateful for being part of her life. Mikǽla's husband didn't want her to suffer, but after some time he was drawn into a deeper understanding of things. It hurt him to see her in pain, but it also forced him to look at his own emotions and to feel more, really going into himself and not just staying at the surface. There are some deep fears in him, and Mikǽla's experiences helped him to take a closer look at those inner fears. Mikǽla's mother wanted to save her, but of course she had to accept that this was a process that couldn't be easily fixed. It really helped Mikǽla's mother to develop her own intuition, self-confidence, and inner wisdom. She has become stronger through it."

"Jeshua," I said, asking the Master to return to our conversation, "when you were in body, did you experience depression, anxiety, or anything we would call mental illness?"

"I needed to withdraw frequently from the world to regain my balance and to remain true to my heart and mission, because I was sensitive, too," Jeshua said. "The energies of other people affected me so strongly that I needed to spend time in nature in order to come back to myself and to feel grounded again, for if one has a strong connection to Spirit or one's soul, then one needs a similar connection to Earth. One also needs to have strong boundaries. If the heart is awakened, one becomes much more sensitive, tunes in more easily to other people's feelings, and can therefore get lost. I didn't experience a mental imbalance or disorder, but I can easily understand how it happens."

"Jeshua, depression and anxiety are so common in the world. How would you advise people to cope with them?"

"If one could look at depression, anxiety, fear, or any other negative emotion as just one part of the self that is confused, then there would be another part of the self that could look at this emotional part with an understanding and a gentleness that would reassure it. But, people tend to identify completely with their depression, anxiety, or fear, and then they feel unbalanced. They cannot find their core, their true self, anymore. The first thing to realize is that *you are not your fear.* You could see the fear, for instance, as a child who comes to you for help. By seeing it that way, you will feel that you are much bigger than the fear. You can get in touch with the child, speak with it, and understand it. Sometimes a therapist can play the role of this parent or guide. The key always is to find a place in your awareness from which to look at the fear and not *be* the fear."

"Jeshua," I said, "earlier when you spoke about how you helped people to heal mental illness, you talked about how they could look into your eyes and reconnect with the essence of their soul. I'm concerned that people who read your words will feel you have an almost supernatural healing ability they do not have. They will want to help loved ones who have mental illness but may feel they can't do what you did."

"They first need to address their own emotions," advised Jeshua. "All kinds of emotions may surface. They may feel that they don't understand what's going on. They may feel rejected by the people who are ill. They may feel alienated from their loved ones. They may feel frustrated. Often, there comes a point at which they have to know their own boundaries, and it requires a lot of courage to take the point of view I had described: simply to be with them, connect with and trust their souls, and allow them to find their own way of healing themselves.

"It's almost impossible to do this if you are deeply, emotionally involved with someone. You want to solve the problems of your loved one, but life challenges you to let go and take a step back. It's a very difficult process, and it may well be the case that you cannot help the other person for some time. The person may need another kind of help, and then your task is just to keep faith in the person, even if he or she seems out of reach. Doing so will often bring you closer to the person. This is part of your own life path: to deal with these emotions of feeling inadequate or left alone.

"Often," he continued, "it takes someone who has experienced mental illness or who has deep experience being with mentally ill people to offer good treatment, because the therapist must be able to understand the person from within since it's not possible to reach out and communicate easily. So, people close to people suffering from mental illness really have to intuit what they can and can't do and when they have to let go and seek another type of help."

From a pre-birth planning perspective, Jeshua had just spoken to one of the primary reasons why some souls choose to experience mental illness: so they may eventually help others to heal. Each of us formulates a mission before we incarnate, and the mission entails some form of service to others and thus the world. The empathic healer is a powerful healer, and empathy comes from personal experience.

"What are your thoughts about conventional psychotherapy?" I asked.

"This can be helpful, but it's very important also to have the perspective of the soul, which often lacks in traditional psychotherapy. Traditional psychiatry and psychology tend to look at issues only from the framework of the current personality, but it's often the case that past-life energies are at play. The perspective of the soul helps people to realize they are much more than their current personality. Bringing them into contact with the soul helps them tap into their self-healing abilities and also make sense of the disorder. Some psychiatrists and psychologists have a subconscious understanding of this bigger perspective, even if they work consciously only with traditional concepts. Healing depends very much on the energy of the therapist. It is the energy, not conscious ideas, that invites people to open up and heal."

"How would an enlightened society handle what we call mental illness?"

"There would be fewer instances of mental illness because people would be taught to remain true to their own inner voice, their intuition, their heart. There would not be as much fear and alienation as there is now. People are fed fearful beliefs, and that is what makes them doubt their own intuition. There would be more acceptance and less labeling of this phenomenon, and it would be understood that the soul sometimes needs to travel very far from Home to truly understand what it is all about. There would be much more respect for people suffering from mental illness."

"What do you say to those who are currently experiencing a lot of pain from any form of mental illness?"

"*You are always loved*," Jeshua said. "People who are in this kind of tremendous pain have a high level of self-judgment. They resent themselves. They often hate themselves. They feel they are failing, and this is so very painful to them.

"Know that you are beautiful and that you can trust life. You may feel completely stuck in life, but there is an energy—you can call it Spirit or God—that never judges you and always tries to offer you new opportunities to get moving again. Life never ends and death doesn't exist, so it is important to trust life. It wants to help you.

"In these times mental imbalance can occur more frequently, because people are awakening and trying to live from the heart. There is a rise in sensitivity in people. No matter how difficult it gets, try to find a place of silence within, and sense that there is more to life than just what you are thinking or feeling. There is a benevolent energy that always envelopes you and always seeks to help. Opening up to help is a major step for people who are completely stuck in self-judgment and fear. Sometimes you need to force yourself to do it. If you open up to life, it will answer your call.

"The truest medicine is self-love and self-acceptance, and you can start right now. Whenever you feel negative emotions or judgment about yourself, look at it with the eye of a gentle parent. Then you can create a space of self-love every minute of your life. That will bring you Home, whether you are struggling with a minor emotional issue or a huge disorder. The power of love is endless. It is a very soft and gentle power. Humanity needs to discover this power again, and that is what is happening now on Earth."

Mikǽla had been quiet, taking in all that had been discussed. I asked if she would like to share her thoughts.

"I deeply appreciate and resonate with what's been said," she responded. "You can be very, very far along on a path of understanding for yourself and channeling for others, feeling connected to your own knowing, and yet there are still human moments when you doubt. It's helpful at times, then, to have a connection through another person. When Pamela puts herself at the service of this book, or when I do that for someone else, there is a cross-connection, a dynamic, that happens. I can actually feel it. It greatly increases the power of the energy. That's why I feel humbled by the fact that we are here in service to something much greater."

"I'm glad you could sense the energy," Pamela told her. "I sensed it strongly, but it's sometimes difficult for me to formulate it into words."

I turned to Jeshua. "Jeshua, what final thoughts would you like to convey?"

"Life can sometimes seem a very lonely path, but even if there is no physical help around you, there are always spiritual energies. The energies of Home are always around you. This is a temporary visit to Earth. You can make it easier if you try to feel the Love of Home every instant of your life. Open up to it. It is already there; you do not have to create it. It is the natural flow of Life. That is my message: Help is always available, and you are never alone.

∽

"If I allow, then this wonderful ease and grace comes, and I … understand the perfection of all creation. Then the story is healed."

These wise words from Mikǽla illuminate the foundation of her healing, which is in truth our healing. What she once judged as bad, she now sees as perfect. What she once attempted to fix, she now permits. What she once viewed as broken, she now knows is whole. Such is the extent of her healing. Within her one lifetime, Mikǽla has allowed and felt to the core of her being the torment of her soul's myriad lifetimes. That allowing and feeling *was* the transmutation of the pain of those other lives. When she allowed that pain to flow through her in whatever form it assumed, it was as though the shutters of a long-abandoned home had been flung open, brilliant sunlight flooding in, fresh breezes sweeping through and bringing renewed life with them.

This she did in service to her soul and, indeed, to you and me since we are all One. Only the most courageous serve their souls through embodiment on Earth, and only the most courageous of those agree to take on what we still call mental illness. As Jeshua told us, many of those who plan this challenge are very old, deeply sensitive souls. To be tender and yet in body on Earth may be difficult under the best of circumstances. To be tender and yet agree to experience literal living nightmares as Mikǽla did is an act of deep love and the utmost bravery. No one who understands this truth can fail to grow in self-love. No one who feels this truth can fail to know greatness.

If you ever suffered from mental illness and judged yourself as bad or broken, know now that all of Spirit stands in admiration of your transcendent beauty. If you ever condemned yourself as weak, realize now that your guides and angels applaud your immense strength. If you ever thought yourself to be unimportant, feel in this moment the boundless gratitude of both your soul and its expressions in other lifetimes, whom you are helping to heal. You are of infinite worth and immeasurable importance, your healing radiating to the far corners of the Universe. Anything less is fiction. Anything else belies your magnificence.

Let us see, too, the equal worth and importance of others who experience mental illness. If we have pitied and thus energetically disempowered them, let us now view them as the majestic souls they truly are. If we have thought them to be our burden, let us now know them to be our teacher, just as Mikǽla was a teacher to her mother, father, and husband. If we have seen them as in need of healing, let us now understand that their mental illness *is* the healing desired and sought by their souls. Indeed, on Earth little is as we have believed it to be.

For millennia we as a race have feared, scorned, pitied, and misunderstood those with mental illness. Now may we see clearly. Through Mikǽla's experience we discover that psychoses can be the bleed-throughs from other lifetimes and dimensions. Far from being out of touch with reality, Mikǽla was simply in contact with *other* realities, perceiving real energies that sought and were in need of healing. Too, her experience teaches us that depression and mania result when one is not sufficiently grounded on the Earth plane, a common result of a soul feeling a moment of doubt or uncertainty before entering body. And yet it was precisely those high, light energies of the manic state that birthed Mikǽla's remembrance of herself as soul. Her mania, which many might judge as a dysfunction of no redeeming value, was in fact a means by which she brought the wisdom, joy, and compassion of her soul into body to share with us. Her courageous willingness, both before and after birth, to plumb the depths of depression and face the consequences of manic behaviors has in many respects made her the teacher she is today. And purposefully did she choose before she was born to have a sensitive nervous system and brain so she might explore the vast landscape of the world within. Though she knew this decision would lead to being tormented by voices, she nonetheless embraced this bold plan in service to her soul and our world. Her obsessive-compulsive disorder was her mind's natural attempt to manage the fear triggered by the nightmares and voices, and bulimia brought to her awareness her doubts about being on the Earth plane.

Though the world may yet see Mikǽla's experiences as forms of meaningless suffering in an arbitrary, uncaring Universe, in truth all were rich with deep meaning and purpose that become clearer during the later stages of healing. It is during those stages that one re-members oneself as soul, just as Mikǽla has. This, as Jeshua eloquently said, is the foundation of all true healing from mental illness or from any other life experience. When Jeshua looked at mentally ill people he saw not illness but Divinity, not flaw but perfection. And as those people saw their reflection in his eyes, they, too, knew themselves as beings of light: holy, eternal souls temporarily enrobed in physical, human bodies. For the first time, in the mirror of his eyes they saw through and beyond the veneer of the body to the loving essence that animates it. It is for this reason that our future selves and many other nonphysical beings refer to healing as re-membering. If you seek to bring healing to yourself, a mentally ill loved one, or the world, allow a felt sense of yourself as soul to seep into your perception. With that felt sense comes the ability, as Mikǽla said, to allow it all to be, the pain and beauty, the torment and joy. Your plan in coming here was to immerse yourself unreservedly, wholeheartedly, and passionately in the sacredness of the human experience.

And all of it is exquisitely sacred.

Epilogue

WHETHER YOUR PATH HAS BEEN smooth or rocky, your life gentle or traumatic, of this you may be certain: You are among the most courageous souls in the Universe. Were that not true, you would not be here now. Your decision to incarnate, your willing agreement to embark on the voyage your soul planned, was an act of profound bravery. Your search for the deeper meaning of that journey is another act of great courage. And your decision to heal is yet another. Throughout the Universe you are honored and revered.

Of this you may also be certain: You *are* healing. You heal as you come to understand that there *is* deep meaning in your experiences. As you see meaning, you free yourself from the reflexive tendency to feel victimized, and you realize that you are the powerful creator of your life. You let go of the learned habit of judging; instead, you trust your intuitive knowing that all is truly well and in Divine Order, even though your logical mind may rail in disagreement. You cease to take your mind's distractions and diversions so seriously; rather, you lean into your heart and rely on its wisdom to set your course. You realize that you are not your thoughts or feelings; you allow negative thoughts and feelings to float gently across your awareness, much as clouds float across the sky. You no longer identify yourself as your fears and worries; instead, you see them as small children in need of your love. And love them you do.

Now you release resistance to life.

Now you wholeheartedly welcome life, both its joys and its sorrows.

In your eternal Home, you knew of the inherent beauty, magnificence, and Sacredness of a lifetime on Earth and so embraced your life-to-be. Now you heal as you embrace your life anew with the same knowing of its beauty, magnificence, and Sacredness you had then.

In your eternal Home, you knew, too, that life on Earth is but a mirror that shows you to yourself. The beauty, magnificence, and Sacredness you now see in life are but a reflection of your own. Were it not within, you could not see it without. Now you heal as you embrace yourself anew with the knowing that you are that beauty.

You are that magnificence.

You are that Sacredness.

References

Bass, Ellen and Laura Davis. 2008. *The Courage to Heal: A Guide for Women Survivors of Child Sexual Abuse.* New York: Harper Paperbacks.

Brodsky, Barbara. 2003. *Presence, Kindness, and Freedom.* Mich.: Deep Spring Press.

Brodsky, Barbara. 2011. *Cosmic Healing: A Spiritual Journey with Aaron and John of God.* Calif.: North Atlantic Books.

Dethlefsen, Thorwald, and Rudiger Dahlke. 2002. *The Healing Power of Illness: Understanding What Your Symptoms Are Telling You.* London: Vega Books.

Friedlander, John and Gloria Hemsher. 2011. *Psychic Psychology: Energy Skills for Life and Relationships.* Calif.: North Atlantic Books.

Goldner, Diane. 2003. *How People Heal: Exploring the Scientific Basis of Subtle Energy in Healing.* Va.: Hampton Roads Publishing.

Hicks, Esther and Jerry Hicks. 2010. *Getting Into The Vortex: Guided Meditations CD and User Guide.* Calif.: Hay House.

Kendig, Irene. 2010. *Conversations with Jerry and Other People I Thought Were Dead: Seven Compelling Dialogues That Will Transform the Way You Think About Dying ... and Living.* Va.: Grateful Press.

Kribbe, Pamela. 2008. *The Jeshua Channelings: Christ consciousness in a new era.* Fla.: Booklocker.com.

Schwartz, Robert. 2009. *Your Soul's Plan: Discovering the Real Meaning of the Life You Planned Before You Were Born.* Calif.: Frog Books.

Shucman, Helen. 2007. *A Course in Miracles.* Calif.: The Foundation for Inner Peace.

Tolle, Eckhart. 2008. *A New Earth: Awakening to Your Life's Purpose.* New York: Penguin.

Walsch, Neale Donald. 2011. *Conversations With God: An Uncommon Dialogue.* Book 1. New York: Putnam.

Zahnow, Carolyn. 2010. *Save the Teens: Preventing suicide, depression and addiction.* N.C.: A Brand New Day Publishing.

Interviewees

Rebecca
mzwrite@frii.com

Bob
robtjbarrett@juno.com

Marcia
Crazycatlady2003@yahoo.com
http://marciaderousse.com

Kathryn
Kathryn@journeytofreedom.ca
www.journeytofreeedom.ca/jtfsociety
www.youtube.com/jtfsociety

Debbie
Wadams58@cfl.rr.com

Carole
Carole@wisdomcoach.com
www.wisdomcoach.com

Carolyn
cczahnow@yahoo.com
www.save-the-teens.com
www.wakeforestsos.com

Beverly
Beverly336@yahoo.com

Please understand that a personal reply to your e-mail cannot be promised.

Mediums and Channels

Barbara Brodsky
www.cosmichealingmeditation.com
www.deespring.org
(734) 477-5848 (Deep Spring Center)

Pamela Kribbe
www.jeshua.net
pamela@jeshua.net

Corbie Mitleid
www.firethroughspirit.com
corbie@firethroughspirit.com
(877) 321-CORBIE

Staci Wells
www.staciwells.com
info@staciwells.com